Praise for *Rise Up!*

"***Rise Up!*** is the most brilliant and accessible synthesis of esoteric wisdom, cycles of time, and cosmic dimensions that I have ever read. With expert guidance, Suzanne Ross takes you into the higher planes over a ten-day course of instruction. As a totally grounded journey into the center of the Universe, this timely self-help manual is a wonderful sequel to her emotional processing book, Wake Up! This is a must-read for any seeker of wisdom. You will see there is nothing to fear as we move rapidly into the Age of Aquarius and remember our divine source."

~ **Barbara Hand Clow,** author of *The Pleiadian Agenda, Alchemy of Nine Dimensions, Revelations of the Aquarian Age* and many more

***

"***Rise Up! Awakening through Revelation, 10 days on the Ascension Path*** by** Suzanne Ross expands upon the masterful "10-day life lesson workshop" she developed in *Wake Up! Awakening through Revelation.* Suzanne reveals the deeper meaning behind life's greatest mysteries in a transformative way which only this empathic author can convey. Readers will discover that the meaning of life is to create, and the purpose is to evolve, so that we may Rise Up! to our full potential. For understanding the mystery that is you, pick up this book and begin the ultimate journey!"

~ **Brad Olsen,** author of *Modern Esoteric, Future Esoteric* and many more

***

"Suzanne Ross' new book is inspiring, fascinating and informative! I highly recommend it."

~ **David Hatcher Childress,** author of *Lost Cities & Ancient Mysteries of the Southwest, The Lost World of Cham* and many more

***

"**Rise Up!** by Suzanne Ross approaches the constructs of spirituality and cosmology from perspectives that are in many ways the opposite of my own. Despite that, time and again we arrive at essentially the same destination in terms of which elements are key to an ancient tradition and their significance. I find quite a lot to recommend in her book."

~ **Laird Scranton,** author of *Sacred Symbols of the Dogon, Science of the Dogon* and many more

RISE UP!
Awakening through Revelation

10 DAYS ON THE
ASCENSION PATH

Book Two of the Up! Trilogy

SUZANNE ROSS

Sacred Dragon Publishing

Los Angeles, California - Sedona, Arizona

Second Edition, Copyright © 2021 Suzanne Ross
ISBN: 978-1-7366793-3-3

Cover Design by Ida Jansson of Amygdala Design

Sacred Dragon Publishing, Los Angeles CA
www.SacredDragonPublishing.com

This book is dedicated to my father
who always encouraged me to
look up at the stars and ponder
what's beyond the horizon.

Table of Contents

READER DISCOUNTS

Subscribe to **SciSpi.Tv** at SciSpi.tv/sign-up/ for access
to all the author interviews referenced in this book.

Enter promo code **RiseUp!44** at checkout to receive your reader discount.

Purchase audio recordings of the **Up! Trilogy** guided meditations
and activations referenced in this book at **SuzanneRossTransendence.com**.

Enter promo code **RiseUp!44** at check-out for your reader discount.

ACKNOWLEDGEMENTS

To my beloved family ~

I will always be forever grateful to my dear sweet husband and the love of my life, Scott Wyatt Tynan, for the unending support and encouragement he has offered me over the past 20+ years. No matter what, he never stops believing in me. He supports my expansive visions even when they seem farfetched. He commutes for hours just so I can live in the spiritual mecca of Sedona, Arizona. He works long hours at a corporate job so that I can have the freedom to write, produce, create and envision. He knows what I do has a positive impact on the collective consciousness and so, in this way, he can support this great cause. He also sees how dedicated I am to my mission and rejoices with me when I receive praise from my colleagues. He knows that everything I do is simply because I dearly love humanity and that's why I dedicate my life to offering inspiration, enlightenment and empowerment. But most of all, he knows I love him with all my heart and am so very grateful every day for all he does and for who he is. He will always be my knight in shining armor. Scottie, I love you for all eternity.

I offer my sincere gratitude to my beautiful, precious sister, Angela Rosenau. She has been there for me since our mother brought me home from the hospital. Growing up, she was always my guiding light. When I couldn't even sit up, she would prop me up against the wall and sing the alphabet to me. Every day after school, she would come to my crib and tell me everything she learned that day. She has always been a role model excelling at everything she pursues. To this day, she offers the support, encouragement and praise I need to inspire me when things don't work out and to celebrate with me when they do. I know she is always just a phone call away and would drop everything to be by my side. She is the best big sister anyone could ever wish for. Psychics have told us that we are twin souls so our motto is "Power Twins Unite!" Sweet sister, you are more than a blessing, you are my forever twin soul. For that, I am eternally grateful. Kimi, I love you with all my heart always.

Lastly, I am forever indebted to my magnificent mother who inspired me every day by waking me up and telling me, "You are the most beautiful, smartest and bravest girl in the whole wide world." She made us believe anything was possible and we could achieve whatever we could dream of. She was a powerful role model as a corporate executive with a master's degree at a time when women weren't welcome in the old boy's club. She became the President of an international women's rights organization to show her support for women worldwide. She has always been passionate about literature, art and theatre. She inspired us to be creative, well-read and well-cultured. She also loved us with all her heart and showed it in every way possible. I am forever grateful for her loving support and encouragement. Mom, I love you for all eternity and am incredibly blessed to have you for my mother and friend.

To my cherished colleagues ~

First and foremost, I would like to extend my deepest gratitude to Barbara Hand Clow, who so generously offered to read my manuscript and then write not only a testimonial but the foreword to my book as well. When her and her wonderful husband, Gerry, came to visit me in Sedona, we both felt an immediate soul connection. She sat for a live discussion which became a 3-part series, which can be viewed at SciSpi.tv/Rise-Up. After that, we stayed in close contact and enjoyed sharing feedback. With her incredibly busy schedule, I feel so very blessed that she took the time to read my manuscript and write the foreword. Dearest Barbara, I am incredibly blessed to call you a colleague but more importantly, a dear friend. Thank you very much for your generous support and beautiful praise.

I would like to extend a special thanks to Carla Rueckert, Don Elkins and Jim McCarty who brought through the Group Ra channelings for the Law of One series and to David Wilcock for referring me to them. I also wish to thank the extended group of people who brought through the channelings for the Urantia book (which I call the Universal Bible).

I would like to extend a sincere thanks to all the authors who contributed to my book by participating in a live or online discussion. I also want to thank them for the use of excerpts from their books and for the opportunity to share their wise teachings. I especially want to thank my dear friend and author, Brad Olsen, for being our tour guide as we visit Central and South America. I want to thank David Childress for his research into the Cham people and their seafaring global migration. I am grateful to Laird Scranton for his research into the Dogon tribe in Africa and his translation of their symbology and cosmology. I am also grateful to Robert Bauval for his discoveries about the Orion constellation and to Andrew Collins for his revelations about the Cygnus constellation. I also want to thank the late Elisabeth Haisch for sharing her past life experiences in Egypt as a high preistess in her book, Initiation. Also, a big thanks to Drunvalo Melchizedek for his two-volume series "The Ancient Secret of the Flower of Life" and to Dr. J.J. Hurtak for his remarkable "Book of Knowledge: Keys of Enoch."

A sincere thanks to Tom Dongo, Maureen St. Germain, Tricia McCannon, Danielle Rama Hoffman, Christine Day, Clifford Mahooty, Mary Rodwell, Amanda Romania, Travis Walton, Kerry Cassidy, Laurie McDonald, Nancy Safford and many more for participating in live and online discussions with me about the magic and mystery of creation and the spiritual and scientific explanations for it all. I am truly grateful to all my colleagues and am blessed to also call them my friends.

Foreword

Barbara Hand Clow

The time has come for me to pass my mantle to the next generation of fine teachers such as Suzanne Ross. Her first book *Wake Up!* offered profound clarity as it guided us to process and dump emotional blocks and addictions in ten days. Then after she finished it, she was inspired to go on a spiritual quest because she could see that *the meaning of life is to create, and the purpose of human life is to evolve.* She realized that to evolve, we must understand the true nature of our origins, the ardent quest that inspired the book you now have in your hands.

Rise Up! is a loving gift from a powerful spiritual teacher dedicated to the wellbeing of others. It offers "Karmic Cause and Effect," a process that teaches us to bring lessons from all our lifetimes into the present time; this frees us to create entirely new experiences. By arriving in the Now, we are released to co-create new realities in synchronicity with the Universe.

Suzanne has interviewed many important teachers. When I first heard from her in 2016, I didn't know who she was, even though her work is extremely significant; we almost did not meet. When we did try to get together, I encountered peculiar communication gaffes and lapses of time, signs of interference from negative forces trying to stop us from linking up. I overrode the blocks, and a few days before Christmas 2017, we enjoyed an excellent three-part interview on *Revelations of the Aquarian Age,* my latest book. I was pleasantly surprised by the scope of her esoteric knowledge and her mastery of my own work. Suzanne is brilliant, determined, and totally dedicated to transformation, even transcendence.

I wanted to support her, so I asked her for a copy of *Wake Up!* But, I had no idea what I was getting myself into! When I got home, I couldn't put it down and stayed up very late. She led me effortlessly through a ten-day emotional processing system that enables anyone to dump the garbage of a lifetime; just dump the negative experiences that keep us from activating our potential. This workbook is a major contribution in the healing arts, so I reviewed it on Amazon and gave it a five-star rating. She was just finishing the manuscript for her latest book, so I asked her if I could read it and write a blurb for it. *Rise Up!* takes us on a deep journey through ancient wisdom while examining our place in the Universe. I couldn't imagine praising it adequately in a few sentences, so I wrote this foreword, my attempt to evaluate it as a contribution to healing ourselves and our world.

I am the author of many books exploring new consciousness since the 1980s, and I was also the co-publisher of Bear & Company from 1983 through 2000 when I helped discover many key teachers. I offer this background because I think my work as a publisher qualifies me put *Rise Up!* in to its proper cultural context. My generation of spiritual seekers, the people born in the late 1930s to the late 1950s, had to use almost all of their energy to break down false paradigms. When I came into my own in the 1980s, human consciousness was left-brain and narrow. Anybody who talked about finding spiritual access, breaking into other dimensions, or transcending time was laughed at. Even though the world had finally gotten past believing God created the world 6,000 years ago and then took Sunday off, the timelines for ancient cultures were far too recent.

The anthropological dogma was that humans have been advancing for the last 5,000 years, but why was the human species declining in my time? My generation rebelled and moved the timeline back for human culture deeper into the past. We assessed the meaning of sacred sites and temples all over the planet, and we felt we might have once been more advanced than we are now, whether the archeologists liked it or not. We challenged left-brain science and history and brought forth intuitive knowledge that ended up being verified. We scaled some of the walls of ignorance by the time Suzanne's generation, people born in the 1960's and '70s, came into their power in the late 1990's and early twenty-first century. Now it is time for my generation to pass the mantle to them. Like a wilderness fire fighter who has fought too many fires, I don't have the energy to do what needs to come next: *It is time to take the great wisdom that we've gathered about our magnificent past into the world and use it to redeem Earth.* Earth must be freed from human ignorance so she can "rise up" in all her glory.

My generation recovered ancient healing methods and found ways to practice them to free Earth from toxicity, which is often sourced in human anger, guilt, greed, and arrogance. The race to avoid succumbing to cancer, or dying from pollution, heart attacks, and addictions, is a race to a finish we cannot yet see. When I was young, to even suggest using alternative healing or developing greater consciousness was considered insane. Meanwhile, Suzanne cuts through the resistance and ignorance by saying, "OK, let's just do it in ten days!" Her emotional-processing workbook actually does show you how to dump your darkness, pain, and resistance in 10 days! Yet, who would ever dream that she also could create a way for students to ascend to the highest planes, the multiple dimensions that encase us all, in only ten days? Well, she actually has.

Dipping into *Rise Up!*, I assumed it would be a fun journey through the essential esoteric teachings in a complete yet simplistic way. Out went that idea when I realized Suzanne based *Rise Up!* on the *Urantia Book*, the 2,000-page tome that journeys through galaxies and universes guided by celestial beings. Speaking of serendipities, I "accidentally" walked into the front office of the Urantia Foundation in 1983 in Chicago when I was in graduate school. It seemed like anybody was welcome, so I sat down with the huge book, read it for many hours, and almost didn't make it home on time. Even though many of the names and places were very foreign to me, truth rang through the pages. Suzanne was very wise to use it as the background for her ascension workbook, since it is the most advanced esoteric source of recent time, amazing cosmic teachings recorded during 1924-35 by an adventurous group that published it in the 1950s. She weaves the wisdom of many other mystic writers along with the *Urantia Book* and lifts you up into a deeper connection with nature and to the universal energy all around you. All you have to do is dedicate ten days. The format for this journey is amazing because as she brings you ancient wisdom, esoteric systems, and sacred places, she walks with you in nature, a brilliant idea.

This morning, as I was taking a walk while enjoying the aroma of grapefruit blossoms and watching hummingbirds zero in on red blossoms and listening to mockingbirds sing, I realized Suzanne had awakened a deeper connection with nature within me just by having the privilege of reading *Rise Up!* I didn't have the time to do the exercises, make notes, and do the meditations, yet just reading it stimulated my senses. My heart connection with everything I was enjoying was so much deeper, and the air and water was shimmering, vibrating with subtle angelic frequencies that were reaching for me. Thank you Suzanne. What a gift from such a gifted writer!

Suzanne accomplishes this by firmly grounding the high esoteric wisdom in the matrix of nature, life expressing itself through many dimensions. So, when she takes you for a walk on the beach and you encounter sand dollars and nautilus shells, you are stunned to see that their shapes and designs are fifth-and-sixth dimensional as if they exist to awaken our inner knowledge of sacred geometry. Hearing birds singing as Suzanne walks with you in the forest accesses your inner seventh-dimensional sound codes, then eighth-dimensional divine light floods your pineal gland. Just being on these journeys with her while contemplating her beautiful art selection activates all of your inner higher-dimensional codes. Based on my nine-dimensional model in *The Pleiadian Agenda* and *Alchemy of Nine Dimensions*, I've taught students how to activate these dimensional codes for twenty-five years. We have advanced so far! Suzanne takes you directly into the zones of living wisdom in nature to activate your inner multidimensional knowledge.

With these ideas in mind, now we have to ask how we are going to move beyond wars, desperate migrations, resource depletion, pandemics, and starvation. The answer is actually in this book. Let us remember that we create with the dimensional fields of Earth; *we* create the dilemmas I just listed above. We've become overwhelmed by these toxic creations because we haven't taken responsibility for creating them and allowing them to continue. The only way out of this conundrum is to purge the negative fields; then activate the creative fields you really want with love in your hearts and intelligence in your minds. This book teaches you how to do it—and fast! After 75 years of loving and serving Earth to pass the wisdom I've found, my own worries are gone because Suzanne Ross and others like her are carrying on. If she could write a book like *Rise Up!* totally grounded in nature, then I can hope our species will rise up and transcend, humans remembering they are the Keepers of Earth.

March 15, 2018

Barbara Hand Clow is the author of *Alchemy of Nine Dimensions* with Gerry Clow, *Revelations of the Ruby Crystal*, and *Revelations of the Aquarian Age*.

Rise Up!

Awakening through Revelation

10 Days on the Ascension Path

INTRODUCTION

I came to a point in my life where I woke up and said, "There has to be more to life than this! There must be more meaning and purpose for my existence! This can't be all there is!" For me at the time, my day looked like this: I would wake up in the morning to a screaming alarm jolting me out of my dream state and plunging me into the harsh reality of having to get up before I'm even done sleeping. The restorative and reparative benefits of sleeping had been rudely interrupted as I was awakened, frightened actually, by the loud bells suddenly clanging in my head! Still sleepy, I would stumble into the bathroom and robotically go through the motions of getting ready for what promised to be a very challenging yet highly unrewarding day. Always the optimist, I would try and think of the positive things I could do or say to improve the quality of the day but, in the back of my mind, I knew I was in the wrong place doing the wrong thing with the wrong people.

This 9:00 -5:00 (or more accurately 5:00-9:00) daily grind did not suit my true nature and I knew it in the very core of my being. At the time however, I felt there was no way out. It was only when I totally surrendered and asked for guidance from a higher power, that I found my way and discovered my true purpose. Only then did my life take on a deeper meaning. I realized later that what that period in my life had offered me as a gift, or reward for suffering, was invaluable. It triggered in me a strong determination to find a greater meaning and deeper purpose to my life. It awakened in me the realization that there had to be more! Even then, somewhere inside of me, I knew there was and that I could find it. And so I did.

It is this type of faith and determination that has driven man for thousands of years to seek out the true meaning and purpose of our existence. Regardless of what it is that leads man to this inherent search for truth, every human being will experience these feelings at some point in their life one way or another. Just by the fact that you are reading this book means that you have reached that point and because of your faith and determination, are now seeking answers. Your interest in universal truth and sacred wisdom shows you have awakened and are ready to evolve!

In my first book, Wake Up!, I share my journey of "Awakening through Reflection" and how it inspired me to set out on a spiritual quest. The book is a 10-day life lessons workshop because I discovered a "Karmic Cause & Effect Analysis" process that reveals the important life lessons we came here to learn while providing the opportunity to balance the karma we've created along the way. I wanted to share this process with others since it has been so cathartic for me. The book also includes journaling, meditations and "Practical Spirituality" — daily practices for balancing ego and spirit. Through this book, you will learn how to intentionally create meaningful experiences so that you can consciously evolve toward more enlightened ones. You will discover that the meaning of life is to create and the purpose is to evolve. This was a huge revelation for me that has transformed my life in many profound ways. It is my sincere desire that it will have this same effect on others. My book *Wake Up!* is available at SacredDragonPublishing and video workshops are accessible at SciSpi.tv/Wake-Up/.

After realizing that the meaning of life was to create, and the purpose was to evolve, I began a quest to discover the true nature and origin of our being which inspired this next book in the "Up!" trilogy, *Rise Up!* My quest has been very fruitful. What I have discovered has filled me with a great sense of awe and wonder. I feel a much deeper connection to nature and to the universal energy all around me. I am so grateful for this opportunity to learn, teach and grow. I embrace every moment of my life with a spiritual fervor that I want to share with all seekers. I have a strong sense of overwhelming love for all that is, and it is this journey of discovery that has inspired me! I wish to share it with you now in the hopes that you will experience the same sense of awe and wonder as we explore the beauty of creation and the mystery of evolution together.

> *"Never cease to stand like curious children before the*
> *great mystery into which we were born."* ~ Einstein

That's exactly what we'll be doing on this adventure!

I am motivated by an intense curiosity that drives me to read and research everything I can get my hands on. My insatiable curiosity fuels my pursuit of answers to the biggest questions: What is the source of our origin? Is there a grand design and if so, what is our role in it? Do we have a greater purpose beyond the everyday struggle and finally, what (or where) is our ultimate destiny?

In an effort to discover, understand and share these answers, I have taken great strides to interpret complex ideas and confusing terminology into everyday language. My goal is to present them in a way that is intriguing and suspenseful. The story of creation is the greatest mystery of all time and should be enjoyed as such. Solving this mystery takes us on a fascinating adventure and it requires turning information into fascination. Fortunately, unlike most people today, I am blessed with the gift of time. I have spent thousands of hours over several years researching a vast array of knowledge on topics ranging from astronomy and physics to spirituality and metaphysics. As such, I have developed a depth of knowledge about these matters only by painstakingly and meticulously going over and over them in detail until I feel I have reached a clear understanding. It became evident to me early on that all of this information was connected and much of it was saying the same thing. I found I was exploring the same concepts just from different perspectives. I even discovered that they were coming up with the same answers to the same questions among disciplines that were supposedly contradictory! The concepts and philosophies were just presented from different perspectives based on their specialized expertise or specific belief system.

I have been able to develop a broad perspective on a wide array of topics because I have maintained an unbiased openness to all of the knowledge. I am not limited by one specific area of research or focused on one religion or spiritual philosophy. As a result, I know a little about a lot and this has allowed me to see the parallels between many different schools of thought. Although unlimited in my breadth of research, I am limited in the specific details and technical knowledge of any one field. However, this book is not intended in any way to be a scientific text or a religious or spiritual doctrine. It is intended for the everyday person who has an open mind and a willingness to explore a variety of ideas and paths. As such, I am opening my book with a blanket statement to clarify my intention:

The theories presented within are purely hypothetical, conceptual and not necessarily factual. I have taken information that I have discovered and contemplated its significance within the context of a broad perspective. I offer this perspective and then develop a theory, or set of ideas, for your consideration. My intention is that the readers discover, consider and decide for themselves what may or may not represent universal truth and sacred wisdom. I encourage this by suggesting further research as well as contemplative meditation.

"The ultimate value of life depends upon awareness and the power of contemplation rather than mere survival." ~ Aristotle

I have found deep contemplation to be an extremely valuable tool which has led to many of my epiphanies and revelations. Einstein called them "thought experiments" and although his were on the level of genius, the concept is still the same. He connected to a greater field of consciousness which led to earth-shattering revelations. We too can access this field and discover our own truths! There are many questions that we as humans do not have absolute factual answers for, so we must "theorize" based on what we believe to be true. For centuries, scientists, spiritualists and theologians have taken what they have knowledge of and formulated what they believed were "truths" based on actual research as well as intuitive insight. It is all a matter of perception. In fact, perception is a major factor in the assessment of the true nature of reality. Honestly, it may be the only one that truly matters!

The Dalai Lama once said something to the effect of: Do not believe anything I say. Listen to and read everything you can get your hands on. Then contemplate what you have learned so you can have your own experience of the truth. This is exactly what I want you to do with the ideas I have presented. I will share as much knowledge as I can from credible sources quoting intelligent and insightful contributors of wisdom (as well as offering my own intuitive insight). In the end, however, it is for you to decide what resonates as true for you. What works for you is whatever you can wrap your head around and apply to your own experience of reality. The most important thing I encourage you to do is to have an open mind. I heard a funny quote by Frank Zappa once:

"A mind is like a parachute. It doesn't work if it isn't open."

In the search for universal truth, it's critical to keep an open mind and not allow preconceived ideas and notions, or fear of the unknown, to stand in the way of new ideas and possibilities. In a book by Shirley MacLaine called "Out on a Limb", I found a wonderful excerpt that inspired me to explore beyond the familiar horizon of my comfort zone:

"Instead of going deeper, most people choose to be comfortable, to just accept the limits and restrictions imposed by safe superficiality, to be successful and well-attended creatures of comfort with protection and warmth and no challenges from what could be frighteningly new and unknown... no challenges from what more we could be, no challenge from what more we could understand, no challenge of how that might threaten us."[1]

When I read this, I thought, "It's like scuba diving. It challenges you to go way outside of your comfort zone as you dive into the freezing water and enter a world of the unknown where you can't even breathe normally! But the fascinating world of incredible beauty and wonder that lies just under the surface is so magical, it's absolutely worth the risk and you are grateful you accepted the challenge!" Just by the fact that you are reading this, shows that you have chosen to accept the challenge of going beyond your preconceived notions and explore new ideas. Motivated by a desire to enhance your life and become more enlightened in your approach to living and being, you may already be very open-minded and that will benefit you greatly on this adventure into the depths of reality.

In the introduction of my first book *Wake Up!* I shared a story about how one day I woke up determined to figure out the true meaning and purpose of life. While on a walking meditation later that day, I was suddenly blessed with a divine revelation. It was so spectacular that it triggered an intense desire within me to reach out and tell everyone what I had learned in that moment. On a walk one day, I was looking down at the ground intensely focused on my thoughts. I was saying over and over in my mind, "Meaning and purpose, meaning and purpose..." when suddenly I felt compelled to look up at the sky. As if I was having a dreamlike vision, I saw clearly written across the sky in puffy white letters:

MEANING — TO CREATE PURPOSE — TO EVOLVE

I knew I was witnessing a miracle and just stood there in complete awe for a few moments. Then a huge sense of relief washed over me. I finally had the answer I had been seeking and it was so simple and yet so profound. From that moment on, I knew I had to devote the rest of my life to creating with meaning and evolving with purpose. I also felt very strongly that this message had been given to me so I could share it with others. I have spent every day since then focused on doing just that. I am either developing a workshop, writing a book, producing videos or conducting interviews. I have interviewed over 50 spiritually inspired thought leaders from around the world and share them on my website at SciSpi.tv/Rise-Up/.

Through my workshops, books and shows, I have inspired and empowered many people around the world just by revealing this one simple truth:

We are extraordinary human beings with the unlimited potential to do, be and have anything we desire with the power of our pure intentions.

All we have to do is believe in ourselves, apply some basic principles and stay focused on our own personal evolution!

This book, however, takes the whole concept of realizing one's potential to a much higher level as we reveal the true power of our 'Creator-consciousness' and the amazing strength of our directed intention. It all starts with a greater understanding of the vibrational nature of reality and our connection to the universal mind! Once I really began to contemplate 'creating and evolving' on a deeper level, it occurred to me that if we truly want to realize the fundamental truths about ourselves, we need to know more about who we really are, where we came from, how we got here, why we are here and where we are going. I knew these were heavy questions, but I also knew I had to find the answers and so I began an exhaustive search through books, archives and religious texts about mythology and history, science and spirituality, quantum physics and metaphysics. I have also referenced material whose source is of an "other-worldly" nature. I discovered some remarkable teachings that were provided by advanced beings through the process of channeling. The knowledge that is revealed in these texts often times far exceeds our own current understanding of reality.

For thousands of years, man has been driven to seek out the origin and nature of his existence. Because of this passionate quest for the truth, there are endless resources of information available about creation and evolution. I will present a vast array of factual, mythological and channeled material and then draw parallels between them. This has proven to be a very effective way of identifying the fundamental truths that have been repeated throughout the ages. The enduring power of these truths stands as a testimonial of their authenticity. Drawing the parallels between different perspectives on the same conceptual truths has been truly fascinating. I will find a sacred text that uncovers some bizarre-sounding myth and then find scientific facts or evidence that actually validate it! The channeled material is absolutely the most revealing. I highly encourage you to open your mind about this as a very credible source of advanced knowledge and sacred wisdom. The stories of Abraham and Moses in the bible are probably the most well-known examples of receiving 'divine' messages from an 'other-worldly' source. Other good examples are Muhammed's encounter with Angel Gabriel or Joseph Smith's interaction with "Moroni" who led him to the "Golden Book of Mormon." Many prophets and seers over the centuries have been blessed with sacred knowledge that they received from an "other-worldly" source. Accounts of gods, demi-gods and angels interacting with humans is a common theme in the ancient world and even today, many people believe in the presence of angels and divine guidance from "above."

I believe channeling is a sincere attempt from higher sources, heavenly or otherwise, to lovingly guide us and teach us in the interest of our evolutionary advancement. In fact, the ancient and modern texts based on insights from these sources contain the most compelling and comprehensive revelations. The "Pyramid Texts" and Sumerian clay tablets along with *The Urantia Book* and *The RA Material* are excellent examples of this and when I align the content with scientific facts and spiritual or religious doctrines, it becomes clear that they are presenting fundamental truths! Some of these truths are rather shocking and have dramatically altered my understanding of creation and evolution. I promise you that this part of the adventure will be extraordinarily fascinating as we crawl through ancient caves, read ancient and modern sacred texts and hang out with extraordinary authors who become our tour guides on this virtual adventure. All of this will bring us closer to the real truth behind the story of creation!

Here are the things you need to put into your backpack before heading out on this adventure:

1) A strong desire to discover the fundamental truths of our existence
2) A deeply inquisitive curiosity about the universe around you
3) An open-mind! This requires a willingness to reserve judgment until all relevant viewpoints have been taken into consideration
4) An ability to set aside preconceived ideas and notions thereby, making space for new ones
5) An expansive mind that can see the big picture beyond ordinary experiences of reality
6) A vivid imagination that can visualize new possibilities about the true nature of reality
7) A commitment to engage in contemplative meditation so inner wisdom can be revealed
8) A dedication to journaling the truths that resonate strongly within the core of your being

Let's briefly discuss journaling as a way of recording your personal revelations. I have suggested that you "journal the truths that resonate strongly." You may be asking, "What does that mean? How will I know what "resonates" for me? Is it a feeling or an awareness? How do I identify 'truths' and develop a 'knowing'?" These are all good questions. Hopefully, I can answer them for you because I had the same ones myself and have given them a lot of thought. I have also been fortunate enough to have had the experience of "coming to a knowing." I believe that to resonate with a truth is to remember it. If something you read or hear about "rings true" for you, I believe you are having a 'moment of recall' just like when you suddenly remember an event or a person from this lifetime because a memory has been triggered.

This type of recall usually occurs when something from your five senses of sight (including visions), sound (including words and thoughts), smell, taste or even touch recognizes something familiar that "rings a bell." It's likely something from the so-called "past" that causes a specific memory to surface. This is common with smells (like perfume) or sounds (like a song). Sometimes we may not even be able to identify exactly where the memory came from as it might feel strange to us like déjà vu. Some memories may even originate from a dream experience or past life. I believe that we have millions of memories from all of our experiences beginning from the first moment of creation. I also believe that if we expand our consciousness, we can greatly increase our ability to tap into these and "recall" many of them. This type of recall presents itself as a familiar truth that you have a certain knowing about and, as such, it resonates with you or "rings true." These truths are the ones that we have had the deepest connection with over many lifetimes. Our akashic records hold the accumulation of all of the experiences we have had since the beginning of time! This is the library of our consciousness and we can tap into the memories within it just by triggering them. Through exploring creation and evolution from a spiritual and scientific perspective, we are triggering deep-seated memories that otherwise may not surface. Of course, journaling, meditating, visualizing and contemplating help to trigger these revelations as well and we will be engaging in all of these practices during each day of our adventure!

Ultimately, the true purpose of our lives is to progress along our ascension paths by creating meaningful experiences that increase our self-knowledge and enhance our ability to love. To "know thyself" and to experience love are the two primary reasons for our existence. Always remember that wisdom and love are the keys to creation, evolution and ascension. This ascension journey presents a unique opportunity to "know thyself" by uncovering the mysteries about our divine origin, true nature and final destiny from both an intellectual and spiritual perspective. It also offers a precious opportunity to develop a greater love for all living beings and a deeper love for all that is. As evolved beings on the ascension path toward self-realization, we can consciously create the most meaningful experiences that fulfill our divine purpose — to gather wisdom and experience love. This deeper meaning and greater purpose lie at the root of our soul's evolutionary journey and reminds me of the divine revelation I was once blessed with:

Meaning: To Create, Purpose: To Evolve

Creating with meaning and evolving with purpose is the divine plan! Let's ask ourselves if we can implement this plan while on our adventurous journey.

What if we could consciously create and purposefully evolve by:

1) Diving deep into sacred texts that reveal profound truths about the energetic nature of reality

2) Taking a closer look at the scientific discoveries revealed by quantum physics, astronomy, and archaeology.

3) Exploring the fundamental truths that lie within the numerous religious and spiritual belief systems.

4) Contemplating and meditating upon all the information that we gather and piecing it together like a puzzle.

Once our exploration of science, religion and spirituality reaches a certain point, pieces of the puzzle will naturally start falling into place and we will have profound "a-ha" moments — or "epiphanies", if you will. What we have really done is triggered a memory from the deep recesses of our subconscious mind. When this happens, we experience a moment of total recall! This is just like the feeling you get when you've been struggling to remember something and suddenly it flashes in your mind. It's a moment of ecstatic recall and you're proud of yourself for retrieving it. Then you have a profound sense of relief that you finally resolved the mystery that had been gnawing at you. All our memories are out there in the vast field of consciousness and we must trigger them if we want to understand the true nature of our being.

Fortunately, many generous and insightful people have already accessed much of this knowledge and wisdom from the universal field and have shared their valuable insight. Whether it has been through exhaustive research, intuitive revelation or spiritual seeking, we have been gifted with a tremendous depth of literary knowledge and sacred wisdom. This is the material I want to share with you along with my own intuitive insight. The truths and possibilities contained within this material have sparked many profound epiphanies and divine revelations for me personally. It is my sincere desire that, after sharing what I have realized on my own path, you too will have personal epiphanies and revelations! Once you discover your own personal truths, you will make significant progress on your own path toward a deep and powerful self-knowing.

The key to fully embracing this adventure will be for you to help me draw the parallels and find the fundamental truths within the revelations. This is our adventure and we are taking it together. I will present you with the material, share my own insights about them and then I encourage you to research and contemplate them as well. I highly recommend that you get a hold of the books I have referenced and check out the contents for yourself. One very unique aspect of this book is that I have had the privilege of interviewing many of the authors whose books I have referenced throughout. I have produced entertaining and informative videos featuring these interviews and you can access them easily at SciSpi.tv/Rise-Up/. This way you can hear directly from the authors themselves and formulate your own conclusions about their revelations and discoveries.

At the end of each day's adventure, you will have the opportunity to sit in contemplative meditation and develop insights of your own. Let's figure this out together! It's our human origin and destiny we are talking about after all! We need to know this stuff if we are going to live in this world with our eyes wide open! This knowledge will allow us to live in our world more fully with a much greater appreciation for the pure wonder and amazement of it all. That makes the whole adventure worthwhile! Plus, we'll have fun along the way!

Now that we're all gathered at the trailhead, let's get inspired to head into this exploration by engaging in the following visualization. This poetic version of the creation story, entitled "I AM", is inspired by the celestial teachings in *The Urantia Book* and as such, I have included several excerpts from this remarkable text. Since this visualization is meant to be thought-provoking, an open mind and vivid imagination will help you to fully embrace the experience.

"Imagination is more important than knowledge." ~ Einstein

The Adventure Begins
I AM
A Creation Story
(Inspired by The Urantia Book and RA Material)

Creation began as a thought — a sudden awareness that emerged out of an infinite ocean of pure bliss. Like a bright idea that sparks one's imagination, this creative thought ignited a spark of brilliant light! Within that single point of light was infinite intelligence and vast energy potential — enough to create the eternal realm of the ever-expanding universe! This "being of light" in the infinite realm is of a triune nature which reflects a trinity of beings. In the nucleus of this ocean of bliss resides the Universal Mother-Father God — the "first source and center" and original "Cosmic Personality." Surrounding this "Nuclear Isle of Light" is a luminous sphere — a reflection of God that embodies his spirit. This is the being of the Eternal Child — the "second source and center" and essence of the "Cosmic Spirit." Expanding outward in this infinite realm is the vibrant sphere of the Infinite Spirit — a co-creative expression of the Mother-Father and Child. This being, the "the third source and center" embodies the "Cosmic Mind." As this trinity of beings, resting in divine unity, became consciously aware of their potential to move beyond just existing into actually experiencing, they were consumed with a desire to "Know Thyself' as the collective "Comic Consciousness."

This inherent longing for self-realization, and the desire to creatively express their infinite potential, inspired these primordial beings of love and light to create in unity as the trinity consciousness of the "One Infinite Creator." They began to realize that in order to create with the energy of love and the light of intelligence, they would have to expand their divine consciousness. From their infinite realm, they would have to co-create an eternal, existential realm within which they could "exist" as manifest beings. This realm would have a beginning but no ending. Their creative consciousness would be projected into an eternal "being" that could actualize their potential in this existential realm. They would call this living, breathing being "The Eternal Realm of Havona." Forever residing in the infinite realm of Paradise, the Divine Trinity realized they could project a reflection of their consciousness into eternity as the Creative Trinity. From Paradise, Mother-Father God could project its "Cosmic Personality" to define all patterns of energy and matter. In Havona, the Eternal Child could project its "Cosmic Spirit" to inspire the creation of life and the Infinite Spirit could project its "Cosmic Mind" to create and illuminate forms. Together, their ability to project their consciousness enabled them to create eternity in four distinct directions with four elemental patterns. Within each of the four directional elements, the trinity was still expressed. With the trinity (3) expressing itself in all four (4) directions, they developed twelve (3 X 4) patterns of consciousness. These twelve patterns became the divine blueprints of perfection for the eternal ones existing in Havona who would later become known as the "Ancients of Days." As 12 male/female divine counterparts, they would become the 24 elders.

Once the Creative Trinity manifested an existential realm of perfection with twelve archetypal beings that could exist and "be", they soon developed the desire to project an experiential realm in which these beings could experience and "do." Already perfect in eternity, they imagined a realm where these beings could "evolve" into perfection by experiencing reality rather than just existing in it. As their collective vision began to take shape, the Creative Trinity taught the eternal children the same technique of reflection and projection that they had used to escape infinity. Just as they had to move out of infinity to create in eternity, the eternal children would have to move out of eternity to create an experiential realm.

From infinity, the Divine Trinity projected a reflection of themselves into eternity. In doing so, they created an inverted triangle that could penetrate a point through which their consciousness could flow beyond infinity. This point is called the Isle of Paradise and will always lie at the center of Havona. This source of consciousness from the infinite sea will always flow into eternity — the creative realm with a beginning but no ending. Now the Creative Trinity would teach the 12 archetypal children of eternity to use the same technique of reflection and projection to expand their consciousness beyond eternity. They developed the ability to project perfect reflections of themselves as holographic images that could suspend in space. Then they created the concept of the "arrow of time" upon which they could travel.

Collectively, they would become one "being" with twelve aspects. Projecting outward into space and traveling on the arrow of time, this being would be called the "Supreme Being." This brilliant technique of holographic projection coupled with the ingenious method of space-time travel would enable the eternal children to virtually experience realms of illusion that would seem very real to their senses. Through the Supreme Being, the 12 archetypal expressions could project their perfect blueprints like soul streams expanding into holographic time and space realms. These realms would simply be a reflection of Havona — the only real and perfect universe at the center of creation. The Supreme Being would create 7 holographic spheres to revolve around Havona as reflections of its 7 energy centers. With 7 universes and 12 archetypes as the perfect patterns of creation, the Supreme Being created holographic worlds with holographic beings to inhabit them based upon these patterns. This grand illusion would offer a holographic "place", or point, where the Creative Trinity could "know" the 12 aspects of thyself through experiences in time and space realms. The further the Supreme Being projected into the farthest reaches of time and space, the more distorted the consciousness of the holographic beings became.

No matter how distorted or chaotic these worlds and beings became, they would always be drawn back to the source of their beingness in Havona as the eternal ones. These "distorted" soul streams would always be sourced from perfection and instinctually be compelled to evolve toward it. In whispers, they would hear their soul calling from Havona and eventually heed the call and turn homeward. These soul-infused "human" beings would always be inspired to seek out their divine source no matter where they were in time and space. At some point on their journey, something would always ignite their divine spark. This would inspire them to set out on a spiritual quest to find the source of this eternal flame. These inspired seekers eventually discover that the source of their being has been inside their own hearts all along. They intuitively find ways to connect into their own heart space and tune into their eternal soul flame from beyond. Eventually, they are drawn into the heart of their home in Havona where they tune into their perfect divine blueprint. When this connection is made, the transformation begins as their soul flame ignites their divine source codes. This sets the seeker firmly on the ascension path and this is where our 10-day journey begins.

The version of creation and evolution you have just read was inspired by the celestial being who shared the following passages in *The Urantia Book*:

"The absolute level is beginningless, endless, timeless, and stateless. This level is Trinity attained by the Paradise deities...Finite realities may not have endings, but they always have beginnings — they are created...Deity may be existential, as in the Eternal (Child); experiential, as in (The Supreme Being — the supreme deity of evolutionary time-space creatures)...undivided, as in the Paradise Trinity. Deity is the source of all that which is divine...Divinity is creature comprehensible as truth, beauty and goodness; correlated in personality as love, mercy and ministry; disclosed on impersonal levels as justice, power and sovereignty. Divinity may be perfect-complete-as on existential and Creator levels of Paradise perfection; it may be imperfect, as on experiential and creature levels of time-space evolution; or it may be relative, neither perfect or imperfect as in certain Havona levels of existential-experiential relationships... Cosmic consciousness implies the recognition of a first cause, the one and only uncaused reality... God, as the first source and center, is primal in relation to the total reality... The Universal (Mother-Father) is the personality of the first source and center and as such, maintains personal relations of infinite control over all coordinate and subordinate sources and centers...The mind forces are converging in the Infinite Spirit (the second source and center) ...The universe spirit forces are converging in the Eternal (Child), (the third source and center). [2]

This remarkable insight gives a sense of order to the creation story and satisfies the pervasive spiritual belief in a beginning-less, endless realm of infinity while still embracing the collective "religious" belief in a Creator as the first cause. This explanation of the trinity as the "triune" nature of God, existing on Paradise fulfills the biblical prophecies and at the same time, helps us to understand them as the source of our personality, spirit and mind. Intentionally projecting their consciousness into the eternal realm allows them to express their creative potential in "Havona" while remaining unified in their divine essence on Paradise. We will continue to explore the creation story as told by the celestial beings in *The Urantia Book* throughout our adventure but this summary helps us to understand the foundation on which it is based.

Within the foreword of this book, I also found an exquisite explanation of the "I AM" principle. This expression has been used repeatedly throughout human history as a divine revelation that embraces the essence of our being. Philosophers and theologians have been searching for the true meaning behind this expression for centuries. In the bible, Jesus, as the word of God, proclaims "I am the bread of life" (John 6:48) and in spiritual literature, "I am that I am" is often presented as a proclamation of our divine nature. I was very intrigued by the explanation offered in *The Urantia Book* and although the terminology used can be somewhat confusing at times, if you focus on the deeper meaning behind the words, the revelations are profound. To convey the meaning, I will present their explanation as a collection of excerpts I have pieced together:

"Reality, as comprehended by finite beings, is partial, relative, and shadowy. The maximum deity reality fully comprehensible by evolutionary finite creatures is embraced within the Supreme Being. Nevertheless, there are antecedent and eternal realities, 'super finite realities', which are ancestral to the supreme deity of evolutionary time-space creatures. In attempting to portray the origin and nature of universal reality, we are forced to employ the technique of time-space reasoning to reach the level of the finite mind. Therefore, must many of the simultaneous events of eternity be presented as sequential "transactions." As the time-space creature would view the origin and differentiation of reality, the eternal and infinite I AM achieved deity liberation from the fetters of... infinity to the exercise of inherent and eternal free will... And this original transaction, the theoretical I AM achieved the realization of personality by becoming the eternal (Mother-Father) of the original (Child) simultaneously with becoming the eternal source of the Isle of Paradise. Coexistent with the differentiation of the (Child) from the (Mother-Father), and in the presence of Paradise, there appeared the person of the Infinite Spirit and the central universe of Havona... The concept of I AM is a philosophic concession which we make to the...finite mind of man, to the impossibility of creature comprehension of eternity existences — beginning but never-ending realities and relationships. To the time-space creature, all things must have a beginning save only the one uncaused — the primeval cause of causes. Therefore, do we conceptualize this philosophic value-level as the I AM, at the same time instructing all creatures that the Eternal (Child) and Infinite Spirit are co-eternal with the I AM; in other words, that there never was a time when the I AM was not the (Mother-Father) of the (Eternal Child) and, with them, of the (Infinite) Spirit." [3]

I recommend reading and re-reading this a few times to fully grasp the meaning and then pausing to absorb the full implications of this profound message. Once the depth of their meaning is understood, however, the reality they portray is magnificent! We begin to fully realize the divine origin and nature of our being. The ultimate truth is that we are each a unique pattern, or aspect, of the Creator's personality. Furthermore, we are endowed with its creative spirit and have unlimited access to its infinite intelligence! Of course, because of our attachment to our ego-identity, it requires a conscious effort to evolve toward this realization, but that's why we are on this ascension journey!

From a more earthly standpoint, I have made a sincere attempt to intertwine scientific theory with the diverse philosophies and beliefs of both religion and spirituality. What I have come to discover, time and again, is that they are intricately intertwined in many ways. Making the parallels between these views truly defines the nature of my approach. As the creation story continues and the formation of the universes get underway, I use this approach to combine science and spirituality into one creative symphony, or uni-"verse". This has inspired me to create a new TV show genre called Sci-Spi, which led me to create my online TV network called SciSpi.tv/.

My quest to merge science and spiritualty inspired me to write this poetic verse:

From a single point of light, the Cosmic Consciousness emerged in a brilliant explosion of infinite energy. Thus, the amazing adventure of creation and evolution began! At first, there were just gaseous clouds and colorful lights but as these continued to expand outward, they began to cool. As they cooled, antimatter and matter engaged in a struggle, but light overcame the darkness and matter emerged victoriously! Atoms began to form out of the gas and swirling strings of vibrating light began spinning to create forms and geometric patterns. The Creator is beginning to realize his infinite intelligence through the creation of these patterns as each one becomes more complex. The ability to creatively evolve in this way gives meaning and purpose to this experience. The Creator's journey of self-realization is underway! Cosmic consciousness is at the core of all creation for it is the first source of all things — the uncaused cause, if you will. The Creator, as the Universal Mother-Father, is the "Cosmic Personality," the bestower of personality and the originator of all patterns of energy — material, spiritual and mindal. The Eternal Child projects the spirit of life into these patterns and in doing so, living beings are created! The Child, as the likeness of Mother-Father God, embodies the pure qualities of love and compassion, peace and joy. These values define the highest consciousness attainable by these created beings. The infinite intelligence of Mother-Father and Child is embraced by the Infinite Spirit who embodies the omnipresent and omniscient "Cosmic Mind." Stars are created that the trinity can admire and planets for beings which they can adore.

We are the Divine Trinity's creations. They created us with the light and energy of their own creative potential which is filled with infinite love and intelligence. As creative aspects of the original trinity, we are filled with the same creative potential ignited by the desire to know and love thyself! In the beginning, these creative beings knew they had the energy potential and free will to create throughout eternity and therefore, to express and self-realize. Their desire to know thyself is so powerful that it drives the eternal expansion of consciousness. They are fully aware of their infinite potential to manifest with an ever-evolving intelligence. Therefore, they use their free will to continue to create knowing the possibilities are always endless. The "One Infinite Creator" as Mother-Father God along with the Eternal Child and Infinite Spirit are proving to be unimaginatively creative as their all-pervasive consciousness intelligently evolves, expands and ascends! We are this cosmic consciousness. We exist within this creative field as eternal spirit beings. We are simply clothed within a holographic vehicle so that we can have experiences in the time-space illusion and therefore, become more self-realized.

"Reality is an illusion, albeit a very pervasive one." ~ Einstein

Our physical and spiritual incarnations in multiple realms enriches our soul's evolution and ascension! As we move through this 10-day adventure, it will become increasingly clear that we must fully embrace every precious moment. We will learn to cherish every opportunity to expand our consciousness. We will become tuned into our higher selves as we activate our divine source codes and ignite the divine spark in our soul. We will be inspired to dedicate ourselves every day in every way to our soul's ascension into the light of pure love!

So, what are we waiting for? Why are we living within this limited view of ourselves as human beings? We truly are spiritual beings having a physical experience and as such, the spirit of the divine trinity and all of their creative potential lie within each and every one of us. We are both human and divine! The creative spirit of the divine is all around us in every living thing and breathing being. It is omnipresent and omniscient. As divine light beings, we can learn to use this omnipotent light, or pure consciousness, to create and manifest. We can absorb this light and use it to ignite our own creative spirit. We can learn how to direct our thoughts intentionally and access the "Creator-consciousness." As we uncover the true nature of our reality, we will learn how to tap directly into it!

With that in mind, let's begin our virtual adventure into the mysteries of creation from infinity to eternity and through time and space realities! Let's set an intention to tune into these realms by opening our hearts and projecting our minds. As we project our consciousness into these realms, we will be developing our own "Creator-consciousness." This will activate our divine potential to create and manifest in these realms. This journey will awaken the creator within us as we tune into the source of our being. We will discover that anything is possible since we are both human and divine. This is how we RISE UP! and ascend, my friends, for this is a journey worth taking.

Many blessing on your extraordinary adventure!

With love in my heart for all beings,

Suzanne

REFERENCES

Introduction cover pic of angels courtesy of: _godsoutreachministryint.org_

Shirley MacLaine, Out on a Limb, Bantam Books, 1983

1. page 166

The Urantia Book Fellowship, The Urantia Book, Uversa Press, 2008

2. Foreword

3. Foreword

TUNING INTO SOURCE

Techniques for Accessing the Light of Wisdom

One day, while on a walking meditation, I was contemplating the origin and nature of light and sound. Several of the revelations I had been exploring, through both research and meditation, were leading me to the conclusion that the sun served as a portal through which consciousness could flow. I began to realize that not only was the sun a source of light, but it was also a source of consciousness. I also knew that the universe hummed with the sound of radiation. It was the vibrational sound of the universe! Then it dawned on me that these four words — source, consciousness, sound and light — were intricately connected. I began to play with various concepts: "Light and sound define the consciousness that emanates from the source", "The source of consciousness is illuminated by light and expressed by sound", etc. Visions of the brilliant spark of light that ignited the creation of all things began to flash in my mind. The sound of this spectacular explosion must have been epic! This flash of light and shockwave of sound symbolized the moment when the creative consciousness expanded wildly in all directions beginning the eternal adventure we are on. I thought of 'God's first words', according to the Bible, the 'words of the source', if you will: "Let there be light!" and had a sense that the greater meaning was "Let there be awareness!", "Let consciousness flow!" Therefore, the sun was created as a portal through which this source could be projected onto creation! I visualized images being created with spiraling waves of light and spinning colors to define the forms. The whole of reality could be viewed as an illusion of vibrating light and color creating an energetic field of consciousness. I began to imagine the source of intelligence — an artiste extraordinaire — swirling around in this field and creating these forms. I knew if I could see the space around me, there would be symbols and patterns crowding every inch of the space around me. Then I thought, "Wouldn't it be cool if I could actually see these invisible energies at work or communicate with the intelligence in charge? Then I could really start to uncover the mysteries of the universe!" It was only then I realized that maybe I already was. These experiences I was calling epiphanies were coming to me in the form of cosmic visions and messages from beyond. I began to realize that by expanding my awareness and meditating daily, I was somehow communicating with a higher source that was showing me answers and sharing inspiration. When I focused my attention in a contemplative state, answers would flow naturally into my mind that I had not previously known. Somehow, I was attracting this information into my own field of awareness. I wondered how I was doing this. I knew there were many people who did this all the time and that this type of communication had been going forever. Ancient cultures were aware of a "cosmic well of knowledge" that could only be accessed by mystics or lamas. The Hindu's called this pre-existing field of knowledge the "akashic records" and relied on enlightened beings to reveal the contents. I became extremely curious as to how and why only certain people could access this field. I also knew that, if it was humanly possible (and apparently it was), anyone could tap into it if they really tried!

As I started to explore this phenomenon, I discovered the concept of a "Zero Point Field" in which every thought, action and event of the past, present and future is stored in a collection of electrical charges. I came to understand that when I intentionally focused on receiving information, that an electromagnetic exchange of energy would take place. Consciousness would flow in on vibrating waves of light and sound. I became aware that I was attracting this information into my field by "tuning into it" like a radio frequency. If thoughts really were stored as electrical charges in a "zero point field", this would mean that I was intentionally sending out an electromagnetic frequency. I began to understand, through studying this concept, that by creating a vibrational field around me, I could attract energy that was vibrating at the same frequency. Thoughts, I realized, were energetic! I was intrigued by these revelations and wanted to share them with my husband. As a mobility engineer, he uses radio frequencies and electromagnetic energy to facilitate the flow of information all day. This is what enables cell communication through all of our devices. I shared with him my discovery that thoughts are stored within fields of electromagnetic energy. I told him that I believed they traveled on light waves as a vibrational frequency and could be accessed intentionally. Not inclined toward anything "woo-woo", he laughed and said, "Well in this reality, my dear, information actually travels on radio frequencies and is transported through fiber-optic cables as light!" I was thinking, "Thoughts, information, consciousness — they create an energetic field and carry an electromagnetic charge. They also travel on waves of light and sound and are energetically exchanged in this way! I wanted to be sure I understood him correctly so I replied, "Are you saying that information is sent through fiber-optic cables as light?" He cocked his head and thought about this for a minute. He then remarked, "Well, I guess you could say that the information is imprinted on the light?" I thought, "Consciousness is imprinted on light too!"

After talking with my husband, it became clear to me that electromagnetic frequencies and waves of sound and light are the mechanisms through which consciousness, or information, flows. I realized that, in my heightened state of awareness, especially during meditation, I was resonating at a higher frequency. This enabled me to access information that was also vibrating at the same high resonance. I was accessing a higher field of consciousness or increasing my band-width, if you will! This reminded me of another conversation my husband and I had recently had. I was explaining how the cells in the body actually used light to communicate with each other. I had learned that information sent from the brain actually travels on light and when cells interact, it causes a very brief flash of light. He just looked at me and said, "Like cell communication?" and we both laughed. That's when we began to associate signals from cell towers like signals from the brain — both attracting specific frequencies within certain bandwidths. He told me that soon technology would allow us to communicate with holographic images and I said, "Ah, the true nature of reality coming to light!" Now we really are demonstrating our Creator-like abilities — a true expression of our Creator-consciousness!

I came to the conclusion that both light and sound can be seen as mechanisms through which the source of consciousness flows. Even though my husband was physically facilitating the flow of information and I was doing it in a spiritual sense, we were both accessing the field of consciousness by using vibrational frequency. I found these revelations to be very illuminating (pun intended) and knew the implications were profound! Ultimately, I believe that, as we become more advanced beings, we will not require the use of mobile devices and computers to communicate or obtain information across distances. I believe we will be able to do it telepathically. According to the pyramid texts found in Egypt, telepathic communication was fairly common. The writings describe "mind-over-matter" practices that were part of the mystic initiations students received inside the chambers of the pyramids. This knowledge later emerged in secret societies like the Freemasons and in the philosophical beliefs and practices of the Rosicrucians, both of which are still going strong today.

Throughout history, sorcerers, sages and biblical characters have performed "miracles" that involved telekinesis, teleportation and telepathy. These enlightened beings were able to move massive objects at will, disappear and reappear as holographic images and relay messages from beyond. They knew that matter was simply a vibrational "thought-form" which had been manifested and that there was also an underlying field of un-manifested energy. In ancient Vedantic philosophy, they called manifest-form "Prakriti" and the underlying pure consciousness, or formless spirit, "Purusha." Those who are enlightened are able to use this knowledge to consciously manipulate both energy and matter at will. They were using their inherent free will and Creator-consciousness in the highest sense! They learned how to resonate with the vibrational frequencies that defined the thought-forms of matter and direct this energy with the power of their intention. I firmly believe that if we focus on evolving consciously, we can begin to master our mind. This will allow us to become more attuned to our inherent abilities and realize our full potential as divine human beings! For now, let's start by learning how to access the field of consciousness and tap into the source of omnipresent intelligence that is swirling around us. As we do so, our unlimited potential to access higher realms of thought will unfold. We will begin to realize the truth that, as children of the Creator, we too have the creative spirit within us. Consciousness is spirit come to life! With free will and intention, we can choose to use these abilities to access universal truth and become more enlightened beings. It's time to explore these possibilities! Throughout our adventure, I will encourage you to engage in four different types of introspection. I have assigned a specific practice to each day depending on the revelations we will be exploring. These practices include:

> Contemplative Meditation
> Walking Meditation
> Visualization
> Lucid Dreaming

They are designed as mechanisms for accessing higher levels of consciousness.

Accessing the Mind-field

I believe that there are three interrelated, yet distinct, aspects of consciousness we can tap into in an effort to gain knowledge and wisdom. The first level of consciousness, that we have the most immediate access to, is our own "higher self". This is the essence of our eternal soul and it is imprinted with all of the accumulated knowledge and experience from this and past lifetimes. It is the primary source of information that our mind draws from on a conscious, subconscious and even super-conscious level. I like to call it the "mind-field" because it is the primary source of the thoughts that enter our mind as consciousness. Our brain is accessing this field as it processes the information it retrieves. Our thoughts are actually outside of us in the "mind-field" rather than inside of our head. Our brain is just an analytical processor receiving and transmitting signals which tune into various frequencies of thought. Our thoughts represent a series of vibrational frequencies strung together in a stream of consciousness. We are concerned, first, with accessing the vast amount of knowledge and wisdom that lies within our own higher consciousness. This mind-field contains all of the knowledge we have gathered in this and past lifetimes. Ultimately, however, we want to reach into the depth of our soul where all of the information we have ever known and all of the experiences we have ever had, both in the physical and spiritual realm, are forever imprinted.

Let's start by talking about the nature of the soul. I believe we actually have an "over-soul" which is essentially the whole expression of our eternal soul and in each lifetime, we are only expressing a certain aspect of it. If we can wrap our heads around the idea of an "eternal present", we may be able to grasp the concept that all of our experiences from the past, present and future are happening simultaneously. As physical beings in time and space, we can only experience them sequentially, within the limitations of our linear mind, so this may be too far out to grapple with. If we can, however, try and embrace the idea of an eternal present, we are more likely to connect with the fullness of our "oversoul". Instead of thinking of past, present and future lives, we can start to think of concurrent lives taking place in a multi-dimensional reality. From this perspective, we can draw upon the experiences which are taking place within all of them. I believe we come into this time and place with a "veil of forgetting" about our so-called past so that we can fully embrace the present, but if the veil is too thin, or if we can penetrate it, we can recall our past lives quite vividly. We can benefit from this greater field of knowledge and experience in order to grasp a better understanding of our true nature and purpose in this one. As souls, we aren't limited by the narrow bandwidth of one single lifetime and just one aspect of our whole self. Psychics, I believe, are able to read the thoughts and see the images that we are projecting not just from this lifetime but from concurrent ones as well. They are accessing our higher consciousness and connecting with the many aspects of our "oversoul". If we have faith in our own abilities as beings of unlimited potential, we too can draw from this abundant source! It just requires a commitment of time and dedication to our practice. The more we recognize that our true nature is that of an energetic "light" being trapped within our physical body, we can start to set ourselves free and connect with the energy all around us! Even though our bodies are also made up of light (as all images are) they appear to be more solid because they are vibrating at a much lower frequency. Our souls vibrate at a frequency closer to that of light so when, through meditation, we learn to resonate at higher frequencies, we can tap into our own "inner wisdom"! Thoughts are energetic and we want to master the exchange of "thought-energy" within the field around us. Once we do, we can learn how to intentionally direct these energetic thoughts at will! Then we will truly begin to unleash our highest potential. I will show you ways in which you can increase the vibrational quality of your environment during meditation so you can resonate with the energetic thoughts of your higher self!

One of the most important skills you will develop is the ability to concentrate and this will serve you well throughout the course of our adventure as we search for hidden truths. During meditation, you will be guided to concentrate on your breathing as it flows in and out of your body. When you first engage in this practice, you will become acutely aware of the overwhelming thoughts that arise in your mind, each one of them competing for space. Over time, you will become more skilled at releasing these thoughts gently without forcing them out or engaging with them. Just like your breath flows in and out, you will be guided to allow your thoughts to arise and dissipate. Then when you feel like your mind is uncluttered like a clear blue sky, you will be guided to focus on a single point in the distance. Concentrating on this single point will cause it to become brighter and you may feel as if you are consciously moving toward it. If a thought arises in your mind and distracts you, just set it on a cloud and send it away so your mind will be like a clear blue sky once again. Trying to stay focused on this single light in the distance will gradually improve your concentration over time. With consistency, you will naturally begin to block out any distractions and your single-pointed focus will become laser sharp. Once your ability to concentrate has been honed-in, you can start to engage in contemplative meditation. Presented with a concept or specific idea, you will be asked to apply your single-pointed focus to decipher every aspect of it. This will challenge you to look deeply into the mind-field. The more you practice this type of meditation, the more epiphanies you will have. You will begin to remember the truths you have known before from experiences in the past. Knowledge and wisdom will come to you that you don't recall being taught or having read. This is when your meditations will become highly productive and your spiritual understanding will begin to grow and develop exponentially. Once you head down this path of discovery, the revelations you have will astound and amaze you. They will come to you as a knowing and there will be no doubt in your mind as to their authenticity. You will discover your own personal truths and make significant progress on your soul's journey of self-realization.

Accessing the Collective Field

Earlier I stated my belief that there are three distinct, interrelated aspects of consciousness that you can tap into. You have the most immediate access to the mind-field we just explored but there is a greater field of consciousness that lies just beyond the horizon of your own soul's journey. You will need to engage in the practice of expanding your energy field now in order to access the interconnected network of the collective soul. We do this every day on a more superficial level but to explore the depths of this vast field of consciousness, you will need to open a channel by engaging in the practice of "running energy" through your chakras. It will be important to create a portal through which the energy from the earth and the light from the cosmos can flow. Along the length of your spine, there are several points of consciousness that we will focus on stimulating in order to create an open channel of communication. At this point, I will also suggest you custom design a shrine containing objects that have a special significance for you on a spiritual level. This may include angels and deities you love and honor or pictures of special people you cherish. Objects from nature show your love of creation and candles (fire), crystal, rocks and water symbolize elements that attract powerful energy.

A clean environment shows respect for the spiritual entities that may help you connect with the divine consciousness. Washing your hands and face is a sign of purification. Choose a place to sit that is quiet and free of distraction. Try and sit in the same place as often as possible as this creates an accumulated field of spiritual energy over time that will be conducive to your practice. I prefer to sit in direct alignment with the sun if it is daylight because I believe consciousness flows through this divine portal. At night, I like to reduce the amount of artificial light and sit facing the starlight through a slightly opened window so the cosmic light and fresh air can stream in. These are my personal preferences though and you need to go with what intuitively feels best for you.

Your posture is important as a straight spine is necessary for a direct, unobstructed flow of energy. Otherwise you can choose to sit on the floor with a cushion or in a chair with your feet on the ground. Just so long as you are connected with the earth and seated comfortably in an upright position. Connecting with this greater field of consciousness goes beyond sitting quietly and focusing on your breath. The single-pointed concentration for accessing the higher self is imperative but, as you progress, you'll need to ripen the conditions for tapping into the collective self. "Spinning" your chakras (energy centers along the length of your spine) will clear a portal through which consciousness can flow. This is also called "running energy" and it will help you connect with the field.

See the following illustration and brief description of each of the ascending levels of consciousness that characterize the seven primary chakras.

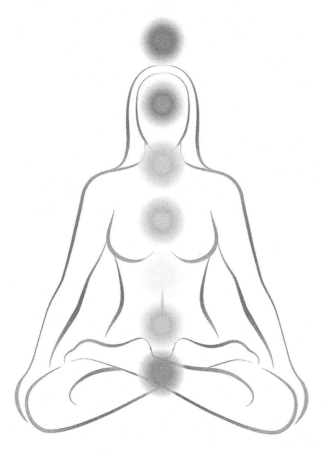

CROWN CHAKRA ~ Divine Consciousness

THIRD-EYE CHAKRA ~ Divine Wisdom

THROAT CHAKRA ~ Communication

HEART CHAKRA ~ Love & Compassion

SOLAR PLEXUS CHAKRA ~ Empowerment

SACRAL CHAKRA ~ Desire & Creativity

ROOT CHAKRA ~ Survival Instinct

Accessing the Cosmic Field

As your practice progresses and you begin to connect with more knowledge and wisdom from the field of consciousness, you will notice revelations of a more divine nature starting to emerge. This is when your practice will take on a greater depth of meaning and you will be elevated to a new level of cosmic awareness. In these higher realms, sacred truth and universal knowledge are revealed. Answers that come to you from this realm will resonate deeply within the very core of your being. You will have no doubt as to the divine nature of these revelations. Sometimes they are so profound that, at first, you feel stunned and then as the truth settles in, you feel a quiet sense of awe and wonder accompanied by a deep inner peace. These revelations come from a higher source. They are a sign that a door has been opened to the infinite field of cosmic consciousness. Once you walk through that door, revelations will start coming to you naturally. You may start to have epiphanies throughout the course of the day when you least expect it. You may even feel the presence of spiritual entities who came through the cosmic portal to teach you and guide you along your path.

You may have already had experiences or feel cosmically connected to a higher source. If so, maybe you would like to deepen your connection. If you don't feel connected, there are more advanced techniques you can use during meditation that will help open a portal to this higher realm. First, you will need to have faith in the existence of inter-dimensional consciousness, or a spiritual realm, and secondly, you must develop your ability to resonate with it. You will need to create vibrational frequencies within your field of consciousness that are much higher than that of the physical realm. You will need to send out the right signals to tune in with the desired frequencies and increase your bandwidth. To reach this more advanced level of communication, you will need to add the powerful energy of light and sound to your practices. In the opening of this chapter, I explored the field of consciousness in which we exist. Light and sound are the essence of this field. In fact, they create the foundation on which reality exists at every level of consciousness. They are the spiritual elements that define reality. This was described to me with beautiful clarity and a depth of insight far beyond this simple explanation by a disciple of Swami Veda. I was recently blessed by the opportunity to speak with him and have transcribed this interview in the last section of my book, "Realization". He poetically explains why the use of light and sound techniques during meditation are so powerful and transcendent.

Let's talk about we can incorporate the use of light into our meditation practice. These techniques can actually be used anytime to bring you into a higher state of awareness and increase your bandwidth. As we know by now, light vibrates at the highest frequency so we can use it to increase our own resonance and attract thoughts into our field that are beyond our normal awareness. The cool thing is that we naturally absorb light, so this ability is inherent in our being. We just have to intentionally develop it if we wish to use it for a higher purpose. There are three access points in which our bodies receive light and the consciousness within it: 1) the pineal gland at the base of our skull, 2) our heart center and 3) our sacral center, or belly button. According to many sources, both scientific and spiritual, the pineal gland is thought of as the seat of consciousness because it absorbs light directly into our being. It is at this sacred point that you receive and transmit light in the form of pure consciousness. It is apparently in the shape of a pine cone (this is how it got its name) and is situated at the base of the skull between the two hemispheres of the brain. According to *The Urantia Book*, this is where our "thought-adjuster" is located and it is the portal for direct communication with God the Father. It can be thought of as your personal line of communication with the source where divine light enters and radiates outward. This is the source of the halo you often see depicted around the heads of "enlightened" beings. From the second point in the heart center, energy flows outward creating a so-called 'toroidal' field. This field surrounds you like a bubble of light. A constant stream of consciousness flows in and out of this bubble. All living beings, including plants and animals, emanate this field and when the light interacts by proximity or even thought, there is a mutual exchange of energy. Remember, thoughts are energetic so it is literally an exchange of consciousness! When you envision this bubble surrounded by an electric blue shield, you are preventing unwanted energy from entering your field. This is especially important when you open portals of communication with other realms. When you fill this bubble with pure unconditional love, you will attract the same type of energy into your field and open a line of communication with the highest realms! Based on the teachings in *The Urantia Book*, the heart center is the access point for the spirit of the Eternal Son to flow into your being. Just like the pineal gland is the access point for the Father, this is the point where the Son fills your heart with pure love and compassion. Finally, you will want to focus your energy at the center of your belly button. This sacral center is the entry point for the life force that keeps your spirit alive. It is the point where your mother shared her life force with you when your souls were united. Once you emerged and were disconnected from this source, you began drawing life force from the omnipresent spirit at this same sacral point. You can visualize the living spirit flowing into your body like an umbilical cord connected to the Infinite, or Holy, Spirit. You can imagine this light entering your being and then radiating outward and spiraling around your body like an electric blue serpent. This symbolizes the spiraling nature of the double helix and the kundalini energy that braids your spine. It is the same sacred spiral that defines the patterns and movement of the entire universe. This is a vibrant visualization that will attract the energy of the Infinite Spirit and help you make a powerful connection with the cosmic consciousness. Now you are radiating a halo of light around your crown, surrounded by a luminescent bubble and embraced by a spiraling serpent. Since light is the highest of all frequencies, you are creating a strong resonance for receiving consciousness from the highest realms! To literally amplify the resonance of your field by using sound, you can choose to recite a mantra or prayer or even softly hum or sing a hymn. You can use the universal mantra "Om mani padme hum" if you don't already have one in mind. If you prefer to use prayer, there are many beautiful ones to choose from, of course, based on your spiritual or religious inclination. Maybe you would just like to start with a simple hymn or verse that you can softly repeat in your mind.

With faith and practice, you will create a line of communication with the infinite source from which consciousness flows. You will find a unique combination of elements that together form an expression of your own spiritual nature. The foundation for any successful practice is a strong commitment. You may want to consider making a silent or written oath to yourself that includes specific times and objectives. If you truly want to progress along your path and access ascending levels of consciousness, you must be dedicated to your goals. It's important to prioritize your spiritual growth and carve out the time it will take to gain deeper realizations. I guarantee however, it will be well worth every single minute that you dedicate to this effort. The ascension path represents the highest aspiration of our eternal soul. Making a conscious decision to intentionally evolve toward a higher consciousness marks the turning point of our spirit. As we gradually reduce our attachment to the material world and turn our attention towards its spiritual nature, a remarkable transformation begins to take place. We begin to see the truth and beauty beyond the form. We develop a lightness of being and gradually begin to replace feelings of anger, confusion and resentment with exuberant joy, faith and compassion. Selfish desires focused on material things are replaced by a generosity of spirit that gives openly to others. As we walk through the world, in this new light, we notice the spiritual essence of all living things and beings. As we begin to connect with this truth, we find comfort in the unity of life. We are united with spirit when we see beyond the form. We become acutely aware that we are truly one with all that is — united in an infinite field of cosmic consciousness.

TRUTH FROM BEYOND

The Reference Material

During our exploration of the creation story, I will be referencing literature that falls under the categories of science, spirituality and religion. The scientific books will provide factual evidence for various theories regarding the creation of the universe. The religious books will rely on scripture and faith to support their version of events. Throughout the ancient scriptures, there are many accounts of "voices from beyond" that have delivered divine messages to various prophets, saints and disciples. Many of the experiences shared in the scriptures are of a 'paranormal' nature and yet, believers accept these messages and miracles as the true gospel based on their faith and devotion. Several of the spiritual books I reference also include messages from beyond that were received in a 'paranormal' fashion. Those who firmly believe in the legitimacy of these accounts, myself included, also have faith in the messengers who delivered them. Two of the main spiritual books I will use that fall under this category are *The Urantia Book* and *The RA Material*. They are both fascinating accounts of channeling that produced remarkable and extensive material about creation, evolution and the true nature of our being.

I have referenced this material because I firmly believe in the existence of "other-worldly" messengers who have an interest in the evolution of our species. These advanced beings play a critical role in the consciousness of our planet and have since ancient times. Based on the teachings in these books, and countless others, the implications are clear: there is one infinite consciousness that permeates everything. This consciousness, as it expands into eternity, is the essence of the "self" that lies within all of us. We are co-creating our experience as individual selves within this omnipresent and omniscient consciousness. As projections, or aspects, of this cosmic consciousness, we are each an integral part of it. The ultimate destination for each individual soul is to reunite with the source from which it came. The whole universal experience represents the journey of self-realization that the "One Infinite Cosmic Creator" is on.

Each of our eternal adventures enriches the journey and enhances the self-knowledge of the Creator. This is our divine purpose as individual souls: to make progress on our own path of self-realization and thereby, contribute to the advancement of the collective soul, or 'whole soul' if you will. As our own self-knowledge increases, we become closer and closer to realizing our divine nature and this is when our path begins to ascend. Ultimately, we will become fully self-realized and at that point, we will become one with the divine consciousness or "One Infinite Creator." This is the essence of my spiritual message on this adventure!

You can call it "God-consciousness", "Cosmic-consciousness", "Divine-consciousness" or even "Unity-consciousness". I like to call it "Creator-consciousness" because the creative spirit is within us acting through us to create in this realm. Regardless of how you label it, the concept remains the same. We, as projections of this consciousness, are on an extraordinary adventure throughout time, space and beyond! We have been cast out into time and space with the mandate to create and evolve. The objective of our adventure is self-realization and the method is experience in these realms! The destination is reunification in the Paradise realms — the divine source from which we all came! Once we recognize our divine nature, we begin our journey on the ascension path home to Havona.

This is what the advanced beings (also expressing the same Creator-consciousness) are teaching us in both *The Urantia Book* and *The RA Material* They reinforce the fact that, because we are of and from the same divine source, we are united within the cosmic consciousness. As advanced beings who are more evolved, however, they have greater access to the infinite intelligence that flows into this vast field of consciousness. Their advanced knowledge represents fundamental truths and universal wisdom. They are compelled to share these truths with us in the interest of universal evolution and the ascension of eternal souls. It is their mandate to reach out and offer guidance to their brothers and sisters in other realms. Teaching is an essential part of their evolutionary journey and it allows them to progress along their ascension path. It is therefore, mutually beneficial not just to us but also to them. This is what "Creator-consciousness" is all about! It is the omniscient, omnipresent and omnipotent creative spirit that inspires everyone and everything!

The Urantia Papers

The teachings in *The Urantia Book* came about as the result of a group listening to the trance channelings of one man over the course of several years. In 1911, a patient of Dr.'s William and Lena Sadler, two highly respected physicians, began channeling celestial beings while sleeping. Upon investigating, they found that he was sharing verbal communication that was of an advanced and sophisticated nature. The voices that were coming through him identified themselves as other-worldly messengers from higher realms that were more advanced. Over time, the communication progressed, and the advanced beings agreed to a Q & A format and a group was formed called "The Forum." Between 1925 and 1955, nearly 500 people participated in this project which produced a 2,097-page book. The book is written as a collection of 196 papers which cover the creation and evolution of a vast multi-verse, the history of our planet (Urantia), and the life and times of Jesus.

The teachings are offered by a multitude of advanced beings residing in different dimensions. On a cosmic level, they are neatly organized into different roles within a structural hierarchy. This multitude of beings govern, orchestrate and direct the entire workings of the universe of universes. Their jobs include administration, justice, teaching and supervising to name a few. As such, they are able to contribute a wide diversity of comprehensive teachings in a collective, yet organized, manner. Although these advanced beings represent a diverse multi-dimensional collective, they share the same fundamental truths about our existence. This excerpt taken from the foreword of *The Urantia Book* describes this phenomenon:

"The universe of universes presents phenomena of deity activities on diverse levels of cosmic realities, mind meanings, and spirit values, but all of these ministrations — personal or otherwise — are divinely coordinated." [1]

I will do my best to represent these astounding revelations as accurately as possible throughout this adventure. The remarkable teachings from this book, sometimes called "The Universal Bible", are mind-blowing to say the least and may dramatically alter your view of reality. They will enhance our experience on this evolutionary adventure tremendously! Here are some excerpts from the foreword of this book, offered by a "Truth Revealer" from Orvonton (the "superuniverse" in which our local universe "Nebadon" resides. This explanation will help to clarify the purpose and intention behind this celestial effort to enhance the knowledge of the human species on this planet they call "Urantia" — our home:

"In the minds of the mortals of Urantia — that is the name of your world — there exists great confusion respecting the meaning of such terms as God, divinity, and deity. Human beings are still more confused and uncertain about the relationships of the divine personalities designated by these numerous appellations. Because of this conceptual poverty associated with so much ideational confusion, I have been directed to formulate this introductory statement in explanation of the meaning which should be attached to certain word symbols as they may be hereinafter used in those papers which the Orvonton Corps of Truth Revealers have been authorized to translate into the English language of Urantia. It is exceedingly difficult to present large concepts and advanced truth, in our endeavor to expand the cosmic consciousness and enhance spiritual perception, when we are restricted to the use of a circumscribed language of the realm. But our mandate admonishes us to make every effort to convey our meanings by using the word symbols of the English tongue." [2]

Here is a brief overview of our world as they describe it in the book. This will provide the foundation upon which their teachings are based:

"Your world, Urantia, is one of the many similar inhabited planets which comprise the local universe of Nebadon. This universe, together with similar creations, makes up the superuniverse of Orvonton, from whose capital, Uversa, our commission hails. Orvonton is one of the seven evolutionary superuniverses of time and space which circle the never-beginning, never-ending creation of divine perfection — the central universe of Havona. At the heart of this eternal and central universe is the stationary Isle of Paradise, the geographic center of infinity and the dwelling place of the eternal God.

The seven superuniverses, in association with the central and divine universe, we commonly refer to as the Grand Universe. These are the now organized and inhabited creations. They are all a part of the Master Universe, which also embraces the uninhabited but mobilizing universes of outer space." 3.

Hang onto your hats because this barely scratches the surface! We will dive much deeper into the essence of these teachings throughout our adventure.

The Confederation of the One Infinite Creator

In 2014, progressive thought leader, Wayne Dyer, God rest his soul, hosted a televised channeling event with author, Esther Hicks, who channels "Group Abraham." This, my friends, was a historical ground-breaking event for channeling as an accepted form of communication with disembodied beings! Although the books written by Esther and her husband, Jerry, are well-known amongst the spiritual community, this exposure helped bring channeling into the mainstream. The more people that start accepting this type of communication, the more we, as a society, can benefit from the advanced knowledge these benevolent beings have to offer. The teachings offered by Group Abraham through Esther Hicks are focused primarily on manifesting by using the Law of Attraction. I have benefited greatly from these teachings and apply their principles everyday with phenomenal results! These valuable truths help us become more enlightened beings and teach us how to consciously evolve. All we have to do is pay close attention to their specific instructions and have faith in what they are teaching (if it resonates with us of course). Discernment is always advised with any teachings that are offered from embodied or disembodied beings!

The RA Material, in the "The Law of One" series, also represents universal truths that were brought forth through the process of channeling. In this case, the advanced beings, or teachers, identify themselves as "Group Ra." This material began to emerge as the result of a meditation group organized by Don Elkins for contacting extraterrestrial beings. He began conducting this "experiment" in 1962 at which time Carla Rueckert joined his group. In 1970, she went to work for Don full-time and in 1974, he decided she needed to focus on developing her ability to channel and, so she did with extraordinary results.

In 1980, shortly after successfully contacting the recently deceased wife of a friend, Carla became aware of a new contact. In her words, "however only a few days later, while working with an advanced meditation student, I received a new contact, one which I had never had before. As I do in all cases, I challenged this entity in the name of Christ, demanding that it leave if it did not come as a messenger of Christ consciousness. It remained, so I opened myself to its channel. Again, I went almost immediately into trance and the entity, which called itself Ra, began a series of contacts with us. This contact is ongoing, fascinating, and, to me, the source of some disquiet." [4] She explains that Don refers to this phenomenon as "telepathic reception in the trance state."

In the introduction to the first book of the "Law of One" series called, *The RA Material*," Don expands on the nature and source of this communication: "Our research group uses what I prefer to call "tuned trance telepathy" to communicate with an extraterrestrial race called Ra. We use the English language because it is known by Ra. In fact, Ra knows more of it than I do. Ra landed on earth about 11,000 years ago as a sort of extraterrestrial missionary with the objective of helping Earthman with his mental evolution. Failing in this attempt, Ra retreated from the Earth's surface but continue to monitor activities closely on this planet. For this reason, Ra is highly informed about our history, languages, etc. Probably the most difficult thing to understand about Ra is its nature. Ra is a sixth density social memory complex. Since Earth is near the end of the third-density cycle of evolution, this means that Ra is three evolutionary cycles ahead of us. In other words, Ra's present state of evolution is millions of years in advance of Earthman's." [5]

Don and Carla were later joined by Jim McCarty in a combined effort to facilitate the telepathic communication with Group Ra. During these sessions, Jim provided spiritual support to Carla in her trance state. These sessions proved to be physically depleting and were detrimental to her health over time. Devoutly committed to the project and determined to satisfy Don's insatiable curiosity about this source of knowledge, she sacrificed her own personal well-being. Those of us who are open-minded enough to consider this communication as a valid source of universal knowledge are forever indebted to Carla for her loyalty and dedication.

Universal mysteries that have confounded man for centuries are clearly explained by Ra in a series of over 100 sessions. The information is both astounding and intriguing and the authenticity of it becomes evident as you compare it to other sources of scientific, religious and spiritual literature. That being said, much of the information is unique to this source and being revealed for the first time. These communications reveal the origin, nature and destiny of our being. They identify the source of our existence and the purpose of our incarnational experiences. I have been blessed with the honor of interviewing both Carla Rueckert and Jim McCarty. Watch their interviews at SciSpi.tv/Rise-Up/.

Their spiritual insight will amaze and inspire you. Carla has since passed. God rest her beautiful soul. She was truly a remarkable being who devoted her life to the enlightenment of others despite the toll this high vibrational channeling took on her physical being. Jim is alive and well and actively involved in the L/L Research that the original group organized in the 80's. We are incredibly blessed to have the opportunity to learn from the remarkable channelings they accumulated over several years of intense communication.

Astral Travel

Another two books which I have referenced, to uncover universal truths, also present experiences of an "other-dimensional" nature. These include "Initiation" by Elisabeth Haisch and "Unveiled Mysteries" by Godfre Ray King. The authors of both books have been "shown" the funda-mental truths of our existence by receiving teachings in the astral realm. Their adventures in astral travel are both intriguing and fascinating. In the book, Initiation, Elisabeth Haisch shares her incredible journey into a past life in ancient Egypt where she was the daughter and wife of a pharaoh. During this past life, she received instruction from her teacher, "Phahotep," on the many wonders and mysteries of the universe. It is well-documented that Phahotep was a very wise and respected teacher in Ancient Egypt.

One of the teachings in the book that I found most interesting concerns sacred geometry. Phahotep teaches Elisabeth, as a high priestess, how these patterns played an integral role in creating the forms of energy and matter which make up our universe. She also went through a process of initiation which includes a cosmic adventure she took while encased in a tomb deep inside the chambers of the Great Pyramid. Her teacher explains that sacred teachings and spiritual initiation was the true purpose of the pyramids and the sarcophogi within them. The revelations that she shares answers many of the questions that have mystified archaeologists and historians for centuries about the architecture and mysticism of ancient Egypt. Her insight will provide a depth of understanding about the true nature of reality unsurpassed by other more traditional sources. We are blessed to have her along on our adventure as an inspiring source of sacred knowledge.

I have also invited Godfrey Ray King along to share his "other-dimensional" experiences. He explores the astral realm with the Ascended Master St. Germain and shares these adventures in his book, "Unveiled Mysteries." Godfre writes about his encounter and subsequent travels with St. Germain in a unique poetic fashion which sweeps you away into a mystical realm of wondrous delight. He challenges the reader to open their mind and heart to the magical presence and power of the Ascended Masters. His experiences, which took place in the fall of 1930 at Mount Shasta in California, were so real and powerful to him that he felt compelled to share them with the world. He inspired a large following after bringing forth the remarkable visions and truths that St. Germain revealed to him during these adventures not just in "Unveiled Mysteries" but in the "I AM Chronicles" as well.

He describes St. Germain as a "Great Beloved Bearer of Light" and in the tribute, at the beginning of his book "Unveiled Mysteries," he writes that he is "one of those Powerful Emissaries from the Spiritual Hierarchy of Ascended Masters who govern this planet."[6] He claims that St. Germain is "indissolubly linked with America's past, present and future for a very important part of his work upon earth is the purifying, protecting, and illuminating of the people of America that she may be the Carrier of the Cup of "Light" to the nations of the earth in the Golden Age that is coming before us." [7] While hiking through Mount Shasta, Godfre stops at a stream to fill his cup when he senses a presence behind him. He turns to see a man who doesn't seem ordinary. The man smiles and addresses him, "My brother, if you will hand me your cup, I will give you a much more refreshing drink than spring water."[8] Godfre writes that "the electrical vivifying effect on my mind and body made me gasp with surprise." St. Germain explains to him, "That which you drank comes directly from the Universal Supply, pure and vivifying as Life itself, in fact it is Life — Omnipresent Life — for it exists everywhere about us. It is subject to our conscious control and direction, willingly obedient, when we Love enough, because all the Universe obeys the behest of Love. Whatsoever I desire manifests itself, when I command in Love." [9]

Thus, the teachings begin, and Godfre Ray King and Ascended Master St. Germain set out on an extraordinary journey that uncovers great truths about the power, we as human beings, have to consciously manifest all of our desires as long as we live in the light of love and our intentions remain pure. The first universal truth that he shares with Godfre concerns the "Law of Love" and the "Eternal Law of Life." In the first chapter, called "Meeting the Master," St. Germain teaches Godfre the following

"Truth of Life." (Note that Godfre capitalizes many words within sentences and uses dashes throughout.)

"It is very important to realize fully that God's intent for every one of His children is abundance of every good and perfect thing. He created Perfection and endowed His children with the same power. They can create and maintain Perfection also and express God-dominion over the earth and all that is therein. Mankind was originally created in the Image and Likeness of God. The only reason all do not manifest this dominion is because they do not use their Divine Authority — that with which everyone is endowed and by which he is intended to govern his world. Thus, they are not obeying the Law of Love by pouring out peace and blessings to all of creation...The personal self of every individual must acknowledge completely and unconditionally that the human or outer activity of consciousness — is absolutely — nothing — of its own. Even the energy — by which one recognizes the Great God within — is radiated into the personal self — by the Great God Self. Love and praise — of That Great Self Within — and the attention maintain focused upon Truth — health — freedom — keys — supply — or any other thing that you may desire for a right use — persistently held in your conscious thought and feeling — will bring them into your use and world — as surely as there is a Great Law of Magnetic Attraction in the Universe. The Eternal Law of Life is that — 'Whatever you think and feel you bring into form; where your thought is there you are — for you are your consciousness; and whatever you meditate upon — you become." [10]

I will share many more of these profound revelations throughout our adventure especially when they enhance the universal mystery we are exploring. Having Godfre along on our journey through creation and evolution will bring us great inspiration just when we need it most!

I have invited many great philosophers, theologians, physicists and spiritualists along on our adventure. We will use the vast amount of resources that are available to us when considering every perspective. This is one way to uncover the truth about the multi-dimensional reality we live in. The other way is by personally connecting with the omnipresent field of cosmic consciousness through the meditations, activations and lucid dreaming visualizations. This field contains an unlimited abundance of universal knowledge and sacred wisdom. All we have to do is tap into it! That's what the next chapter focuses on. I want you to be well-prepared with all the necessary tools you will need to make the most of this extraordinary adventure through time, space and beyond!

REFERENCES

The Urantia Book Fellowship, The Urantia Book, Uversa Press, 2008

1. Foreword:1.1

2. Foreword:1-2

3. Foreword:5-6

Elkins, Rueckert, McCarty, "The RA Material" The Law of One: Book 1, Whitford Press, 1984

4. p. 49

5. p. 2

Godfre Ray King, Unveiled Mysteries, Saint Germain Press, 1934

6. Tribute:vii

7. Tribute:vii
8. p. 3
9. p. 3-4
10. p. 5-6

ASCENSION

An Overview

Ascension is both an individual and collective shift into higher consciousness. *The Urantia Book* teaches us that our souls are engaged in an "ascension career" and that, regardless of the cosmic age we are in or where our planet is in the solar system, our individual souls will naturally advance to the next dimension when we achieve mastery in this one. We can advance more rapidly if we make a focused effort, just like any other career. As a collective shift into a higher dimension, there are certain periods in the space-time continuum when a planetary consciousness is accelerated by solar alignments with other star systems and with the galactic center. Starting in December 2012, according to many sources, our solar system began moving into many critical alignments. Approximately, every 26,000 years, our solar system aligns with Alcyone, the great central sun of the Pleiades star system, and super-charged particles travel on solar flares that impact our planet and raise the frequency of the collective consciousness. Author, Andrew Collins, has discovered that we also receive super-charged solar rays from Deneb, the central sun of the Cygnus constellation.

These powerful solar rays carry encoded light just like information traveling on fiber optic cables at the speed of light. So not only do these super-charged particles raise the frequency of our consciousness but they carry codes of higher intelligence that enlighten us in preparation for an acceleration of consciousness into a higher dimensional reality. These encoded photons also carry the love frequency which elevates unity consciousness and increases our capacity to express universal love and compassion. The most powerful alignment, however, is with the supermassive black hole at the center of our galaxy. The extreme gravitational pull at the "event horizon", or threshold of this massive portal, warps the fabric of space-time so profoundly that it can propel a consensus reality into another dimension of time and space. Intelligent forces, conducting the symphony that universally harmonizes all dimensional realities, "harvest" only those souls who are prepared to jump dimensions at the time of these alignments, according to the Law of One channelings with Group Ra. This 6D advanced race also teaches us that every 75,000 years, there is a major "harvest" and that our collective consciousness is now entering that phase. They describe this as a choice the soul makes but essentially the soul's frequency determines its readiness to move into a higher dimension. If the soul isn't ready, it just makes another round on the 3D ferris wheel to gain more self-knowledge and to develop more self-love.

Those of us who are awake and aware are anxious to transcend this mundane realm of suffering and create more joy, beauty and grace in our lives and in the lives of others. We are well aware that our 3D reality fell into chaos and out of divine alignment due to many planetary events over time. We want to be part of a collective effort to realign our earth plane and our own energetic pattern with their original divine blueprints of perfection. We want to make a conscious effort to accelerate our consciousness and raise our frequency right here and now. We know we are divine beings who are of and from the same divine source and that we can activate our dormant DNA and bring our brain fully online. This is the major focus of our 10-day journey on the ascension path. Every day, we learn how to create an expanded experience of reality out in nature and then how to tune into higher guidance and our own heart space by activating our energy centers and stimulating our right and left brain.

There has been a lot of speculation about what global ascension might look like and how this process will unfold. In The Book of Knowledge: Keys of Enoch, Dr. J.J. Hurtak offers a scientific explanation and detailed diagram of how the 3D earth plane will merge with the 5D earth plane and then pull apart. He also describes the effect of powerful alignments that will send supercharged solar rays into the earth's core, heating it up and causing it to expand. When this happens, the earth experiences a dramatic pole shift which can result in major catastrophic events that annihilate many species. This is exactly what has happened in past ages at the end of a 26,000 year cycle. Some sources claim that, this time around, the "Sphere Alliance" made up of higher dimensional beings in favor of saving our species, have placed blue spheres around earth's stratosphere to shield our planet from the high intensity of the solar rays. The purpose of this would be to prevent a catastrophic pole shift by gradually filtering through these super-charged particles. This would also give us a grace period within which to increase the vibrational frequency of the collective consciousness so we are better prepared to absorb these high-frequency rays. The bestowal of this grace period and the opportunity to accelerate our consciousness before the ascension energies hit is one of the reasons so many of us are awakening at this time. There are many galactic emissaries who have been sent here to have a human incarnation during this time on a special mission to teach, guide and herald in the higher dimension for humanity. If those of us who have awakened and are raising our frequency can reach back and assist others to do the same, we can prepare humanity for the time when the Sphere Alliance moves out and we are exposed to the full intensity of these super-charged solar rays.

In Barbara Hand Clow's book, The Alchemy of Nine Dimensions, she offers a diagram of the nine dimensions that make up our physical reality in this galactic realm. She shows 3D as the plane we are now experiencing on earth's surface and 4D as a sort of canopy over this dimension. She calls 4D the astral plane and it's a realm we must transition through on our way to ascending into 5D. It is the realm of angels and demons, essentially, and our opportunity to choose to connect with the positive forces who emanate the light of love. If we manage to emerge victorious without being tempted by the demons, we can move onto 5D with our newfound awareness and accelerated frequency.

With regards to how the ascension might manifest, some thought leaders have speculated about the "100th Monkey Effect." In case you do not know what this effect is, it got its name based on an observation by a group of scientists who discovered that a certain species of wild monkeys, who were isolated in a remote area, had started to wash their sweet potatoes in the river. When the 100th monkey washed its sweet potato, suddenly monkeys of this same species all over the globe started washing their sweet potatoes at once. This observation supports the theory that each species has its own consciousness grid and that when enough of the conscious beings (100 to be exact) who are entangled in this grid behave or believe in a certain way, it suddenly spreads across the entire grid all at once. This relates to global ascension, in that, many believe when enough of humanity raises its frequency to a 5D vibration, that in an instant, that vibration will spread like a wave across the entire consciousness grid. In a flash, all of humanity will resonate at the 5D frequency and as a consensus reality, collectively shift into a 5D experience of reality.

Drunvalo Melchizedek has described what it might look like to witness our 3D reality transform into 5D. He says that the platonic solids as patterns of reality may suddenly appear in colorful shapes like small spheres, cubes and triangles in the corners of the room and then dissipate as the reality disintegrates. He warns us not to feel any fear because this will jolt us right back into 3D. If we can just express gratitude and embrace the opportunity to ascend, we will transition into the experience of being in a void for 3 ½ days. In this void, we will experience a sense of oneness with God. When we wake up out of this void, we will be like a baby in this new higher dimensional reality. We will observe our parents as tall luminescent beings who love us in a deeply profound way unlike anything we ever experienced in 3D.

Another theory is that the transition into 5D is happening now and it's affecting everyone and since 2012, everyone's vibration is speeding up as is time itself. Author Carl Johan Calleman theorized, based on Mayan calendar research, that with each new age, time increases by 20%! So for those of us who think time is flying by, it actually might be! Many believe also that, as human beings are exposed to this accelerated vibration, their physical being is actually transforming gradually from a carbon-based being to a silicon-based being and finally to a crystalline being with a translucent "light-body." Of course if the shift happens suddenly with the 100th monkey effect, we could theoretically transform instantly into a crystalline being. Regardless of how the ascension unfolds, most thought leaders agree that we have transitioned into a phase on this planet where the opportunity to shift into a fifth dimensional reality is upon us. We may actively be shifting in and out of momentary experiences in 5D already.

No matter what environmental conditions may be impacting our consciousness, it is always in our best interest to engage in practices that raise our vibrational frequency. This effort can be as simple as being more present and expressing more gratitude and kindness toward others. It can be as advanced as engaging in powerful initiations and activations specifically designed to raise the light quotient of your physical and spiritual being. On our 10-day journey, we will engage in the entire spectrum of ways that we can raise our frequency, not just to prepare for the ascension, but to enhance our everyday experience of this precious gift we simply call... life.

A HANDY TRAIL GUIDE

There is divine meaning and purpose within every aspect of the creation story. It is this element of the story that transcends the chronological order and details of the specific events. The divinity behind the events is what gives them such great symbolic significance. Revealing the symbolism behind the creation story, and within the evolutionary progress, is my primary intention and why I named the subtitle of this adventure: **Awakening through Revelation**! As you witness the divine plan unfolding throughout the progressive adventures, the meaning and purpose of your own life will be revealed. You will find that your plan and the divine plan are one and the same:

Self-realization through the descending and ascending of spirit.

The Urantia Book refers to "God's ever-expanding self-realization in the time-creatures" [1]

The creative trinity is self-realizing through each one of our experiences and therefore, our path becomes theirs! Understanding the creative and evolutionary events, and virtually experiencing them through this adventure, will take us one step further along on our ascension path. It is after all, our divine purpose!

The key to understanding the meaning and purpose of life lies in the discovery that they are essentially one and the same. They are interwoven into the fabric of life. Once you discover you have a divine purpose, suddenly your life has more profound meaning! Understanding the life lessons you came here to learn, through the workshop in my first book, "Wake Up!," also gives your life more direction and symbolism as the moment to moment events in your life take on a much greater significance. Your life becomes a series of synchronistic events in this higher state of awareness as you weave your pattern of consciousness through many time and space realms in this sequential book in the trilogy, "Rise Up!" Similarly, the cosmic events that led to our creation and evolution take on a deeper symbolism and greater meaning when we bring our awareness into the synchronicity that is so exquisite and divine in the eternal now moment. In the final book, "Lighten Up!", you will learn how to activate your light body so you can transcend time and space realities and live in the eternal now moment while still interacting with the dimensions of time and space.

Within the Purpose, Lies the Meaning

When we realize our purpose is to evolve toward a higher level of consciousness, we can then find profound meaning in the process. It is an exquisitely creative process as we consciously manifest with a higher level of awareness. As we progress toward a greater self-realization, we accumulate wisdom based on the fundamental truths that are revealed. Of course, there are fundamental truths within the larger, divine truth but what we know so far is this:

- The meaning of our lives lies within the divine purpose of self-realization.
- This meaningful process is the manifestation of experiences within which 'knowledge of self' is revealed.

- So, the meaning then lies within the experiences and, more specifically, the creative manifestation of them.
- Within these truths, we can see that the whole purpose of creation, or creative manifestation, is self-realization.
- These truths provide a strong motivation for seeking the truth about creation itself.
- Let's consider the Creator's first moment of self-realization ~ the first step on his path ~ from my imaginative point of view:

The Creator couldn't recognize himself in his unmanifested state because he couldn't see a reflection of himself. So, in essence, he created a 'mirror' in which he could recognize himself and the reflected image became his Eternal Child. At this exact moment, a light went off like 'a spark of recognition' and instantly the Infinite Spirit came into being!

"Back in eternity, when the Universal (Mother-Father's) first infinite and absolute thought finds in the Eternal (Child) such a perfect adequate word for its divine expression, there ensues the supreme desire of both the 'thought-God' and the 'word-God' for a Universal and Infinite agent and mutual expression of combined action. In the dawn of eternity, the (Mother-Father) and (Child) became aware of their interdependence and so they entered into a divine covenant ~ an everlasting and infinite divine partnership. The very instant that God the (Mother-Father) and God the (Child) conjointly conceive an identical and infinite action ~ the execution of an absolute thought-plan ~ that very moment ~ the Infinite Spirit springs full-fledgedly into existence ~ they are all three existent for eternity." ~ The Urantia Book [2]

My vision continues ~

He was so inspired by the magic of this reflective mirror that his imagination ran wild! Once he saw himself reflected in the mirror image, he wanted to create more images! Creating gave his life meaning and actualizing his creative potential became his purpose. Therefore, recognizing himself, or knowing thyself, through the creative manifestation and experiences of his "thought-forms" gave his life a deeper meaning and greater purpose. "The physical universe as idea construction" is a concept Jane Roberts spoke about in her book, "Seth Speaks."

We are these "thought-forms" or spirit-infused holograms projected by the Supreme Being within this divine plan. This evolutionary plan through the illusion of time and space is being carried out through us. In this way, each of us are an integral part of the plan, each with a very important role! Our own self-realization enhances the divine self-realization individually and collectively! In this way, we are in a sort of partnership with the creative trinity! So, as holographic reflections of a divine origin, this becomes our destiny: the meaningful and creative manifestation of experiences that fulfill the divine purpose for which we came. When we are consciously engaged in the process of self-realization through creative manifestation, we are serving our divine purpose and therein lies the true meaning of our lives. Once we realize that we are not serving God insomuch as God is within us as us and we are all serving the highest good, God-realization transcends self-realization.

"Self-realization is necessary before God-realization." ~ Sham Hinduja

Our adventure will start with the Creator's first moment of conscious awareness, the "I AM" recognition of itself reflected in the spirit of the Eternal Child and we'll see how this gave rise to the reflection of the mind of the Infinite Spirit!

"The mind is a reflection of the soul. The soul is a reflection of God. The soul and God are eternal and unto each other." ~Shirley MacLaine

Then, as this perfect 'trinity of beings' expands beyond the timeless, spaceless and dimensionless realms of infinity, we will follow their divine path toward self-realization through the creative manifestation of all experience, physical and spiritual! This will lead to our experience as evolutionary creatures of time and space sourced from the highest realm!

Virtual Travel

Soul travel is an advanced skill that was taught to initiates in the ancient mystery schools of Egypt, India and China. It involves shifting one's consciousness into other realms and dimensions. This ability is a precious gift for those who wish to tune into all aspects of their many soul extensions experiencing different time and space realities. Once we realize that there is no such thing as time in the true nature of reality, we can begin to grasp that all expressions of reality are happening all at once. So rather than speaking of past lives, we can refer to these as concurrent lives. Since these concurrent realities are happening simultaneously, we can easily tune into them, participate in them and observe them. We can observe who we are "experiencing" in these other realms and in doing so, reunite the various aspects of who we truly are as "whole souls."

In Theosophical schools, students are taught that they are expressing 12 aspects of being in this octave of existence as a "soul extension." The soul is always expanding into larger expressions of its "self," however, and as a "monad," it expands into 12 souls each still expressing its 12 aspects. Now there are 144 expressions of our "self" experiencing in a myriad of both material and non-material realms. Ultimately, the self gets even bigger with choices to become logo expressions like planets, solar systems and galaxies! With this in mind, we can only begin to imagine how many lives we are actually experiencing all at once in the bigger picture of things.

The sole purpose of taking this virtual journey into other time and space realities that were, or are, significant in our human evolution is simply because it's highly likely we have all had, or are having, experiences there. On the first half of our adventure, I take you into your own natural surroundings by encouraging you to walk along a nature trail nearby. I take you with me to the ocean and then into the mountains and this is where you will start to practice visualization. As you picture the scenes I am describing, you will use your imagination to place yourself there alongside me. On the second half of our adventure, we start to travel internationally and this is where you will develop the technique of projecting your consciousness into these far off places. Once we start visiting ancient sites like the Mayan Temples and Egyptian Pyramids, you will advance your skills of consciousness-projection and begin to experience soul travel. Traveling to these sites virtually will trigger deep-seated memories of lives you may have had, or are having, there. It is a profound experience to reunite with other aspects of who you are as a whole soul. I like the theosophical term "soul extension" although "soul projection" might be more accurate when we consider our whole soul is actually projecting these various expressions of itself into these different realms of time and space.

Coming into an awareness of who you are at these different levels, and in these other places, is a critical part of your soul's "self-realization." Each time you re-member the fragmented pieces of your dismembered soul, you are coming into a greater sense of wholeness. At each juncture on your ascension path, you will retrieve another aspect of yourself and this will result in elevating your consciousness to whole new levels! You will become much more multi-faceted as you re-member skills and abilities you are expressing in other realms. You will make significant progress as your ability to tap into these other personalities expands your human potential. You will actually become a larger expression of yourself as your potential explodes while tapping into knowledge and skills you could not access before. You have likely attended the ancient mystery schools as an initiate or even a high priest or priestess. In these schools, you may have mastered soul travel, telepathy, alchemy and telekinesis. Imagine how your potential will increase and expand as you merge with these multi-dimensional aspects of your whole soul! This is an incredibly important part of our 10-day adventure and why I have chosen to make it a virtual one. The meditations and visualizations along with the initiations and activations all greatly enhance the reunification of your soul.

At the end of each adventurous day, you will be guided through a variety of different visualizations, activations and lucid dreaming. These are all designed to help you tap into your higher consciousness so that you can access the vaults of your own inner wisdom. As you learn to tune into your whole soul and even your monad, you will unveil vast amounts of knowledge already innate within you. These represent your own personal akashic records. Beyond that, you will develop the ability to access the universal field of consciousness and tune into infinite wisdom and knowledge. All of the records from the beginning of time are held within the vastness of this field also known as the cosmic akashic records. By learning to access this field during these advanced practices, the ultimate truths we are seeking will be revealed!

Listen to the audio version on the Up! Trilogy Books tab at www.SuzanneRossTranscendence.com.

An incredibly unique part of this adventure is the multi-media experience it offers. The exciting opportunity to engage in the interviews I've conducted with the authors I am referencing takes our adventure to a whole new level! The authors become virtual tour guides as they come to life on the screen in front of you and explain in person the concepts and revelations from their intriguing books.

Watch the interviews at SciSpi.tv/Rise-Up/.

The multi-dimensional aspect of this adventure takes it way beyond the experience of just reading a book. You will be engaging in this virtual adventure in many different ways that will stimulate all of your senses. It will trigger memories, expand your consciousness and vastly increase your potential. You will become a greater expression of your radiant soul and this will bring you an abundance of joy and prosperity. Your level of enthusiasm for life and ability to engage in it fully will bring you more fulfillment than you ever thought possible. You will experience a whole new expanded awareness that will leave you in awe and amazement of every precious moment. If you embrace this adventure fully by engaging in all it has to offer, it will transform your life in many profound ways. Your life will take on a much deeper meaning and you will be guided to fulfill your divine purpose. The ascension of your soul is the ultimate purpose and now you can pursue it wholeheartedly!

This promises to be an extraordinary adventure full of exhilarating revelations and profound implications. So — hang onto your hat and prepare to be blown away by this life changing experience! This exploration may significantly alter your perception of reality and change the way you think about, well.... EVERYTHING!

The Divine Plan

There is in the mind of God a plan which embraces every creature of all his vast domains and this plan is an eternal purpose of boundless opportunity, unlimited progress and endless life. And the infinite treasures of such a matchless career are yours for the striving! The goal of eternity is ahead! The adventure of divinity attainment lies before you! The race for perfection is on! Whosoever will may enter, and certain victory will crown the efforts of every human being who will run the race of faith and trust, depending on...the guidance of that good spirit of the (Eternal Child), which so freely has been poured out upon all flesh.[3]

REFERENCES

The Urantia Book Fellowship, The Urantia Book, Uversa Press, 2008
1. page 37
2. pages 90-91
3. page 365

Day One

Search for a Sacred Symbol

For the first day of our outdoor adventure, we'll embark upon a search for a sacred symbol. This will be a shape or symbol that recurs in nature and shows up in many forms. We will start by following the stream that winds through the countryside in my own backyard. As we gather at the trailhead and plan our first route, let's take in all the glorious sights and sounds of nature. Notice the vibrant green foliage and clear blue sky. Listen to the sweet songs of birds and rustling of the leaves. Feel the warmth of the sun on your face and shoulders and the soft cool breeze through your hair. Take a nice deep breath to inhale the crisp freshness of the clean air and smile with appreciation for the beauty of your surroundings. Now let's head out on our extraordinary adventure through time, space and beyond! Full of anticipation and curiosity, we'll choose a path adorned by colorful foliage and follow the trickling stream.

As we head out on our search for a symbol in nature, I will share the following story about one I recently discovered, and you can virtually experience it with me! I was inspired by an intuitive friend who suggested that I go out and look for a recurring shape or pattern in nature that felt particularly symbolic to me. She said that this symbol would show up in all of creation if I could heighten my awareness enough to see it. I was enthusiastic about my quest for a sacred symbol and, so I headed out with my eyes and mind wide open. It wasn't long before it showed up in all its glory in every living thing and being. It was a radiant spiral! I recognized it in the very first flower — a point in the center from which life radiates outward in a continuous spiral. This was especially evident in the lovely roses with their spiraling layers emerging out from the inner core. I could see it in the bright yellow daisies too with their pedals exploding outward from a spiraling center just like rays from the sun! I even noticed the radiant spiral in the stream as I tossed in a pebble and watched the symbol emerge. The wind around me seemed to create spiraling vortexes of energy that would spin blades of grass and tall weeds in its path. Everywhere I looked, there it was! I squinted at the sun and there it was! I peered into the flowers and there it was. I gazed upon the stream — there it was! The radiant spiral, that's it — a revelation, indeed!

At this point, I felt deeply connected with the nature around me and in my heightened state of awareness, I began to see everything in high definition and hear every sound in high resolution. I was able to see further than I'd ever seen before and could hear sounds from way off in the distance. Close-up, every color seemed so vivid and every sound was amplified. The grass looked florescent green and the water sparkled like diamonds. The snap of a twig under my feet sounded like cracking thunder and the birds chirping in the trees were like an orchestra. I recognized this experience, I call "merging", because I have had it before. Absorbed in nature, I suddenly become acutely aware that my life-force is merging with that which surrounds me. I am open to the living spirit and truly feel at one with all beings. This sense of oneness fills me with joy and I find comfort in the unity of life. I become overwhelmed with an unconditional love for all living beings as my heart opens and my mind expands. Exploring the meaning of the symbols out in nature, I begin to ponder my new discovery — the radiant spiral.

I imagine the Creator painting with stardust in a vibrating swirl of energy. Bringing life to all things in a harmonious symphony of light and sound, he spins shapes and patterns into energy and matter. He keeps his creation close to his heart by the gravitational force of pure love. And so, all planets, things and beings swirl forevermore in a continuous spiral around his core. He creates a radiant spiral of celestial light to brighten the day and glow in the night.

This revelation inspired me to write a little poem:

The creator himself had a brilliant idea!

A radiant spiral — that's what it will be!

The pattern from which all life will spring,

A flower, a tree and each living being!

And so, it was, in one great spark

His idea came to life

And light overcame the dark!

~ Suzanne

Of course, this leads into an exploration of how it all began. Naturally, we'll start at the beginning of creation and unravel the mysteries as they unfold! To kick off our adventure, I would like to share some excerpts from a remarkable poem written by Ed James Weldon Johnson in a book called "The Book of American Negro Poetry." Although it is written from an African American perspective in 1922, it transcends race and time and all beings at any time can appreciate its poetic beauty and eternal grace. It is truly a timeless and precious gift to us all and I am blessed to offer it here.

The Creation

And God stepped out on space,

And he looked around and said:

"I'm lonely –

I'll make me a world."

And as far as the eye of God could see

Darkness covered everything

Then God smiled,

And the light broke,

And the darkness rolled up on one side,

And the light stood shining on the other,

And God said: "That's good!"

Then God reached out and took the light in His hands,

And God rolled the light around in His hands

Until He made the sun;

And he set that sun a-blazing in the heavens

And the light that was left from making the sun

God gathered it up in a shining ball

And flung it against the darkness,

Spangling the night with the moon and stars.

Then down between

The darkness and the light

He hurled the world;

And God said: "That's good!"

The cooling waters came down.

Then the green grass sprouted,

And the little red flowers blossomed,

The pine tree pointed His finger to the sky,

And the oak spread out his arms,

The lakes cuddled down in the hollows of the ground,

And the rivers ran down to the sea;

And God smiled again

And the rainbow appeared,

And curled itself around His shoulder.

Then God raised His arm and He waved His hand

Over the sea and over the land,

And He said: "Bring forth! Bring forth!"

And quicker than God could drop His hand,

Fishes and fowls

And beasts and birds

Swam the rivers and the seas,

Roamed the forests and the woods,

And split the air with their wings.

And God said: "That's good!"

And God said: "I'm lonely still."

Then God sat down

On the side of a hill where He could think;

By a deep, wide river He sat down;

With His head in His hands,

God thought and thought,

Till he thought: "I'll make me a man!"

Up from the bed of the river
God scooped the clay;
And by the bank of the river
He kneeled him down;
And there the great God Almighty
Who lit the sun and fixed it in the sky,
Who flung the stars to the most far corner of the night,
Who rounded the earth in the middle of His hand;
This Great God,
Like a mammy bending over her baby,
Kneeled down in the dust
Toiling over a lump of clay
Till He shaped it in His own image;
Then into it, He blew the breath of life,
And man became a living soul.
Amen. Amen.
~ James Weldon Johnson (1871-1938) [1]

Aw, yes. Let's just take a few moments to breathe that in and reflect upon the visions this poetic verse inspires.

Whenever you're ready, close your eyes and project your consciousness back to the path along the stream.

One day, as I was walking through a flower garden, I noticed something extraordinary. Right there in front of my eyes was a little rainbow suspended in the air! It looked just like a holographic image. I realized there was a light mist coming from the sprinklers that, when combined with the sunlight, produced this hologram of a tiny rainbow! As I started to think about this image, it became increasingly clear to me that it symbolized the true spectrum of all forms in nature. I began to imagine all the forms around me as holographic reflections of light!

The prism of color within the light gives shape and definition to all forms. As a form myself, I extended my arms out in front of me and observed them from a different perspective now. I became acutely aware of the true nature of my material form as a colorful hologram of vibrating light. I had formulated an idea about myself as a projection of the Creator's consciousness and so, imagining a ray of light emanating from the source, I thought, "Aha, that must be how it's done! The Creator projects thought-images, or consciousness, by using vibrating rays of light!"

The prism of color gives definition to the forms!" I also felt, deep within my soul, that the Creator loves all of his forms dearly and immensely enjoys the experience of creating them. I could feel the love within the light! I am always filled with joy and delight when I am out in nature observing and admiring the life forms around me. These experiences give my life profound meaning and I am always spurred on to find out more about their significance.

When I got home, I shuffled through my collection of books, hoping to find out more about the holographic nature of reality. I wanted to explore the idea that form was simply a projection of consciousness. I had already read about the concept of "thought-forms" in the *The RA Material*. I chose this book and three others: "Initiation", *The Urantia Book* and "Sacred Geometry." After several days of reading, highlighting, taking notes and thinking deeply, I began to form concepts in my mind about the creative process. My visualizations start with the infinite realm beyond time and space before the explosion of creation.

In the Urantia Book, it refers to the "absolute level":

"The absolute level is beginningless, timeless and spaceless." [2]

In the book, Initiation, it talks about a "first source":

"The first source of all truth and of all manifestation is the eternal being — God. But God is in the un-manifested state beyond time and space, and only his manifestations appear as projections in the three-dimensional world." [3]

As we head into this part of our exploration, I'd like to take a moment to honor Elisabeth Haisch, the author of the book "Initiation" for her courage and willingness to share the exquisite details of her past-life recall. She is no longer with us in the physical realm, but we are still blessed by her generous spirit as she reveals profound truths about the mysteries of creation. I highly encourage you to purchase this book for yourself, so you can fully appreciate all the extraordinary teachings. Thanks to Elisabeth, we can clearly see, through the following descriptions and illustrations, how sacred geometry lies at the very heart of every creation story.

First, let's imagine the One Infinite Creator as the Mother Womb existing in an infinite realm of pure consciousness. Inspired by the teachings in *The Urantia Book*, let's imagine that the first source emerging from the womb is the Universal Father, the second source is his reflection, the Eternal Child and the third source is the Mother Spirit.

1.1

"The Universal Father achieves free will liberation from the bonds of infinity and the fetters of eternity by the technique of trinitization, threefold deity personality." [4]

In her book, Elisabeth describes this "trinitization" from a different perspective: "...the creator recognizes himself in the created, ... In this condition, the recognizer, the recognized and the recognition are one and the same." [5]

The infinite source and Mother Womb is the Divine Mother who births all of creation. Her firstborn becomes the "Creator" and "recognizer" as the Universal Father. The second source becomes the "recognized" and "Created" Eternal Child and the third source, the "recognition" and "Creative" Mother Spirit is the Infinite, or Holy Spirit.

Note: The Urantia Book refers to the Eternal Child as the Son (literally a "Sun" analogy) but this being is clearly androgynous.

Here is where we will begin to explore sacred geometry as an explanation of how the One Great Self awakened in the infinite realm and transformed into the Divine Trinity. The trinity "rested" in perfect unity until the desire to create overwhelmed them and through the process of reflection and projection, they transformed into the Creative Trinity and created a realm called eternity. It's time to concentrate on these concepts by envisioning them with an open mind. Let's continue to follow the teachings that Elisabeth shares in her book: "...this divine state in which the creator recognizes (itself) may also be expressed symbolically by numbers: 'God in (its) state of resting within (itself) is 1 in 3 and 3 in 1. 1 and 3 are still an unseparated unity. In the field of geometry, the form of the equilateral triangle is the symbolic image of God in which the recognizer, the recognized and the recognition are one and the same: 1 in 3 and 3 in 1...Divinity in its primordial state of resting within itself, always manifests in the form of a triangle. The triangle represents perfect harmony and perfect equilibrium at the three corner points all exactly the same distance from each other." [6]

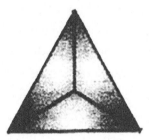

The equilateral triangle represents the divine trinity 'resting" in an "existential" state expressing only their potential in the experiential realm. *The Urantia Book* expands on this state of being:

"The Father, Son and Spirit are — existential in actuality (though all potentials are supposedly experiential)." [7] The Creator recognizes its potential for experience and wishes to realize it by expanding its consciousness beyond the dimensionless state. To do this, the Creator uses the creative concept of "reflectivity" to create a triangle within the divine triangle. It is inverted because it is a reflection. We can call this newly created form "the creative triangle" as the trinity moves from the un-manifested into the manifested state. Within the creative triangle, there are four smaller triangles which becomes significant as "the four faces of God" and the four elements!

Let's return to "Initiation" to continue with the sacred geometry perspective: "... When the aspect of God to which we refer to as resting within itself moves out of the dimensionless state, beyond time and space and into the three dimensions, it becomes the creative aspect of God and always manifests itself in the number four... (When the numbers 1 and 3 emerge from the divine condition of unity, they separate, and out of the 1 in 3 there emerges 1 and 3 and that makes 4). The equilateral triangle contains, hidden within itself, four smaller equilateral triangles." [8]

At this point, the trinity has moved into its creative aspect and is ready to emerge into time and space to create form. Together, the trinity focuses with intention on condensing their combined energy, or consciousness, into one point of light. The book, "Initiation", describes a 'projection of consciousness' from the dimensionless state into the first dimension starting as a single point. Then, after a time, the point becomes a 'point of departure' as it moves out into a line. In the realm of infinity, the book explains, this line would be represented by the number one, but now that this energy has moved into the realm of time and space, it has a beginning and ending, and therefore is represented by the number three. The line has three aspects: a beginning, a middle and an end, as described: "Thus the line represents the number three, the key number for the one-dimensional world. This line also represents the first dimension — length." [9]

This next step in the creative process represents the pivotal point when a separation from unity takes place. So, before we move into the second dimension, let's hear what this book has to say about how and why a sense of unity is maintained in the reflective process.

"Reflection vs. Separation"

" . . . There is no possibility of manifesting or of finding the number 2 in a unity. As a matter of fact, after the first manifestation of the point, which represents only one single factor, we immediately jumped to three factors, without the number two...In order for the number 2 to arise, there has to be a splitting of unity. The number 2 can only be born when two units are set beside each other. But because nothing has any real existence outside unity, unity must project a reflection outside itself." [10]

The book then describes how this single line becomes a flat rectangular plane as all the points on the line project away from it with the same force and for the same time. Now, the second dimension is born and the number five becomes significant. This number represents the four sides plus the un-manifested space, or spirit, within. Five becomes the key number for the second dimension.

Then the climactic moment — 3D reality comes into being! This climax of reality manifestation feels to me like a crescendo in a symphony as the flat plane moves out from its four points and becomes a cube. Then Ta-Da! The symphony ends and applause erupts. The third-dimension is born! The conditions for experience in 3-D are ripe! The cube represents the key number for our world, the number seven. The seven aspects of the cube include its six sides plus the un-manifested space, or spirit, within. We will be referring to the number seven repeatedly in our adventures throughout time and space because it has tremendous significance in all of creation.

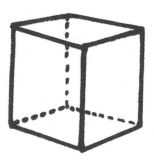

Within this cube, lies the divinity that created it which is, and always will be, represented by the equilateral triangle. This cube may also represent the so-called, "Metatron's Cube", which is said to be the cube from which the Platonic solids emerged. The book, "Initiation" states that, "...the form of matter is the cube. The basic crystals are built in conformity with this law...or the basic elements of the cube in various aspects and variations." [11] As you will see, the platonic solids are in fact, crystals, and as such, they manifest the four aspects of the elements and a fifth "variation."

At this point, since we have emerged into a 3D experience of reality, we will focus our attention on the five Platonic solids as they provide the foundation for the manifestation of form. Of course, the Platonic solids got their name from the ancient philosopher, Plato. He associated the Platonic solids with the four elements. The fifth solid, the dodecahedron, the Platonian philosopher, Timaeus, described as "a fifth combination which God used in the delineation of the universe." [12]

As we move into a discussion about the platonic solids, it's interesting to note that this philosopher, "Timaeus," believed that these solids were the true elements of the material world and refers specifically to the triangle and the square. "The true elements of the material world, Timaeus says, are not earth, air, fire, and water, but two sorts of right angled triangles, the one which is half a square and the one which is half an equilateral triangle. The above two sorts of triangles, we are told, are the most beautiful forms and therefore God used them in constructing matter. By means of these two triangles, it is possible to construct four of the five regular solids, and each atom of one of the four elements is a regular solid. Atoms of earth are cubes; fire, tetrahedron; of air, octahedron; and of water, icosahedra." [13]

The significance here is that the Platonic solids brought forth the four elements. Fire was produced by the tetrahedron, air by the octahedron, water by the icosahedron and earth by the cube. The dodecahedron as "ether" seems to contribute some type of embracing principle, possibly the force of gravity (a personal speculation). Another intriguing revelation within the Platonian philosophy, is that the platonic solids are crystals which gives them a reflective property capable of projecting thought-forms of vibrating light within the spectrum of seven rays!

The first Platonic solid is the tetrahedron and it is hidden within the cube. It can be exposed by cutting off all four corners of the cube, as demonstrated in "Initiation."

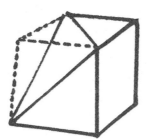

The book explains, "Just like the equilateral triangle which makes its mantle, the tetrahedron is the very incarnation of harmony and equilibrium. Each of its corner points is equally distance from each of the others, there is no strain or tension in a tetrahedron, but rather a condition of resting equilibrium. By way of contrast, the corners of the cube, just like those of the square, lie at different distances from each other, and this means that both in the square and in the cube, there is a condition of everlasting stress....(This tension creates a resistance which is necessary in the world of form. Without it, everything would collapse into the source from which it came!)...The matter in our three-dimensional world is built in cubic form, but hidden within itself it contains the form of the tetrahedron based on divine equilibrium. Matter cannot exist without the divine content...No one suspects that the tetrahedron (the divine self)...so different from the outward cubic shape...is dwelling within!" [14]

Here in lies the profound meaning that is revealed in this symbolic nature of the creative process. According to the book, the cube represents our material form and the tetrahedron within symbolizes our divine self. Man, therefore, has two choices based on this truth. He can either choose to identify with the cube, his body, or with the tetrahedron, its divine content. The suggestion is that the flat surface of the cube should only be used as a secure base.

The author explains: "hidden and invisible within this body, however, is a higher, divine self — life — eternal being! Only man is able to manifest his higher self (through) his thoughts, words and deeds, when he identifies his consciousness, not with his body, but with his spiritual content — with his 'self'. As long as a person identifies himself only with his body, he is like an opaque cube in that he reveals only the characteristics of matter, crowding the divine creative principle into a latent, unmanifested state." [15] This clearly defines the ego-self. It is this strong identification with our physical form that detracts from our identification with our spirit-self.

The author expands on this concept: "on the other hand a person may use his body, his thoughts, words and deeds to manifest the divine creative principle, while leaving the characteristics of his physical existence — his person — in the unmanifested state — such a person, to continue using the same figure of speech, is like a cut cube whose corners and inner content are turned outward so that the inner triangles — the equilateral triangles of the divine tetrahedron — are visible. Such a person uses the material, square shape only as a secure base in the three-dimensional world, allowing his weight to rest on this base." [16]

As I read on, I was fascinated by the next revelation that, if the 'cut cube' is turned inside out, what you have now is the shape of the pyramid. With this, "the pyramid is the symbolic form of the God-man, who reveals his divine, selfless nature and completely manifests God on earth. The salvation of the earth, the spiritualization of matter, is completed in the person of the God-man. The divine self–the Creator–is seated in complete Majesty on his throne and rules over matter, over the body." [17] Of course we realize how significant the pyramid was in Egyptian times and now we have a better understanding about why that might have been!

Now a major revelation emerges as the book shows us what happens if we don't reveal our divine self within, symbolized by the tetrahedron, and identify only with our body, the cube:

"This symbolic representation of materialistic man who uses his intellect for the service of his material being is the cross — or a "T"- formed out of the four squares making up the surface of the cube. On his cross...the secret, indwelling divine self is crucified." [18]

The book explains: "In such persons, divinity is robbed of its power. It cannot manifest and is subject to the laws of the material world. It is crucified on the two great beams of the three-dimensional world — on time and space — and dies on this cross of matter. Its death, however, is not final! Even in the consciousness that has sunk down to the lowest level, the divine creative self sometimes undergoes resurrection and saves the suffering human being. Materialistic man, in his ignorance through crucifying his own higher self — God within himself — creates ceaseless tortures and sufferings for himself; he becomes the criminal who is also crucified beside the divine one. The pains awaken him; his higher consciousness is aroused, and with the resurrection of his divine self, he experiences his own salvation because he recognizes himself in him!" [19]

As I read this, the stories in the Bible came rushing to the forefront of my mind. How symbolic is it now that Jesus was crucified on a cross?! The divine self was crucified, and divinity was robbed of its power on this 'cross of matter' by materialistic man in his ignorance. In this way, he crucified the God within himself and thereby, created endless suffering! Even the reference to the criminal, "he becomes the criminal who is also crucified beside the divine one" is just like Barabbas in the Bible who was crucified beside Jesus. I promised you in the introduction that the creation story would hold profound meaning that would transcend the details behind the creative process itself. This is a perfect example!

It's necessary to refer to the cube now so we can continue to explore how the creative force moves forward into the manifestation of form. From the tetrahedron that we found inside the cube, we can also find its complementary half reflected by cutting off the other four corners.

This exposes the star-tetrahedron and according to the book, this symbolic shape represents "the innermost law of the recognizable world: the inseparable relationship between the two complementary halves — positive and negative — which, self-contained each within the other, form a perfect equilibrium and sit, (as co-creative spirit and matter), on the right hand and on the left-hand of divinity. In creation they rule as two opposite laws: the law of spirit and the law of matter. Spirit is life, matter is resistance. The law of the Spirit is radiation, giving, selflessness. The law of matter is drawing inward, cooling off, paralysis." [20]

This resistance that the author refers to reminds me of the "divinity tension" spoken of in *The Urantia Book*:

" . . . The eternal and infinite I AM achieved deity liberation from the fetters of unqualified infinity to the exercise of inherent and eternal free will, and this divorcement from unqualified infinity produced the first absolute divinity tension." [21]

So we can see that the moment the Creator moved out of infinity and into time and space, the first 'divinity tension' was produced. This also represents the 'separation from unity' that is the nature of the 3-D world of time and space. It is the difference between spirit and matter and is recognized as tension or resistance. In the cube, or square, for instance the corner points lie at different distances from each other and this produces everlasting stress as opposed to the tetrahedron, or triangle, where the three corner points all lie the same distance from each other in perfect harmony and equilibrium. In "Initiation," the author describes this more clearly:

"Without the resistance of matter, creation would be impossible. In unmanifested divinity, all creative forces are still resting in unity, in complete repose, in equilibrium, representing merely potential, only power possibilities. Creation begins in that one force separates itself from unity and sets itself up opposite to the Creator as resistance. That is the "first born (child)" of God, the spirit of resistance which (God) sends out to act throughout eons and eons of time as a negative and opposite pole to its self, to bear the frequencies of creation, and by resisting them make it possible for creation to take place. This spirit of resistance is the opposite pole to the manifesting aspect of God. By virtue of its centripetal, chilling and coagulating characteristics, it is the cause of the creation of matter." [22]

From the star- tetrahedron, the two tetrahedrons are contained within each other as the equilibrium between two opposite poles are demonstrated and this law operates in the crystallization of matter too! The next platonic solid is the octahedron and it is also symbolic of the tetrahedron reflecting its opposing self as two pyramidical shapes connected at their bases.

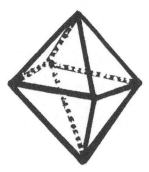

I have come to believe, through further research and illustrations, that with the creation of the octahedron, the sphere came into being. Spinning on its axis and rotating, it created a sphere around itself!

This is another extremely important point in the creative process as the sphere represents the symbolic center of all of creation. We will come right back to the sphere as soon as we finish our discussion of the Platonic solids, the last two being the dodecahedron and the icosahedron.

The dodecahedron represents the shape of a Pentagon and, at first, I didn't understand why this crystal deviated from the symbolic triangular shape. Then I realized that this shape comes into being when the bases of five triangles are connected! The pentagonal dodecahedron, which has 12 pentagonal faces, also introduces the possibility for more complex geometric equations as the Creator begins to advance his use of geometry in his creative endeavor. The book "Initiation" simply says, "The pentagonal dodecahedron reveals further laws of the long path of the consciousness." [23]

Lastly, we have the icosahedron which has 20 triangular faces increasing the potential for advanced mathematics even more!

And there you have it — the five Platonic solids! As we mentioned in the beginning of this discussion, the Platonic solids are related to the elements. In the book, "Sacred Geometry" by Stephen Skinner, he writes, "the five Platonic solids were associated with the four ancient elements and ether (upper air) and are the only perfectly pure regular solids." [24]

Now we can move on to our sphere. "Initiation" points out how the number of faces on the geometric shapes of the Platonic solids combine to give us the degrees in the circle. It explains,"if we take the number of faces of each of the geometric bodies we talked about — the tetrahedron, cube, pentagonal dodecahedron, and icosahedron, we get the numbers 2, 3, 6 and 10. If we multiply these numbers together, we get the number 360, the number of degrees in the circle. And if we add these numbers together, we get 21, the number of possible connections between the seven factors of the key number of the three-dimensional world, the number 7!" [25]

The sphere, or circle, and the number seven are both critical aspects for the creative manifestation of our 3-D reality! This sphere becomes the shape from which the pattern of creation emerges and the number seven represents the three aspects of the Creator, (the trinity), plus the four elements, sometimes called the "four faces of God." To understand how the sphere came into being, we need to refer to the octahedron because, as Drunvalo Melchizedek discusses in his book, "The Ancient Secret of the Flower of Life," this Platonic solid created the spherical shape. When the octahedron spins on its axis, it creates a 'rotating octahedron' which then becomes a 'spherical octahedron' and the sphere emerges!

Another pivotal point in creation begins as we move from shapes into patterns. These patterns will become the basis for all recognizable forms of matter and energy. The first of the patterns to emerge from the sphere is the 'Vesica Pisces' which represents a sphere projecting a mirror image of itself. It is simply a reflection of the first sphere. At the intersection of the two spheres (where the two become one) is the fish shape, or symbol for Pisces. This is always sometimes referred to as the third eye in the center. Then a pattern called the "tripod of life" emerges which may be a representation of the trinity. These two patterns may also represent the first and second day of creation and the following four patterns, each with an additional sphere, may represent the six days of creation.

With the creation of each sphere, the spirit increased its mathematical knowledge and creative skills. At the end of the six days of creation, there were seven spheres forming "The Seed of Life" pattern which is the basic pattern of existence and is perceived as sacred.

And on the seventh day, the Creator rested.

Conclusion

From a consciousness perspective, we can clearly see how the Creator manifested thought into form by first reflecting upon his own image with the creation of the Eternal Child. Upon recognizing the mirror image, the Infinite Spirit came into being! The Eternal Child reflects the Creator's spirit and the Infinite Spirit reflects the Creator's mind. The Creator retained its personality by diffusing itself in this way. In this sense, God is personality, the Eternal Child is spirit and the Infinite Spirit is mind. I will expand upon these concepts in the next chapter, but you can see how the universal aspects of consciousness (as personality, spirit and mind) were created within this divine trinity.

Moving out of the realm of infinity, where the trinity was at rest within itself as a perfect equilateral triangle, the primal consciousness emerged as a single point with one dimension. This point, then, became a point of departure as the creative energy moved for the first time ever outside of infinity. The Creator projected a line in time and space with a beginning, a middle and an end and, in doing so, created the key number of the first dimension: 3. From this first line, a series of points, the creative force moved out and projected energy forward to create a flat, rectangular plane. Thus, the second dimension emerged and is represented by the key number: five.

From the four corner points of this rectangular plane, the Creator projected his consciousness by moving out into the third dimension and in doing so, created a cube. This primal cube contained within itself the original perfection of the trinity — the equilateral triangle expressing its three divine aspects. From within this cube, the five Platonic solids emerged, which brought forth the four elements. As crystals, these solids brought forth fire (from the tetrahedron), air (from the octahedron), water (from the icosahedron) and earth (from the cube). The dodecahedron may represent the so-called "ether" or "upper air" but I'm beginning to suspect that this crystal (which Timaeus thought, "delineated" the universe), may have something to do with gravity.

The Trinity-consciousness, upon projecting the five crystals in time and space as elements and "ether," began creating energy patterns. As the octahedron spun on its axis and created a sphere, the spherical octahedron came into being. Once this first sphere was created, it reflected a second one just like it and the Vesica Pisces emerged as dual consciousness, representative of the Mother-Father and Eternal Child. This was the first day of creation. On the second day, a third sphere emerged, the Infinite Spirit, symbolic of the trinity, and became known as the tripod of life. On the three consecutive days that followed, one sphere was added to the pattern each day until on the sixth day, there were seven spheres. This pattern became known as the seed of life and is the basic energy pattern of all living beings. Once this pattern becomes active, life emerges! Finally, the seed of life flourishes as the Creator expands its consciousness and moves into the realization of its creative potential with the flower of life pattern!

1.2

Once I realized that the Platonic solids represented the four elements (and possibly gravity), and that the spheres represented the six days of creation, I naturally thought of the creation story in The Holy Bible.

"In the beginning God created the heavens and the earth." ~ Genesis 1:1

It starts with a void, maybe with an imperceptible pinpoint of light, and then as the creative force moves, the point becomes a line and then a plane and finally a 3D cube. We can think of this point of light expanding its consciousness as it moves and upon creating the cube in 3D, its light becomes expansive and overcomes the void of darkness.

"The earth was without form, and void; and darkness was on the face of the deep.
And the spirit of God was hovering over the face of the waters. Then God said,
"Let there be light"; and there was light." ~ Genesis 1:2-3

At this point, we can imagine the spheres as days and in the beginning, there was just one single sphere — God alone in infinity. Then on the first day, the Creator creates a second sphere — the Vesica Pisces — as its reflection. The Creator "divided" its self and in doing so, created an essential nature of creation: the 'complementary half'.

"And God saw the light, that it was good; and God divided the light from the darkness."
"God called the light Day and the darkness he called Night. So the evening and
the morning were the first day". ~ Genesis 1:4-5

On the second day, the trinity, or three spheres, came into being and this made possible the manifestation of creation. Of course, the platonic solids are necessary for the crystallization of matter so, at this point, the first two elements come forth as the crystals work their reflective magic! Fire and air emerge as creation swirls within what the bible calls the "firmament" or other texts call "ether." This fifth solid may even be expressed as a gravitational force embracing the elements within the stratosphere). Remember, Timaeus referred to it as the "delineation" of the universe.

"Then God said, "Let there be firmament in the midst of the waters,
and let it divide the waters from the waters."
"Thus God made the firmament and, and divided the waters which were under
the firmament from the waters which were above the firmament; and it was so.
"And God called the firmament Heaven. So the evening and the morning
were the second day." ~ Genesis 1:6-8

On the third day, when the spheres start to multiply, the platonic solids become very effective with their advanced mathematical capability and water and earth emerge!

"Then God said, "Let the waters under the heavens be gathered together
into one place and let the dry land appear"; and it was so.
"And God called the dry land earth and the waters he called Seas.
And God saw that it was good." ~ Genesis 1:9-10
"So the evening and the morning were the third day."
~ Genesis 1:13

On the fourth day, we have five spheres. At this point, all five platonic solids are active. The bible refers to the seasons and therefore, acknowledges the four elements as seasons. The book, "Initiation" refers to "the four faces of God."

"Then God said, "Let there be lights in the firmament of the heavens to divide the day
from the night; and let them be for signs and seasons, and for days and years."
~Genesis 1:14
"So the evening and the morning were the fourth day."
~ Genesis 1:19

As we move into the fifth day, all six spheres come together to create the seed of life, the basic pattern of all living beings. Incredibly, the Bible's story aligns perfectly as life emerges in the sea below and in the air above!

"Then God said, "Let the waters abound with an abundance of living creatures,
and let birds fly above the earth across the face of the firmament of the heavens."
So God created great sea creatures and every living thing that moves,
with which the waters abounded, according to their kind, and every
winged bird according to its kind. And God saw that it was good.
And God blessed them, saying, "Be fruitful and multiply, and
fill the water in the seas and let birds multiply on the earth
So the evening and the morning were the fifth day." ~ Genesis 1:20-23

And now, we come to the awesome sixth day when the spheres begin to multiply rapidly as the Creator expands its consciousness and creates a pattern with the highest potential — the amazing "flower of life"! As this pattern, with its profound mathematical potential, becomes active, more advanced creatures evolve. This leads to the climactic emergence of Man! In beautiful and sweet synchrony, the Bible confers.

"Then God said, "Let the earth bring forth the living creature according to its kind:
cattle and creeping thing and beast of the earth, each according to its kind";
and it was so. And God made the beast of the earth according to its kind,
cattle according to its kind, and everything that creeps on the earth according
to its kind. And God saw that it was good. Then God said, "Let us make man
in Our image, according to Our likeness; let them have dominion over the
fish of the sea, over the birds of the air, and over the cattle, over all the earth
and over every creeping thing that creeps on the earth." So God created man
in his own image; in the image of God He created him; male and female
He created them. Then God blessed them, and God said to them, "Be fruitful
and multiply; fill the earth and subdue it; have dominion over the fish of the sea
over the birds of the air, and over every living thing that moves on the earth."
~ Genesis 1:24-28

"Then God saw everything that He had made, and indeed it was very good.
So the evening and the morning were the sixth day." ~ Genesis 1:31

Of course, on the seventh day, the Creator rested, pleased with all of the images he had projected.

"Thus, the heavens and the earth and all the host of them, were finished. And on the
seventh day God ended His work which he had done, and He rested on the seventh
day from all His work which he had done. Then God blessed the seventh day and
sanctified it, because in it He rested from all his work which God had
created and made. This is the history of the heavens and the earth when they
were created, in the day that the Lord God made the earth and the heavens."
~ Genesis 2:1-4

And there it is — the seven days and that magic number once again. The three (**3**) aspects of the Creator (the trinity) + the four (**4**) faces of God (the elements) ~ the key number for the third dimension: **7**. Isn't the synchronicity beautiful? A sweet harmonious symphony swirling and spinning just like the radiant spiral from which it emerged!

It's been a long but very interesting adventure on this first day of exploration, but we covered a lot of territory! We figured out how all of creation came into being and along the way discovered many sacred symbols. We started out searching for one and ended up finding the most sacred of all symbols, the triangle, as well as the shapes and patterns that created the 3-D world that we live in! I hope you've enjoyed this journey of self-discovery as much as I have.

Let's move to a quiet place now where we can sit and perform the following contemplative meditation, "Symbols of Love, Light and Life," that I have designed for today's adventure. This guided visualization will lead you into a reflective state where you can access your own inner wisdom. This will enable you to piece together in your own mind what makes the most sense to you. You will simply start to "get it" when the truths that resonate within you fall into place perfectly. This is a process of 'remembering' as you connect with the divine truths. As an emanation of the Creator-consciousness, you have access to this knowledge, you just need to re-member it!

Let's express our gratitude for this remarkable experience and rejoice in the One Infinite Creator, whose love is omniscient, omnipresent and within.

There is no life, truth, intelligence, nor substance in matter.
All is infinite mind and its infinite manifestation, for God is all-in-all.
Spirit is the immortal truth; matter is mortal error.
Spirit is the real and eternal; matter is the unreal and temporal.
Spirit is God and man is his image and likeness.
Therefore, man is not material; he is spiritual.
~ Carol Beckwith & Angela Fisher

Symbols of Love, Light and Life
A Guided Visualization
(Audio version available at www.SuzanneRossTranscendence.com)

Find a comfortable place to sit in a posture that is most conducive to your meditation. Start by inhaling and exhaling — just soft natural breaths flowing in and out. Drop your shoulders and relax your muscles. Relax into the floor beneath you. Focus on the feeling of the breath moving past your upper lip, flowing in and flowing out. Focus on that spot where you feel the breath. Now draw your attention to the base of your spine and feel your energy centered there. Imagine a red disc spinning clockwise at the very base of your spine. This is your primal "root" chakra and as it spins, imagine light radiating out from its center. As the brilliant red disc gets larger, it spins faster. This disc represents the consciousness of survival and it reflects your most primitive instincts. These natural instincts protect you from harm by alerting you to danger and driving you to seek food and shelter. So as this disc spins at the base of your spine, connect with these primal instincts and experience your most basic level of consciousness.

Before progressing to higher levels of consciousness, we are going to connect with the earth beneath us. To stay grounded to Mother Earth, imagine a dark green column of light leaving the base of your spine and penetrating the ground below. This is called your "grounding cord." As the column of light starts radiating into the earth beneath you, imagine it spiraling downward — first through the dirt and gold flecked rocks, where it picks up the gold sacred energy, and then down through the crystalline rocks where it picks up the violet divine energy. Imagine the cord spiraling downward now through the hot orange lava and into the fiery point of light at the center of the earth. Your being is now connected to the sacred core of Mother Earth. You feel unified with her spirit and comforted by a deep inner knowing that she dearly loves you and all her children.

Now, pull that motherly love back up toward the base of your spine. As the light travels upward from the center of the earth, it spirals back up through the fiery core picking up the energy and intensity of the heat. Swirling upward past the thick lava, it emerges from the heat and penetrates the crystalline rock and the gold flecked earth. Finally the spiraling cord penetrates the ground beneath you as it emerges from the earth and connects with its origin at the base of your spine. The intense energy from the spirit of Mother Earth spins your root chakra and then splits into the form of two electric serpents as it progresses from this point. Ascending from your root chakra, this serpentine energy braids your spine as it spirals upward. At the level of your second chakra, located behind your sexual organs, the energy converges and spins this wheel of wanting.

This bright orange chakra represents the consciousness of desire. As it spins clockwise, it radiates light outward from its center and any shadowy debris blocking the chakra is flung off as it rotates faster and wider. Feel the emotions attached to the consciousness of desire. Envision negative thoughts of greed being flung off as more virtuous desires arise. A strong wish for the prosperity of all living beings arises and pure light radiates out from the center. As it expands, the orange disc becomes brightly illuminated. Now emerging from the second chakra, the electric blue serpents ascend, braiding your spine, as they move toward the bright yellow chakra at your solar plexus behind your belly button. This chakra represents the consciousness of power. Spin that chakra clockwise and allow the light to radiate through it. Any debris on that chakra which represents negative attachments to power — like the need to control and manipulate others — are flung off. As the debris flies off into space, your chakra becomes a shimmering gold wheel spinning faster and wider. As it expands, you are filled with a sense of pure empowerment — the power to create that which will benefit all living beings.

Emerging from that chakra now, the serpents intertwine ascending into the fourth chakra of pure, unconditional love. This chakra is located directly behind the heart and its fluorescent green energy illuminates the wheel as it spins faster and wider. Any negative emotions of hate, anger, fear or resentment are flung off and immediately replaced by compassion and forgiveness which spread far and wide. You are filled with unconditional love for all living beings and this makes you smile.

Now, the serpent's energy rises up your spine and travels between your shoulder blades converging at the base of your throat. This is where your fifth chakra is located, and it represents communication or communion. This is the brightest chakra of all and it sparkles with a clear blue energy just like the sky. As it expands, you feel a strong sense of communion with all of your brothers and sisters on this planet. You are at one with these beings and you imagine that you are all united as a community of souls.

Now, at the base of your throat, feel the serpentine energy rising into the sixth chakra at the back of your skull. This is an indigo blue wheel which represents all of the inner wisdom you have accumulated since the beginning of eternity. This is the portal to all of the knowledge and experience which has been gathered by your eternal soul. You are filled with an inner knowing that all of the truths from the beginning are stored within your aura and you have access to them whenever you are connected with this sacred chakra. Now imagine a "third eye" at the center of your forehead looking back at you. An image of this eye emerges from a single point of light. You can clearly see this indigo blue eye flashing on the screen in front of you. This third eye is the essence of your eternal soul and seeing it confirms that you are now deeply connected to it. You have opened a portal of clear communication with your whole soul.

Now, the serpentine energy rises and ascends to the very top of your skull where it converges into one single point. This point marks the center your seventh chakra. This chakra represents the highest consciousness which is divine in nature. It represents faith and worship. It is your connection to the cosmic consciousness and to all of the spirit beings who lovingly guide you. Opening this portal allows divine energy and cosmic wisdom to flow into your being. This wheel is illuminated by a bright violet light and as it expands, you feel a strong connection to the spiritual realm. As it spins wider and faster, you see a powerful beam of light emerge from the center and expand outward in all directions. You are now connected with the infinite field of cosmic consciousness. As this divine source flows into your being, you feel a powerful flash of electric blue light race down the length of your spine. Your vertebrae tingles with the power of this source and the fluorescent blue serpentine glows brightly.

You have a clear line of communication now from the center of Mother Earth through the vast realms of the infinite cosmos. You have created a clear portal for pure consciousness to flow. Let's go deeper now by connecting with the loving spirits we have drawn into our field:

Opening salutation:

"Thank you spirit beings who have joined us to illuminate the divine secrets of creation — the mysteries that lie within the universal knowledge. Please help us understand how all things came into being in the realms of time and space. Please show us how the divine trinity emerged from "resting in perfect unity" and reflected upon itself to become the creative trinity manifesting into form."

(Contemplate this and pause to receive. Allow the cosmic consciousness to flow into your being and just listen to what arises in your mind as you do.)

Imagine a point at the base of the skull where you connect with the light of pure consciousness from the Creator. Now imagine a point at the center of your heart where you receive the light of pure spirit from the Eternal Child. At the solar plexus, imagine a point where you absorb the light of pure awareness from the Infinite Spirit. These three points of light represent the Trinity-consciousness — the first expression of consciousness unified in the infinite ocean of bliss. Here, the trinity is resting in its most divine aspect. (Pause to contemplate this.)

As the trinity projects this pure consciousness into the realm of eternity, it merges into a single point of light and rests. Now the trinity is resting in its creative aspect in this realm that has a beginning but no ending. In this realm, the possibilities are endless and consciousness is unlimited. From that single point, the energy moves out to a line projecting into time and space and then stops in this realm where consciousness is limited with both a beginning and an ending. This line consists of points and from these points, the consciousness projects itself outward creating a flat rectangular plane. Like the point represents just one dimension, the plane now represents a two-dimensional experience. Now, from the rectangular flat plane, consciousness is projected outward creating a cube and the third dimension is born. Inside of that cube is still the divine energy of the Trinity consciousness. Let's look inside and go beyond the form.

You are now exploring spirit which is beyond the physical form. So, as we explore how form was manifested in dimensions as geometric shapes and patterns using light, color and sound, we keep in mind that it is the spirit beyond the form that underlies all manifestation. The origin of that spirit is the infinite realm — consciousness beyond time and space, consciousness beyond form. Reuniting with that consciousness is the gateway to transcending form and ascending on our path. From the three points of light, one which radiates light at the base of your skull causing a halo to form, one which radiates light outward from the center of your heart creating a field of circulating light all around you and one which radiates light from your solar plexus causing light to spiral around your being in a continuous flow from head to toe. These three lights merge to create an aura of light all around you which radiates in all directions — outward, circulating and spiraling. As your light radiates, it merges with your co-creative guides. Both lights merge to create one radiant light that spreads and fills the space. The energy that is driving the expansion of this light is pure love. As we close this meditation, we will remain bathed in this light throughout the remainder of the day. Unified in spirit and filled with unconditional love, deeply inhale radiant light and then gently exhale and smile.

Closing salutation:

"Thank you, spirit beings, who joined us to bring a deeper awareness into our meditation. Thank you for sharing your wisdom and thank you for sharing your love. With gratitude and joy, I bless you and I bless my co-creative friends." Draw your hands together in a prayer position at the center of your heart. "I bless the Creator, the Trinity, the Archangels and Ascended Masters. Namaste."

Your Personal Revelations

_____

_____

_____

_____

_____

_____

_____

_____

_____

_____

_____

_____

_____

_____

_____

_____

REFERENCES

Illustrations:

Chapter cover image courtesy of: https://pngpix.com

p 39-44:Personal photos

1.1. Image courtesy of: https://pngpix.com

1.2. Image courtesy of: https://nuryourselfen.wordpress.com

Text:

1. |Internet website: www.poetry-archive.com/j/the_creation.html The Urantia Book Fellowship, *The Urantia Book,* Uversa Press, 2008

2. (Foreword: 7.6)

4. (Foreword: 3.4)

7. (Foreword: 7.3)

21. (Foreword: 3.14)

Elisabeth Haisch, *Initiation,* Aurora Press, 2000

3. page 226

5. page 226

6. page 228

8. page 229

9. page 229

10. page 230

11. page 230

14. page 230

15. page231

16. page 232

17. page232

18. page 232

19. page 233

20. page233

22. page 234

23. page 236

25. page 238

Bertrand Russell, *A History of Western Philosophy,* Simon & Schuster, 2007

12. page 146

13. page 146-7

Stephen Skinner, *Sacred Geometry,* Octopus Publishing Co. Ltd., 2006

24. page 55

Day Two

Beyond the Form

Good morning! I hope you are well-rested and ready for another adventurous day of self-discovery! Today we are going to the beach! It's time to engage your creative imagination as we set out on our virtual exploration. Let's start by visualizing an expansive beach with the sun reflecting off the sand. In the sunlight, the white sand sparkles like a vast array of tiny crystals. Imagine you are standing in the direct light of the sun embraced by its warmth and consumed by its brilliance. In this moment, you are aligned with a powerful source of radiant energy that ignites your spirit and illuminates your soul. Your feet are sunken deep into the soft, warm sand and you feel connected to the energy of the earth. You realize that a strong force of energy is flowing through you now as you absorb the power of both the radiant sun above and the living earth below. In the distance, you can hear the rhythmic sounds of the ocean's breath — exhaling as the waves are expelled onto shore and inhaling as they return to their source. You start to synchronize your own breathing with the rhythm of the waves and a profound sense of inner peace consumes you. At this moment, you are merging with the living spirit all around you and pure ecstasy fills your soul. This feeling of ecstatic peace is like a quiet celebration in the stillness of your mind.

Guided by the living spirit, let's head down to the ocean and take a walk along the water's edge. As we do, I will share a powerful revelation that I had earlier this year while walking on the beach with my husband. I encourage you to let your imagination flow as I virtually recreate my experience. Let the adventure begin…

Offering from the Ocean

After spending weeks with my head buried in research, my husband suggested that we take off and have some fun in the sun. I had been intensely focused on preparing material for my "Consciousness Expansion" classes and wholeheartedly agreed that we could both use a break. Pismo Beach is the perfect getaway because it has sand dunes we can play on in our dune buggy and an expansive beach we can run on with our dogs. We love taking road trips in our R.V. and at Pismo, we can park it right on the beach! Another great thing about having an R.V. is that my babies (our two dogs) can come along. They both go crazy every time we start to load up the R.V. and race around in ecstatic anticipation. Their pure joy is contagious and we all feel a sense of freedom as we climb in and head out.

In the weeks before we left on our trip, I had been researching sacred geometry and the fundamental patterns of life. This had led me to the discovery of the seed of life, the flower of life and finally, the awe-inspiring tree of life. I was enthralled by the beauty of these patterns and felt a strong connection to their symmetry. I spent hours drawing them and deeply contemplating their significance. I was trying to grasp a clear understanding of exactly how these patterns showed up in nature. So the following week while my husband and I were walking along the beach, I was still consumed with these thoughts. Suddenly my husband broke my concentration by stopping me dead in my tracks. He was pointing excitedly at the sand beneath our feet. Splayed out in front of us were literally hundreds of perfect little sand dollars. My husband commented that he had never seen so many in one place before. We couldn't recall ever seeing them in Pismo before. I squatted down to pick one up, so I could examine it more closely. As I began to realize what I was seeing, I became breathless. Painted clearly on every single sand dollar was none other than the seed of life pattern. I was stunned. Then slowly I turned the sand dollar over to examine the other side. In the very center was a tiny hole with perfect little tree branches emanating from it. "Whoa", I thought, "the tree of life?!"

Pismo Beach, California

2.1 **Site where I received a Divine Offering of Sacred Gifts**

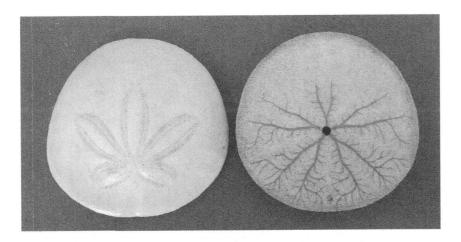

2.2 **Hundreds of Perfect Sand Dollars with the Seed of Life
on the front and the Tree of Life on the back!**

Just as I was concentrating intensely on how these patterns manifested in creation, there they were! The fundamental patterns of creation were clearly imprinted on the forms laid out right in front of me. The truth that I was seeking had been magically revealed. I looked up in the sky and thanked God for responding to my inquiry with this divine miracle! It reminded me of when I was inquiring about the meaning and purpose of life and sky writing appeared above me with a clear and definitive answer. These experiences are affirmations of the saying "Ask and you shall receive." I couldn't believe it and exclaimed to my husband, "Wow! These patterns really do show up in nature after all!" He had read my presentation on "The Seed of Life" before we left. He grasped the significance of what had just happened and we both knew it was a miracle made manifest. Did we manifest it? We began collecting them like they were lost treasures that had finally been found. Well, to me, they were...

My husband and I were speechless as we walked back to the R.V. each of our pockets bulging with sand dollars. Once inside, we took them out one by one and carefully laid them on towels to dry. I couldn't wait to share this experience with my students. Instead of just explaining the 'seed of life' and 'tree of life' to them, now I could show them the manifestation of these patterns clearly expressed in form! I wanted each and every one of them to have their own special sand dollar so I gathered up the most exquisite ones I could find. They came in all different shapes and sizes and even ranged in color. Some were a shade of pale green and others were a soft brown or smoky grey. There were literally hundreds to choose from and they weren't even cracked or broken! They were all perfect. It was fantastic!

Back to our adventure —

Let's take a break from walking along the shoreline now and find a nice place to sit on the sand. Facing the ocean, it feels like we are peering into infinity as the horizon merges with the ocean. We can clearly see the colors of the sky above reflected in the ocean below affirming our revelations about the reflective nature of reality! Let's breathe in the awe and wonder of it all.

2.3

This reflective aspect of creation is fascinating to me and on yesterday's adventure, we clearly saw how this concept of mirror imaging was reflected in the divine and creative trinity. We were shown this in the Platonic solids as the first pyramid reflected an exact image of itself to create the octahedron — one of the first sacred forms with the divine trinity expressed in the upright tetrahedron and the creative trinity reflected in the inverted one. This is especially apparent in the sequence of spheres. The second sphere reflects the first and so on and so on…until finally the seed of life and the flower of life are formed. Creation reflects upon itself to create more and more images just like the first until more complex forms emerge!

Let's explore this concept of reflectivity a little further now. Remember how the Platonic solids were referred to as crystals by the ancient philosophers? I believe we can gain a deeper understanding about the reflective nature of reality if we take a closer look at these forms of crystallized consciousness. We will begin our exploration by first summarizing the creation events from the last chapter in a more progressive sequence. Let's pull a pen and paper out of our backpacks because this time, I want you to 'experience' the creative sequence by drawing the progressive symbols yourself. When I did this, the creative concepts became much more 'real' to me and I developed an inner knowing about these fundamental patterns rather than just an intellectual understanding of them. We'll start with the trinity of beings emerging from the Mother Womb in infinity and moving into the experiential realm of eternity. Please engage in this visualization with me:

Inspired by a brilliant epiphany, the trinity gathers all its energy and condenses it into one point — a single point of light in the void of darkness. Highly motivated by the desire to create, this point of consciousness moves out and expresses itself as a line with a beginning, middle and end. With this act, the trinity consciousness has entered, or created, the first dimension! Inspired by the success of this movement, their unity consciousness moves out from all the tiny points that make up the line and together, they create a flat, rectangular plane. The second dimension emerges! Realizing the power in the points, they expand their consciousness out from all the points of the flat plane and create the sacred cube which becomes the first 3D manifestation!

The line is a series of points which are simply a reflection of the original point and similarly, the lines in the flat plane are reflections of the original line. Of course, the cube is simply a reflection of the first flat plane and this reveals an important truth about the reflective nature of all forms in 3D.

They are simply reflections of the source consciousness from which they are projected. As we learned yesterday, the trinity has often been depicted as an equilateral triangle and that this triangle, then, represents the trinity in its "divine aspect." Once the trinity becomes aware of its desire and ability to create, it moves into its "creative aspect" and a second triangle emerges within the first. This process of reflecting within the divine consciousness becomes the key mechanism for creating in eternity. To demonstrate this, we can see how the divine triangle in infinity manifests an inverted triangle to create through a portal into eternity while still manifesting within the divine triangle. Still embraced by the divine energy of the infinite womb, the creative trinity can manifest forms in eternity!

The Creative Trinity within the Mother Womb

This also brings the number four into play as the creative trinity reflects upon itself inside the larger divine triangle. Looking closer within the larger triangle, we can actually see four smaller triangles. This is a sacred symbol that represents the spiritual cosmology behind creation which recognizes the infinite watery womb as the divine sea within which all of creation unfolds:

As referenced in "The Return of the Divine Sophia": "I am...She who exists before the All... I move in every creature...I am the Invisible One within the All...I am both Mother and Father since I procreate Myself...I am the Womb that gives shape to the All...I am the glory of the Mother." The author, Tricia McCannon explains, "This is the Virgin of the World, the self-created One, who gives birth to the cosmos...she is also the Creator herself who gave birth to both the Divine Father and Mother, who in turn gave birth to the Divine Daughter and Son." [1]

I recommend watching my full interview with Tricia McCannon to witness her revelation of the Divine Mother in action as she so beautifully describes it. Watch the interview at SciSpi.tv/Rise-Up/.

In this sacred symbol, we see the inverted triangle of the Creative Trinity within the upright and original triangle of the Divine Trinity. However, we also see 4 individual triangles emerge within the Mother Womb representing the birth of the Mother, Father, Son and Daughter. Notice the Mother is still in the center with the inverted triangle representing the womb creating in eternity.

Now, let's imagine this creative triangle, with the 4 divine beings inside, manifesting in 3D as the Platonic solids. We can clearly see the Platonic solids emerging starting with the 2D triangle manifesting in 3D as the tetrahedron, or fire element, which reflects upon itself to create the octahedron, or air element. The creative intelligence continues to manifest by reflecting mirror images and three more solids emerge to produce the elements of water, earth and the ether. This is how the Divine Trinity expresses through the Creative Trinity to manifest within the infinite womb.

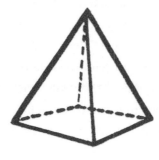

Learning about the creative process in this way empowers us to refine and resurrect our own Creator-consciousness knowing all the while...We are That Which Creates as the original I AM. Say out loud, "I Am That I Am." This is the most powerful statement we can make when developing our ability to manifest as creators in this realm. So let's continue our exploration of the creative process:

As the creative trinity progressively creates mirror images, from a simple point to increasingly complex patterns, it is always learning more about its creative ability. Driven by the infinite intelligence of its divine source (which we can tap into) the trinity realizes the mathematical possibilities within geometric forms. They exponentially increase their creative potential with sacred geometry reflecting and spinning their triangular form into a progressive series of increasingly complex patterns. With the platonic solids, they create the elements! The Creator-consciousness becomes aware that with each progressive pattern, more possibilities emerge! They realized that by spinning the octahedron, they could create a sphere. The first world emerges as a conscious being within a sphere!

This first sphere rests within its self, until it recognizes the next step of self-realization. By reflecting, it creates a mirror image opposite of itself and the Vesica Pisces is born. Within the Vesica Pisces, notice how the divine self (the equilateral triangle) still rests perfectly in the intersection of these two spheres. This intersection represents the Pisces or fish as well as the Cosmic Egg. The

Vesica Pisces is symbolic of the Divine Mother and the Divine Father merging to create the Eternal Child who always has the divine essence within! We are that eternal child who always has the divine within our heart space. These intersecting circles also represent polar opposites which are always a reverse of the original image. Standing in front of a mirror, you will see how you have just become two. You are witnessing the reverse and opposing image of your original self. You are now having a direct experience of the creative process of 'mirroring'! Look into your eyes and you will see the divine light shining through them!

The love created by the union of the Mother, Father and Child ignites a spark of divine light and the Infinite Spirit comes into being. A third sphere emerges and now we have the Sacred Trinity expanding in creation with the Divine Trinity at its core. The creative consciousness loves this game as the Infinite Spirit is now expressed and another sacred symbol emerges.

Each progressive sequence of spheres still contains the original octahedral energy. The next progression of Platonic solids is the icosahedron — multiple triangles emerging from the octahedron to create a sphere with 20 triangular faces and the element of water comes into being!

From these faces, five triangles split and move about until all their bases connect and form a pentagram in the center. Out of this pentagram, seven more emerge and the 12-faced pentagonal dodecahedron is born. This allows for the creation of an even more complex energy pattern and the fifth solid which may represent the force of gravity holding all the other elements together in one sphere like a world or universe or all of creation for that "matter"! Pun intended.

Now we can really start to see how the Platonic solids and the progressive spheres are truly the fundamental patterns of creation. When the fourth sphere is created, the four elements are activated! Each of the Platonic solids represent an element: Fire (Tetrahedron), Air (Octahedron), Water (Icosahedron) and Earth (cube). The earth and the atmosphere around it are now prepared for the emergence of life.

The bible says that on the fourth day, one half of creation was complete. The next half is the creation of life. Once the fifth sphere emerges to embrace life in its grasp, the star-tetrahedron is activated! The two opposing tetrahedrons, one divine and one human, merge! Instead of two triangles connected at their bases, like an octahedron (air), these opposing triangles intersect and realize a greater part of their consciousness by merging. They express the perfect complement of both male and female energy. The merging of this powerful "dual-consciousness" creates life which begins swimming in the water below and flying in the skies above.

On the exciting sixth day of creation, the seed of life is complete and four-legged creatures emerge on dry land! Upon seeing these life forms, the Creator said, "Go out and multiply!" and the consciousness within the spheres expands wildly.

And on the seventh day, shining in the seventh light, God paused to admire all the living things and beings that had been created. With divine love and light imprinted upon each and every being, they go onto to become their own creative pattern personalities accessing the Creator-consciousness within. This increasingly intelligent consciousness projects its original patterns of creation from the eternal universe into time and space as holographic reflections. These pattern-personalities create ever more imaginative beings and worlds in multidimensional realms using their creative abilities.

2.4

We are destined to take this amazing journey through time and space as an integral part of the Creator-consciousness. If we make a sincere effort to evolve toward the highest level of consciousness in each incarnation, our creative abilities will continue to be enhanced and each incarnation will become increasingly more magnificent and expansive! The ascension path promises to be extraordinarily rewarding and breathtakingly beautiful! Well worth the effort, don't you think!?

With that in mind, let's continue our exploration of the Platonic solids as crystallized patterns of consciousness. Let's consider the possibility that the solids as crystals are fundamental patterns of consciousness. If we think of consciousness as a field of vibrating light, color and sound, we can equate light with consciousness. Crystals may be 'frozen light' or crystallizations of consciousness. I have concluded that the five platonic solids plus the star tetrahedron and Metatron's cube (5+2=7) represent seven progressive levels of 'crystallized' consciousness. I believe the seven "chakras", or energy centers, literally "reflect" this consciousness and can be crystallized energy. These seven levels of consciousness are projected as colorful light rays which then become frozen or crystallized as "chakras". Each of these crystal forms and the colors they project have increasingly higher vibrational frequencies as they ascend through higher levels of consciousness.

Patterns of Consciousness	Expressions of Consciousness	Levels of Consciousness	Chakra Color	Vibrational Frequency
Cube	Earth	Survival	Red	400-484
Tetrahedron	Fire	Desire	Orange	484-508
Octahedron	Air	Power	Yellow	508-526
Dodecahedron	Ether (Upper Air)	Love	Green	526-606
Icosahedron	Water	Communion	Blue	606-668
Star-tetrahedron	Duality	Wisdom	Indigo	668-700
Metatron's cube	Divinity	Worship	Violet	700-789

*Some of the information above was obtained from the website *www.buzzle.com*.

The fundamental patterns of creation are projected outward in a 360-degree radius when the light shines from within the crystal solids. When I asked my husband what he thought about this speculation, he simply said, "Think of a disco ball. The light inside the ball causes the geometric patterns to be displayed on the surrounding walls in 360-degrees!" What an epiphany! That's it — a disco ball! The brilliant light of the consciousness within the crystal causes the projection of its geometric patterns. These patterns create the holographic images that define our view of the world like one giant discotheque! Our spirits are all dancing in their forms on the great big dance floor of life! It's ingenious!

2.5

From eternity, the pattern personalities are reflected on the edges of the universe and the illusion of reality is created. It's a spectacular 3D movie: "The Eternal Adventure" — featuring holograms of dancing shapes and swirling patterns all vibrating in a glorious spectrum of light and sound! Bravo!

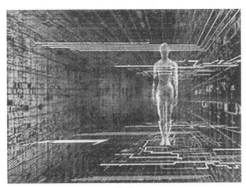

2.6

And it's all for a divine purpose: to create the ultimate experiences in multidimensional time and space realms. It's a never-ending and wildly imaginative journey of self-realization!

Now, let's try and visualize the force of consciousness emanating from the core of each crystal. Imagine the energy it must take to keep the forms spinning in such a wide spectrum of color and sound. My guess is that its love — the most powerful force in the universe and the passion that drives creation. Now let's consider that we are limited by our perception and may only be experiencing a fraction of the consciousness being emanated from the crystalline patterns. To elaborate upon this visualization, let's consider the following excerpt from the book, "Initiation":

"All energy, all the forces of the universe, are movements which emanate from one point — their own center — and radiate in circular waves in all directions, manifesting themselves as vibrations or oscillations...The fact that the creative force manifests itself on each level of innumerable possibilities means that there are countless different wave lengths, wave forms and frequencies. As long as we are in the body with its limited perceptive ability, we can perceive only a certain number of these wave forms because our organs of sense are limited...The shorter the waves in which a form of energy manifests itself, the less our consciousness records a sensation of matter. To the vibrations that are sent directly to our consciousness by our organs of sense we give names: matter, sound, electricity, heat, taste, smell, light. The still higher, immaterial energies and radiations perceptible only by means of our brain and nerve centers, we call thought waves, idea waves. Beyond them are still higher, more penetrating rays and frequencies, all the way up to the very highest all-pervading frequencies of the divine creative power: life itself! We can only perceive these frequencies as a state of consciousness." [2]

Whoa. We might want to re-read that a few times to grasp its full meaning! Then we can sit and contemplate these powerful revelations. From energy and matter to thoughts and ideas, it's all vibrating within a vast field of divine consciousness — the infinite intelligence of the Mother Womb within which all of creation is immersed! With this revelation, we can begin to appreciate the spectacular creativity behind the divine plan taking place within the watery womb.

O.K. so we've talked about points, lines, rectangles and cubes. Then, we discussed the divine triangle and all its progressive manifestations including crystal shapes and spheres. We concluded with Metatron's cube and the emergence of consciousness! Wow! Let's not forget that we figured out the whole reflectivity concept with the light of consciousness emanating from crystals. Without our disco ball revelation, we wouldn't be able to grasp all this nearly as well!

It's time to get up and stretch. Stand up and take a big inhalation while you sweep your arms up and then exhale as you release them down. Now flex your knees and sway right and left moving your arms in a sweeping motion as you do. Inhale and sway right, exhale and sway left. Repeat this a few times. Now reach for the sky and inhale up and then exhale as you fall forward and reach for your toes. Hold it there to stretch your back and hamstrings. Now roll up one vertebrae at a time and draw your hands to your chest in a prayer position. Drop your shoulders and follow your breath as it gently flows in and out. Close your eyes and imagine the powerful energy swirling all around you. It's the underlying vibration of pure consciousness. As we absorb the beauty of this truth, let's bow in appreciation for all that is.

Bathed in the warmth of the sun and inspired by its brilliant light, let's move away from the shore now and hike into the dunes that lie beyond. As we walk and admire the beauty that surrounds us, let's engage in a discussion about the power of numbers. We have already seen how the seven primary patterns translate into seven levels of consciousness. Remember in the book, "Initiation", the author showed us how the number seven is the key number for the third dimension? She explained the significance of the number seven as the sum of the trinity (the three divine aspects) + the four elements (the primary "faces" or expressions of consciousness): 3 + 4 = 7. From this analogy, the number twelve also emerges as the three divine aspects within each of the four faces of the pyramid: 3 X 4 = 12.

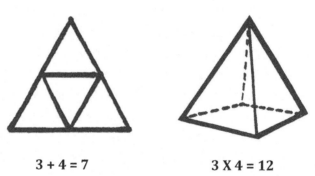

3 + 4 = 7   **3 X 4 = 12**

The numbers seven and twelve are both sacred and symbolic. The number seven expresses the divine nature of the third dimension. The number twelve symbolically defines its characteristics.

Let's focus on the sacred number seven for now and we'll end our exploration with the symbolic number twelve, how does that sound? O.K., so let's back up a little and start with one:

1 = Unity, the origin, the essence. Starting as a point and progressing into a line — the first dimension with a beginning, middle and end: 3 aspects in one.

2 = 1 + 1, Separation from unity, division, duality, opposition, the reflection. The second dimension as a rectangle with four lines and the space in between: 5 aspects in one.

3 = 1 + 2, The divine trinity, the triangle, body/mind/spirit. The third-dimension expressed as a cube with six faces and the space contained within: 7!

4 = 1 + 3, The foundation, the four directions, the four winds, the four elements, the four faces or expressions of the Creator.

5 = 2 + 3, Duality + Trinity, the characteristics of man: duality in spite of his trinity origin. Five fingers, five toes, five points (1 head+ 2 arms + 2 legs) The five platonic solids and the pentagram.

6 = 3 + 3, The trinity reflected, trinity manifested on Earth = The six days of creation.

7 = 3 + 4, The trinity (three aspects) + The foundation (four faces) The totality = six days of creation + one day of rest. 6 defines creation, 7 begins the evolution.

(8 symbolizes transcendence, or ascension, and 1-8 represents a complete 'octave')

*Some of the information above was taken from the website: *www.corax.com/tarot*

Seven has always been my lucky number. Even when I was a little kid, I insisted that seven was "my number." When I learned how to write and spell, I discovered that each of my names, first, middle and last all had seven letters: Suzanne Michele Rosenau. Now, some 40 years later, reflecting on my life, I started to think about seven in years or cycles. I thought about human life in seven-year stages and it occurred to me that the number seven has been significant all along! Check this out — we typically enter first grade at the age of 7, then we go through 7 years of school (grades 1-7). Most kids are around age 14 when they enter 7th grade. After 7th grade, a huge transition takes place as kids enter high-school and begin to 'grow-up'. Soon they get their get their driver's license and take on more responsibilities. The next significant age is then 21! Now they are officially an adult! I am sure there are significant changes at 28, 35, . . . but I haven't thought that far ahead yet. Maybe you can reflect upon your own life and see! My friend who is an esthetician told me that hormonal changes take place within the human body every seven years that significantly affect the nature of our skin cells! This made me think about the hormonal 'seven-year itch'! Of course, there are seven days in a week and this may be based on the seven days of creation. I wondered if we have different levels of consciousness on different days of the week. Then I thought, "Of course we do! The first day, Monday, is the beginning of work (creation), Tuesday — Friday we are involved in the process of working or creating and on the 6th day, the fun day — Saturday, we celebrate! Sunday is a day of rest and most of us rejoice by honoring creation — either going to church, spending time with family or enjoying the beauty of nature. Are you feeling a strong connection to the number seven yet?!

The seven crystal shapes and the seven spheres (seed of life) represent the origin and reflection of the seven levels of consciousness just like the seven colors of the rainbow! Let's dig deeper now and look more closely at the true significance of the number seven as it relates to the colors of consciousness, the corresponding energy centers and even the universes at large. This will be fun! Let's start with the seven levels of consciousness that are represented in the chakras. I think of chakras as energy centers where a certain type of consciousness is condensed or crystallized. Chakras are like crystal wheels that spin and vibrate at 7 points along the vertebrae. These points affect our central nervous system as they radiate spiritual energy in the corresponding color that matches their frequency. The lowest frequencies (red, yellow and orange) start at the base of the spine and represent survival, desire and power. As we ascend through the higher levels of consciousness — love, communion, wisdom and worship — the frequencies get higher as reflected in the colors green, blue, indigo and violet. The primary colors of these energy centers naturally correspond to the colors of a rainbow — the prism within a single ray of light. Chakras are spinning crystallizations of energy emitting and responding to the varying frequencies of emotion, color and sound. These frequencies can be measured in wavelengths and heard as sounds or tones. Some spiritual practices use certain tones, or musical notes, to harmonically balance chakras as each tone vibrates with a specific chakra due to their matching frequencies!

The Seven Chakras	Levels of Consciouness	Colors	Tones	Wavelengths (nm)
Root	Survival/Instinct	Red	C	620-750
Sacral	Desire/Creativity	Orange	D	590-620
Solar Plexus	Power/Fear	Yellow	E	570-590
Heart	Love/Harmony	Green	F	495-570
Throat	Expression/Freedom	Blue	G	450-495
Third Eye	Wisdom/Intuition	Indigo	A	425-450
Crown	Worship/Unity	Violet	B	380-450

(The 8th chakra is 'the soul chakra' and represents transcendence or infinity).

Chakras are primarily used in spiritual practices as a mechanism for balancing the energy centers that may be blocked. Since Balance = Harmony, harmonizing the frequencies of these centers clears blockages and 'balancing' is achieved. I found the most fascinating description of how this works in Book I of "The Law of One" series: *The RA Material*. Don Elkins is asking Group Ra about balancing energy centers and clearing blockages:

Don asks, "How does an individual go about balancing himself? What is the first step?" Ra replies, "I am Ra. The steps are only one; that is, an understanding of the energy centers which make up the mind/body/spirit complex." This understanding is summarized as follows:

"The first balancing is out of the Malkuth, or Earth, vibratory energy complex, called the red-ray complex. An understanding and acceptance of this energy is fundamental. The next energy complex, which may be blocked is the emotional, or personal complex, also known as the orange-ray complex... The third blockage resembles most closely that which you have called ego. It is the yellow-ray or solar plexus center. Blockages in this center will often manifest as distortions toward power manipulation... The center of the heart, or green-ray, is the center from which third-density beings may springboard, shall we say, to infinite intelligence...Blockages in this area may manifest as difficulties in expressing what you may call universal love or compassion. The blue-ray center of energy streaming is the center which, for the first time, is outgoing as well as inpouring...Those blocked in this area may have difficulty in grasping the spirit/mind complexes of its own entity and further difficulty in expressing such understandings itself...The next center is the pineal or indigo-ray center. Those blocked in this center may experience a lessening of the influx of intelligent energy...As you can see, this is but one of many distortions due to the several points of energy influx into the mind/body/spirit complex. The indigo-ray balancing is quite central to the type of work which revolves about the spirit complex, which has its influx then into the transformation or transmutation of third density to fourth density, it being the energy center receiving the least distorted outpourings of love/light from intelligent energy and also the potential for the key to the gateway of intelligent infinity. The remaining center of energy influx is simply the total expression of the entities vibratory complex of mind, body, and spirit. It is as it will be, balance or imbalance has no meaning at this energy level, for it gives and takes in its own balance. Whatever the distortion may be, it cannot be manipulated as can the others and, therefore, has no particular importance in viewing the balancing of energy." [3]

This is very powerful information. These books also support the concepts of reality as a reflection of vibrational "thought-forms" and refer to the patterns from which they are constructed as "distortions" of infinite energy. The message is that the illusion ("an illusory separation"), and the patterns ("distortions") are created for teaching the Law of One which emphasizes absolute love and total unity as the original thought of the Creator. For further clarification of these concepts as described personally by Carla Rueckert and Jim McCart, watch their interview at SciSpi.tv/Rise-Up/. Before channeling Group Ra, Carla Rueckert had contacted a divine being named "Hatton". In the introduction to Book I, Hatton explains:

"The original thought,...another term for our word "love",...implies a unity that is so great that we do not simply see each other as close friends , or brothers and sisters, but ideally, as the Creator; and we see each other and ourselves as the Creator, we see one being...all of the thought that exists is the thought of our Creator...All of His parts communicate with all of the creation, in His entire and infinite sense...This, my friends, is what Man of Earth must return to if he is to know reality: this simple thought of absolute love, a thought of total unity with all of his brothers regardless of how they might express themselves or whom they might be, for this is the original thought of the Creator...the creation of the Father has a very simple nature, a nature in which love is the essence of all things and of all their functions." [4]

What a profound and yet simply beautiful message! Now let's move onto the profound complexity of the "Universal Bible" — *The Urantia Book* — and check out how the number seven is expressed on a grand universal scale! According to *The Urantia Book*, there are 7 super universes rotating around the Central Universe of Havona. This makes up the Grand Universe. Guess what super universe we inhabit? The seventh one! Based on this revelation, we can think of universes expressing levels of consciousness as well. Of course, they do! They are simply projections of the Creator-consciousness after all! We can picture the Grand Universe as "One Being" expressing all seven levels of consciousness within its seven super universes! These seven super universes rotate around the center of this one being. This being at the core would represent the eighth level of consciousness — infinity or transcendence! This one being we could simply call: The One Infinite Creator.

Seven Super universes revolving around ONE Central Universe

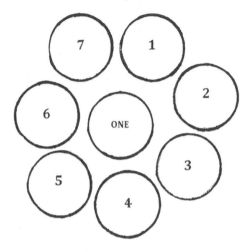

ONE Infinite Creator and Seven Levels of Ascending Consciousness

The celestial teachers in *The Urantia Book* explain that the seven levels of consciousness, within the seven super universes, are reflected by the nature of their unique purpose(s):

"There are seven major purposes which are being unfolded by the seven super universes. Each major purpose in super universe evolution will find its fullest expression in only one of the seven super universes, and therefore does each super universe have a special function and a unique nature… Orvonton, the seventh super universe, the one to which your local universe (Nebadon) belongs, is known chiefly because of its tremendous and lavish bestowal of merciful ministry to the mortals of the realms. It is renowned for the manner in which justice prevails as tempered by mercy and power rules as conditioned by patience, while the sacrifices of time are freely made to secure the stabilization of eternity. Orvonton is a universe demonstration of love and mercy." [5]

We should take a moment to consider the importance of this statement and ensure that our personal and societal reflection of these divine qualities prevails. Don't you agree? Let's make a commitment, individually and collectively, to uphold these universal values of love, mercy and patience that are unique to our super universe settled in the seventh light! *The Urantia Book* gives many examples of the significance of the number seven in the manifestation of all creation and also discusses universe reality as a projection of patterns. On page 10, in respect to pattern, it says, "Pattern can be projected as material, spiritual or mindal, or any combination of these energies. It can pervade personalities, identities, or nonliving matter…. Pattern is a master design from which copies are made…Pattern may configure energy, but it does not control it. Gravity is the sole control of energy-matter." [6]

To understand the seven levels of consciousness as patterns of energy, it's important to understand that this energy, according to the book, is transmitted by the Creative Trinity as Father, Son and Spirit through circuits. More clearly explained, "Any and all things responding to the personality circuit of the Father, we call personal. Any and all things responding to the spirit circuit of the Son, we call spirit. Any and all that respond to the mind circuit (of the Infinite Spirit), we call mind — mind in all its phases. Any and all that respond to the material-gravity circuit centering in nether Paradise, we call matter — energy-matter in all its metamorphic states." [7]

The energies from these circuits combine to form the patterns of our consciousness. The basis for the seven levels of consciousness expressed can be seen in "The Seven Master Spirits". This explanation of the seven ways in which the Creator as "Father", Child as "Son" and Infinite Spirit express themselves separately, and in various combinations, clearly shows the universal significance of the number:

"In the sevenfold creative act of self-duplication the Infinite Spirit exhausted the associative possibilities mathematically inherent in the factual existence of the three persons of deity. Had it been possible to produce a larger number of master spirits, they would have been created, but there are just seven associative possibilities, and only seven, inherent in three deities. And this explains why the universes operate in seven grander visions, and why the number seven is basically fundamental in its organization and administration. The Seven Master Spirits thus have their origin in, and derived their individual characteristics from, the following seven likenesses:

1. The Universal Father
2. The Eternal Son
3. The Infinite Spirit
4. The Father and the Son
5. The Father and the Spirit
6. The Son and the Spirit
7. The Father, Son and Spirit [8]

These teachers go on to tell us that there are seven "Reflective Spirits" stationed on the headquarters of each super universe to "...variously reflect the natures and characters of the seven possible combinations of the associations of the divine characteristics of the Universal Father, the Eternal Son, and the Infinite Spirit...one of each of the seven types is required to ensure the perfect reflection of all phases of every possible manifestation of the three Paradise Deities." [9]

Later in the book, the spirit guides talk about "seven evolving levels of 'mind-consciousness'" which are listed in order of evolutionary attainment. They are also described as "energy circuits transmitted by the Universe *Mother* Spirit." Finally the matriarchy emerges!

1. *The spirit of intuition:* Quick perception, the primitive physical and inherent reflex instincts, the directional and other self-preservative endowments of all mind creations;

2. *The spirit of understanding*: The impulse of co-coordination, the spontaneous and apparently automatic association of ideas. This is the gift of the coordination of acquired knowledge, the phenomena of quick reasoning, rapid judgment, and prompt decision.

3. *The spirit of courage*: the fidelity endowment-in personal beings, the basis of character acquirement and the intellectual root of moral stamina and spiritual bravery. When enlightened by facts and inspired by truth, this becomes the secret of the urge of evolutionary

ascension by the channels of intelligence and conscientious self-direction.

4. *The spirit of knowledge*: the curiosity-mother of adventure and discovery, the scientific spirit; the guide and faithful associate of the spirits of courage and counsel; the urge to direct the endowments of courage into useful and progressive paths of growth.

5. *The spirit of counsel*: the social urge, the endowment of species cooperation; the ability of will creatures to harmonize with their fellows; the gregarious instinct among the more lowly creatures.

6. *The spirit of worship*: the religious impulse, the first differential urge separating mind creatures into the two basic classes of mortal existence. The spirit of worship forever distinguishes the animal of its soulless creatures of mind endowment. Worship is the badge of spiritual-ascension candidacy.

7. *The spirit of wisdom*: the inherent tendency of all mortal creatures toward orderly and progressive evolutionary advancement. This is the highest of the adjutants, the spirit coordinator and articulator of the work of all the others. The spirit is the secret of that inborn urge of mind creatures which initiates and maintains the practical and effective program of the ascending scale of existence; that gift of living things which accounts for their inexplicable ability to survive and, in survival, to utilize the coordination of all their past experience and present opportunities for the acquisition of all...Wisdom is the acme of intellectual performance. Wisdom is the goal of a purely mental and moral existence.[10]

The guides in *The Urantia Book* also teach about "seven levels of 'personality-consciousness'" and these are considered endowments from the Universal Father.:

"The Universal Father bestows personality upon numerous orders of beings as they function on diverse levels of universe actuality...personality is diverse, original and exclusive; and the manifestation of personality is further conditioned and qualified by the nature and qualities of the associated energies of a material, mindal, and spiritual nature...personalities may be similar... but they are never identical."

They go on to clarify that; "Creature personality is distinguished by two self-manifesting and characteristic phenomena of mortal reactive behavior: self-consciousness and associated relative free will...The relative free will which characterizes the self-consciousness of human personality is involved in:

1. Moral decision, highest wisdom.
2. Spiritual choice, truth discernment.
3. Unselfish love, brotherhood service.
4. Purposeful cooperation, group loyalty.
5. Cosmic insight, the grasp of universe meanings.
6. Personality dedication, wholehearted devotion to doing the Father's will.
7. Worship, the sincere pursuit of divine values and the wholehearted love of the divine Value-Giver. [11]

Furthermore, the guides reveal that:

"The bestowal of the divine gift of personality upon such a mind-endowed mortal mechanism confers the dignity of cosmic citizenship and enables such a mortal creature forthwith to become reactive to the constitutive recognition of the three basic mind realities of the cosmos:

1. The mathematical or logical recognition of the uniformity of physical causation.
2. The reasoned recognition of the obligations of moral conduct.
3. The faith-grasp of the fellowship worship of Deity, associated with the loving service of humanity.

"The full functioning of such a personality endowment is the beginning realization of Deity kinship. Such a selfhood, indwelt by a pre-personal fragment of God, the Father, is in truth and in fact a spiritual son of God. Such a creature not only discloses capacity for the reception of the gift of the divine presence but also exhibits reactive response to the personality-gravity circuit of the Paradise Father of all personalities." [12]

These powerful realizations of our own divine nature should inspire us to express the highest virtues in all of our thoughts, words and actions. Out of pure gratitude and respect for the divine gifts that have been bestowed upon us, we can make a sincere effort to reflect these traits. In reflecting these divine traits, we develop a "kinship" with the Creator and become more receptive to direct, personal communion.

Now let's continue on our adventure and jump from the 'Universal Bible' to the Holy Bible. Let's explore the Book of Revelations where the number seven is highly symbolic and walk through the apocalyptic predictions and stories of human suffering and courage together. The intention here will be to try and apply a consciousness perspective to the biblical references. We'll see if we can make parallels with the seven levels of consciousness we have outlined above in the chakras and spirits with the seven revelations in each symbolic description.

In the Book of Revelations, there are several references to the number seven: seven seals, seven trumpets, seven bowls, seven heads of the beast, seven kings, seven golden lamp stands, the seven thunders, the mystery of the seven stars, just to name a few! The first one that struck me as being symbolic for Man was the seven heads of the beast (us being the beast, of course! Never mind that the "Universal Bible" just referred to us earlier as "lowly creatures." Pay no attention to these references. We know that we are both human and divine! We know that we are advanced beings on the ascension path).

As I researched the symbolism and various translations of the Holy Bible, I discovered that the revelations are marked primarily by judgments and apocalyptic events that occur over the duration of man's time on Earth. It seems to me that the judgments are related to the beliefs and actions of man and the apocalyptic events, including plagues, represent the associated punishment for disbelieving or bad behavior. From a more benevolent perspective, we could see the seven seals, trumpets and bowls as levels of consciousness and the divine guidance or intervention along the way as the reward for good behavior. This, for me, is a classical representation of the struggle between good and evil.

I immediately think of the need for balance between the two. Our lives, or series of incarnations, become one big balancing act: a search for 'balance', or harmony, as we move through the evolutionary stages of our consciousness. This is how I am seeing it. Maybe you see it differently and are prompted to journal or do some research of your own. That's exactly what I want you to do — search and discover your own personal truth! Realizing the truth of your 'self' becomes powerful when you begin to contemplate the possibilities!

The 'Law of One' series of books offers another enlightening perspective on consciousness. Let's take a moment to consider the earth we are standing on. These books talk about the earth itself representing seven different levels of consciousness. This made me think about chakras, or energy centers, within the earth. I thought about the seven chakra colors reflected in the levels of the earth. The center of the earth is red hot (survival) which transforms into bright orange lava (desire) which creates yellow gold (power). The inner core represents the lower chakras. The higher energy centers are expressed on the surface as green on the land (love) and blue as water (communion). Love and communion prevail on the surface! The skies above represent the highest chakras as the pale blue skies transform into a deep indigo blue extending high up into the stratosphere where the band of energy defining our atmosphere is pure violet! Wisdom and worship prevail at the highest levels!

We can imagine that the earth is also moving through the seven evolutionary stages of consciousness just like we are. In the Law of One Books, Group Ra refers to these evolutionary stages as "densities." It seems the lower stages are representative of thicker physical densities with lower frequencies and the higher stages with less physical density expressing higher frequencies. A "lightness" of being seems to emerge as we evolve through the "densities." Group Ra tells us that the earth is vibrating at the fourth density and we, as a society, are still vibrating in the third density. Ultimately, this will resolve itself, or harmonize, as third density beings who are ready to make the shift into the fourth and fifth densities remain here. Those who are not prepared for the shift may reincarnate on a third density planet where they can harmonize within a 3D illusion until they are ready to shift. Of course, this is only one possibility for how the "ascension", or shift, might go down. Others believe in the 100th monkey effect wherein enough of us elevate and shift our consciousness into a higher frequency that in one spectacular moment, the entire matrix of 3D consciousness will pop into a higher dimensional experience of reality as 4 or 5D beings. Only time will tell.

These prophecies concerning the transformation of our world actually parallel with the apocalyptic biblical revelations that predict major shifts in the earth's energies along with the shifting human experience which becomes either suffering or salvation. Since 3D is considered the realm of suffering, as in Buddhism, and salvation relates to being saved from that, the parallels in perspectives are clear. The Book of Revelations talks about one-fourth of the earth's inhabitants dying off and then, as judgment passes, the "chosen ones" get to stay. You hear this same prediction in the prophecies of the Jehovah Witnesses. The information provided by Group Ra parallels with these prophecies. As the earth transitions, those who are not ready to evolve to a higher level of consciousness will physically perish and reincarnate on a 3D sphere (suffering) and those who "evolve" will remain on earth (saved).

I prefer to hold the vision that everyone is saved and no one suffers and therefore am a fan of the 100th monkey effect. Regardless of the global prophecies, each and every one of us can intentionally progress on our ascension path right here and now and create our own higher dimensional experiences of reality in pockets across the planet. Let's focus on harmonizing, or balancing, the seven levels of our consciousness so we can progress through the evolutionary stages of development. Group Ra speaks of eight levels of consciousness and refers to them as "octaves of existence." These octaves repeat through higher and higher levels of evolutionary consciousness from physical incarnation in the lower realms to a spiritual experience in the higher realms. This gives us fascinating insight into the infinite realms of possibilities — octaves of consciousness within densities of existence in a constant state of evolution throughout eternity! This may represent the true nature of our evolutionary journey of self-realization. The destination of course is the ultimate realization as we reunite with our true self, our eternal soul, residing in Paradise at the center of all creation. I like the sound of that — Destination: Paradise!

We must keep in mind however, that the stages of evolutionary development we are moving through now, as physically incarnated beings, are reflective of our own personal choices and free will actions. Remember we must harmonize with the sphere we are inhabiting and, according to Group Ra, our planet has now moved into the fourth density. We can harmonize with it by respecting it and loving it. Realizing that the life force pulsing through our veins is the same one that causes trees to blossom and animals to thrive, reinforces our connection to Mother Earth. Our planet has levels of consciousness just like we do, and this recognition gives us a greater appreciation of her as a conscious being. Let's take a moment to reach out and gently touch the leaves on the trees. Let's crouch down and lovingly stroke the earth and express our deep gratitude for the sustenance and support that she so generously provides. Of course she wants all of her children who she loves so dearly to join her on her ascension journey.

Back to our adventure! Now that we've reached the sand dunes, let's stand in awe of the huge rolling hills of white sand. As we look across the vast expanse of the dunes, it feels surreal, almost as if we are on another planet all together — one that is made purely of sand — one that would simply be called "Dune".

2.7

The edge of the dunes are lined with trees which are providing some nice cool shade. Let's head in that direction and have some refreshments while we continue our discussion. As I promised, we will conclude today's journey with an adventurous exploration of the magical number 12. We will uncover the secrets and mysteries that lie within this highly symbolic number and see how and why it dominates our experience of reality. First, let's talk about the prevalence of the number 12 in our everyday lives: 12 hours on the clock for starters! 12 months in a year, 12 inches in a foot, 12 in a dozen, 12 astrological signs.

Let's deepen our search for answers by revisiting the explanation in the book "Initiation" concerning the pyramid with four triangular faces and three divine aspects within each triangle: 3 x 4 = 12. Here we are seeing the trinity expressed in each of the four sides of the pyramid which also face in the four cardinal directions: North, South, East and West. These directions are called "the four winds" and along with the four elements are referred to as "the four faces of God". The author explains this in further detail:

"The four sides of the pyramids symbolize the four faces of God, each of which taken alone and by itself manifests the three aspects of the first source, the pyramid reveals a living reality, the living law, that God manifests himself in the material world, and because he does so he is in-dwelling in everything that has been created. From every point in the universe God manifests himself four-fold. In each of the four directions of the earth and sky he radiates with a different effect...You will find this four-fold manifestation in everything that has been created, most noticeably in the four characteristics of the great currents of air, the winds." [13]

The book describes the differing effects of the four major winds depending on the direction from which they are flowing and compares them to the four faces of God.

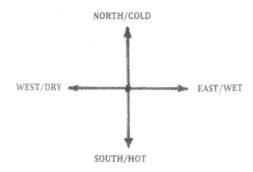

The author continues, "Whenever the divine creative principle leaves its timeless spaceless condition in the unmanifested state to come out into the three-dimensional world and become matter, it manifests itself -even while keeping its three aspects-in the number four...Thus the pyramid manifests four times three: the number 12." [14]

This concept of the four faces, each representing the trinity within, is critical in a greater understanding of the divine manifestation of the number 12. The book, "Initiation" refers to this as a "twelvefold manifestation which is present at every point of the universe and is acting in everything that exists...the earth receives the twelvefold radiation of the force of the four faces of God from the direction of various constellations of stars. Taken together, these constellations surround us like a wheel. We call this huge wheel the "zodiac". [15]

To understand the twelve signs of the zodiac, as the four faces of God each expressing itself in three aspects, it's important to understand the different characteristics of the four faces:

"The first face-the north face-is fiery and has a vitalizing effect. That's why the south wind brings heat and stimulates all living creatures to conceive new life."

"The second-the west face-is airy and cool. It makes everything movable, and that's why the east wind is refreshing."

"The third face of God-his eastern face-is damp, wet and lukewarm. It brings heaviness, inertia, warmth, dampness and precipitation, making all living creatures sleepy. Their consciousness withdraws into their bodies."

"And lastly, the fourth face-the south face of God-is cold. It has a contracting, astringent, crystallizing, materializing effect. It brings cold and calms the nerves." [16]

There is an incredible stone monument at the ancient Bayon Temple in Angkor Wat that shows four faces carved into what looks like a massive cube with a pyramidical cap. On each of the four sides of the cube is a face with each one facing in each of the four directions — north, east, south and west. Check it out!

2.8

It is fantastic and a spectacular representation of the "four faces of God." One day, I will go to Cambodia and see the ancient ruins at Angkor Wat. This site and many other ancient ruins around the globe are incredibly sacred. These temples and ancient artifacts offer the best clues to our ancestry and origin. Here we will find the answers to the mysteries of the universe if we just look closely enough and someday I will!

The most fascinating aspect of the book, "Initiation," is that it represents a period in Ancient Egypt when the Giza pyramid had underground chambers that were used as 'mystery schools' to teach students, or initiates, the secrets of the universe. In this book, the author is retelling events in very specific detail that she is recalling from her past life as a priestess. Her teacher, the High Priest Phahotep, is preparing her for 'Initiation' by teaching her how to harness the laws of the universe with the highest intentions. This special knowledge and divine connection will benefit both herself and her kingdom. The ancient philosophies of the Freemasons and Rosicrucians are based on the Pyramid Texts that divulged much of this knowledge. We will dive head first into the esoteric teachings offered within these Pyramid Texts in the third book of the "Up" trilogy, *Lighten Up! Activating Your Light-Body*, since these mystery school teachings are all about activating higher consciousness.

For now, let's continue with our exploration of the zodiac as is being taught to the priestess by Phahotep. What he is showing her is that the four faces of God, or four cardinal points, each contain three divine aspects and that essentially gives us 12 'radiations' in a 360 degree circle. The characteristics represented by each of the 12 points are essentially being radiated from them. Doesn't this sound similar to the "energy circuits" that *The Urantia Book* speaks about through which divine forces radiating from the Father (personality circuit), the Son (spirit circuit) and the Spirit (mind circuit) are projected onto the created beings?

Ptahhotep explains this concept to the high priestess:

"The three fiery aspects of the first face of God, or the first group, are revealed in the three constellations called Aries (Ram), Leo (Lion) and Sagittarius (Centaur). The Lion is the first manifestation of God and consequently the great father of the entire zodiac. That's why all three manifestations of the first face of God have a fatherly, life-giving character." [17] Here the face is in north facing south and the element represented is fire. "The three aspects of the second group, of the earthly-material face of God are: Taurus (Bull), Virgo (Virgin) and Capricornus (Goat). All manifestations of this face of God reveal a motherly character." [18] This face is in the east facing west and the element is earth. "The three aspects of the third group, the vaporous face of God, are: Gemini (Twins), Libra (Balance) and Aquarius (Water Bearer). The vaporous combination state arising through this radiation gives movement. That's why these three constellations are favorable for the manifestation which require free and unhindered movement. They are spiritual in nature." [19] This face is in the south facing north and the element is air. "The three aspects of the fourth group, the aqueous face of God are: Cancer (Crab), Scorpio (Scorpion-Eagle) and Pisces (Fishes). The three manifestations of this face of God have an emotional character which manifests itself in feelings." [20]

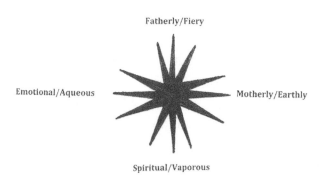

Of course, the 12 characteristics, or forces, radiating from each of these 12 points are very symbolic and explain a great deal about our own interior nature as well as the exterior nature of our environment. These forces combine to create the states of consciousness we experience through various stages of our life as well as through multiple incarnations. This can be seen in how we react to these forces on a daily, weekly, monthly, yearly and even epochal time. If we tap into the multidimensional aspects of ourselves existing all at once in different time-space realms, we can experience how we are all of these signs at once in the eternal now moment. Literally, we are being affected by all of these forces, or expressions of being, at different times and in different places on many levels. I encourage you to do more research on the zodiacal points and forces if this interests you. The most fascinating aspect of exploring these possibilities is discovering the effects these forces have on you personally based on what sign you were born under and in each of the months these signs are in play throughout the year.

You may see your own personal nature reflected within your 'sign' or you may find that your varying states of consciousness, or experience of life, reflect aspects of the constellations. I, myself, see many parallels within my own conscious experience of life even down to the direction I have been facing at different times. For instance, when I was in the northeast (facing southwesterly), I had a completely different experience of both my individual consciousness as well as the collective consciousness then when I was (or am) in the southwest facing northeasterly. My experience of the collective consciousness in the southwest is much more calm and positive, idealistic and spiritualistic than it was in the northeast which I experienced as more chaotic and intense, realistic and materialistic. I even discovered in the "Law of One" books that it was important to face northeast when attempting to connect with spiritual forces! When I read that, I said, "Aha, now I get it!" Of course, each of our experiences will be unique since it is the combination of forces that create the pattern of consciousness we respond to individually. However, I think we can clearly see, from this explanation of the zodiac, how the number 12 influences our experience of life!

We can look to another remarkable example of the power of this number by referring to the philosophical science behind "The Yugas". Joseph Selbie and David Steinmetz wrote an extraordinary book called "The Yugas" based on the teachings of Sri Yukteswar and Paramahansa Yogananda. I had the great privilege of interviewing Joseph Selbie. Watch the interview at SciSpi.tv/Rise-Up/. For now, however, I would like to highlight their teachings regarding "The Yugas". I will do my best to explain the basic concepts that underlie this philosophy as it concerns the cyclical nature of our universe (which is based on the number 12!).

Now that we have come to the end of our adventurous day and night is falling, let's go back to our campsite and get settled. Close your eyes and virtually create a scene where we are all sitting around a campfire and peering up at the stars. This visualization will be conducive to our exploration of the Yugas. Are you ready for a trip around the galaxy? Let's go!

Start by visualizing the Milky Way and look for the dark rift in the center (which we now know is a massive black hole!). Then let's imagine our planet as a member of the solar system which is traveling around the galaxy in a 26,000-year cycle. At certain times throughout this span of time we are, of course, closer to the center of the galaxy and, at other times, further away. According to the book, "The Yugas, Sri Yukteswar believed that the position of our solar system, with respect to its distance from the center of our galaxy, has a tremendous effect on the consciousness of our planet. There is a rather complex explanation as to why Sri Yukteswar claims a 24,000-year cycle of the 'yugas', or ages, as opposed to the 26,000-year cycle. This has to do with the inconsistent rate of the precession of the equinox which I will explain more about briefly.

According to this fascinating book, in this 24,000-year trip around the galaxy, we can imagine two 12,000-year-round trips. One trip's destination brings us closer to the center of the galaxy (which Sri Yukteswar refers to as the "grand center" or the 'source of Brahma'). The other trip's destination takes us farther away from this center or source. Sri Yukteswar refers to this elliptical path as the 'ascending arc' moving closer to the source and the "descending arc' moving away from it. He teaches us that our position on these arcs throughout the 24,000-year span dictates the consciousness that we are experiencing in different ages, or yugas. Essentially, he is teaching us that it is our proximity to 'Brahma', or the 'source, that determines the higher or lower frequency of our consciousness due to the spiritual forces emanating from its center. This affects our level of spiritual awareness and knowledge of sacred wisdom as we make this ascending and descending roundtrip.

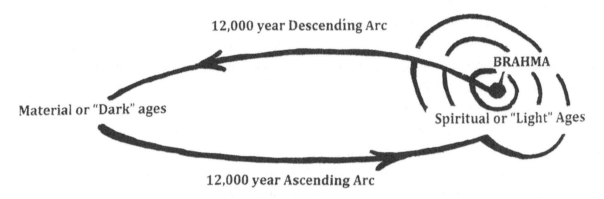

We have seen from the previous discussion that we are deeply affected by the position of our planet with respect to the Zodiacal constellations. This positioning determines the nature of the radiations we are receiving from the great cosmic wheel. These two philosophies — astrology and the philosophy described in "The Yugas" — have many parallels conceptually. However, instead of radiating a different type of consciousness within a 2160-year cycle (the time spent in each constellation), the 'yugas' represent an ascending and descending level of consciousness as the solar system passes through a 24,000-year cycle. The amount of time spent in these different levels is broken down into "four ages" throughout this 24,000-time period.

Once we have a greater understanding of these four ages, it will be very interesting to compare them with the effects of the constellations at any given time. In this way, we can look at our past, present and future as a human race on this planet in a whole new light! We should have a much more enlightened vision about both the type and level of consciousness we have been in, are in and are going toward. Of course, this will enlighten us about our own human experience, collectively and individually, since we know we are susceptible to the forces outside of us as an entire species but also to the unique forces from within our own inner wheel.

This depth of experience is what I was referring to in the introduction when I said that we would not just be looking at creation as a chronological series of events but from a much broader perspective that transcends the historical sequence. In this way, we are revealing the greater meaning of our existence within the context of our evolutionary experience! This will be much more adventurous and illuminating than just revisiting a historical account of the creation. It will help us to have a deeper 'realization' about it and this will translate into a greater understanding of our 'self' within it. In this way, we progress along our path toward 'self-realization'. Are you with me? Of course, you are! We're in this together after all!

On that inspiring note, let's keep progressing with our eye on the prize and dive back into the remarkable book, "The Yugas" to see what more we can learn about our true nature! In the book, the authors tell us that Sri Yukteswar offered his precious teachings with the same goal of 'self-realization' in mind! As such, he has presented us with the knowledge of the yugas due to his profound connection with this sacred wisdom. Although we have come to an understanding about the 26,000-year cycle around the sun, Sri Yukteswar has been made aware of the fact that although our planet aligns with the sun in exactly the same position at each spring and fall equinox annually, we always fall just short of the zodiacal revolution. This is due to a "slight backward movement of the equinoctial points round the zodiac and is a well-accepted astronomical phenomenon". [21] This goes back to the rate of the precession of the equinoxes I was referring to earlier which is inconsistent and this "may explain the discrepancy between the current estimate for the precession which is 26,000 years and Sri Yukteswar's phrase that it takes "about 24,000 years" to complete a cycle of the yugas". [22] As I mentioned earlier, the book explains that this 24,000-year cycle represents two 12,000-year cycles — one ascending (moving toward the center of the galaxy) and one descending (moving away from it). The number of years spent within each of the four ages that mark the 12,000-year arcs are listed in the book as follows:

Kali Yuga = 1,000 years
Dwapara Yuga = 2,000 years
Treta Yuga = 3,000 years
Satya Yuga = 4,000 years

It is further explained here that there is also a transition period before and after each cycle that is 1/10 of the duration of the yuga, i.e. The period of Kali Yuga would be 1200 years because 1/10 of its duration (1000 years) would be 100 years: 100 + 1000 + 100 = 1200.

We can calculate the length of the yugas along with their transition periods and come to a 12,000-year cycle:

1200 + 2400 + 3600 + 4800 = 12,000 years [23]

O.K., now that we know the duration of the yugas, let's look deeper into their meaning and more importantly, their effect on mankind's consciousness throughout the ascending and descending cycles! Finally, we will discover where we're at now!

For this explanation, I will be referring to the center of the galaxy (aka 'a black hole') as 'the source'. In "The Yugas," it explains 'Brahma' which emanates from this 'grand center' as "the creative force that brings the universe into being." From Sri Yukteswar's perspective, "our solar system and all of its inhabitants are profoundly affected by subtle vibrations or the "universal magnetism" emanating from the "grand center" (which may well be the center of our galaxy). It is this influence that elevates mankind as we come nearer to the source, and which causes mankind to decline as we go farther from the source." [24]

Let's examine the nature of the ages as described in the book:

Kali Yuga — "The Material Age," "the darkest of all"

Dwapara Yuga — "The Energy Age," "the whole of mankind can comprehend...the "fine matters and electricities" that comprise all matter.

Treta Yuga — "The Mental Age," "mankind can comprehend the "divine magnetism" that underlies all energy."

Satya Yuga — "The Spiritual Age," "mankind can "comprehend all, even the spirit beyond this visible world."[25]

So how do these four ages compare with what we know about the epochs of human history? To answer that question, the authors first look at the time periods that are associated with these ages. As we walk along the beach, please try and virtually experience the time periods by looking around at the environment and imagining it as you think it might have looked back then.

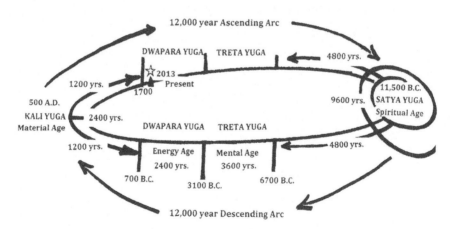

In the year 11,500 B.C., our solar system was at the apex of the Satya Yuga, or "Spiritual Age" and traveling away from the source along the descending arc. This 4,000-year age has a 4800-year total duration with its 400-year transitional periods. The authors teach us that this correlates with the time between 11,500 B.C. TO 6,700 B.C. This period, as they explain, represents two very different levels of consciousness amongst the inhabitants of the earth. This is so fascinating because they point out that we have the archaeological proof of mankind's existence during that time which shows that there were, at once, two ways of 'being'! One is a picture of a very primitive man hunting and gathering and the other is a vision of a very "enlightened people living lightly on the earth." Regardless of the varying conditions of man's existence during that time however, the authors point out that both types of man had a high level of spiritual awareness and were intimately connected with the universe.

This book teaches us that the next age on the descending arc is the 3600-year Treta yuga, "The Mental Age." The time periods corresponding to this age span from 6,700 B.C. to 3,100 B.C. and is marked by a "devolution" of mankind. The authors tell us that, while still highly spiritual, there seemed to be a veil between the recognition of God the Spirit and the ability to draw directly from this life force. Apparently, this is evidenced by the spiritual texts from that time.

The next 2,400-year period is marked by the descending Dwapara Yuga, "The Energy Age" which spans from 3,100 B.C. to 700 B.C. The authors teach that the Sumerian, Egyptian, Early Chinese and later Mayan civilizations marked this time and they tell us that they were all, in many ways, still far more advanced spiritually and even technologically than we are today. As one example, they point to the megalithic stone monuments that were erected during this period which defy gravity and remain a mystery.

Next, the book explains that we move into the 1200 year "Material Age" of Kali Yuga, (700 B.C. — 500 A.D.), the darkest age along the descending path, (which, remarkably, is literally referred to by modern historians as "the dark ages"!) Fortunately, this is the shortest age and the most highly advanced age is the longest! The authors teach us that, although enlightened Masters like Buddha, Krishna and Lao Tzu emerged during this time to try and reduce the impending suffering, these dark times were primarily marked by barbarianism and highly destructive tribes like the "Huns." They describe how large-scale destructions of people and their civilizations were occurring all over the globe and these crusaders seemed hell-bent on destroying libraries of knowledge that represented thousands of years of accumulated wisdom.

Then, literally, by the grace of God and at the height of the dark ages, a miracle is bestowed upon the planet and her people — the birth of Jesus! Switching briefly to "The Urantia Book," the wisdom teachers explain that in a universe that has over 10 million 'inhabitable' planets, ours was hand-picked by the Creator Son himself for a 'personal bestowal' mission. It is my strong belief that the Creator Son, Michael of Nebadon, who literally 'created' the specifications for our universe, and who oversees and directs all universe activity, physically manifested as the savior, Jesus Christ, in our time of desperate need and intense suffering. His miraculous 'virgin' birth is the trademark of Creator Son bestowals upon their planets, according to *The Urantia Book*. His lifelong mission to spiritualize mankind and pull him out of the darkness and into the light was a tremendous privilege which, unfortunately, was not fully appreciated at the time. His teachings did however inspire his disciples to bring them forth and as a result, we were blessed with the messages in the New Testament. Significant change takes time and even though we were given a great gift of inspiration, it was another 500 years until we swung around the curve of the great arc described in "The Yugas" so we could begin our ascension back to the source!

Keeping on track with the remarkable version of sequential events as described by the authors of "The Yugas," we are still in Kali Yuga as of 500 A.D., but now we are on the ascending arc. We don't enter back into Dwapara Yuga, "The Energy Age", until 1700 A.D. The authors point out that tremendous advancements in culture and knowledge took place over this 1200-year period but the spirituality of this age, in the U.S. anyway, was primarily marked by the power, control and authority of the church. Only amongst the 'secret societies' of the Freemasons and the Rosicrucians was the sacred knowledge of the prior ages preserved while more ancient belief systems still dominated in the Middle and Far East.

So now we know what age we are currently in "The Energy Age" of ascending Dwapara Yuga! According to "The Yugas" this is a time when "The common theme of scientific discovery in the twentieth century, and now in the twenty-first, is energy…it's as if the material cover of matter has been peeled back to reveal a pulsating, ceaselessly vibrating world of what Sri Yukteswar described as "fine matters and electricities." [26] The authors show how our ability to understand the true nature of matter has contributed to major technological advances as opposed to the purely mechanistic advances of the previous age. Of course, this continues at a stunning rate as we understand more and more about quantum physics, atoms and molecules. Spiritually, we have a long way to go back to harnessing the pure life force energy of the universe, but at least were ascending! It feels to me like we are becoming more open-minded as a society about religion and spirituality. The global nature of communication contributes to this development as we are exposed to diverse belief systems. A 'spiritual' culture has emerged in the U.S. which continues to flourish as people realize the tremendous benefits of meditation and embrace the need for universal love as opposed to the divisiveness of religion.

The merging of the yugas and the zodiac gives us a strong foundation for both the level and type of consciousness that our solar system is experiencing which translates to our own planet and ultimately to us! As individuals, of course, we still have free will and can make the conscious choice to evolve spiritually regardless of the outside forces and radiations of our environment! The authors of "The Yugas" expressed this oh so eloquently towards the end of their remarkable book:

"Our examination of the past has revealed many ways man has understood and expressed the knowledge and awareness of each yuga. We hope that, as you explored the ancient past and the potential future with us, you have come to appreciate that all forms of spiritual expression have their origin in man's own, inherently spiritual nature. From the first stirrings of intuitive awareness of energy to the liberating experience of self-realization, man is only rediscovering his essential nature. We do not need to wait for the slow unfolding of the yugas to find self-realization. In the personal future of each one of us, enlightenment awaits. It is ours to claim. Self-realization is within reach of anyone, in any age." [27]

Yes! We are in charge of our own conscious evolution during this physical incarnation! The gift of incarnation in the physical realm is a precious one and must not be wasted. The diversity and multitude of experiences offer tremendous opportunity for our soul's growth. From this perspective, we can view both suffering and joy as gifts that have been bestowed upon us for the mere purpose of our progressive evolution and ultimate ascension. It all comes down to the way in which we perceive reality, the choices we make and how we react to any given situation. If we apply the highest thoughts, words and actions (with pure intention) to our experiences, we can consciously ascend! This shows that we're using our experiences to move toward a higher consciousness! I once heard a spiritual master say: spiritual truth + physical experience = perfect wisdom! That's why the Buddhists say that this life as a human is so precious. It is a rare opportunity to seek spiritual truth while incarnated in a physical body with an intuitive mind! We are oh so blessed, my friends.

Now that the sun is beginning to set, we can see its bright orange glow on the horizon. Enlightened by the teachings of the day, let's head back to our base camp on the sandy beach below the dunes. As we hike back through the dunes, we can admire the glorious sunset. Vibrant colors of purple, indigo and fuchsia streak across the sky as the bright orange disc melts into the ocean.

2.9

The scene is breathtaking, and we are stunned by the effect of the sky reflected upon the ocean below. We are reminded of the illusory nature of this 3D reality and by seeing the mirror reflection of the sky upon the ocean, we can imagine our own physical beings as merely a reflection of our true selves in the stars above. We can't help thinking of the verse "As above, so below" and so we feel blessed by the presence of heaven on earth. We know that we are of a divine origin and that all that we see, think and feel is a projection of a much greater reality in the pure land of Havona. Beyond Havona, the perfection of Paradise and the unconditional love of the trinity illuminates the vastness of all creation and expands into eternity. Everything is always expanding. We are always evolving and yet, eternally present.

In the magic of the eternal present moment, we have a strong connection to the spiritual realm, to our own higher selves and to the source of our being. Standing in awe of the stunning glory of the sunset, breathing in the tremendous grace and beauty of this moment, we feel totally engaged in the present and deeply connected to the omnipresent spirit. We know we are incredibly blessed to be alive and well on this most beautiful planet right here and now. Sustained by the pure love of Mother Earth below and blessed by the unconditional love within the Mother Womb, we feel a deep sense of inner peace and divine harmony wash over our entire being. Suddenly we have a strong sense that all is one and we are one with it. We can see our reality as images dancing on the screen of the one infinite mind. We can feel our spirits floating within the essence of the omnipresent spirit. Here we are connected to all of the other spirit beings on earth, in the heavens, in the entire universe and beyond.

We feel the power of the light shining down upon us from the stars that have appeared in the skies above. We look for our own star and feel particularly drawn to one specific star shining brighter than all the others. We sense that our higher self is reaching out to us from this distant star and we know that whatever aspect of our being we are expressing here on our home away from home, its merely a projection of our whole self in eternity. As we evolve and progress along our path however, we are able to express more and more of our higher self in our home star. We are able to live from that place and draw from the light of the source, not just from the light of our home star but from its eternal source in Havona and ultimately, the Paradise Core — the omnipotent source of all that is and ever will be.

Let's prepare our camp around the fire and set up our sleeping bags in the soft sand. After a light dinner, we will lie under the stars and dream about the infinite possibilities in the spiritual realm.

Instead of doing a guided meditation at the end of today's journey, we're going to practice lucid dreaming as a means of going within to discover important truths. Bringing your 'super-conscious' awareness into your dream state can produce profound revelations! As you get tucked in for the night, I would like you to start by recalling the day's adventures. Think about those things that really stood out for you as particularly meaningful and important. Maybe something resonated deep within the recesses of your mind almost like a distant memory. It could be as simple as an "a-ha" moment or a sequence of truths that fell into place and suddenly made perfect sense to you. Whatever comes to mind for you, just lie with it and visualize the symbols or events that seem most inspiring. This recall is setting an intention for the content of your dreams.

I highly recommended summoning a spirit guide to accompany you during your astral travel. You can call on anyone in the spirit world who you have an intimate connection with. One last thing — before nodding off, tell yourself that you will remember your dreams in the morning. You can just say it out loud or in your head: "I will remember my dreams." It's that easy! To give you an example of how truth-revealing lucid dreams can be, please allow me to read you this bedtime story. It is intended to illuminate your spirit while your physical body rests. Then I will guide you into the lucid dreaming state.

Sleepwalking on Secret Beach

Last summer, I visited my husband's aunt in Kauai. We were going to beach spots all along the coastline. Then one day she pulled off at the top of a cliff and said that we were going to hike down to a very special beach. In a soft whisper, she told me it was called "Secret Beach." I was immediately intrigued and felt like I was privy to a hidden treasure reserved only for those with special knowledge of its existence. As we hiked down the hillside, I became aware of a certain stillness. Even the other beachgoers were silent. It was if we were observing the sacredness of this place by honoring it with our silence. I could see huge rays of sunshine streaming through the trees from the open beach below. Then suddenly it came into view and I became breathless. It was so expansive! The sand shimmered like white diamonds and I couldn't tell where the ocean ended, and the sky began. I felt like I was looking into infinity. I just stood there and let the sun warm my shoulders while I inhaled the spectacular beauty of it all. My body felt light and tingly as if I was shimmering just like the sparkling sand and crystalline water. I had the sensation of merging with the sights and sounds of nature that surrounded me. I knew this place would remain forever etched in my memory for all of eternity and that I could draw upon it anytime for divine inspiration. Secret Beach became a sacred rendezvous for my spirit guides and I to go during meditation or lucid dreaming. I travel here often in my dream state to receive special teachings and sacred wisdom from them. One night after focusing on the significance of sacred symbols, I fell into a lucid dream state where I had the following experience:

In my dream, Angel Gabriel guides my spirit to a special place on Secret Beach where we meet with Creator Son Michael. In response to my request, he shares secrets with me about the universe he created. We are aware that the Universal Mother-Father God is looking upon this gathering with approval. They want all of their children to have access to the sacred knowledge and universal abundance. Michael motions the angelic guide Gabriel and I to be seated on the beach. He sits down beside us forming a circle. He is holding a stick and starts to draw in the sand as he instructs me. He draws a 0 and says simply, "spirit". Then a 1: "unity" As he draws each number, he conveys its symbolic meaning:

0: "spirit" — single point

1: "unity"- one line

2: "division" — two lines

3: "trinity on earth" — three spheres

4: "divinity on earth" — triangle above

5: "spirit on earth" — sphere below

6: "spirit connecting earth to the heavens" — sphere on earth opening to the heavens

7: "man on earth" — image of man

8: "spirit above and below: sphere above and below (as above, so below)

9: "spirit connecting heaven to the earth" — sphere above reaching below

10 (1+0): "unity in spirit"

11 (1+1): unity of self and other

12 (1+2): unity within duality

I begin to understand deep within my soul the spirit values represented in the numerical sequence.

He then demonstrates with letters. Try and imagine the letter as a symbol and equate the meaning with the shape. You will be amazed at how the symbol itself defines the meaning!

A: "day one — the creative manifestation"

Divine Creative Triangle — A

B: "day two — the creative Father and the created Son"

Vesica Pisces (Father + Son) — B

C: "day three — the emergence of the holy spirit"

The Third Sphere — C

D: "day four — half of creation manifested on earth"

Half of Holy Spirit manifested on Earth — D

E: "day five — life reflects the trinity (3) manifested on earth"

Trinity (three 3 — reversed E) — E

F: "day six — four-legged creatures walk on earth"

F rotated as a four-legged creature — F

G: "day seven — God rests in the soul of man"

One sphere: half God, half-Man — G

H: "day eight — as above, so below"

One column of light, Heaven Above, Earth below — H

I: "day nine — unity in God and man"

One column of light — I

J: "day ten — "Man recognizes God above"

Spirit of Man ascending to Heaven — J

K: "day eleven — "Man seeks balance between heaven and earth"

K rotated to represent a balancing scale — K

L: "day twelve — "God blesses Man below"

Spirit of Heaven descends on Earth — L

We all remained seated as the profundity of this knowledge left us in a state of dreamy awe and wonder. After a few moments, he indicated for us to stand and hold hands in a unified embrace and bow our heads in sacred recognition to the all-loving one.

Then before we departed ways, he motioned for me to come close, so he could whisper one last secret in my ear. He said,

"The key to Man's self-realization is to reverse the trinity starting with himself: Man, Infinite Spirit, Eternal Child & Mother-Father God, the Creator.

First, reflect on the divine nature of man (spirit), then reveal the power of the Infinite Spirit (mind) and finally, realize the qualities of the Eternal Child (love). This is the gateway to reunification with the One Infinite Creator."

The next morning as I headed downstairs to make my coffee, the phrase that kept repeating over and over in my head was, "reverse the trinity, reverse the trinity". As I started to recall my dream,

I took out a piece of paper and wrote, "The gateway back to God is to reverse the trinity."

These teachings were so profound and beautiful, and I had never realized this remarkable symbolism in numbers and letters! I was so blessed to be receiving these incredible teachings and I knew I was meant to share them.

You too can prompt whatever dream experience you desire by setting an intention and calling on a spirit guide to assist you in your travels. I will guide you through a method of inducing "lucid dreaming" that has been very effective for me. You will be prompted to reflect upon today's adventure as you fall asleep and then in the morning, you can journal the truths that were revealed. Like I said, it may not happen the first time but if you keep making a sincere effort and have faith, eventually it will, and you will be blown away!

Good luck and sweet dreams.

Inter-dimensional Adventures
A Lucid Dreaming Experience
(Audio version available at: www.SuzanneRossTranscendence.com)

To induce a state of lucid dreaming, it is important to set an intention before going to sleep. This requires a quieting of your mind. Start by letting go of the thoughts of the day and being present. Become aware of yourself in your present space by saying "I am." Become aware of the spirit residing within. Repeat a mantra or prayer of your choice to connect with spirit. I like to say the words of the Lord's Prayer in the Aramaic version as follows:

O Cosmic Brother, all radiance and vibration,
Soften the ground of my being
And carve out a space within me in which you can reside
Fill me with your creativity that I may be
Empowered to bear the fruit of your mission
Let each of my actions bear fruit in accordance with my desire
Endow me with the wisdom to produce and share
What each being needs to grow and flourish
Untie the tangled threads of my destiny that binds me
As I release others from the entanglements of past mistakes
Do not let me be seduced by that which diverts me from my true purpose
But illuminate the opportunities of the present moment
For you are the ground and the fruition,
The birth, power and fulfillment
As all is gathered and made whole once again

By saying a prayer or repeating the mantra, you are connecting with spirit. You are connecting with your higher self and with the higher spiritual realm of divine beings who are ready to guide you through your lucid dreaming experience. I suggest that you call upon protective spirits such as Archangel Michael or Angel Gabriel to prevent any lower energies from penetrating your space. To protect yourself, imagine that you are surrounded by three rings of light. One light emanates from the pineal gland in the center of your skull and the light that radiates from this point produces a halo around your head. The second light emanates from the center of your heart. From your heart center, the light radiates out producing a protective bubble all around you that spreads far and wide. The third light emanates from your solar plexus and as this light leaves your belly button, it spirals around you from head to toe.

These lights create three rings which represent Mother-Father God, the Eternal Child and Infinite Spirit. Now that you are surrounded by the higher energy of spirit and protected from the lower energy of darkness, you are ready to set an intention. Decide what experiences you would like to have during your astral travels. Think about what truths you would like to reveal or places you would like to visit. Call upon a spirit guide to assist you in these travels. Before releasing your spirit, imagine a thin silver cord that will keep your spirit attached to your body as it ascends into the astral realms. Then imagine your spirit ascending through the ceiling of your bedroom and rising up above your house, then above the neighborhood, above your city, state and country and as you look back, you see all that you are leaving behind getting smaller and further in the distance.

As you ascend higher and higher, you now have a vision of the entire globe as the solar system comes into view. You admire the luminous sun and all of the planets revolving around it. Now you look in the direction of outer space and you see the Milky Way galaxy. In the center of this galaxy, you see a dark rift and you know that is your destination. You are aware that it is a sacred portal where divine consciousness is centered. Once there, you will connect with your spirit guide who will help you travel safely through this portal and onto the other side. You reach up and take the hand of your spirit guide as you both sail through the portal and are whisked away to the other side. You speed through a wormhole illuminated by a soft pink light and then suddenly you break through into a heavenly realm and see a very bright light in the distance. This is your ultimate destination. This is where you will connect with pure consciousness.

You and your spirit guide fly toward the light and within moments, you find yourself gradually floating, descending upon the most beautiful paradise you've ever seen. You see a huge waterfall plummeting down into a clear blue lake shimmering with diamonds. It is surrounded by fluorescent green foliage adorned by exotic flowers. Everywhere you look, the trees, the plants and flowers are enormous and bright. You realize there are animals who look strange and colorful. They exude a loving warmth and you are not afraid.

Then your spirit guide takes your hand and you walk toward a jeweled stairwell that leads to a golden platform. Upon this platform, many deities and angels are seated in a circle around a large luminous being who is seated upon a throne. This is where you will receive teachings. This is where you may ask questions and request to visit other realms. This is where the truth-seeking astral experience begins. Just let the celestial experience unfold according to your desires. You have set a pure intention, asked for guidance and surrendered to the divine will. You will have an extraordinary experience. Just before nodding off, you must repeat three times:

I will remember my dreams. I will remember my dreams. I will remember my dreams.

As soon as you awake in the morning, be prepared to immediately journal your dream experience before arising. Your dream journal will become a very important part of your spiritual journey. You will make significant progress on your path by using lucid dreaming as a method of enlightenment. Stick with it. Be consistent and it will be worth it, I promise!

Your Personal Revelations

_____

_____

_____

_____

_____

_____

_____

_____

_____

_____

_____

_____

_____

_____

REFERENCES

Illustrations:

Chapter cover image courtesy of: http://echinoblog.blogspot.com

1 - 3. : Personal photos

4. : Image courtesy of: http://www.Crystalinks.com

5. : Image courtesy of: http://www.YouTube.com

6. : Image courtesy of: http://www.wakingtimes.com

7. : Personal photo

8. : Image courtesy of: http://www.Pinterest.com

9. : Personal photo

Text:

Tricia McCannon, *Return of the Divine Sophia*, Bear & Company, 2015

1. p. 319

The Urantia Book Fellowship, *The Urantia Book,* Uversa Press, 2008

5. (15:14.1)

6. (Foreword: 6.10)

7. (Foreword: 6.1)

8. (16:0.1)

9. (17:3.1)

10. (36:5.6-12)

11. (16:8.7)

12. (16:8.8)

Elisabeth Haich, *Initiation*, Aurora Press, 1994

2. p. 211

13. p. 241

14. p. 243

15. p. 244

16. p. 242

17. p. 247

18. p. 248

19. p. 249

20. p. 250

Elkins, Rueckert, McCarty, *The RA Material* The Law of One: Book 1, Whitford Press, 1984

3. p. 144

4. p. 22

Joseph Selbie and David Steinmetz, *The Yugas*, Crystal Clarity Publishers, 2010

21. p. 7

22. p. 7

23. p. 5

24. p. 8

25. p. 5

26. p. 41

27. p. 319-20

Day Three

The Seventh Light

Good morning brave adventurer! It promises to be another fascinating day full of light, truth and beauty! Today, we are going to virtually travel around the Grand Universe until we narrow in on the seventh super universe. It is also known by the celestial guides in *The Urantia Book* as the "Seventh Light" and it is within this light that our local universe spins and swirls. We will see how all universe activity is connected by circuits of gravity and emanations of light within a web of "space-time." It will also become clear how gravitational attraction is the true expression of divine love as the curvature of "space-time" allows the Creator to literally embrace all of creation and keep it spinning around the core of its being. We will also see how gravity circuits are used as a way of projecting consciousness and how the atom is a mechanism for doing so. Finally, we will look deeper into the core of the atom to uncover the true source of its vibrational nature!

For today's adventure, we are going to travel deep into a remote region of Africa to visit the Dogon tribe of Mali. At the trailhead, we will be joined by author, Laird Scranton, who will teach us about the Dogon cosmology. This tribe claims to have received their wisdom from the star people of Sirius long ago. Their version of the creation story is based on an advanced knowledge of quantum physics similar to our own modern scientific theories. Their Dogon cosmology, however, is ancient and has been passed down through oral traditions. They claim it was taught to them by their cosmic family in the Sirius star system. You will be amazed by the parallels between our modern discoveries and their ancient knowledge!

Are you ready? Let's throw on our backpacks and set our sights on the country of Mali, in the West Continent of Africa! First, we will gather at the trailhead and plan our long trek through this desert region. Our destination will be the Dogon villages which are scattered amongst the sandy plains. As we near the villages, we will stop and set up camp along the Niger River near the city of Bandiagara. This is where we will meet our guides before entering the villages. We will need special permission and a translator before heading into this protected territory. Let's prepare to project our consciousness into the Mali region of Africa while intentionally connecting our hearts and minds with the Dogon people who revere this sacred land. Trail map and compass in hand, I will guide you through the sandy plains and rocky ridges pointing out all the beautiful sights and sounds along the way. Let's head out on the path toward the Dogon villages.

3.1

Greeting us at the trailhead is author Laird Scranton. He is a renowned authority on Dogon glyphs, symbology and cosmology. In his books, Sacred Symbols of the Dogon and The Science of the Dogon, he shares the wisdom of the tribal elder "Ogotemmeli." These teachings were originally given to a French Anthropologist named "Marcel Griaule" in October 1946. Griaule was granted the privilege of spending thirty-three days with the elder, Ogotemmeli, learning all about the religious traditions and oral history of the Dogon people. We are primarily interested in their version of the creation story. The Dogon cosmology is based on knowledge they claimed to have received from the sky gods. Griaule reports that these deities are believed to have come from the star Sirius "the star of the Sigui." To this day, they perform ceremony and ritual to honor these sky gods by dressing in costumes that resemble them.

3.2

I have chosen to visit this tribe and learn about their cosmology because of the remarkable parallels between the Dogon symbolism and the recent discoveries of modern physics and astronomy. As we hike toward the villages, let's take a closer look at the scientific theories posited by modern astronomy and cosmology. This will give is a better foundation for our comparison.

A Scientific Perspective on the Creation Story

To better understand these parallels, we will review the more recent explanations of the emergence of our universe based on scientific research and astronomical observation. I have invited Bill Bryson along for this part of our exploration. He wrote a book called, "A Short History of Nearly Everything" and his sharp wit and creative story-telling make the scientific explanations much more entertaining than a standard textbook. In his chapter entitled "How to Build a Universe," he describes the Big Bang Theory and the Inflationary Universe Model in a way that we can easily relate to and therefore, visualize in our mind. These two theories, as far as I can tell, vary in that the "Big Bang" proposes that all energy and matter needed to create a universe exploded into being in one flash while the inflationary theory says that only 98% of matter was created (the lighter elements) and the heavier ones emerged later from exploding supernovae, or "neutron" stars.

This variance brings me to an important observation I have made during my search for truth. I have found time and again that each reasonable theory holds some truth and that it is the combination of these theories that often paints the bigger picture. I don't know if there is an insatiable need to be 'right' that is inherent in humans, but an attitude prevails that says, "This is right and that is wrong" when in actuality, the whole truth is often revealed when all perspectives are taken into consideration. I believe that the intersection of ideas, discoveries and theories almost always reveals the greatest truths, especially when the concepts are complex. This goes for religion, science and every discipline seeking truth. That's why it's so important to keep an open mind and consider all possibilities and perspectives.

I was watching an episode of "Through the Wormhole" one day and picked up on a great story that exemplifies this point perfectly. Here is the gist: There were a group of physicists deeply embroiled in the study of string theory but were confounded by the fact that their version of this theory was actually five different theories rolled into one. Then there was one lonely physicist who held that there were 11 dimensions and that incorporating these into string theory would resolve their dilemma. Even though he had been ostracized to the point of ridicule, he maintained his theory. One day, the "string theorists" went out on a limb and applied the 11 dimensions to their model and "BAM!" the five theories coalesced into one. String theory became an astounding revelation about the true nature of reality once the group opened their mind to new possibilities. The reputation of the lonely physicist was redeemed and they all worked together to formulate a new model for what is now the most widely accepted theory explaining the vibrating energy behind everything!

The most glaring example of 'right and wrong' and 'this or that' is the division between religions and worse yet, between science and religion. The more research I do, the more I come to find that they are all saying the same thing just in different terms! It's astonishing and I just shake my head and say, "That's exactly what the last book was talking about only using different terminology." I love it when that happens because I know that now I am getting down to the truth of the matter. Even the biggest controversy of all time — Darwin's Evolution vs. Intelligent Design — is falling into place! It's becoming obvious that it is a process of intelligent design giving way to natural evolution (with some divine intervention along the way!) In my opinion, most often it is not "this or that." It is more likely "this and that!" An open mind allows all the information to flow in without being too discriminatory and then gradually sifting through it with discernment. I feel that this applies to the "Big Bang vs. Inflationary Universe" debate as well and that there is more of a continuous spiraling in and out of energy with periodic explosions, or bangs, when a collective group mind shifts into a higher dimension. This collective shift occurs spontaneously in what we could call a "singularity moment" (although this has other meanings as well) because it indicates a sudden transition through the singularity in the center of the group mind's galaxy which is always a supermassive black hole. This happens when a planetary consciousness has collectively evolved beyond the level of its current dimension and is ready to ascend its consciousness to a higher dimensional experience of reality. But we will get more into that as we continue to reveal the spiraling nature of a multidimensional reality designed for evolutionary beings and then you can decide for yourself! Meanwhile, let's look at what Bill Bryson has to say about these different models and see if we can piece them together to give us a bigger picture. Here's what he has to say about building a universe:

O.K. "You are ready to start the universe...get ready for a Big Bang. Naturally, you will wish to retire to a safe place to observe the spectacle. Unfortunately, there is nowhere to retire to because outside the singularity there is nowhere. When the universe begins to expand, it won't be spreading out to fill a larger emptiness. The only space that exists is the space it creates as it goes. It is natural but wrong to visualize the singularity as a kind of pregnant dot hanging in a dark, boundless void. But there is no darkness. The singularity has no "around" around it. There is no space for it to occupy, no place for it to be. We can't even ask how long it is been there — whether it just lately popped into being, like a good idea, or whether it has been there forever, quietly awaiting the right moment. Time doesn't exist. There is no past for it to emerge from. And so, from nothing, our universe begins. In a single blinding pulse, a moment of glory much too swift and expansive for any form of words, the singularity assumes heavenly dimensions, space beyond conception. In the first lively second (a second that many cosmologists will devote careers to shaving into ever-finer wafers) is produced by gravity and the other forces that govern physics. In less than a minute the universe is a million billion miles across and growing fast. There is a lot of heat now, 10,000,000,000° of it, enough to begin the nuclear reactions that create the lighter elements- principally hydrogen and helium, with it — (about one atom in 100 million) of lithium. In three minutes, 98% of all the matter there is or ever will be has been produced. We have a universe. It is a place of the most wondrous and gratifying possibilities, and beautiful, too. And it was all done in about the time it takes to make a sandwich." [21]

Don't you love his writing style? No big, fancy technical language — just a "matter-of-fact" common sense approach (with a dose of humor) that we can wrap our heads around! Moving forward from the Big Bang event, let's explore how we got here from there. Bill tells us that a "junior particle physicist . . . named Alan Guth" became inspired to focus on the birth of the universe after hearing a lecture on the Big Bang. What he came up with, after many years of research and intuitive insight, was "the inflation theory." Let's hear how Bill explains Guth's theory in his witty, yet eloquent, fashion:

"A fraction of a moment after the dawn of creation, the universe underwent a sudden dramatic expansion. It inflated-in effect it ran away with itself, doubling in size every 10 to the 34th seconds. The whole episode may have lasted no more than 10 to the 30th seconds — that's 1 million million million million millionths of a second — but it changes the universe from something you can hold in your hand to something at least 10,000,000,000,000,000,000,000,000 times bigger. Inflation theory explains the ripples and eddies that make our universe possible. Without it, there would be no clumps of matter and thus no stars, just drifting gas and everlasting darkness. According to Guth's theory, in one ten-millionth of a trillionth of a trillionth of a trillionth of a second, gravity emerged. After another ludicrously brief interval, it was joined by electromagnetism and the strong and weak nuclear forces-the stuff of physics. These were joined an instant later by swarms of elementary particles-the stuff of stuff. From nothing at all, suddenly there were swarms of photons, protons, electrons, neutrons, and much else-between 10 to the 79th and 10 to the 89th of each...Such quantities are of course ungraspable. It is enough to know that in a single cracking instant we were endowed with a universe that was vast-at least 100 billion light years across, according to the theory, but possibly any size up to infinite-and perfectly arrayed for the creation of stars, galaxies, and other complex systems." [22]

It turns out that the term "Big Bang" was coined by the famous cosmologist, Fred Hoyle, as a sarcastic way of ridiculing the theory. He proposed a steady-state inflationary universe where the heavy elements critical to our survival were born out of supernovae explosions. Remember earlier we were posing the problem with the Big Bang theory that only 98% of matter (the light gases-helium, hydrogen and lithium) was created leaving out the heavy elements (carbon, nitrogen and oxygen)? To create these elements, you needed the intense heat and energy of the Big Bang but since there was only one, Hoyle theorized that they were produced by exploding supernovae. Bill explains this further:

"Hoyle favored a steady-state theory in which the universe was constantly expanding and continually creating new matter as it went. Hoyle also realized that if stars imploded they would liberate huge amounts of heat-one hundred million degrees or more, enough to begin to generate the heavier elements in a process known as nucleosynthesis...Hoyle showed how the heavier elements were formed in supernova explosions...According to Hoyle's theory, an exploding star would generate enough heat to create all the new elements and spray them into the cosmos where they would form gaseous clouds-the interstellar medium as it is known-that could eventually coalesce into new solar systems. With the new theories it became possible at last to construct possible scenarios for how we got here." [23]

From this, we can see that both theories can be true at the same time! We can hardly have a complete discussion about the Big Bang without including insight from Stephen Hawking. Before researching, I thought he actually coined the term! In fact, I have a book by him, "A Brief History of Time — From the Big Bang to Black Holes", which is fascinating. I like his insight on what happened right after the primal explosion because it describes more specifically how our universe went from a purely gaseous state to the formation of matter. In a chapter entitled, "The Origin and Fate of the Universe", he asks the question, "Does the universe in fact have a beginning and an end?" He starts out with an amusing story I think you will enjoy:

". . . my interest in questions about the origin and fate of the universe was reawakened when I attended a conference on cosmology organized by the Jesuits in the Vatican. The Catholic Church had made a mistake with Galileo when it tried to lay down the law on a question of science, declaring that the sun went around the earth. Now, centuries later, it had decided to invite a number of experts to advise it on cosmology. At the end of the conference the participants were granted an audience with the Pope. He told us that it was all right to study the evolution of the universe after the Big Bang, but we should not inquire into the Big Bang itself because that was the moment of Creation and therefore the work of God. I was glad that he did not know the subject of the talk I had just given at the conference — the possibility that space-time was finite but had no boundary, which means that it had no beginning, no moment of Creation. I had no desire to share the fate of Galileo, with whom I feel a strong sense of identity, partly because of the coincidence of having been born exactly 300 years after his death!" [24]

Isn't it incredible that only a few hundred years ago, seekers of the truth were condemned for their 'heretic' ideas? This was especially true if these notions fell outside of what the church wanted everyone to believe or if they threatened the egocentric idea that we must be at the center of the universe! I love Stephen Hawking's humor but am dismayed that there is still resistance from the Vatican regarding scientific explanations about 'God's Creation' and look forward to the day when science and religion truly coalesce. I feel strongly that just because there is a scientific explanation doesn't mean it can't still be "the work of God." Of course, it is! In my mind, it's just an explanation of how it was done! Intelligent design, Darwin's theory of evolution and physics all have a place in a universe where all thoughts are unified within one collective field of consciousness. Keeping an open mind allows the seeker to explore all possibilities to see how and where different ideas might converge to reveal a greater truth.

Stephen Hawking's explanation gets very technical and surpasses my ability to fully comprehend, so I will share just bits and pieces from his lengthy explanation of the "Hot Big Bang Model" in order to convey the gist of it. I will also make some comparisons with the biblical account in Genesis because the parallels are fascinating!

"At the Big Bang itself, the universe is thought to have zero size, and so to have been infinitely hot. But as the universe expanded, the temperature of the radiation decreased...At this time the universe would have contained mostly photons, electrons, and neutrinos...and their antiparticles, together with some protons and neutrons..." [25]

Take a note of the "zero size" of the pre-Big Bang nothingness and consider the biblical verse:
"The earth was without form and void, and darkness was upon the face of the deep. And the Spirit of God was hovering over the face of the waters." ~ Genesis 1:2

The "spirit of God was hovering" as he contemplated moving out of the dimensionless realm of infinity and into time and space and then "Bang", suddenly there were photons (light), electrons (energy) and neutrinos (possibly dark matter) and their antiparticles.

"Then God said, "Let there be light"; and there was light. And God saw the light, that it was good; and God divided the light from the darkness." Genesis 1:3-4

This division of the "light from the darkness" sure sounds like the separation of matter from antimatter (antiparticles) and possibly photons and electrons from neutrinos

I must stop here at the word: "antiparticles." This is important because it is only because matter overcame antimatter, that we exist at all! Also, the neutrinos may have been "sourced" out of the dark matter that we know pervades the universe!

I have a theory that dark matter is simply a form of antimatter that pre-exists the formation of matter. It's like a blank screen vibrating with the pure potential of dark energy. It's only when a Creator Son and Creative Daughter project their co-creative powers of intention into the pure energy that a new possibility for creation emerges. On the blank canvas of dark matter, they activate the potential of dark energy and spin a new universe into being. The story of creation begins to play as they project it onto the blank screen. The movie begins with two spiraling arms of creative energy, one male and one female, forming and swirling in opposite directions to create a galactic center. In Act II, dark energy begins spiraling toward a white hole, or singularity, in the center. On the other side of the singularity, the pure potential of the dark energy is actualized as it enters a cooler environment. Here, the male and female energies combine to transform darkness into light. In Act III, the co-creative pair project colorful images of swirling gases onto the screen of their new universe. The neutrinos and anti-neutrinos form both electrons and anti-electrons that annihilate each other to create photons of light.

This is the action of the Infinite Spirit working through the creative pair to illuminate the new creation! As electrons begin to outnumber the anti-electrons, matter begins to form and the new universe takes shape! A new creation spirals into being on the "other side" of the dark world which has sourced it with its dark energy potential. Or...is this universe merely an illusion being projected onto a movie screen from the dark world? Using the processes of reflectivity and projection that we revealed in yesterday's exploration, the forms on the screen would simply be mirror reflections illuminated by the light of the "projector." The images, as information, go into the dark lens, or black hole, and come out on the other side, the white singularity. On this side, the images are illuminated by the light being projected onto the screen.

The intelligent codes written into the dark matter and exist only as dark energy potential. Once they become illuminated on this side of the "light" world, the codes are activated and the elements form on the screen. If we could see it in action, we would see intelligent codes inside crystallized stars projecting forms onto the screen of our world. Remember, the world only exists because we perceive it, so this movie is actually playing across the screen of our minds.

With that in mind, let's see what Stephen Hawking says happens next:

Stephen tells us that, at its starting point, the universe contained photons (light) and electrons (energy) and neutrinos (possibly sourced from dark matter as pure energy potential). He goes on to explain what happened next:

"As the universe continued to expand and the temperature dropped, the rate at which electron/antielectron pairs were being produced in collisions would have fallen below the rate at which they were being destroyed by annihilation. So, most of the electrons and antielectrons would have annihilated with each other to produce more photons, leaving only a few electrons left over. The neutrinos and antineutrinos, however, would not have annihilated each other, because these particles interact with themselves and with other particles only very weakly. So, they should still be around today. If we could observe them, it would provide a good test of this picture of a very hot early stage of the universe. Unfortunately, their energies nowadays would be too low for us to observe them directly. However, if neutrinos are not massless, but have a small mass of their own, as suggested by an unconfirmed Russian experiment performed in 1981, we might be able to detect them indirectly: they could be a form of 'dark matter', like that mentioned earlier, with sufficient gravitational attraction to stop the expansion of the universe and cause it to collapse again." [26]

Now, here comes the climax:

"About one hundred seconds after the Big Bang, the temperature would have fallen to one thousand million degrees, the temperature inside the hottest stars. At this temperature protons and neutrons would no longer have sufficient energy to escape the attraction of the strong nuclear force, and would have started to combine together to produce the nuclei of atoms...Within only a few hours of the Big Bang, the production of helium and other elements would have stopped. And after that, for the next million years or so, the universe would have just continued expanding, without anything much happening. Eventually, once the temperature had dropped to a few thousand degrees, and electrons and nuclei no longer had enough energy to overcome the electromagnetic attraction between them, they would have started combining to form atoms." [27]

The first atoms are born! This is truly a monumental point in the evolution of creation! I can't help but wonder how this unfolding of events, as described by Stephen, synchronizes with our earlier interpretations of the Platonic solids and patterns of life. Keeping in mind that I am only conducting a thought experiment here and this is purely conjecture, I invite you to play along with me and maybe you can conjure up your own ideas or already have the parallels formulated in your mind:

So, what we have first is the presence of light gases (helium, hydrogen and lithium) followed by the emergence of the heavy elements (carbon, nitrogen, oxygen) It all begins with the light ignited by the Infinite Spirit and all manifestations of matter are vibrational expressions of this spiritual energy — light translated into form or "trans-formed", everything is light transformed! Light vibrates at the highest frequency and is always contained within the lower vibrational form that condenses around it. Just like we showed in the last chapter where the divine spark is always contained within the patterns of creation. In the first moments after the new universe spirals into being, the forces of gravity, electromagnetism and the weak and strong nuclear forces come into play. These are the forces that intelligence energy uses to create holographic time-space universes. The creator beings project these thought-forms with the power of intention on gravity-circuits from eternity. Hydrogen atoms must come first because it is the fusion of these, due to intense gravitational forces, that forms helium. This nuclear fusion creates intense heat and light and FIRE, the first element, the tetrahedron, is formed! The first platonic solid is created by the divine trinity in action which reflects upon itself to create the second solid, the octahedron.

 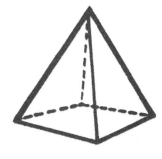 

The heavier elements are born within the stars as they age and fuse helium within their core — AIR (oxygen), the second element, is born! This element is equated with the octahedron. Now that we have hydrogen and oxygen — WATER, the third element, is made possible and it is equated with the icosahedron.

Then, finally the heaviest and most stable element is created within the core of the star — Iron — and the elements for EARTH emerge, the fourth element equated with the cube! Four of the Platonic solids are expressed. The fifth, the dodecahedron is the most complex solid and may represent the force of gravity that holds the other patterns within a biosphere by forming a stratosphere around it.

The patterns of life, or 'patterning', takes off within that sphere at that point and the periodic table extends beyond the basic elements and the complexity of elements increases. The number of protons within the nucleus and the configurations of electrons around it determines the atomic and molecular structure, or coding, of the complex forms which evolve. It all started with the male and female spiraling arms swirling around each other to create a new child. The laws of physics were created in the interlocking spheres of the Vesica Pisces and then the trinity forms. Replication through reflection introduces more interlocking spheres and the mathematical complexities and creative possibilities increase with each petal as the flower of life emerges and expands!

Interjecting these creative visualizations into the scientific explanation is the key to developing our own Creator-consciousness.

Let's pick up where we left off with Stephen Hawking's description when only hydrogen and helium atoms were born out of the light. At this point, we just have the intense heat of the first element — fire.

"The universe as a whole would have continued expanding and cooling, but in regions that were slightly denser than average, the expansion would have been slowed down by the extra gravitational attraction. This would eventually stop expansion in some regions and cause them to start to collapse. As they were collapsing, the gravitational pull of matter outside these regions might start them rotating slightly. As the collapsing region got smaller, it would spin faster — just as skaters spinning on ice spin faster as they draw in their arms. Eventually, when the region got small enough, it would be spinning fast enough to balance the attraction of gravity, and in this way disc-like rotating galaxies were born. Other regions, which did not happen to pick up a rotation, to become oval-shaped objects called elliptical galaxies. In these, the region would stop collapsing because individual parts of the galaxy would be orbiting stably round its center, but the galaxy would have no overall rotation." [28]

I must interject as the image of the 'rotating octahedron' that we learned about on Day One comes to mind. Air, or oxygen, is the element that the octahedron represents and as you will see, the spinning motion Stephen talks about leads to the creation of oxygen! Check it out:

"As time went on, the hydrogen and helium gas in the galaxies would break up into smaller clouds that would collapse under their own gravity. As these contracted, and the atoms within them collided with one another, the temperature of the gas would increase, until eventually it became hot enough to start nuclear fusion reactions. These would convert hydrogen into more helium, and the heat given off would raise the pressure, and so stop the clouds from contracting any further. They would remain stable in this state for a long time as stars like our sun, burning hydrogen into helium and radiating the resulting energy as heat and light. More massive stars would need to be hotter to balance their stronger gravitational attraction, making the nuclear fusion reactions proceed so much more rapidly that they would use up their hydrogen in as little as a hundred million years. They would then contract slightly, and as they heated up further, would start to convert helium into heavier elements like carbon or oxygen." [29]

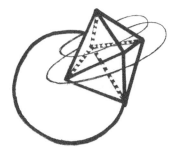

Ta-da! Oxygen emerges from the spinning octahedron! And like I said before, now that we have hydrogen and oxygen, water is made possible! Metaphysics meets Quantum Physics! YES!

This is where the evolution of the star souls projecting this patterning gets even more interesting:

At this point, the star experiences an energy crisis and begins to collapse. This is when a supernova, or possibly even a black hole, is created as the star collapses inward creating an extremely dense core. When this explodes, look out! This explosion is almost as powerful as the Big Bang itself and if it has the potential to create black holes, it may even be the precursor to one! Imagine an exploding star creating a black hole — a portal to a whole new parallel universe! This is one creative star soul who is ready to expand and create a whole new parallel universe. Here is how Stephen explains it:

"What happens next is not completely clear, but it seems that the central regions of the star would collapse to a very dense state, such as a neutron star or black hole. The outer regions of the star may sometimes get blown off in a tremendous explosion called supernova, which would outshine all the other stars in its galaxy. Some of the heavier elements produced near the end of the star's life would be flung back into the gas in the galaxy, and would provide some of the raw material for the next generations of stars. Our own sun contains about 2% of these heavier elements because it is a second or third-generation star, formed some five thousand million years ago out of a cloud of rotating gas containing the debris of earlier supernovas. Most of the gas in that cloud that went into forming the sun got blown away, but a small amount of the heavier elements collected together to form the bodies that now orbit the sun as planets like the earth." [30]

So, this one creative soul star explodes into space and has the potential to create a black hole into a whole new parallel universe AND throws off debris that can ultimately form new stars and planets to swirl around them. Of course, we are made from stardust too and like the stars and suns and planets, we are all infused with the spirit of the star soul who created us! All matter is infused with the Infinite Spirit and patterned after the Divine Source from which it came. On that note, let's move into the emergence of solar systems within galaxies within parallel universes — complex concepts within which we are finding the divine simplicity.

This is very exciting because now we are getting very close to home! Before we explore how our own solar system came into being, let's examine our local universe (within the larger super universe) a bit more closely so we can envision the surrounding realm of space in which our Sun was born. There are very specific values of elements and forces that make the existence of our universe possible. Bill Bryson points out that:

"If the universe had formed just a tiny bit differently — if gravity were fractionally stronger or weaker, if the expansion had preceded just a little more slowly or swiftly — then there might never have been stable elements to make you and me and the ground we stand on. Had gravity been a trifle stronger, the universe itself might have collapsed like a badly erected tent, without precisely the right values to give the right dimensions and density and component parts. Had it been weaker, however, nothing would've coalesced. The universe would have remained forever a dull, scattered void... This is one reason that some experts believe there may have been many other Big Bangs, perhaps trillions and trillions of them, spread through the mighty span of eternity, and that the reason we exist in this particular one is that this is the one we could exist in." [31]

It's as if this universe was custom-made according to very specific standards by creative beings endowed with the artistic liberty to create at will. Their universe would be special and, while fashioned after the super universe within which it resides, it would retain a uniqueness that reflects their own brand of creativity. It's just like how each of us resemble each other but are still unique in our own special way.

We discovered that the number seven is of significance to our three-dimensional world and, according to *The Urantia Book*, to our superuniverse as a whole since it is, in fact, the seventh one. So, it was no surprise to me when Bill Bryson pointed out a finding that the astronomer, Martin Rees, discovered:

"For the universe to exist as it does, requires that hydrogen be converted to helium in a precise but comparatively stately manner- specifically, in a way that converts <u>seven</u> one-thousandths of its mass to energy. Lower that value very slightly from 0.007% to 0.006%, say, and no transformation could take place: the universe would consist of hydrogen and nothing else. Raise the value very slightly — to 0.008% — and bonding would be so wildly prolific that the hydrogen would have long since have been exhausted. In either case, with the slightest tweaking of the numbers the universe as we know and need it would not be here." [32]

Bill tell us that "Martin Rees, Britain's astronomer royal, believes that there are many universes, possibly an infinite number, each with different attributes, in different combinations, and that we simply live in one that combines things in the way that allows us to exist. He makes an analogy with a very large clothing store: "if there is a large stock of clothing, you're not surprised to find a suit that fits. If there are many universes, each governed by a different set of numbers, there will be one where there is a particular set of numbers suitable for life. We are in that one." [33]

I would like to add, from a personal perspective, that our universe is suitable for life *as we know it* — a universe made specifically of the elements our Creator Son and Creative Daughter chose to use in the design of their unique universe, like paints for their artist's palette — and they chose the number 7. Why? Because our local universe spins and swirls in the seventh super universe of creation. There are only seven super universes rotating around the Central Universe and we are in the 7th one.

So, if we imagine that our universe is unique and distinguishable from the others, how is it contained within itself? Should we imagine our universe enclosed within a bubble to distinguish it and protect it from others that aren't suited for our particular brand of existence? Fortunately, Bill Bryson takes us to the edge of our universe, so we can peer into the possibilities. Here he explores the space-time curvature:

"Now the question that has occurred to all of us at some point is: What would happen if you traveled out to the edge of the universe and, as it were, put your head through the curtains? Where would your head be if it were no longer in the universe? What would you find beyond? The answer, disappointingly, is that you can never get to the edge of the universe. That's not because it would take too long to get there — though of course it would — but because even if you traveled outward and outward in a straight line, indefinitely but pugnaciously, you would never arrive at an outer boundary. Instead, you would come back to where you began (at which point, presumably, you would rather lose heart in the exercise and give up). The reason for this is that the universe bends, in a way we can adequately imagine, in conformance with Einstein's theory of relativity. For the moment it is enough to know that we are not adrift in some large, ever-expanding bubble. Rather, space curves, in a way that allows it to be boundless and finite." [34]

Now we can see how our universe distinguishes itself from the other universes around it and likely how the super universes that contain the local universes form a space-time curvature around their boundaries.

O.K. Now that we have a better grasp on our modern understanding of the creation from a scientific and metaphysical perspective, let's project our consciousness back into Mali and tune into the Dogon wisdom. Picture the scene below as we proceed on our virtual adventure. The Dogon village where we will be receiving the ancient teachings from the tribal elder, "Ogotemmeli" is situated in the sandy Seno-Gondo Plains:

3.3

The Dogon villages are built into the sandstone and as such, they live in harmony with their natural surroundings. These structures resemble the ruins of the Native American indigenous sites that can be found throughout the Americas. Indigenous people around the world found ways to reside in harmony with the landscape disturbing it in the least way possible. I feel such a resonance with this way of flowing with nature in honor of it rather than dominating and destroying it for our own selfish needs. Let's make a mental note of these villages. Maybe it will inspire us to build self-sustaining unity communities in our own background that flow with the harmony of our natural surroundings in honor of Mother Earth and her creation.

3.4

Inspired by the Dogon way of life, let's hear what author Laird Scranton has to teach us about the Dogon creation myth. Listen carefully for the parallels to the scientific explanations we've been exploring. He will also point them out as we go along.

The Dogon Creation Myth

In the "Dogon Cosmology", the God "Amma" is the creator of the universe and her egg is described as "a primordial body having existed before the creation of the universe and is said to have housed all of the potential seeds and signs of the future creation...When Amma broke the egg of the universe, it released a whirlwind that spun primordial matter in all directions — matter that would eventually come to form all of the galaxies, stars and planets."[35] This myth alone may sound simplistic but as it continues, we see similarities with the modern knowledge of atoms and their subatomic particles (which is fascinating considering the remote and secluded nature of this tribe) but their knowledge is based on an ancient oral tradition that has been passed down for millenia. Laird Scranton continues to translate the myth shared by Ogotemmeli. He describes what the Dogons believe to be the first work of Amma — a tiny seed called a "po". This seed can be compared to the atom as a fundamental building block of matter. They believe that "po is the very image of the creator (and) Amma's creative will is said to be located inside the po." As the elder goes on to explain the inner workings of the po, it becomes evident that he is describing the substance and function of the atom as we know it. According to the myth, the smaller elements of the po are called "sene seeds" (what we would call "subatomic particles"). These sene seeds "combine together at the center of the po and then surround it by crossing in all directions to form a nest." In his book, Laird points out that their description aligns perfectly with the modern atomic theory of electrons encircling a nucleus.

Picture of a sene seed

He points out in his book that this resembles a known orbital path of electrons around a nucleus. There are four main orbital paths that electrons will make around a nucleus. The path which resembles a four-petaled flower is called a "d-orbital." This symbol is repeated throughout ancient and modern texts and regarded as sacred.

The Dogon myth goes beyond the structure and function of the atom, however, and dives into the subatomic nature of it as well. They believe that the sene seeds are germinated by 266 fundamental seeds. Laird helps us to understand the modern scientific explanation of quarks by explaining that there are three quarks in each proton and neutron and that scientists have now identified over 200 types! According to Laird, quarks are categorized by their rotational property or "spin". He goes on to translate the mythological explanation by citing a Dogon drawing he describes as: "four spiked circular figures each of which reflects the rotational attributes of one of the four spin categories."[36] This, he explains, aligns with the four known quantum forces: gravity, electromagnetism, and the weak and strong nuclear forces.

As if that's not compelling enough, now things really start to get intriguing as the Dogon myth starts to describe the concepts of "String Theory." This theory wasn't proposed by modern physicists until the 1980's! The modern concept of this theory is that tiny vibrating strings are the most fundamental elements of all energy and matter. According to the myth, as translated by Laird:

"the formation of matter begins with tiny vibrating threads woven by a mythological spider named Dada". [37] They believe that these threads are the source of the 266 primordial seeds, or in modern terms — the root of the "quarks" in the subatomic protons and neutrons.

As we hike to our campsite, we will talk more about "Calabi-Yau" spaces but they are essentially loops within which seven dimensions are wrapped up in bundles at every point in space-time. With the help of Laird Scranton's teachings, we can compare this modern scientific theory with the ancient Dogon myths. Their myth speaks of "...an egg that is the mythological home to seven successive vibrations of matter." They drew it as "seven rays of a star, each of increasing length." This produces the appearance of a spiraling coil drawn according to the dimensions of a Fibonacci sequence or Golden Mean spiral! I encourage you to try drawing a star with seven rays each increasing in length. Then, starting at the point in the center, trace the endpoints of the rays around to form a coil. These practices enhance your Creator-consciousness and ultimately, your creator abilities to manifest form in this realm!

Laird goes on to explain, "Descriptions of string theory tell us that after the seventh vibration of a string, a new Calabi-Yau space tears and then bends in a new way to form another Calabi-yau space." [38] According to the Dogon cosmology: "the vibrations in the egg can progress only after the thread "has broken through" the wall of the egg. This event is described as the eighth and final stage of the first egg and as the initiating step of a new egg." In the "Law of One" series, Group Ra speaks of "Octaves" (eight vibrations within each dimension — seven progressive vibrations plus the eighth transitional one). Once you pass through the seven vibrations (or chakras), you can ascend through the eighth which is a sort of portal into another dimension or Gateway to infinity (symbolized by the number 8!). The "tearing through" of another Calabi-Yau sure sounds like breaking through to another dimension. According to Laird, modern "superstring" theory proposes that there is a Calabi-Yau space at every point in space on the vast web of creation. It reminds me of how some Native American tribes refer to the mother of creation as Grandmother Spider weaving her web one super-string at a time.

Let's take a moment to sincerely thank the author, Laird Scranton, for his incredible insight. I am truly grateful for his ability to translate and share the ancient Dogon creation myth in a way that clearly shows astounding parallels with modern quantum physics. These parallels are the key to uncovering the universal truths we are seeking. For a much more in-depth conversation about the Dogon Cosmology directly with Laird Scranton himself, watch the full one-hour interview at SciSpi.tv/Rise-Up/.

Let's also thank the French Anthropologist, Marcel Griaule for bringing the Dogon myth alive for the rest of the world to appreciate and learn from. And finally, let's acknowledge the Dogon elder, Ogotemmeli, for trusting an outsider enough to share these advanced initiate teachings that his tribe considers sacred.

Now as we near our campsite, let's consider how the Dogon's Sene Seeds cosmology compares with the atom as a fundamental building block of creation. Before diving into the purely scientific theory however, please allow me to offer this whimsical perspective for your consideration.

Think of the atom as a vehicle upon which consciousness can travel. From the core of creation where consciousness is centered, the atoms become vessels upon which thoughts can travel on gravity circuits into the expanding creation. The concentration of pure love at the core continues to exert a gravitational pull on all the projected thought-forms. This is a feature that is inherent in the atomic structure. Think of love and attraction. In the atom, the attraction of the protons is what keeps the electrons swirling around the nucleus (or heart center). Imagine that the protons and neutrons within the nucleus are held together by pure love. The orbiting electrons are attracted to this love just like we are drawn to the pure love of the Creator — at the heart-center of our creation.

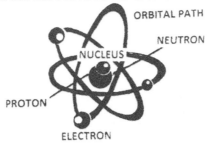

From this perspective, atoms represent the essence of our own true nature. The negatively-charged electrons are inherently attracted to the positive energy of the protons in the nucleus. You know the saying, "Opposites attract!" As I considered the role of the neutrons, I pondered their neutrality and imagined the possibilities! If the nucleus represents pure consciousness and the neutrons represent neutrality (balance) while the protons represent the attractive force of pure love, what do the electrons represent? The electrons represent pure potential! They are more creative while the protons are more stable which reflects our own feminine and masculine qualities. Polarity defines our own true nature and atoms are at the foundation of it!

Let's find out more about the creative potential of electrons:

Electrons seem to exist as seeds of potential, or mere possibilities, as they pop in and out of existence unpredictably until they mysteriously translate into form or trans-form. Ooh, elusive and mysterious — how intriguing! Research has shown that what makes the electrons transform, or "actualize", is the action of observing or measuring them. They are pure potential popping up here and there until the presence of an observer determines how they will "set" into form (and it's based on the expectation or intention of the observer!) The form that electrons actualize into from pure energy potential is based solely on what the observer expects or intends to perceive. This mysterious behavior of both electrons and photons is caused by their "wave-particle duality." When they are not being observed, they act like waves of endless possibilities. In the presence of an observer, they become particles taking on a definite form. In a recent episode of "Through the Wormhole" with Morgan Freeman, he described this phenomenon explaining that: "The subatomic world remains a blur of possibilities until the moment someone looks at it when those probabilities gel into one definite reality." The show goes on to prove mathematically and observationally how this applies to the universe at large.

I found this to be a fascinating concept because it clearly implies that the subatomic particles that define our reality are subject to the consciousness of the observer perceiving them. More accurately, they are "directed" by the subconscious mind of the observer who, in most cases, is consciously unaware of the intention or expectation they are projecting into this energy potential. WOW! This says a mouthful about how the power of intention works in manifesting the forms which create our perception of reality. It also says a lot about how we subconsciously create the forms in our reality with our positive and negative expectations. The electrons swirling around the nucleus are just waiting for our mind to tell them what to do! Our individual and collective perception of reality is defined by the thoughts being projected into the pure energy potential of the subatomic world. The electrons and photons are simply manifesting the forms they are instructed to by the individual and collective minds programming and perceiving them! That's why we refer to our world as a "consensus reality." Together, as a "group mind", we are creating the images which define our reality.

This is true on an individual level too as we create our own little worlds with the power of our intention or subconscious expectation. We are simply perceiving exactly what we consciously intend, or subconsciously expect, to experience. We actually project the thoughts in our mind onto our experience of reality. These projections create the picture of reality that unfolds before us as we walk through each moment of our lives. Think about that as you move through your day with the realization that you are creating every moment with the power of your mind. How will you create the moments that unfold? A positive mindset will create positive images and a negative one, likewise. It's all a matter of perception and reality is based purely on your perception of it. Your mind simply projects the thoughts and you experience them accordingly. It's up to you what you choose to project into and imprint onto your version of reality. It's your movie and you are both the director and producer of it. You can do it consciously as an awake and empowered creator or as an asleep and powerless witness. This choice is what creates a Creator mindset or a victim mindset. Your reality is either happening because of you or just to you. You can use your free will wisely by intentionally making conscious choices to become an empowered creator! Then you can manifest the forms in your reality that serve the highest good for all. That's how you can make a powerful and positive difference in the world always in all ways.

This knowledge can either be super empowering or very intimidating. That's why it's so important to focus on mastering our mind before we create with the power of our intentions. Just remember, we create our reality within a vast field of consciousness that affects everyone in the matrix. That's why this power in the wrong hands has such a devastating effect on the collective consciousness. We, however, are focused on creating the highest good for humanity with the power of our pure intentions so we always choose our thoughts wisely. We will explore these concepts much more in Book 3 of The Up! Trilogy — *Lighten Up!* In it, we will apply the Creator-consciousness we're developing now so we can learn to manifest skillfully and wisely.

From a purely scientific perspective, atoms are the fundamental building blocks of the light, energy and matter that make up our world. From a more spiritual perspective, they are simply the mechanism that the omnipresent spirit uses to express itself. I believe that spirit is the true source of energy underlying all manifestation. Spirit has the power to transform energy into form and endowed with this spirit, we all have this innate potential within us. Understanding the structure and function of the atom and how Spirit uses it as a vehicle and mechanism for projecting thought into form, will give us greater insight into our own innate potential. All we have to do is tune into Spirit so that we can activate the divine spark within us. Infused with Spirit, we will always create in alignment with the divine source. When we are in alignment, we step into divine synchronicity and create in divine order and with divine timing. There is a profound transcendent meaning which lies <u>beyond the form</u>. Exploring this will unleash our unlimited potential to intentionally create meaningful experiences so we can consciously ascend toward more enlightened ones!

While researching sacred texts, I discovered a book by Ralph Waldo Trine written in 1910 called, "In Tune with the Infinite". The essence of this inspired work aligns perfectly with the creative concepts we have been exploring. As such, I would like to share with you the following excerpts from pages 11-13 of his remarkable book entitled, "The Supreme Fact of the Universe and of Human Life". The book itself is an excerpt from a parent book entitled, "In Tune with the Infinite or Fullness of Peace, Power and Plenty."

The Supreme Fact of the Universe
By Ralph Waldo Trine

The great central fact of the universe is that the Spirit of Infinite Life and Power that is back of all, animates all, that manifests itself in and through all; that self-existent principle of life from which all has come, and not only from which all have come, but from which all is continually coming. If there is an individual life, there must of necessity be an infinite source of life from which it comes. If there is a quality or force of love, there must of necessity be an infinite source of love whence it comes. If there is wisdom, there must be the all-wise source back of it from which it springs. The same is true in regard to peace, power and what we call material things. There is, then, this Spirit of Infinite Life and Power back of all which is the source of all. This infinite power is creating, working, ruling through the agency of great immutable laws and forces that run through all the universe, that's around us on every side. Every act of our everyday lives is governed by the same great laws and forces. Every flower that blooms by the wayside, that springs up, grows, blooms, fades, according to certain great immutable laws. Every snowflake that plays between earth and heaven, forms, falls, melts, according to certain great unchangeable laws. This Spirit of Infinite Life and Power that is back of all is what I call God. I care not what term you may use, the Kindly Light, Providence, the Over Soul, Omnipotence, or whatever term may be most convenient. I care not what the term may be as long as we agree in regard to the great central fact itself…God, then, is this Infinite Spirit which fills all the universe with himself alone, so that all is from Him and in Him, and there is nothing that is outside. Indeed, and in truth, then, in him we live and move and have our being. He is the life of our life, our very life itself. We received, we are continually receiving our life from him…There have been and are highly illumined souls who believe we receive our life from God after the manner of a divine inflow…if God is the Infinite Spirit of Life back of all, whence all comes, then clearly our life as individualized spirits is continually coming from this Infinite Source by means of a divine inflow." [1]

Whoa, so beautifully expressed and such a powerful affirmation for all we have been exploring today. And so timely as we have arrived at our campsite and are ready to set up and then settle into a lively discussion around the campfire. Let's project our consciousness back into the Mali landscape and imagine that we can camp at the base of the Dogon village.

Close your eyes and envision the scene as we gather around the campfire and share our thoughts from today's exploration. To guide our reflection, let's explore how we can align our consciousness with the divine streams of consciousness flowing in from the source. In my dream experiences, the spirit guides have shown me how vortexes of energy are like portals through which powerful streams of divine consciousness can be directed into our collective mind matrix. This is a wonderful illustration of how the eternal creator beings project thoughts to create in space-time.

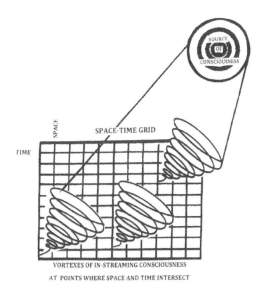

Einstein's Special Theory of Relativity basically says that the laws of physics are the same for all creators regardless of where they are in space-time. With this in mind, let's perform a "thought-experiment" just like Einstein did to reveal profound truths about reality. All you have to do is follow along and then see what arises in your own creative mind:

Einstein's General Theory of Relativity attempts to explain gravity by predicting the existence of a space-time grid in which matter can bend or "curve" space in time. In his theory of gravity as a "space-time curvature", the existence of matter causes "waves" in the grid as it moves through it. Light and sound travel on these waves as it bends and curves around matter.

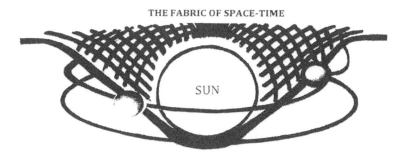

Einstein's theory addressed gravity not as an attractive force but rather a result of this "space-time curvature" in which larger objects in the space-time field, or web, cause the smaller ones to rotate around it.

In a field of "space-time", there are intersecting lines that form the grid and then there are the spaces in between. The linear, or horizontal, lines that move forward and backward represent time — the "now" and the vertical lines that connect systems to the source represent space — the "here." A space-time field is thus created giving us the "here and now." The points where these lines intersect can be thought of as "nodes" and they are very powerful "points of access." They are thought to be the connection points or "links" between inter-dimensional realms. They may represent a transition between realms or a portal into a realm beyond space and time.

Like links on a chain-link fence, space and time wrap around each other to give us the interwoven fabric of space-time. The spaces in between represent our experience of space and time — the "here" and "now" — the linear past, present and future of our 4-dimensional reality (with the 4th dimension being time itself).

SPACE-TIME POSSIBILITIES

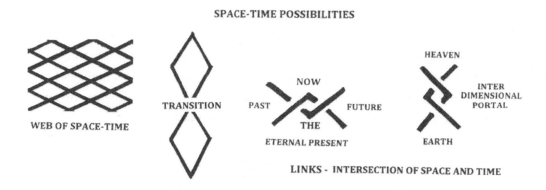

These points have also been referred to as the "eternal" present where time and space intersect, and a portal is created. Through this portal, the timeless-spaceless realm of eternity may be accessed. Using these portals, thoughts originating from the eternal realm can be projected into time and space realities. All "events" that we see as occurring in linear time "here" sometimes called the "arrow of time" — the "past, present and future" — occur simultaneously in the eternal present "now."

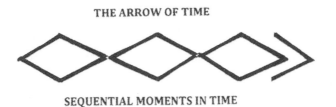

THE ARROW OF TIME

SEQUENTIAL MOMENTS IN TIME

SIMULTANEOUS MOMENTS IN ETERNITY

Time stands still and loses its sequential meaning in the eternal now moment. There is no past or future as we know it, just now.

At powerful moments in our lives, time seems to slow down or even stand still and they are imprinted on our memory forever. Think about times when the world around you seemed to stop and you were fully engrossed in a powerful moment where time stood still. The "Fullness of Now" is a magical place to connect with. It represents the power of the present moment. It's a powerful place to tune into and create from because it represents the true source of reality rather than the illusion of space-time. Similarly, when we are truly embracing the beauty of the present moment for all its worth and seeing "God" in everyone and everything, we are touching the truth and it resonates strongly within the core of our being as a powerful knowing. We are connecting with our divine nature and experiencing the true reality of our "being" in God as the god within us.

How does this all work? How can we tune into the eternal now moment to create at will? More importantly, how can we create in the field of space-time applying what we know about electrons and photons and their "wave-particle" duality? How does the Creator do it? It starts with an intention which projects a stream of energy into the field like a vibrational wave rolling across the ocean of consciousness. A "thought-form" is projected and it causes a wave sometimes referred to as distortions or interferences in the field. Group Ra talks about "distortions of consciousness" in the "Law of One" books and the book "Initiation" refers to "interferences which cause condensations and materialization".

These intentions projected into the field with emotion set energy into motion (e-motion). Condensations of energy start spinning around a point in space-time which is exactly what propels the pure energy potential of electrons and photons to condense into form in our atomic reality. Atoms are the vehicle for manifesting the intentions. The nucleus becomes the node where space and time intersect. The electrons are pure energy potential just waiting to be actualized by the power of intention propelled by emotion.

This is defined by the wave-particle duality of all subatomic particles in which they exist as waves until they intentionally become particles. When consciousness is projected, and it begins to condense as a spinning vortex, the potential for a new creation manifests into form! The spinning motion is intensified by the strong gravitational force of the core and a "space-time curvature" is created. As the gravitational core of this "space-time" curvature attracts more energy into it, this energy spins into matter and creations like stars and planets spiral into being!

In the beginning, it all started with the Infinite Source breathing as a sea of pure consciousness. In one divine in breath, the self within source suddenly became aware, and this realization caused a wave to erupt in the ocean of consciousness. This knowing caused the divine source to reflect upon its self and the first image of its reflection was born as its "child." The recognition of this image sparked the Infinite Spirit to ignite and the light of awareness overcame the darkness of infinity. The divine trinity rested in perfect unity enjoying this state of pure bliss until suddenly they felt a strong urge to know thy self through experience. Realizing they couldn't create in infinity as a divine tetrahedron, they reflected upon themselves and created a portal into eternity. As a creative octahedron, they could merge their divine immortal self with their creative eternal self and create in the realm of timeless perfection. With the power of their passion and intention to create, they broke free of the bonds of infinity and emerged into the realm of eternity! With the power of free will and ever-increasing intelligence, spirit began to manifest form by creating the perfect mechanism upon which thought could flow — the atom. With the positive attraction of pure love at its core and pure potential swirling all around it, this would be the vehicle for expressing their creative will. Through this mechanism, all the laws of nature could be expressed, the forces could flow, and the energy potential could manifest into form. A symmetrical universe would unfold swung into form and sung into being by the harmonious symphony of pure spirit. One harmony, one verse — a uni-verse.

Let's move into this scientific explanation still inspired by spiritual revelation:

Our universe came into being with a bang — a spiraling explosion of super-hot pure energy flowing in through a portal into a point in space-time where the creator projected his intention to create. Through this spiraling vortex of pure energy potential, a space-time curvature began to form within which this universe could gravitate. The core of this field would always be the source of pure love attraction as the gravitational force holding it into place — a center where this universe could swirl around as it creates things and beings to adore. As this space-time field begins cooling, particles of matter are formed.

This "cooling" takes place as an intelligent response to the intention to create. A field (now known of as the "Higgs field") is intentionally activated. When this field is "turned on", it provides the resistance necessary for particles to slow down to a speed less than that of the speed of light (photons being the exception). Scientists explain that, below a certain temperature, the Higgs field is produced which "gives off" the "Higgs Boson". An energy exchange takes place within the field in which the Higgs boson gives mass to some particles. Without this field and the bosons, it produces (which were only recently proven to exist), we couldn't have the atoms that make up the stuff of the universe.

Remember how we discussed the need for resistance on the first day of our adventure? In the book, "Initiation", Phahotep was teaching the high priestess that without the resistance of matter, creation would be impossible. Phahotep predicted this field of resistance and Elisabeth drew it according to his description. Phahotep explained how the trinity was expressed in the equilateral triangle and then moved into its three-dimensional form as the tetrahedron: 'Just like the equilateral triangle which makes up its mantle, the tetrahedron is the very incarnation of harmony and equilibrium." (page 231 — Initiation) He called it the divine tetrahedron and he said, like the pyramid, it symbolizes "God-man" who "reveals his divine, selfless nature and completely manifests God on Earth." He goes onto explain the manifestation of the field: "Thus you can see that in every one of its points, three-dimensional space is based on the divine tetrahedron representing absolute harmony and absolute equilibrium." (Page 237 — Initiation) Modern physicists call it "symmetry".

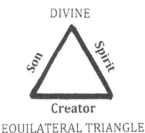

DIVINE

Son   Spirit

Creator

EQUILATERAL TRIANGLE

3-D DIVINE TRIANGLE

THE TETRAHEDRON

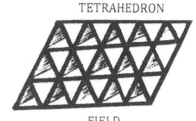

TETRAHEDRON

FIELD

We just recently proved the existence of this field of resistance and called it the "Higgs Field" after the leading physicist who predicted it — Peter Higgs. It provides the necessary resistance for the possibility of creation to unfold. It is the physical "field of consciousness" required for a physical reality with energy <u>and</u> mass to unfold within. According to Einstein's equation, E=MC2, energy (E) must be slowed down to a speed far less than that of the speed of light (C) to convert into mass (M). Conversely, mass must be sped up to convert to energy. E=MC2 simply defines the conversion, or exchange, rate between energy and mass.

The Higgs field provides the resistance necessary for the energetic particles to slow down enough so they can cool off and convert to mass. In addition, the particle this field "gives off" allows other particles to acquire mass when they interact with it — a perfect design, of course!

THE GASEOUS EXPLOSION OF THE BIG BANG ENCOUNTERING RESISTANCE & ACQUIRING MASS

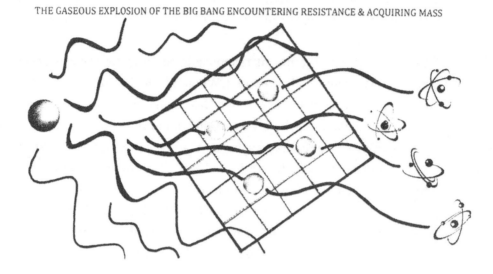

The following is an explanation of the Higgs Field as I understand it. I have pieced together this general description from various resources:

The rise of the Higgs field is due to a "breaking of the symmetry" of the "electroweak interaction" which causes components of the field to give mass to elementary particles. The "Higgs mechanism" refers to the "symmetry breaking" of the electroweak interaction. We don't have to understand the specifics for our purposes here (of course, you can always research them if you like) but it is the "symmetry-breaking" that will become important for us to understand.

It has been proposed that it is the "successive symmetry breaking" of the Higgs field at "phase transitions" (transformations of energy and matter into different states) from which the presently known forces and fields of the universe arise. Without this symmetry breaking caused by the Higgs field, there would no mass — no universe to arise. There would be no stars, no planets, no us!

It was this "successive symmetry breaking" that really caught my attention and I will tell you why. Apparently, physical laws have a certain symmetry at every point in space-time called a gauge symmetry. Particles have intrinsic properties (like their electrical charge +, −, or 0 spin frequency and mass) which are called the properties of their gauge symmetry. When these are "broken" during "phase transitions" within the Higgs field, it is proposed that the forces and fields which make up our known universe arise. You will see later that, as described in Laird Scranton's book, "Sacred

Symbols of the Dogon", the Dogon Tribe speak of seven "successive" vibrations. You will also learn of a phenomenon he presents (known to modern science as the "Calabi-Yau" space) in which seven dimensions are wrapped up in bundles at every point in space-time and after the seventh vibration, a new space tears, or "breaks" through, and then bends to form another space. When these points in space-time are penetrated, it causes a "spatial rift" in space-time — the symmetry is broken as a phase transition takes place within the field. There must be a correlation with the symmetry-breaking caused by the Higgs field.

Let's consider this from a "Sci-spi" perspective merging science and spirit synchronistically:

Scientifically, this successive symmetry breaking represents a phase transition which leads to an energetic shift. An exchange of energy and mass takes place which changes the vibrational frequency of the particles in the field.

From a spiritual perspective, it represents a transformational shift in the field of consciousness. Plain and simple. The Dogon speak of seven successive vibrations. We know from our adventure yesterday that there are vibrational frequencies (or chakras) associated with seven distinct levels of consciousness. A transformational shift in frequency takes place between levels as we break through one and transition into the next. The "Law of One" refers to seven densities that we move through each with a successive vibration. Of course, these represent major shifts in frequencies, but we experience minor shifts in our vibration all day as our "moods" shift up and down and we go through different phases. We are constantly breaking our symmetry as we phase transition in and out of different states of consciousness just like the subatomic particles we are made of!

If our experience unfolds in a field of consciousness and we live in a 4-dimensional reality (3-dimensions of space + 1-dimension of time), this field is also a field of "space-time". The Higgs field is this "field of space and time" and it clearly shows the interconnectivity of everything that takes place within it. We slow, or cool, spinning electrons into form with the power of our mind all the time! In this way, we create our own Higgs field by cooling our reality into the forms we perceive simply by observing it. Of course, we can do this intentionally. This reveals our creative power as a Creator-being! It is within this interconnected "web" of reality that space-time is woven. It is the fabric that we are interacting with as we move through our experience of reality. Every vibrating string that makes up this fabric of space-time is just like every individual soul creating within it. The Dogon speak of matter as being "woven" and many Egyptian hieroglyphs symbolize "weaving" as an important aspect of creation.

Expanding on the "Calabi-Yau spaces" I mentioned before, theoretical physicists speculate that there are seven dimensions wrapped in bundles at every point in space-time. These bundles at the intersection of space and time are called "Calabi-Yau" spaces after the physicists who discovered them (Calabi and Yau). They propose that these are the seven dimensions which didn't manifest at the time in which our four-dimensional universe unfolded. However, those seven dimensions plus our four make up the eleven dimensions that are the foundation for string theory! How cool is that?!

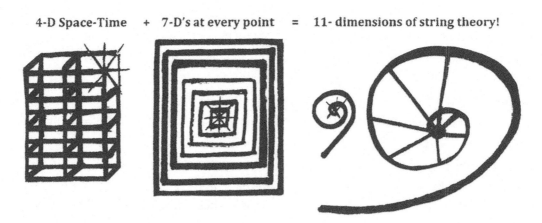

4-D Space-Time   +   7-D's at every point   =   11- dimensions of string theory!

Laird Scranton writes in his book, "Sacred Symbols of the Dogon", that the Dogon believe that the vibrating strings underlying all of reality spiral outward from a center point, or star, with seven rays each increasing in length (seven successive vibrations ranging in frequency).

In the "Law of One" series, Group Ra also speaks of seven "rays" correlating with the seven colors (or densities) of the chakras — red, orange, yellow, green, blue, indigo and violet — each increasing in frequency. The eighth ray is the "gateway-density" and represents a transition between dimensions. Laird Scranton explains in his book, on page 35, that the Dogon myth says "the vibrations in the egg can only progress after the thread has broken through the wall of the egg.

This event is described as the eighth and final stage of the first egg and as the initiating step of a new egg. There must be something very significant to this concept of symmetry breaking which takes place during phase transitions. Whether on a minuscule scale, like minor shifts in consciousness, or on a larger scale, like major transitions between dimensions, the number seven defines the progressive journey and the eighth — the "breaking through", the gateway to the next point or dimension in the fabric of space-time.

We will continue to explore atoms and subatomic particles as the fundamental building blocks of creation but underlying these, many physicists now believe, are the tiny strings which vibrate inside the quarks of these particles. The celestial guides in *The Urantia Book* also confirm that vibrating strings are the most fundamental elements which define the true nature of reality. When we speak of reality being woven, it's only natural to think of strings or threads! We already know that all matter has a certain spin (or frequency) and yesterday we learned about the seven vibrational frequencies which give us the primary colors and basic tones which define our experience of reality. When you pluck the strings on any string instrument, they vibrate and produce different tones based on the frequency created. String theory seems like a perfectly natural explanation to me and theoretical physicists are working hard to prove it. In the meantime, let's focus back on what we know about our subatomic reality and the recently discovered Higgs field. I obtained the following statement from Wikipedia and have provided the appropriate reference:

"The Higgs field doesn't create mass out of nothing. In Higgs-based theories, the property of mass is the manifestation of potential energy transferred to particles when they interact within the Higgs field which had contained that mass in the form of energy." (Max Jammer, Concepts of Mass in Contemporary Physics and Philosophy, (Princeton, NJ: Princeton University Press, 2000) pp 162-163 — provides many references in support of this statement).

This "exchange of energy potential within the field giving rise to mass" is an incredibly important aspect of the true nature of reality which we will explore throughout our journey of self-discovery. The discovery of the Higgs field has opened the door to endless possibilities and unlocked many secrets of the universe which have tremendous implications for human potential. As we evolve, we will learn how to use our inherent ability to manifest form (or mass) out of the energy potential in this field with the power of intention. It's simply "mind over matter." What we will come to discover is that the mere act of looking at the electrons that shape our reality changes their velocity, or spin, and thus determines the form they take on. It's a transfer of energy from the light of our spirit that we shine on our reality. We project this light into our reality and this transfer translates our thoughts into forms. We now know that the energetic nature of the thoughts we intentionally (or unintentionally) project determines the nature of the reality that unfolds. Once we understand how to control the nature of the energy we project in order to create the intended nature of the reality we wish to experience, we will begin to master the art of manifestation and unleash our creative potential!

If we want to learn how to control the nature of our experience, we need to understand the true underlying nature of reality itself! So, let's turn our attention now to electrons and the gravity circuits that control their behavior. Then we will look at the important role that gravity, or density, plays in the conduct of atoms. From a spiritual perspective, we will see how the field of gravity is the conductor of the universe. The atoms and its electrons are the instruments that create this symphony. Who's playing these instruments? Spirit, of course!

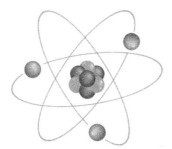

Let's review some basic background information about electrons and then take a closer look at what I find to be the most fascinating aspect of these subatomic particles — the origin and nature of their orbital paths. There are some remarkable spiritual implications in the design of these paths.

| 1 s-orbital | 3 p-orbitals | 5 p-orbitals | 7 f-orbitals |
| The symbol of one | The trinity pattern | The pentagonal | The sacred seven! |

**The four-standard electron orbital paths — s, p,d & f, each containing a maximum of 2 electrons.
Take note of the numbers represented and the symbols they produce.**

The most basic atom is the hydrogen atom which has one proton, one neutron and one electron. Then, since electrons are inclined to pair up, two hydrogen atoms combine to form H2. Beyond the hydrogen atom, the subatomic nature of atoms becomes more complex. As matter and energy increase in complexity, so do the electron configurations. The patterns, behaviors and arrangements of the subatomic particles within an atom determine the form of energy or matter it produces. Every form of energy and matter has a distinct pattern. Let's reference *The Urantia Book* to clarify these concepts from the same consciousness perspective we've been exploring:

Patterns, according to *The Urantia Book* are determined by the Creator alone and cannot be changed only reproduced or duplicated, for he is the originator of patterns. He creates the pattern, or personality of the universe. The Son duplicates and creates images projecting his creative spirit into the universe, creating the spirit of the universe. The Spirit breathes life into these images causing them to manifest in time and space, creating the mind of the universe. This is a good time to integrate the celestial teachings in *The Urantia Book* with what we have learned about modern physics. Here we will clearly see the spiritual significance of the electron configurations and the gravity-circuits that control their behavior.

We will also see how these circuits determine the patterns and behavior of the atoms which define everything, including us! Setting aside the patriarchal references, these divine teachings depict a harmonious reality within which the trinity of the Father, Son and Spirit use their magic wands to direct these circuits like conductors of a symphony. With the power of their intention, they create the vibrational frequencies of color and sound which define our experience. We can think of the fermions as their instruments and the bosons as the force that plays them. The Higgs boson is like the players which give rise to the performance and the field the auditorium in which the symphony takes place. These celestial visions will create a divine experiential as we snuggle into our sleeping bags and stare up at the starry night sky.

Commentary on "The Urantia Book" Version of Creation

The Urantia Book" gives some extremely fascinating insight into how our universe came into being (albeit in incredibly complex detail). To simplify these explanations, I will be presenting generalizations of the concepts and centering my attention on the consciousness aspects of it. Since we are going into lengthy discussions now about a "Creator-God", I feel it is important to stress the consciousness viewpoint I am focused on here since I realize the topic of God may be controversial to some readers. I empathize with this and as such, want to introduce a passage out of the book, "The Yugas", that conveys these sentiments. As we know from yesterday's adventures, this book is based on the teachings of Sri Yukteswar and Paramhansa Yogananda. Under the heading "Pure Consciousness", the authors write:

"God is a loaded word today. It conjures up different meanings for different people based on their backgrounds and cultures; often it conjures up a wide variety of positive and negative feelings… Sri Yukteswar wryly observes that God is not a "venerable personage, adorning a throne in some antiseptic corner of the cosmos! God is pure consciousness, beyond form and limitation, and our own consciousness, our very being, is an inextricable expression of this consciousness as part of the pure consciousness of God." [2]

This is a valuable perspective with which to approach the following teachings presented in this beautiful description of the "Creator-God", which they also refer to as "the first source and center." It talks about the "eternal purpose" of creation as being "the ascension scheme for spiritualizing and training the mortals of time and space." Yes! Our divine purpose is revealed! It refers to the experience of "time and space beings", as essentially being the ground-floor, or training ground, of our "ascension career". We have spirit experiences at the higher levels that contribute to our ascension progress as well. So, this gives us a definite purpose: to ascend from training in the physical realm to spiritualizing in the higher realms! This also indicates that we are being guided toward this ascension as the Creator fulfills his eternal purpose! Right on. So, how is the Creator projecting this ascension scheme? Through creating time and space, of course! And how did he go about creating time and space? Well, that's what we're exploring here today. Let's consider this symbol of infinity from *The Urantia Book* — three concentric circles emanating from a single point in the center.

We can try and imagine that these circles represent the creative expression of the Universal Father, the Eternal Son and the Infinite Spirit. As their consciousness expands outward from the source, energetic circles are formed, one within the other. Just like *The Urantia Book* teaches us, these spirit personalities are radiating out from the center as first, second and third "sources and centers" of creation. According to the book, the Father, as the first source and center, is the universal personality which he projects through the "personality-gravity circuits." The infinite aspects of his personality represent the emerging potential for all of creation — the created beings and things.

The Son, the second source and center, is responsible for initiating and controlling the "spirit-gravity circuits" as he represents the creative spirit of the living beings. The Infinite Spirit, third source and center, projects the "mind-gravity circuits" — the creative mind of all living beings.

Here's where the atom comes in and science and spirit converge! Please engage in a "thought-experiment" with me as I imagine how these gravity-circuits perform their role as conductors of the symphony. If the atoms are the instruments, picture how the conductor directs the music they play. Envision an atom in your mind and the circuits become obvious! The circuitous route the electrons take around the nucleus are the gravity circuits projected by the Father, Son and Spirit! According to the book, the maximum potential of their combined potential is seven! Whoa there's that magical number again! 7!

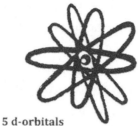

1 s-orbital 3 p-orbitals   5 d-orbitals
1)The Father 1)Father 2) Son 3)Spirit 1)Father 2)Son 3) Spirit 4)Father-Son 5)Father-Spirit

7 f-orbitals
1)Father 2)Son 3)Spirit 4)Father-Son 5)Father-Spirit 6)Son-Spirit 7)Father-Son-Spirit

If we consider gravity in terms of a field, like we discussed earlier, we can clearly see how the circuits of the Father, Son and Spirit intersect to create the tetrahedron pattern of this field.

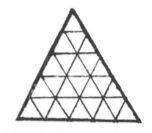

The Father Circuits The Son Circuits The Spirit Circuits The Gravitational Field

All the matter and forces of the known universe arise from this field and are clearly a manifestation of the divine potential from which they came. The forms of energy and matter that emerge from this design reflect the consciousness that created it. Projecting from the Father, Son and the Spirit are many, many levels of spirit beings that become involved in universe creation and control. According to the book, this spiritual energy is very organized and as beings emerge with personalities, spirits and minds, they are divided into groups and a hierarchy evolves. Eventually, headquarters for the administration and justice of the developing universes are formed and training schools are erected for the development of the emerging potentials. As thoughts originating from the source travel on gravity-circuits out into the universe, they become more intelligent and evolved. This is a very general interpretation of the creation and evolution of the universes as I understand it in the context of these teachings. Within this tremendous and ongoing expansion of eternity, whirling vortexes of energy-potential develop wherever the sources and centers of consciousness are projected.

So, what about the emergence of our universe? *The Urantia Book* tells us that 987 billion years ago an "inspector" searching for condensations of energy discovered our emerging potential in the

"Andronover Nebula." We are taught that, "an associate force organizer and then acting inspector #811,307, of the Orvonton series, traveling from Uversa, reported to the Ancients of Days that space conditions were favorable for the initiation of materialization phenomena in a certain sector of the then easterly segment of Orvonton."[3] Remember, Orvonton is the 7th super universe. The universe controllers logged the coordinates and his discovery was so noted but apparently it takes billions of years for this energy to coagulate into something more than a spinning vortex. It wasn't until 87 billion years later when the "Uversa Council of Equilibrium" issued a permit to the super universe government "authorizing a dispatch of force organizers and staff to the region" and thereby executing a mandate calling for the "organization of a new material creation." The "staff" upon arrival engages in activities which result in the emergence of a new physical creation!

As we discussed on yesterday's adventure, our vortex world emerged within the seventh super universe of Orvonton. Within this super universe, our local universe of Nebadon spins around its core. Let's pull back for a moment to get a wider view of the surrounding "Grand Universe" before narrowing in on ours:

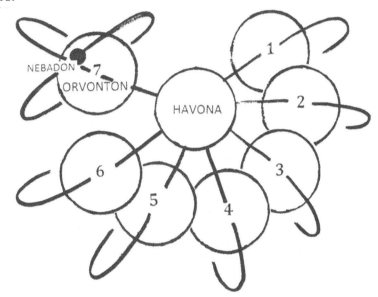

Does this pattern look familiar? Of course, it does! It is just like the known 7-orbitals of the electron in the f-orbital pattern that we explored above. Or the seven petals on the Flower of Life created during the first seven days of creation. As we look deeper into the patterns of the microcosm, we discover that they reveal the synchronicity of the macrocosm. These fundamental patterns are repeated in a synchronized universe. Just like in a music verse, there are major scales and minor scales which synchronize to produce a symphony. What appears to be complex is really quite simple and the true beauty lies within the sheer simplicity of it all. What's more is that there is a divine plan hidden within this multi-verse and we are revealing its secrets!

Remember from our discussion yesterday, that each of these super universes, starting with one and evolving through seven, represents an ascension of consciousness. With the emergence of each new super universe, a higher level of consciousness is expressed just like the evolutionary system of chakras we are familiar with. These energy centers ascend from a primitive survival consciousness up through the evolutionary levels of desire, power, love, communion, wisdom and finally, cosmic, or universal, consciousness. From this perspective, the seventh super universe within which we reside represents the highest attainment of consciousness within the Grand Universe!

Under the heading, "Purposes of the Seven Super universes", it is written:

"There are seven major purposes which are being unfolded in the evolution of the seven super universes. Each major purpose in super universe evolution will find full expression in only one of the seven super universes, and therefore does each super universe have a special function and a unique nature. Orvonton, the seventh super universe, the one to which your local universe belongs, is known chiefly because of its tremendous and lavish bestowal of merciful ministry to the mortals of the realms. It is renowned because justice prevails as tempered by mercy and power rules as conditioned by patience, while the sacrifices of time are freely made to secure the stabilization of eternity. Orvonton is a universe demonstration of love and mercy. It is, however, very difficult to describe our conception of the true nature of the evolutionary purpose which is unfolding in Orvonton, but it may be suggested by saying that in this super creation we feel that the six unique purposes of cosmic evolution as manifested in the six associated super creations are here being inter associated into a meaning-of-the-whole;" [4]

This statement would suggest that the super universes have progressively evolved in their level of consciousness expression, if you will. Therefore, the seventh super universe could be thought of as the embodiment of the highest and most evolved consciousness in the Grand Universe! The bodies that reside within it would then be an expression of the highest level of creativity and intelligence. How fortunate we are to be residing within this highly evolved consciousness! Another thing to be grateful for!

Back to the Grand Universe! To provide a clearer picture of the "Grand Universe", I have presented the following "plan of universe organization" offered by *The Urantia Book* which lays out the divine "plan of universe organization":

Superuniverses...7

Major Sectors...70

Minor Sectors...7,000

Local Universes...700,000

Constellations...70,000,000

Local Systems...7,000,000,000

Inhabitable Planets...................................7,000,000,000,000

(Inhabitable Planets are referred to as "worlds" in the following chart)

Each of the seven superuniverses is constituted, approximately, as follows:

One system embraces, approximately.......................... 1,000 worlds

One constellation (100 systems) ....100,00 worlds

One universe (100 constellations) ....10,000,000 worlds

One minor sector (100 universes) .... 1,000,000,000 worlds

One major sector (100 minor sectors) ....100,000,000,000 worlds

One superuniverse (10 major sectors) .... 1,000,000,000,000 worlds[5]

From this universal plan, we can see that each super universe has the potential to manifest 100,000 local universes. Within each local universe, there is the potential for 10,000,000 inhabitable planets to emerge. So that would mean that within a super universe, there is the potential for 1,000,000,000,000 inhabitable planets.

WOW! If this book is accurate, we really aren't alone after all! The thing about the accuracy of this book is that so many aspects of the historical data it discusses, in relation to the emergence of life and the evolution of beings, so closely aligns with our known record of events, it naturally follows that the rest of the information would be accurate as well. In other words, if we can verify the accuracy of one aspect of the book with our recognizable experience of reality, the accuracy of the entire book becomes plausible. Why would these higher spirit beings speak the truth on one topic and then alter the truth on another? I believe we can only verify that which our limited perceptual minds can grasp but would benefit greatly from opening our minds to that which lies outside of our known reality. In this way, we expand our consciousness and allow it to be illuminated by infinite possibilities. I have chosen to let the light in so that it can overcome the darkness of my ignorance about the world around me! At the same time, I use what I can of my rational and cognizant mind to be discriminating and discerning. The proclamations of truth that are revealed in *The Urantia Book* feel very true and accurate to me, so I am allowing the light of this information in. I invite you to consider these truths as well and then you can see for yourself what rings true for you.

According to the book, our universe originated in a great "nebula" called the "Andronover Nebula" and it took over 500 billion years to evolve into a system of suns. This evolution is described in detail. I have briefly summarized it here:

About 100 billion years after the "emerging potential" was discovered and, "the enormous Andronover Nebula was duly initiated, only the presence of the force organizer and the liaison staff was required to inaugurate the energy whirl which eventually grew into this vast cyclone of space. After the initiation of such nebular revolutions, the living force organizers simply withdraw at right angles to the plane of the revolutionary disk, and from that time forward, the inherent qualities of energy insure the progressive and orderly evolution of such a new physical system. "[6] This is just like the spiraling vortexes of energy we discussed earlier which create a space-time curvature within which a new system can spin into being! This "emerging" energy potential, or Higgs field, is activated so it can start spinning around a core and cool into matter to create a new physical system.

It took another 500 billion years for the Nebula to evolve into a "Sun System". This evolution is also described in detail but here's a summary:

Primary stage: Marked by circular energy patterns (200 billion years):

"All evolutionary material creation is born of circular and gaseous nebulae, and all such primary nebulae are circular throughout the early part of their gaseous existence. As they grow older, they usually become spiral, and when their function of sun formation has run its course, they often terminate as clusters of stars or as enormous suns surrounded by a varying number of planets, satellites, and smaller groups of matter in many ways resembling your own diminutive solar system." [7]

Secondary stage: Marked by spiral energy formations (300 billion years):

"The ever-increasing rate of whirling was soon to throw enormous suns off into space on independent circuits. And this is what happened in Andronover ages upon ages ago. The energy wheel grew and grew until it attained its maximum of expansion, and then, when contraction set in, it whirled on faster and faster until, eventually, the critical centrifuge stage was reached, and the great breakup began." [8]

And finally, this solar light show reaches a climactic crescendo:

"500 billion years ago the first Andronover sun was born. This blazing streak broke away from the mother gravity grasp and tore out into space on an adventure in the cosmos of creation. Such young suns quickly become spherical and start out on their long and eventful careers as the stars of space." [9]

Awesome! I love the dramatic flair! The beings who contribute their knowledge in this book obviously want to impress upon us the magnitude of these celestial events. I am in awe of the magnificent explosions of creation and love how they so eloquently describe them. This is what I want to share with you — the awe and wonder of the magnificent grace and symmetry.

Various astronomical events and evolutionary processes take place over the next 425 billion years and then, 75 billion years ago marked a turning point in the evolution of our universe during the height of the "sun-family" stage when, "the majority of the Suns possessed themselves of systems of planets, satellites, dark islands, comets, meteorites and cosmic dust clouds". [10]

"25 billion years later, the Nebulae had given birth to 876,926 Sun systems" [11] ...and then...

"by the end of the terminal breakup (and birth of our planet's sun) over 6 billion years ago, the Andronover Nebula had given birth to 1,013, 628 suns and sun systems."! [12]

I fully realize that our scientists and astronomers have pegged the birth of our Universe at 13.89 billion years ago and I am not about to try and reconcile with these figures but there are a couple of interesting things to point out here that might help explain this.

First, we have to back up a little, well a lot — 400 billion years ago actually. This is when a very important event took place that was primal to the creation of our universe. A Creator Son chose the "emerging potential" of our Universe to express his own infinite potential! The space aggregation of energy and matter was like a blank canvas upon which the Creator Son was given artistic license to create at will. It is written, "Michael of Nebadon, a Creator Son of Paradise, selected this disintegrating nebula as the site of his adventure in universe building." [13]

This topic of "Creator Sons" deserves more attention because this extraordinarily creative being has great significance not just to the creation of our universe but is, the "Father of our Universe" who together with the "Creative Daughter of the Infinite Spirit", or "Mother of the Universe" created a "child" within the Mother Womb of Creation. We are ultimately, children of the original Mother-Father Creator-God emerging from the Mother Womb of Creation. Each and every one of us is infused with a spark of their divine personality and therefore, have a personal connection with them. We have a direct connection to these creator beings of our local universe through the "indwelt adjuster" and "mystery monitor" imprinted within our being.

Here's the shocker — *The Urantia Book* claims that the Creator Son of our local universe, "Michael of Nebadon" personally manifested upon our planet, Urantia, as "Jesus of Nazareth" and this "personal bestowal" of a Creator Son on a planet of his choosing is extremely rare and a great honor. This story is a topic for another time, but I wanted to point out the connection here.

Further information is provided as to the nature of the Creator Son and accompanying Creative Daughter:

"At the head of all personality in Nebadon stands the Creator and Master Son, Michael, the universal father and sovereign. Co-ordinate in divinity and complemental in creative attribute is the local universe Mother Spirit...And these creators are in a very literal sense the Father-Son and the Spirit-Mother of all the native creatures of Nebadon." [14] "When energy- matter has attained a certain stage in mass materialization, a Paradise Creator Son appears upon the scene, accompanied by a Creative Daughter of the Infinite Spirit. Simultaneously with the arrival of the Creator Son, work is begun upon the architectural sphere which is to become the headquarters world of the projected local universe. For long ages such a local creation evolves, Suns become stabilized, planets form and swing into their orbits, while the work of creating the architectural world which are to serve as constellation headquarters and system capitals continues." [15]

The first order of business, upon the arrival of the Creator Son and Creative Daughter 400 billion years ago, was to begin construction on the universe headquarters worlds, the "Architectural worlds of Salvington". So, "Salvington" then becomes the name of our "universe headquarters." We are taught: "Almost immediately the Architectural Worlds of Salvington and the 100 constellation headquarters groups of planets were begun... 300 billion years ago, the Andronover solar circuits were well-established, and the nebular system was passing through a transient period of relative physical stability.... About this time the staff of Michael arrived on Salvington, and the Uversa government of Orvonton extended physical recognition to the local universe of Nebadon." [16] According to the teachings, over the next 295 billion years, a long period of "sun dispersion" takes place and some of these take on planets, satellites and dark islands. About 6 billion years ago, our sun was born bringing the total number of suns to about 1,014,000. Then about 1.5 billion years later, 4.5 billion years ago, our solar system produced planets: "The great column of solar gases which was thus separated from the sun subsequently evolved into the 12 planets of the solar system." [17]

Here, modern science and *The Urantia Book* agree on the dates of the birth of our solar system and subsequent formation of our planet. However, the dates for the birth of our universe differ by hundreds of billions of years. I will speculate on some various possibilities that could help explain why modern science would have detected a monumental eruption 14 billion years ago that would seem to indicate the birth of our universe. Of course, I invite my readers to join me in this speculative search for answers if you too are interested in reconciling this difference.

In *The Urantia Book* chronology of celestial events, the period of 25,000,000,000 to

10,000,000,000 years ago was marked by tremendous explosions and dramatic nuclear eruptions within the Andronover Nebula. This period of sun disbursement was one of terrific cosmic upheaval as the Mother Nucleus of the great nebula went through billions of years of convulsions liberating over 1 million suns. From my perspective, any one of these massive eruptions taking place in the Grand Universe could have been the birth of our own local universe.

On the other hand, there is another description in the book of a "primary eruption", with a very different nature and cause, which I found intriguing and may very well be the "spiritual flash" that science calls "The Big Bang." This eruption occurred when the Creator Son proclaims that life is to be projected into the newly organized universe. Check this out: "Upon the Paradise recognition of this declaration of intention, there occurs a reaction of approval in the Paradise Trinity, followed by the disappearance of the spiritual shining of the Deities of the Master Spirit in whose super universe this new creation is organizing."

Meanwhile, the other Master Spirits draw near this central lodgment of the Paradise Deities and subsequently, when the Deity-embraced Master Spirit emerges to the recognition of his fellows, there occurs what is known as a "primary eruption". This is a tremendous spiritual flash, a phenomenon clearly discernible as far away as the headquarters of the super universes concerned; and simultaneously with this little understood Trinity manifestation there occurs a marked change in the nature of the Creative Spirit presence and power of the Infinite Spirit resident in the local universe concerned. In response to this Paradise phenomenon there immediately personalizes, in the very presence of the Creator Son, a new personal representation of the Infinite Spirit. This is the Divine Minister. The individualized Creative Spirit helper of the Creator Son has become his personal creative associate, the local universe Mother Spirit." [18]

Let's take a closer look at what seems to be an incredibly complex (and foreign) idea and try to make some sense out of it. What stood out for me was that there was a marked change in the local universe, "the new creation that was organizing", and this was proceeded by "the disappearance of the spiritual shining" of the super universe Deities. It's as if the new creation is emerging from a purely spiritual realm and into the recognizable physical realm and this coordinates with the recognition of the Creator Son's intention to project life! This recognition also brings about a change in the Creative Spirit, "the breath of life", as she becomes the "local universe Mother Spirit"!

The book describes this event as a "stupendous drama... a momentous transaction... instantaneous, inscrutable, and in comprehensible;" It says that, "the secret of the technique and procedure resides in the bosom of the Paradise Trinity." [19] The remarkable significance of this "transaction" is described in the following passage: "To all practical intents and spiritual purposes, this manifestation of Deity is the divine individual, a spirit person. And she is so recognized and regarded by the Creator Son. It is through this localization and personalization of the Third Source and Center in our local universe that the spirit could subsequently become so fully subject to the Creator Son that of this Son it was truly said, "All power in heaven and on earth has been entrusted to (her)." [20] The book doesn't associate a specific time for this "primary eruption" but when I read that this "spiritual flash" could be seen across the entire super universe, I thought, "this could potentially be the Big Bang." This moment of spirit illumination, in response to a declaration by the Creator Son that he intended to project life into his new universe, could be the moment when the emerging world "lit up" as a physical creation. A huge explosion of light could have occurred that transformed the universe from an emerging potential to an actualized phenomenon wherein the universe became illuminated in time and space! The Higgs field is activated igniting a new space-time field as a divine spark lights up all of creation!

When I shared these speculations with my father, who is also fascinated by this remarkable book, he said something simple, yet profound: "your guess is just as good as anyone else's!" I thought, "You know what, he's got a good point." No one really knows for sure what happened at the beginning of time, right? All we can do is speculate based on whatever knowledge or scientific evidence we have access to. So, from that perspective, my guess is just as good as anyone else's and so is yours! We don't have to be theologians or physicists to develop a picture of creation in our minds that may be just as plausible as any other. This is especially true when we go within and consult with our higher selves or connect with a greater part of the infinite field of consciousness where a much broader perspective is attainable. I firmly believe that is how Moses, Einstein, Plato, Nostradamus, Edgar Cayce, and many others attained their remarkable insights. They had access to a much wider field of consciousness than the average person. They had a "wider band width", if you will, and a very strong signal which allowed them to receive this knowledge directly (just like the gentlemen who channeled the advanced beings offering these teachings in *The Urantia Book.*

I highly encourage you to partake in this contemplative speculation about creation and evolution with me. For it is only in the continued search for truth that we will all find the answers we are seeking. This profound search is a highly valuable pursuit because when the truths of our origin and the mysteries of our evolution are revealed, we progress on our path of divine self-realization and this brings us closer to the Creator. We are, after all, fulfilling his divine purpose by discovering our own!

Let's reflect upon how the theory of seven successive vibrations of matter aligns so perfectly with everything we have learned so far on our adventure. On the first day, we learned about the significance of the number seven in creation. On Day Two, we talked about the seven chakras and corresponding levels of consciousness as well as the seven vibrational frequencies of sound and color. Today we learned about the seven super universes as ascending levels of universal consciousness and now the seven successive vibrations of matter in each dimension. I am astounded as I write this because I am discovering this material in such a way that one teaching builds on the next and it is not something I can take credit for. It hasn't been planned that way. I believe it is the result of spirit guiding these teachings.

I have found that when I am open to spirit and surrender to its will, I can easily follow the energy. For example, I had barely looked at this book about the Dogon people (or even remembered I had it) prior to writing this chapter. One day, as I was taking a shower and thinking about where we would go on this day of our adventure, it just came to me. The voice inside my head literally said, "Check out a book you have in your collection about the Dogon people." Still in my towel, I followed the calling of Spirit downstairs, pulled the book off the shelf and then sat on the stairwell glued to it for over an hour. I knew it would be perfect for today's adventure and it was! I sincerely hope you enjoyed these remarkable myths as much as I did.

Now it's your turn to follow spirit! We have covered a tremendous amount of material today between the gravity-circuits of the Father, Son and Spirit, the Big Bang and inflationary theory, and the intriguing myths of the Dogon people. Once again, the knowledge shared by advanced other-worldly beings converges with the known facts of science! I love it! We owe a debt of gratitude to both sets of advanced minds, in this world and beyond, for the great strides they take to help us unravel the mysteries of the universe. This is how we evolve as a species! Let's take the knowledge we have learned today and think deeply about its significance.

Today's adventure has given us some extraordinary insight into the sacred truth behind the ancient tribal myths of the Dogon people. Just as they were taught by the "star people" of Sirius long, long ago, we in the modern era continue to receive celestial teachings today. The channeled information in *The Urantia Book* and "The Law of One" are two excellent examples. These "inter-dimensional" beings continue to enlighten us with their advanced knowledge and sacred wisdom. As we wrap up today's extraordinary adventure and prepare to go within, I would like to inspire your creative imagination with the following sacred verses transmitted through automatic writing in 1880.

OAHSPE
Chapter III

1. *THUS spake Jehovih; by the light of kosmon proclaimed He these things amongst the nations of the earth.*

2. *Man looked upward in prayer, desiring to know the manner of all created things, both on earth and in heaven. And it Jehovih answered him, saying:*

3. *The whirlwind made I was assigned to man of the manner of my created worlds. As thou beholdest the power of the whirlwind gathering up the dust of the earth and driving it together, know that even so do I bring together the a'ji and ji'ay and nebulae in the firmament of heaven; by the power of the whirlwind create I the corporeal Suns and moons and stars. And I commanded man to name the whirlwinds in the etherean firmament, and he called them vortices and wark; according to their shape called he them.*

4. *By the power of rotation, Swift driving forth in the extreme parts, condense I the atmosphere he and worlds that float in the firmament; and these become My corporeal worlds. In the midst of the vortices made I them, and by the power of the vortices I turn them on their axes and carry them in the orbits I allotted to them. Wider than to the moons of the planet have I created the vortices, and they carry the moons also.*

5. *Around about some of My corporeal worlds have I given nebulous belts and rings, that man might comprehend the rotation of My vortexan worlds.*

6. *For each corporeal world created I a vortex first, and by its rotation and by the places in the*

firmament wither it traveleth, caused I the vortex to conceive the corporeal world.

7. *A great vortex created I for the sun, and, within this vortex and subject to it, made I the vortices of many of the corporeal worlds. The sun vortex I caused to rotate, and I gave it power to carry other vortices within it. According to their density and position are they thus carried forth and around about the sun.*

8. *Think not, O man, that I created the sky a barren waste, and void of use. Even as man in the corporeal form is adapted to the corporeal earth, so is he in spiritual form adapted to My theory and worlds. Three great estates have I bestowed on man: the corporeal, the atmospherean, and the etheran.* [39]

Note: "Oahspe" is the title of a book that was written in 1880 by John Newbrough and is based on the automatic writing he produced while channeling other-worldly knowledge.

Let's take a moment to express our sincere gratitude to all the divine beings, both in the spiritual and physical realms, who shared their profound revelations with us today. Thanks to their tremendous insight and comprehensive research, we can appreciate the many diverse perspectives of the creation story on a much deeper level. Now it's time for us to go within and discover what aspects of this story resonate within the core of our being. As I have said before, we already know the truth, all we must do is look deep inside to uncover these hidden memories. The main purpose of our adventure is to trigger these memories. By exploring many different possibilities and then searching for the truth within ourselves, we will discover the true nature of our origin and gain profound revelations about our ultimate destiny.

As night falls on our campsite, let's watch the last streaks of sunlight blaze across the sky. In the distance, we can see the glowing flames from the campfires the Dogon tribes are gathered around.

3.7

We can envision what types of ritualistic dances or ceremonies they might be performing. Maybe the elders are telling stories about the ancient star people who once landed right here on these very plains to help the inhabitants of Earth progress along their evolutionary path. To help us continue to progress, I have designed a meditation that will allow you to go within and reflect upon the sacred teachings we received today. This meditation called "The Divine Light of the Seventh Ray" will help connect you with spirit as you contemplate eternal truth and infinite beauty! After that, you can journal your own creative thoughts and profound revelations from today's excellent adventure.

The Divine Light of the Seventh Ray
A Guided Meditation
(Audio version available at: www.SuzanneRossTranscendence.com)

Protected by the Angels and embraced by the Golden light, become fully aware of the higher frequency of spirit residing within you as it energizes and illuminates your being. Feel a subtle vibration resonating throughout your body. Imagine a white swirling cloud of light suspended above your crown. The shimmering light enters your being and swirls through your forehead, cheeks and jaw relaxing them and transforming your entire head into bright shimmering light. As the light descends into your neck and shoulders, running down the length of your arms and into your hands, they too relax and shine with bright white light. The light swirls from the top of your chest down into your abdomen, hips and buttocks. Your upper torso shimmers and vibrates. The light now travels down the length of your thighs, into your knees and down to your calves and feet. Your lower body is now illuminated and energized by the light. Take a deep inhalation breathing in the glorious white light and upon exhaling, release any remaining tension or dark energy.

Your being is now fully illuminated and bathed in the white light of love and serenity. You are filled with a deep, inner peace and feel an underlying vibration of pure joy. You are both exuberant and peaceful at the same time. You are one with Great Spirit. Repeat "I am one with Great Spirit." It is flowing into your crown and swirling around your entire being. You feel light and airy as you vibrate at a higher frequency. You feel as if you could elevate and suspend your body within this light of pure spirit that surrounds you. You suddenly feel a strong desire to connect directly with the highest energy in the spirit realm. Before allowing your spirit to ascend, release a cord from the base of your spine that penetrates the ground below you and connects to a point at the center of the earth. As you pull the cord back up from the center of Mother Earth, bring with it all of the energy of the fire, lava, violet crystals and shimmering gold that lies deep within her heart. As the cord penetrates the ground beneath you and travels back up into the base of your spine, it spins your root chakra. This bright red wheel of survival energy spins and throws off any dark debris of fear, anger or resentment. This allows the bright white light from the center to radiate outward and fill the chakra with shimmering red light.

The spiraling energy travels up from the root chakra and into the desire chakra where it forces the wheel to spin at a higher frequency and throw off any lust or greed residing therein. It becomes a bright orange disc illuminated by the light radiating from its sacral center and it spins far and wide. Your being is filled with a strong desire to lift the hearts and minds of your brothers and sisters. You are filled with a desire to help alleviate suffering and bring happiness to all. As the energy from that chakra ascends upon the electric blue serpentine braiding your spine, it penetrates the bright yellow chakra of your solar plexus. Residual energies of control and dominance are thrown off as the disc spins faster and grows wider. The radiant light of the Infinite Spirit transforms this disc into a shimmering golden wheel of empowerment. Illuminated by the Infinite Spirit, you have the power to make a positive change in the world. You have the power to enlighten others with a message of hope, love and faith. You are empowered by a strong desire to serve.

As the energy ascends toward the fluorescent green chakra of pure love at your heart, your entire vertebrae comes alive with a violet light of the highest frequency. Imagine your entire being erupting in violet flames and say out loud: I am the violet flame, I am the violet flame, I am the violet flame. Become aware of the presence of Ascended Master St. Germain who teaches about the power within this flame. Embraced by this violet light, your attention goes back to the love chakra which spins around your spine directly behind your heart center. Any feelings of hatred, anger or resentment are discarded as this fluorescent green wheel glows brightly and spreads far and wide with the essence of the pure unconditional love. Repeat "I love all beings without exception."

Filled with the loving spirit of the Eternal Child, imagine the light emerging from your heart center and traveling to the base of your throat. Here is the center of compassion, or passion for communion, where unity and communication come together to form the essence of community. Filled with a strong desire to reach out, you know you have the power of unconditional love and the communication skills to express it. Spin your throat chakra and release any fear or anxiety associated with communicating or reaching out to the world around you. In doing so, this pale blue chakra becomes illuminated with sparkling light and it expands into the far reaches of the world around you opening the channels of communication between humanity on earth and divinity in heaven.

Now you are seeking the wisdom to enrich the knowledge and ignite the intelligence we all have access to when we vibrate at the highest frequency and send out a clear intention to receive. Send out an intention to receive sacred truth and universal wisdom so that you can share it with others for the benefit of all. As this indigo blue light fills your entire head, imagine the right and left hemispheres of your brain becoming illuminated with sparks of pure energy. Indigo blue sparks flash in your mind and the third eye at the center of your forehead opens and looks back at you.

You can clearly see this indigo blue eye with a bright white pupil looking back toward the base of your skull where it sees your pineal gland. Your awareness causes this pinecone of light to explode with white light and a halo forms around your head. This is the sacred point where you absorb the divine consciousness of the One Infinite Creator. The thoughts of the divine Creator become yours and you are inspired to embrace the essence of your highest self and express the highest virtues in every thought, word and action. This is the access point for direct communication with the Creator and as you absorb his light, you also respond with pure gratitude and infinite love.

Now you are drawn into the seventh light — the highest chakra at the crown of your head where you worship and express faith in the One Infinite Creator, the Eternal Child and Infinite Spirit. This divine trinity is fully expressed in the seventh Universe as the seventh light of creation. Repeat: "I honor the divine and creative trinity. I honor the Divine Father expressed in the Creator Son of our local universe. I honor the Divine Mother expressed in the Creative Daughter of our universe and I honor Mother Earth for we are her children. We are the children of the Sun. We are the children of the Stars. These deities, Angels and light spirits love us dearly. They love us more than we can possibly imagine, and we embrace this love for we are bathed in it for all of eternity.

As you honor these beings, honor yourself always as one of them. Spin the violet chakra of divine consciousness at the crown of your head far and wide into the infinite realms and celestial heavens. Spinning this violet chakra opens the portal through which pure consciousness can flow in and out of your being. It flows from the point at the center of Mother Earth to the point at the center of Paradise where the trinity resides. From Paradise, they radiate the brilliant white light of pure love into the vast realms of infinity to illuminate the eternal creation of all divine beings.

Surrender to the will of the One Infinite Creator. Repeat "I am the love of the Creator. I am the image of the Eternal Child. I am the light of the Infinite Spirit. I am the seventh light! I am love. I am truth. I am beauty. I am divine and I am blessed."

Now bring your palms together at your chest where they connect with your heart center. Nod your head and honor the God and Goddess within you and all living beings. Say out loud: Namaste. As you look up, open your eyes and bring your awareness back to your spiritual being in the physical realm knowing that the power of your radiant spirit has been ignited so that your light shines far and wide. Make a strong determination to spread universal love and wisdom everywhere you go just by the kindness, compassion and joy you express in subtle yet powerful ways. Spread compassion, spread joy, radiate love and express beauty and truth in every thought, word and action. And always remember, you are the sacred seventh light expressing divine love in creation. This light of love is within you and all around you always. Amen.

Your Personal Revelations

_____

_____

_____

_____

_____

_____

_____

References

Illustrations:

Chapter cover image of golden star courtesy of: http://www.treeleavesoracle.org
1. Image courtesy of: http://www.paradiseintheworld.com
2. Image courtesy of: http://www.otherworldmystery.com
3. Image courtesy of: http://www.pixabay.com
4. Image courtesy of: http://www.paradiseintheworld.com
5. Image courtesy of: http://www.moxon.net
6. Image courtesy of: http://www.mobes.info
7. Image courtesy of: http://www.paradiseintheworld.com

Text:

Ralph Waldo Trine, *The Supreme Fact of the Universe and Human Life,* Kessinger Publishing
1. Joseph Selbie and David Steinmetz, *The Yugas*, Crystal Clarity Publishers, 2010
2. p. 129
The Urantia Book Fellowship, *The Urantia Book,* Uversa Press, 2008
3. (57:1.3)
4. (15:14.1-3)
5. (15:2.10-11)
6. (57:1.6)
7. (57:2.1)
8. (57:3.4-5)
9. (57:3.6)
10. (57:4.2)
11. (57:4.3)
12. (57:4.8)
13. (57:3.8)
14. (37:0.1)
15. (32: 1.5)
16. (57:3.8)
17. (57:5.7)
18. (34:1.1)
19. (34:1.3)
20. (34:1.4)
Bill Bryson, *A Short History of Nearly Everything*, Anchor Canada, a division of Random House of Canada Limited, 2003
21. page 9-10
22. page 14-15
23. page 38
31. page15
32. page 16
33. page 15
34. page 16-17
Stephen W. Hawking, *A Brief History of Time,* Bantam Books, 1988
24. page 115-6
25. page117
26. page 117
27. page 117-8
28. page 119-20
29. page 119-2
30. page 120

Laird Scranton, *Sacred Symbols of the Dogon,* Inner Traditions, 2007
35. page 31
36. page 33
37. page 34
38. page 34-5
39. Oahspe — DVD-ROM: *The Internet Sacred Text Archive,* Evinity Publishing, 2011

Day Four

Communion

GOOD MORNING! Are you ready to venture out into another day of mind-blowing revelations about the true nature of reality? Today we will breathe in the fresh mountain air and spiritual essence of Lake Tahoe in Northern California. Nestled in the pine trees just outside of this bustling town is the smaller and much quieter community of Truckee. The very first time I camped here, I instantly knew it was a magical place and told my husband we would buy a summer home here someday. The perfect home base for our adventure will be in a little campground simply called

Lakeside. Here we will set up camp right along the edge of the reservoir which is a smaller version of the lake in Tahoe but still just as beautiful. It is also surrounded by majestic pine-covered mountains but much more peaceful and serene. From this spot, we can hike up into the mountains and appreciate breath-taking vistas amidst the sweet-smelling pines. We can picnic alongside the streams and listen to the water tumbling over the rocks. We can search for the source of the fresh spring water and see if we can find a waterfall plunging from the mountain's peak. It promises to be a glorious day, so let's close our eyes and project our consciousness into this vast wilderness.

Gathered at our campsite alongside the reservoir, let's sit and prepare for today's journey by opening our mind and expanding our consciousness. This will help us get into the right mindset, so we can absorb the wonders of the day with a greater appreciation for their divine significance. I would like to start by sharing the following revelation. It helped shed some light on a theory I had been playing with ever since I returned from my own magical trip to Lake Tahoe last summer. As our adventure unfolds, I will share the remarkable insights I received while hiking in this mountain paradise. I always carry my phone so that I can record my experiences and I suggest you do the same. You might be surprised at how often you touch divine truth and beauty throughout your everyday experience of life.

Exaltation

On a particularly beautiful morning last summer, the sun was coming up in a blaze of glory as I hiked along the edge of the lake. Basking in the brilliant orange glow, I found myself pondering the source of the purple and fuchsia streaks painted across the horizon when suddenly I had an epiphany. These moments of clarity come to me when I'm pondering some aspect of reality and suddenly, I just get it. Often, I have placed another piece into the puzzle or made a connection between different perspectives — say, a discovery in quantum physics suddenly synchronizes with an inscription on an ancient text. So, I'm hiking and thinking when my disjointed thoughts suddenly come into focus and I say into my recorder:

"One aspect of our eternal soul is having a 3D finite experience within time and space limitations. Other aspects of our personality are focused in other dimensions throughout time and space. Our higher-self, or whole soul projects and oversees all aspects of our space-time experiences from the star we call home. Our destiny and origin, however, our true home, lies in Paradise — the time and space transcendent realm of infinity."

Later, when I listen to it, I nod my head and think, "Ya, that's it." As usual, these thoughts often lead to more questions than answers but that defines this eternal journey of self-realization — baffling questions lead to elusive answers which just lead to more questions...It's a never-ending exploration of our "self." Fortunately, we have all of eternity to figure it out!

Let's explore this concept of a star-residence — a sort of home-base for our whole-soul. What if stars are forms of crystallized consciousness that the trinity projects "source-consciousness" into? These stars are like brilliant sparks of awareness, each a different point from which to view the space-time experience. The Eternal Children are a projection of the Divine Mother-Father God who emerged from the Mother Womb of Creation to achieve self-realization through experience. We, as the created beings, then, reflect the light of the Father, the love of the Mother and the spirit of the Child. Upon emergence, we are enlightened by the mind of the Spirit! From this perspective, we are truly an expansion of the trinity-consciousness and each of their divine aspects are united in the depth of our being — our whole-soul — which resides in a star. What if a star is born when the trinity intentionally projects a pattern of light into a specific point in space where it then becomes frozen as a way of "storing" that unique pattern? Crystals are simply frozen light and at the core of every star there lies a perfect crystal which may contain the essence of the consciousness that was projected into it!

When a universe is born, the stars which contain the crystallized consciousness begin to emerge. As they evolve, some explode into space fulfilling their mandate to create new worlds. Others become suns destined to attract and illuminate a whole new family of planets. Mature stars may become white dwarfs after they go supernova and remain in the sky as guardians — wise beings or old souls — enlightening us for many billions of years. We know stars are born in the stellar nurseries called nebulae which spin and swirl inside galaxies. We can imagine then that each star has a creative consciousness which is projected onto the realms of time and space. Crystals are made of silicon and both our bodies and the body of Mother Earth are covered with this reflective element. We are crystal beings of frozen light living on a crystal ball surrounded by crystalline structures called stars! These are all forms of crystallized consciousness! It's all a play of light — a sort of "light-refraction" which creates a multi-dimensional reality. Vibrating at different frequencies, this light is projected here and there across time, space and beyond!

When this light is frozen, it creates a crystalline structure. This helps to explain the reflective nature of our holographic experience of life. Just like the light inside the disco ball is the source of the holographic images it displays in 360 degrees, the light from our home star may be the source of our holographic experience here on Earth. The light, or crystallized consciousness, from within displays the holographic images that define our space-time experience in 360 degrees!

I believe the whole essence of our soul is contained within the unique pattern of our home star. From this star, various aspects of our soul are projected into the many dimensions of time and space. International best-selling author, Barbara Hand Clow, teaches us about the multi-dimensional realms of time, space and beyond in her phenomenal book, "Alchemy of Nine Dimensions." She actually has a model for these dimensions which shows the progression of these dimensions from 1D to 10D. In the introduction, she offers an illustration called "The progressive structure of the vertical axis of consciousness." Here are the dimensions as she describes them in her book:

1D — Iron Core Crystal of Earth

2D — Telluric Realm/Deep Hot Biosphere: Elementals

3D — Linear Space & Time Humanity

4D — Collective Mind: Annunaki

5D — Love and Creativity: Pleiades

6D — Morphic Fields/Sacred Geometry: Sirius

7D — Galactic Informational Highways of Light: Andromeda Galaxy

8D — Cosmic Order/Galactic Federation: Orion

9D — Milky Way Galactic Center: Tzolk'in

10D — Andromeda Galaxy

Her entire book is chock full of fascinating insights about these multiple dimensions and a must-read! She has also published 12 other phenomenal books that are equally as intriguing and insightful. What I found most interesting about this "vertical axis of consciousness" in her book "Alchemy of Nine Dimensions" is how consciousness is first projected into the iron core crystal of Mother Earth and then moves up into the next dimension to become the elementals that are the foundation for our earthly bodies. Our bodies are actually made up of these earth elements that we know are sourced from supernova stardust! Of course our physical bodies are infused with our own unique spiritual essence and DNA coding. 4D becomes the collective mind where our consciousness is projected into the astral realm and our feelings and emotions are reflected back as mythological beings and light and dark entities. In 5D, consciousness is seated within the love and light of our Pleiadan star family and lovingly projected into our realm. 6D consciousness is seated in Sirius and as we know from yesterday's adventure, the Dogon's claim to have received their cosmology from their ancestors in Sirius. These are the wisdom keepers. 7D consciousness travels along the Galactic Informational Highways of Light and is directed by the Anromedans. In 8D, consciousness is elevated to Orion where the Galactic Federation reigns and Cosmic Order is adjudicated and balanced. The 9th dimension is where consciousness is centered in the Milky Way Galaxy. This is the center of consciousness that embraces and defines our entire galaxy! In 10D, consciousness is projected beyond our galaxy as it is drawn through the supermassive black hole at the center of the Milky Way and projected into the next galaxy — the Andromeda Galaxy! WOW! Just yesterday, we were discussing how consciousness is projected through the singularity to birth a new realm and drawn back through the black hole to expand into a new one! Brilliant. Watch my fascinating interview with bestselling author, Barbara Hand Clow at SciSpi.tv/Rise-Up/, to witness first-hand her extraordinary revelations about the multiple dimensions of time and space realities.

Just like consciousness progresses through multiple dimensions, our whole soul projecting from our home star is constantly creating and evolving. The light of the trinity, or source-consciousness, is perpetually shining upon all dimensions throughout time, space and beyond. This light is guiding us as we create an ever-evolving experience defined by our own unique pattern of consciousness. The stars are a vehicle through which the light of the source can shine upon the souls and spirits of all living beings in its ever-expanding journey of self-realization. If we are to reach a state of enlightened self-realization, then we must align with our star by harmonizing with our higher self or "whole-soul." Once we do, then we will also be united with the source of its light — the divine Trinity in eternity sourced from the Mother Womb in infinity.

I had a dream once in which a voice kept repeating over and over: "The key to reunification with the source is to reverse the trinity." When I awoke and reflected on the dream, it became clear that the ascension path starts by connecting with our own higher self. Once we do this, we can connect to the light of the omnipresent spirit. Feeling at one with the Infinite spirit all around us, we then begin to sense a deeper connection with the Eternal Child (created in our own image. Finally, we reach the point where communication with the Universal Father, the Creator, connects us with our divine Masculine source and ultimately, we connect directly with the Divine Mother, Sophia, who embraces us in her womb and reassures us that we are one. As a reflection of the One Infinite Source, we are compelled to seek answers about the true nature of our being and we start to grasp the concept that you and I and the divine Mother-Father are on this journey of "self-realization" together.

This brings us to the recognition that we are in "communion" with the Divine Mother and the Divine Father. We, as the Divine Sons and Daughters, are the creative expression of their divine feminine and masculine source-consciousness. When I was able to fully comprehend this revelation, a feeling overwhelmed me that was so powerful I couldn't even think of words to describe it. Then the word "exaltation" popped into my mind, so I looked it up and discovered the profound meaning of this powerful word: "a state or feeling of intense, often excessive, exhilaration or well-being." Another definition says, "a state of being carried away by overwhelming emotion" and then Charles Dickens is quoted: "Listening to sweet music in a perfect rapture." That explains so beautifully how I felt when the true essence of being "in communion with the divine" washed over me and settled in my heart space — rapture, bliss, elation, exhilaration... all of it at once and I have never felt alone again. Inspirational revelations like this fuel my desire to know more and more about this tremendously exciting journey of self-realization that we have embarked upon. What an incredibly vast and extraordinarily imaginative "consciousness experience" we are engaged in! It is a true exploration of infinite possibilities within an endless sea of emerging potential just waiting to be realized!

With this inspiration, let's start today's adventure by taking a short hike down to the edge of the reservoir. Just like crystals are frozen light, water is liquid light and it adds to the reflective experience! Therefore, it is a perfect place to sit on the shore while we engage in the practice of reflective inquiry. This means that we will pose questions to some of the bigger mysteries, reflect upon what we have learned so far and examine what becomes clear in the process. The Dalai Lama talks about reading and researching to a point where you then just set aside the material and reflect upon it. We're going to take his advice and do just that! Be sure to bring your journals (and your creative imagination) for this promises to be an exhilarating experience. If you make an effort to free your mind, liberate your spirit and expand your consciousness, your own personal revelations will emerge!

To begin our reflective inquiry, I will tell you about a movie I recently saw depicting the life of Buddha. As you can clearly see from our adventure thus far, I am extremely intrigued by ancient philosophy. My fascination with Buddhism influenced my ever-expanding spiritual quest and ignited my interest in ancient civilizations. I tried to imagine the kingdom that Prince Siddhartha, who later became the Buddha, must have lived in. Thanks to the movie "Little Buddha", starring Keanu Reeves, I was able to experience an incredibly inspired depiction of the life of Prince Siddhartha. The movie itself was an enlightened expression of creative potential. It illuminated the experiences that led from suffering to seeking to realization with powerful emotion and profound imagery. Ultimately, the Buddha is bathed in the light of communion as he merges with the source of pure consciousness. Reunited with the source, he experiences the full realization of enlightenment. His journey is wrought with human suffering and temptation, doubt and frustration (just like ours) but he never gives up. Something inside of him knows that if he is persistent in his search and dogged in his determination, his faith will prevail, and he will transcend the suffering. In order to release his attachments, he has to face his "maras" one by one.

These "maras" are the sensual desires and earthly emotions that keep him attached to the physical realm. As he releases his attachments to the material world, he becomes more and more connected to the spiritual realm. He gradually moves out of the darkness of human suffering (marked by birth, aging, illness and death) and into the light of spiritual bliss. The most inspirational aspect of the life of Buddha is his selfless determination to alleviate human suffering. Upon discovering the suffering in the streets, he leaves the illustrious kingdom and sets out on a treacherous journey. First, he becomes an ascetic completely deprived of, not just the sensual pleasures, but also of food and water. Thin and frail, he finds that he doesn't have the mental or physical strength to reach enlightenment in this way. He continues and encounters many temptations along the way. Finally, he settles in under the boddhi tree and faces each of his maras one by one until he becomes completely "untangled" from all his attachments (or entanglements). No longer distracted by his senses, he can transcend the material world and ascend into the higher realms. What he discovered is the potential to experience the inner peace and pure bliss of the spiritual realm while still living in the physical one. This is the realization that he wanted to share with everyone. He wanted to teach them how to get in touch with their higher consciousness and then to live from that place in the physical realm. Many people who touch the light of spiritual bliss are naturally compelled to share the experience with others so that they too can live a more peaceful and joyful life here on planet earth.

Our desire to share the bliss is a beautiful representation of the power of love we inherently have for one another. It is a natural extension of the exaltation of "communion" and clearly exemplifies our unity consciousness. We want to comm-uni-cate and share our love and joy with the comm-unity around us! So that will be the focus of our discussion today — unity-consciousness in the spirit of communion! So, let's spread out our blanket and sit by the rolling waters. We can draw from the life-force, or prana, in the stream while we are illuminated by the source-light of the sun! Inspirational environments like these are highly conducive to connecting with divine consciousness.

Let's start by doing some simple breathing exercises. Just sit comfortably and let the air flow through you as you breathe in and out of your nostrils. Sometimes it helps to count to 7 as you inhale and then 7 as you exhale until your mind feels focused and then you can breathe naturally. Now let's pull the energy up from the earth by imagining a green cord of spiraling energy exiting the base of our spine and traveling through the earth, the gold-flecked rock and the violet crystal caves. The cord descends into the hot orange lava and then into the raging fire. As it reaches the core of the Mother Earth, it connects to her crystal heart at the very center. As you pull the cord back up through the earth, imagine that it is bringing back all the energy from her spirit as it travels back up through the fire, lava, crystals and gold it passes along the way. Once it returns to the base of your spine, the energy spins your base chakra, the red survival center. At this point, the cord becomes electric blue and splits into two intertwining cords which braid your spine on the way to the second chakra, your orange desire center behind your sexual organs, spinning it clockwise. Picture the intertwining blue cords traveling toward your third chakra now which is the yellow power center behind your navel. The energy from the dual-serpents spin this chakra and as it expands, a strong sense of empowerment arises from the very core of your being. As you spin these chakras, try to experience the true nature of the energies they represent from desire to power to love! The blue cords that braid your spine represent the dual life-force that surges through you, me and every living thing.

It is the dual Mother/Father energy of the source — one cord ascending from Mother Earth and the other descending from the heavens as the Universal Father! As the cords reach your fourth emerald green chakra of unconditional love, imagine the feeling of love filling your entire chest and illuminating your heart like a vibrant emerald jewel. Think about the pure feeling of unconditional love for all living beings. Now feel the electric blue energy of the spiraling cords fill the space between your shoulder blades as it approaches the base of your throat where it will spin the sky-blue center of communion, or communication, with all that is. This is a bright chakra that sparkles with flashes of connectivity to both inner and outer communion with spirit. Now feel the back of your neck and head light up as the blue serpents of complementary forces become unified as one powerful cord of electric blue energy. With all the energy from the other centers united as one now, a powerful force of unity-consciousness explodes into the swirling indigo wheel of wisdom. This chakra is located in the center of your head directly behind the space between your brows and as it spins, you suddenly feel enlightened by the depth of your own inner wisdom.

Imagine the third eye at the center of your forehead looking back toward this spinning chakra. At the center of your skull between the right and left hemispheres of your brain, picture a brightly illuminated pinecone splaying golden light in 360 degrees around your entire head like a halo. This is your pineal gland and the source of its light is the direct in-streaming of consciousness from the divine source of knowledge — the cosmic consciousness of the Great Self! Now you have greatly increased your access to the entire field of consciousness and significantly increased your band width. You have a 6G connection! At this point, you are ready to connect with the highest source of knowledge — the primal consciousness itself — the source of the source! This 7G connection will bring you the most profound downloads of pure wisdom. Imagine the electric blue cord, now containing the combined energy of all the other centers, emerging from your wisdom chakra and ascending into a point at the center of your crown.

With a brilliant flash of white light, the core of the most sacred chakra is ignited, and this violet wheel of pure consciousness begins to vibrate. As the light spreads throughout the vast span of this divine wheel, it begins to spin wildly. A brilliant column of light explodes from the core and ascends with a powerful force into the infinite realms beyond time and space connecting to the very source of pure consciousness at the Paradise core of creation. A peaceful feeling of pure bliss consumes you and your entire being is brightly illuminated by a golden light. You feel an exhilarating vibration of energy wash over you and a calm, yet exuberant, feeling of pure joy emerges as a soft smile forms on your lips. You are connected to the omnipotent source of divine consciousness and at one with the omnipresent spirit of divine love.

Now that you have a powerful flow of energy keeping you connected to the earth consciousness of the planet and the source consciousness of the cosmos, you are PLUGGED IN! This is the optimal state of receptivity for the deeper answers we are seeking. As I lead this search with my personal insights, try and stay connected to the divine source so you can explore the possibilities from within your own heart and mind. It's not unlikely that your perspective will differ from mine and that's what I encourage — your own unique point of view. We are all vibrating at different frequencies and have access to different sources of information. Also, our life experiences inform our perceptions as well.

Just keep your mind open to new possibilities and try to prevent preconceived ideas or ego-skepticism from standing in the way of your progress (like I have regretted doing many times before!). Try to stay as clear as possible letting everything in first and then gradually you can filter out what doesn't resonate or ring true for you.

Let's continue to pursue our own self-realization with a strong desire and persistent determination, just like the enlightened Buddha, peeling back the layers of the collective human experience. As we sit by the stream, I encourage you to engage in "reflective inquiry" by truly experiencing the thoughts, emotions and images within the following reflections. During these reflections, try and stay focused on the awareness that each of our experiences, yours and mine, are an integral part of the collective experience and therefore, very meaningful within the divine plan. From this perspective, even though I am sharing my own personal thoughts and experiences, they essentially become yours too. My experiences are an essential part of both the human and divine "self-realization" just like yours are. What we come to realize is that we are both human and divine and we all have an inherent underlying awareness of this collective "oneness." As our connection with each other and with the divine source is experienced deep within our souls, we begin to grasp our oneness with the whole of creation! We sense an underlying spirit that transcends the physical creation. We begin to see beyond the form and sense the omnipresence of the Infinite Spirit. We feel the depth of love within the Divine Mother womb that embraces us all. We rejoice in this revelation because it helps us realize we are never alone on our spiritual quest. Realizing our unity with all of creation makes us realize that we are also an integral part of the universal or "cosmic" consciousness and therefore, intricately connected to it as well. This became clear in Barbara Hand Clow's description of our galactic families in higher dimensions.

In Shirley MacLaine's book, "Out on a Limb", she shares the following profound message about the importance of each human soul. This message was relayed to her friend, David, by an inter-dimensional being that he encountered in Peru, who called herself "Mayan." It encompasses the essence of 'cosmic consciousness' beautifully:

"...in all the cosmos, nothing is valued more than the individual, nothing was valued as highly as one living soul, and in the value of one living soul lay the value of the entire cosmos...humankind follows a spiral projection upward, that although it may appear we are not progressing, that is in fact, not true. With each rebirth and afterlife reflection, humankind finds itself on a higher plane, whether we realize it or not...with each individual's soul progression, the machinery of the movement of the entire cosmos is affected because each individual soul is that important!...Man has a habit of reducing his understanding to the perception of his own mind, that it is difficult for us to break through our own frames of reference and allow our imagination to take quantum leaps into other dimensions, transcending the limits imposed on us by lifetimes of structured thinking." [1]

Shirley MacLaine herself had many profound revelations while visiting Peru which she shares in her book. These revelations came from her direct experiences with truth during both meditative and waking states of pure enlightenment when her connection to spirit was heightened. Here is an example of the messages she was receiving from the spirit of truth:

"Nothing is as powerful as the collective human mind — that infinitely elastic web of strength called human consciousness and represented by communal energy people refer to as their souls... maybe one human soul is everything." [2]

Shirley's friend, David, shares one final message from Mayan that inspired the title of her book:

"Mayan always says, "Love God, love your neighbor, love yourself, and love God's work, for you are part of that work. Remember that. And something else. She told me not to forget to tell you one thing. She said that in order to get to the fruit of the tree you have to go out on a limb." [3]

That's what we're doing, going "out on a limb", so that we can "get to the fruit of the tree" which brings to mind a verse from the Aramaic version of the "Lord's Prayer":

"O cosmic brother, all radiance and vibration...
fill me with your creativity so that I may bear the fruit of your mission...
let each of my actions bear fruit in accordance with my desires." [4]

What is the fruit? From my perception, it is the divine truth of the soul's potential and the mission is the soul's progression toward the complete understanding of that truth. To know and express the truth in every thought, word and action allows us to "bear fruit in accordance with our desires." In the bible, it says, "The truth will set you free." I like the sound of that — liberation through truth, that's what we are seeking!

There are moments when I feel deeply connected to the divine truth and it is always when I am fully aware of the 'eternal presence' of the moment. At these precious times, I know that I am touching the truth and experiencing the omnipresence of the Infinite Spirit. This is possible for each one of us at any time so let's take a moment to just appreciate the full essence of the moment. Breathe in every smell, take in every sight and feel the objects around you. Make a practice of doing this regularly just by saying "Moment!" and then becoming fully present. Just imagining the true essence of the moment reinforces the profundity of it and you will experience an overwhelming sense of the deeper meaning within it. This knowing also reveals the awareness that the divine spirit is within you and seeing this reality through your eyes. If you are with someone else, you can imagine that their eyes are a reflection the divine spirit as well! Try to imagine this divine presence within others and the omnipresence of the cosmic consciousness in everything. This is a sure way to touch divinity at any time and in any place. This is especially effective out in nature when you are in the presence of the pure, unaltered creation. Just admiring the perfection of a flower or a bird is an excellent way of experiencing divine truth and beauty and it helps you become completely absorbed in the essence of the moment. Realizing that you too are an artistic expression of this divine perfection. This will give you a sense of oneness with all of the beautiful things in nature — every flower, bird, animal and tree. I have experienced a deep sense of this "unity with spirit" on a few occasions which stood out as being particularly profound. As I share the following one, please try to experience it with me by deeply connecting to the sights and sounds as well as the feelings and emotions.

One glorious day last summer, while engaging in a walking meditation, I was admiring the snowy white egrets perched upon the rocks along the stream. I call them "angel birds" and I like to try and communicate with them. I stand perfectly still and softly tell them how lovely they are while intentionally sending them love. When they turn their head and look directly at me, I know in that moment I have made an energetic connection. Once I establish this bond, they will follow my dogs and I along the trail, appearing and reappearing for the rest of the walk no matter how far along the stream we go. On one very special occasion, I became acutely aware of the potent energy of these precious connections. I had just broken into a run when suddenly I realized that the egret soaring just above the stream, my dog running along the embankment and I, running on the path, were perfectly synchronized. Our spirits were in perfect harmony as our energies aligned. The 'synergy' was incredible and as the magic of this moment hit me, I became so overwhelmed with joy, tears ran down my face and I smiled from ear to ear. I was truly grateful for this precious opportunity to feel so alive! I knew I had been divinely blessed by this "communion with spirit." I was also grateful for my expanded awareness which enabled me to fully appreciate the harmony and grace of this magical moment.

Another one of these "communions with spirit" happened right here in Truckee! This magical experience kicked off a series of profound revelations I would continue to have over the course of my trip. As we hike toward the meadow where it happened, I will tell you about the miracle I was blessed with and how it inspired the rest of my journey. It all started when my husband and I were off-roading through the woods and we spotted a beautiful meadow. The sun seemed particularly brilliant over this spot and it was making the whole meadow look fluorescent green. He stopped without even being prompted because he knows I love meadows and would want to jump out and run through it. He's fully aware of my ecstatic connection with nature by now. There was a large rock right in the middle of the meadow and I felt compelled to run toward to it. When I got there, I stood on top of it, closed my eyes and inhaled the pure air.

4.2

With my arms outstretched toward the sun, I felt incredibly alive. Suddenly, I became aware of a presence, so I opened my eyes and discovered that a beautiful monarch butterfly was fluttering all around me as if to say, "Hi there! Welcome to my meadow." I very slowly extended my finger toward the lovely little work of art and was breathless when it accepted my offering and landed right in my hand! I knew this was a precious moment and a special recognition from Spirit. In that moment, I heard a message: "Thank you for recognizing the beauty of my creation and this gift is an expression of my gratitude."

I love to go to this magnificent spot just outside of Tahoe because it is so very peaceful. There are vast expanses of untouched wilderness to explore. I will take off on foot with my dogs in tow and hike for hours. It is during these times when I have my most profound epiphanies. I decided there must be a source of energy in Lake Tahoe that is especially conducive to connecting with spirit. Later I read in one of Drunvalo Melchizedek's books, "The Ancient Secret of the Flower of Life":

"In conjunction with the sacred sites, the creators also used mountains because of their vortex energy...the spiral (of kundalini energy) leaves the coast of California, it passes through Lake Tahoe, Donner Lake and Pyramid Lake." [5]

There is no doubt in my mind, this vortex of energy is still spiraling through these mountains and swirling through these streams! As I was hiking along the stream and contemplating the prana, or life-force, that kept the water rushing over the rocks with such exuberance, it occurred to me that it was inspired by the force of gravity (which you already know I believe is a pure expression of love!). I realized that Mother Earth was drawing the water closer to her heart by pulling it down from the mountains and bringing it to the lowest point where it could rest — peacefully united with the lake or ocean from which it was drawn.

4.3

Just like the water in the stream, our souls are gravitationally attracted to the heart of the divine Mother source. While incarnated on the planet, we are attracted to Mother Earth, but when we leave the physical body, our souls are attracted to the divine source. Then I started to think about the heavens from which our souls emerged and the ultimate reality at the Paradise core of creation. This reminded me again of the illusion we are in. I began to ponder how our illusion of reality is merely a reflection of the only true reality that exists in what *The Urantia Book* calls "Havona." In this place, time and space are transcended and every magical moment is eternally present all at once. That's why, when we are acutely aware of the fullness of any moment, embracing the "eternal present", we feel in awe of it and know that we are touching divinity or experiencing Heaven on Earth! Aha, now I felt like I was going somewhere with this line of thinking, but something was still gnawing at me — HOW? How was the true reality on Havona projected (or reflected) to create the time and space illusion on Earth?

As I walked and pondered, I noticed that the sun was setting, and my husband would be getting worried about me, so I set aside that thought for the time being and headed back. He was relieved to see me and gestured for me to lie down in the lounge chair next to him, so we could enjoy the magnificent sunset together. We just sat there deeply contented with the silent beauty of this time and place. The feeling of love, trust and faith are strong at these times and there is no need for senseless chatter. We are unified within the field of pure love and the comfortable silence speaks volumes about the inner peace we feel when we are together.

Normally we can see very few stars in the sky back at home, only the brightest ones. But here, the sky is a vast sea of sparkling lights. It reminded me of a crowded city where each individual is a spark of light. Thinking of stars as people made me giggle at the silliness of my thoughts. As I sat there enamored by the stars, I thought about the Platonic solids and the four elements of fire, air, water and earth. They were all forged within the stars and since the Platonic solids are crystals or "crystallized forms of consciousness", I began to wonder if that's what the star is reflecting — pure consciousness. Maybe the star itself is a complex crystal and since crystals have a 360-degree reflective property... Suddenly I realized, "That's how it is done!!! The stars are crystals and they are simply reflecting the consciousness which is projected into them from the source! Then, succinctly, they project that consciousness into creation and it becomes a reflection of the original source."

I began to imagine that the Paradise core of creation itself was a magnificent crystal from within which the trinity consciousness could project the first perfect universe of Havona. Like a light inside a crystal ball projects holographic images all around it in 360 degrees, the trinity projected their colorful consciousness in this way. As the trinity used this reflective technique to move beyond the fetters of infinity and expand their consciousness into the eternal realm, they began to realize their unlimited potential to create more and more complex images within the prism of light. Inspired by this realization, they exploded with creativity and the vast beauty of Havona became a magnificent work of art.

According to *The Urantia Book*, Havona, the central universe, is the only perfect and settled universe that transcends time and space. All future universes in dimensional space-time are merely a reflection of this first perfect model. This is where the stars come in! They are used as a mechanism through which the universal source of consciousness — the Paradise trinity and eternal souls in Havona — can be projected onto the worlds of time and space and into the beings who inhabit them! These worlds become a playground where the universal spirit can have a so-called "physical" experience and both the individual and collective souls can grow and progress!

These concepts prompted me to reflect upon the following visual offered in *The RA Material* which depicts source-consciousness expanding into Paradise and illuminating Havona. This perfect universe becomes the one true reality and these images are projected into time and space to create the 7 holographic universes that make up the grand universe. As these images of universal perfection get further from the source, they become distorted and create imperfect worlds. The source projects its consciousness onto these worlds and manifests itself as star-souls. These perfect souls become points of light above the worlds of time and space.

In *The RA Material*, Group Ra describes this streaming consciousness as love/light and the illusion of planets and individuals as fields of electromagnetic energy:

"RA: I am Ra. Picture, if you will, the One Infinite. You have no picture. Thus, the process begins. Love creating light, becoming love/light, streams into the planetary sphere according to the electromagnetic web of points (or nexi of entrance). These (love/light streams) are then available to the individual who, like the planet, is a web of electromagnetic energy fields with points or nexi of entrance." [6]

As I thought about individual souls, I began to think that maybe that's why there were so many stars crowded in the night sky. Each one represents an aspect, or point of view, a "nexi of entrance", as an individual soul within the collective soul. From every point in time and space, Spirit has a unique point of view represented by an individual star or soul and this light shines through the star or eyes of each one! It's like each star is a spark of awareness within the omnipresent light of the source. As I stared into the night sky and pondered these possibilities, I became aware of a profound oneness with the cosmos. I felt deeply connected to the source and I knew the illusion of reality that I was experiencing was simply a projection of the greater truth from beyond. I became aware that even the stars were holographic projections of light. I realized that all things and beings in time and space were holograms vibrating within the prism of projected light. It's all spirit just vibrating with the energy of pure love! All beings are united by this spirit. They are this spirit and all is one within it. There is total oneness within the womb of the Divine Mother!

After dinner that night, we settled into our comfortable R.V. to watch a movie together on our big screen T.V. I know, really "roughin' it"! As much as I connect with nature, I'm still not ready to sleep outside with the critters. I must admit that I enjoy ending our day of outdoor activity in the nice, cool indoors with all of our creature comforts. So be it. As I shuffled through our collection of DVD's, I came across one called, "Stardust", and I thought, "How appropriate!" I hadn't recalled ever seeing it before and asked my husband if this one would be O.K. He had apparently seen it and replied, "Oh ya, you'll love that one!" He was right. It was an inspired movie and I was shocked by the parallels with my earlier revelations! A shooting star turns out to be a beautiful girl who looks like an angel (and glows like one too- but only in the presence of love!) I was amazed by the divine synchronicity and knew I was being guided every step of the way. That night, my dreams were filled with people ascending and descending between their home in the stars and their lives here on earth.

Back to our adventure —

Up ahead in the distance, there appears to be a clearing and like all meadows, the sun seems to be shining a spotlight on it. As we come nearer, a feeling of serenity descends upon us and there is a sacred silence which gives us a sense this place has been blessed.

4.4

I believe that meadows were created as a gathering place for people to worship and honor creation. Within this circle, one has a 360-degree view of the surrounding foliage filled with chirping critters and adorned with shimmering flowers. Amongst the fluorescent green canvas, vibrant splashes of color appear. Between the tall blades of grass, blossoms in dazzling shades of yellow, violet and orange sparkle in the sunlight. Trees, young and old, towering and blossoming, surround the meadow creating a lush green fortress for our sacred gathering. Many birds flock to this special gathering place as well. They come to pollenate the flowers and nest in the branches. They too recognize that the meadow is a blessed place and rejoicing, they sing their little hearts out. Listening carefully, we can make out several different tunes that all harmonize to create a lovely symphony. We bow our heads and thank them for welcoming us to their meadow with this sweet serenade. Like the splashes of color in the grass, we notice there are vibrant sparks in the sky as well. As we narrow our focus, we see that they are butterflies, little works of art, flittering all around us. If we stand motionless, they will fly close enough to show off their beautiful designs. As we stand in this sacred circle, we each have a panoramic view of this lovely meadow and its wide-open space allows us to expand our consciousness.

This ability to both focus and expand our awareness at once is a special gift of our senses and when we appreciate it in this way, we can become fully present and completely immerse ourselves in the moment. If we go deeper into the true essence of the images before our eyes, like the little butterflies, we can picture them as swirling forms of energy vibrating within the prism of light. Within the brilliant light, emanating from the source and shining down upon the meadow, all of the images, including ourselves, are shimmering. The true essence of all life-forms is revealed when they are illuminated by the light. The forms we attract are a reflection of our spiritual essence — a creative expression of our true nature. Our spirit is like a swirling vortex of energy spiraling in and around our form. This energy is always vibrating within a wide range of frequencies, as we have seen, the slower and lower the vibration, the more dense the form and likewise, the faster and higher, the more translucent.! Regardless, each and every form is an expression of spirit all vibrating within the omnipresent light. This glorious meadow is the perfect spot for pondering the mystery within the light and that's exactly what we are going to do.

Let's gather around in the center of the meadow and make a sacred circle within which we can continue our reflective inquiry. To inspire our inquiry, let's reflect on the concept of star souls and see what comes up. Let's revisit the movie from last night and just imagine the possibilities: A star falls from the sky and becomes a girl who glows in the presence of love. Hmmm. Would she be falling from her home star and if so, would she be a holographic projection of her higher-self sourced from her eternal soul in Havona? Would she be reflecting just one aspect of her multi-dimensional self? If home stars really are multi-faceted crystals projecting holographic images on the walls of our 3D sphere, the images would still reflect the light of the eternal soul housed inside. The girl who came to earth would be projecting an aspect of her whole soul but like any hologram, her whole essence would still be in every fragment. Her image would be sourced by that stream of consciousness from Havona that is focused on the star (or nexi of entrance) in space-time. Her higher self would be housed in that home star and from there choose a nexi of entrance into the earth plane to express itself. If her divine self in Havona is projecting into her home star and her higher self is streaming into her hologram on earth, what are we really talking about here? We are talking about a direct connection between our eternal soul in Havona and our holographic soul here on Earth. Our home star is our base for streaming consciousness between Havona and the earth planes.

Let's picture two tetrahedrons stacked at their bases, one being a reflection of the other. One houses the divine eternal soul and the other houses the mortal human soul. They are joined at their bases to form an octahedron. Then the two triangles merge to form a star-tetrahedron. A 'star' is born! Within the heart of the star, I pictured a brilliant crystal that contains a divine spark. I was reminded of a Buddhist image I once saw that looked something like this:

**Inspired by image
"The Phenomenon Source"**
4.5

When these two tetrahedrons merge, the divine spirit merges with the human soul. They are always united by the source at the center which is the divine spark within. The spark between the two is like the crystalline star which streams divine consciousness into the human soul from its sparkling light up above.

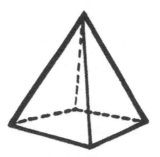

Knowing that the star tetrahedron represents two evolving patterns of crystallized consciousness:, I began to imagine the possibilities. If the elements are created within the stars and those elements are represented by evolving patterns which become crystallized forms of consciousness, then 'patterns of consciousness' are evolving within each star. That's what going on in the stars! Elemental patterns of crystallized consciousness are projected into the star and then an evolutionary process begins. Unique patterns are captured within the frozen 'light' of a star. These crystals then reflect unique pattern-personalities which become the creative expressions we call beings. *The Urantia Book* teaches us that the Creator, the Universal Father, is the originator of these patterns and only he can project personalities, or creation codes. Each living being, each soul and every star, is a totally unique pattern that can never be duplicated! Within each of our eternal souls, there is a unique code which is our frequency signature for all time. All patterns are a product of the intelligence codes that inform the creation of their being and subsequently their evolutionary course. Therefore, each and every living thing and being, including elements and minerals, all have a unique energy signature of creation codes that inform and instruct their creation and the evolutionary development of their being. These codes are projected into the stars as "encoded light" which defines its soul's frequency signature.

To summarize this reflection:

Stars are living patterns of consciousness that receive encoded light from the original pattern personality in Havona. These points of light become a nexi of entrance for light streaming in from the original pattern encoded by the Creator. The source of the codes streaming into the star is the perfect divine blueprint of its pattern personality. Our eternal souls in Havona are the perfect pattern personalities streaming encoded light into our home stars. As perfect souls, we are projecting these codes into our stars in space-time in the form of encoded light. We do this so we can project our pattern personalities onto different earth planes. In this way, we can have so-called "human" experiences that enhance our self-knowledge and allow our souls to experience love. Whole souls are contained within stars so that its 12 aspects can be expressed in different forms and in many different realms all at once. In the time-space transcendent world from which their whole soul originates, all is eternally present. Therefore, all aspects of their personality, can be projected from their home star and imprinted on different planes all at once. Between incarnations, these fragmented souls can reunite with their eternal soul and rejoice with their soul families. They can console with their divine guides to review their mortal journey in time and space. They can recalibrate their consciousness, receive new teachings and upgrades and then decide to reincarnate or possibly to serve in a different way.

The linear human mind is limited by the concept of time and can only consciously experience one aspect of its whole soul at once. There are times however when the veil is thin and one can experience aspects of these other selves as bleed-through feelings, emotions and identities. This happens when these concurrent lifetimes in other realms come into their current awareness. This is usually subconscious but can be witnessed consciously. Of course, we can always intentionally tune into our higher self in our home star. We can also tune into our concurrent lives in other realms and dimensions. We usually feel compelled to do this once our soul becomes aware of its divine source. We may experience a strong desire to realign with our perfect divine blueprint and become aware of our eternal soul in Havona. Once we start tuning into the multi-dimensional aspects of ourselves, we start becoming whole again. We will be exploring many powerful techniques for doing this in Book 3 of the Up! Trilogy, *Lighten Up! Activating Your Light Body.* For now, it's important to understand that there is one single star for every soul. Within that star are the unique codes that define our soul's pattern-personality. Our soul's frequency signature is projected into the forms that we take on in different space-time dimensions. From our home star, our soul can project a stream of consciousness onto any dimension it wishes to experience. These streams can be thought of as fragments of our soul's personality and each experience will be specially designed to complement our whole soul evolution. Once our soul has integrated these experiences and the fragments begin to reunite, our soul starts gathering up all of its pieces and gets ready to return home to its source. This is when we become fully aware that we are on an ascension path and we begin seeking answers and yearning for soul reunification. We feel a deep longing for our home in the stars and a knowing that we are eternal. We rejoice that we have star families in the cosmos and that we have an eternity of experiences ahead.

Let's sit and ponder these revelations for a moment. Let's tune into our homes in the stars and imagine what that might look like. Let's project our minds into Havona and tune into our eternal souls. What do we look like? What do we feel like? Are we simply an ethereal essence like a wave of consciousness? Explore it. Envision it. Feel into it. Now open your heart space and allow the love of the Divine Mother to flow in. Be seated in her womb space where you feel safe and warm. Here you feel such a powerful force of love penetrating every soul of your being. You know she is always with you. She is the source of who you truly are as a divine spark in human form. She is you. You are her. All is one.

As we leave the meadow where I was blessed by a miracle, we feel grateful for the experience and know that it has allowed us to progress personally and evolve spiritually. Feeling peaceful and connected, we walk in silence listening to the sounds of the forest. Gradually, the sound of rushing water becomes louder and we feel compelled to move toward it. Maybe it's a magnificent waterfall! Emerging from the trees, we find ourselves standing on the edge of an embankment. At the bottom, water is rushing through the stream and we look up for the source of its energy. Low and behold, a tremendous waterfall is blessing us with all of its exuberance and glory! What a refreshing place to sit and re-energize! Just imagine absorbing the powerful life-force pouring down from the mountains peak like prana flowing in from its source in the heavens.

4.6

As we sit on the embankment, a beautiful white egret descends and perches on a rock in the stream. We have an inner knowing that this is a gift from above — an angel with a divine offering. This winged angel symbolizes the spirit which, descending from above, blesses those below. This special blessing is a divine reflection of our own angelic spirit, pure as white snow like the egret who has blessed us. We have been shown this symbol to remind us of the angelic spirit within us. Whenever we radiate the light of love from our heart, our angelic nature shines through as our pure spirit in form. When we shine our light on others and love permeates our soul, this energy extends to all beings. It's an expression of our divine spirit and we become like the winged angel.

Let us bow our heads and send love and gratitude to this messenger of light. As we do this, we feel a strong connection with its radiant spirit and we know that we are one with its source. In this magical moment, we are truly experiencing the essence of communion: the unity of spirit and the oneness of being within the heart of the Creator. We are blessed. We are one in the love and the light of the Divine Mother and One Infinite Creator.

Let's rest in the fullness of this realization and meditate quietly on it for a few moments. Close your eyes and experience the omnipresence of spirit. There is only one spirit that embraces all things. You are that spirit and it dwells within you as the divine spark that ignites your soul.

4.7

Enlightened by the depth of this profound realization and feeling refreshed from a short break, let's dive back into the revelations we were exploring earlier which were inspired by my experiences in Truckee:

When I got back home from my trip, I went in search of the bible. I wanted to look once again at the verses from Genesis to see if these poetic verses might shine some light on my new "star-soul" theory. Let's see…Genesis, Chapter 1:

Now, according to Genesis 1:14-31, (days 4-6), a second phase of manifestation takes place starting with the creation of "lights in the firmament" (stars) for "signs and seasons" on day four: "Then God said, "Let there be lights in the firmament of the heavens to divide the day from the night; and let them be for signs and seasons, and for days and years."

Really? Lights, or stars, in the firmament on day four for signs and seasons?! Like four directional signs — N, S, E & W — SPACE! It follows: "and seasons" — four seasons — "and for days and years" — TIME! On day four, when God, the Creator, wished for the lights in the firmament to be for "signs and seasons", space (four directions) and time (four seasons) came into being! If the fabric of time and space was created when the stars were placed in the firmament, then maybe they were placed there to project from points on the grid like divine sparks. From there, they could project onto the worlds of time and space, a mirror reflection of the dry land and seas which were already created in the heavens.

Within each star, the four elements — fire, air, water and earth (four Platonic solids) emerge as crystals. These points of light, as crystallized consciousness, were "set" as stars in the firmament of the heavens to give light on the earth. And here we are, back to my original conclusion that the light of our spirit, or soul, is contained within a star and there is one star for each soul. Our souls are projected by the stars onto the worlds of time and space just like the dry lands and seas. They are all forms of "crystallized consciousness" — a way for the source to project its consciousness into the world of experience.

This is God's consciousness in action. He already created "Heaven" with dry lands and Seas <u>before</u> he created the stars and <u>before</u> he asked that the lights be for signs (space) and seasons (time). And with the creation of the firmament (the fabric of space-time), he could project his consciousness into the stars and they would appear like sparks of awareness at every point in space-time. Each one would become a unique point of view from which the Creator could experience his new worlds. These points of light, each shining with their own creative brilliance, would forge the elements necessary to build an entire universe.

Those stars that matured would explode and disperse these elements out into the universe far and wide, so the worlds of time and space could be created. Others would become suns, so they could start a family and illuminate their own new worlds. Each star, with its own unique pattern of crystallized consciousness would project the illusion of reality in 360 degrees. Within each star, a whole soul lives and breathes and from its special place in the cosmos, every aspect of its personality may be projected onto many dimensions all at once. Each star-soul is on a remarkable journey of self-realization as its spirit descends, ascends and evolves throughout time and space.

"Let them (the stars) be for lights in the firmament of the heavens to give light on the earth"; and it was so. Then God made two great lights: the greater light to rule the day, and the lesser light to rule the night. He made the stars also. God set them in the firmament of the heavens to give light on the earth." Genesis 1:15-17.

So, at the end of the fourth day, we have light on earth because of the stars in the heavens where dry land, seas and life already exist. You can probably already guess my interpretation of this but here goes:

The lesser light on earth reflects the greater light in the heavens. The illusion of the dry land, seas and life on earth is a mere reflection of that which was already created in the land of "Havona" — the first perfect and "eternal" universe upon which all other universe realities in time and space are merely a reflection. *The Urantia Book* tells us that Havona is dimensionless, timeless and spaceless. It exists within the magic of the eternal present where all events are concurrent rather than sequential. The divine perfection of this magical place is the experience of reality we can choose to have on earth. We can do this by connecting with spirit and living in the higher chakras of love, communion, truth and faith. We can touch the magic of the eternal now by being truly present in the moment. We can rejoice with gratitude for all that is. This light from the heavens is filtered through the fabric of time and space which gives it layers upon layers of dimensions. The lens through which this divine perfection is projected gets more distorted the further the soul descends and gets more clarity as the soul ascends. The energy vibration gets progressively lower as the soul descends into the lower dimensions and its form takes on more density. That's why our consciousness gets distorted and things move out of alignment with the divine order and perfection of its source. When we move out of divine order and alignment, chaos reigns and persists until we realign with our perfect divine blueprint. We can realign with intention and restore our perfection! All we have to do is RISE UP! and remember the divine source from which we came. Together we can do this and restore the collective consciousness one divine spark at a time.

In Carla Rueckert's book, "The Aaron/Q'uo Dialogues", she channels a being "Q'uo" who shares this:

"...there is an intelligence moving through all that is, which does, indeed perfectly creates each of you day by day, inasmuch as you can allow it; and as you bear witness in a life of faith to this true nature that continually and perfectly transforms all that there is, you may see the face of creation blossom and infinitely expand in love reflected in love. So, as you bring it down into the life of faith the energy of the spirit of love that strengthens the heart, that it may move further downward into each darkened space within, so the reflection upward begins, and the heart is informed by the energies that it may make its return to the alpha and the omega of all that there is. All things from the beginning to the end of creation are implicit in this present moment. And the cycle or circle that is process and learning and growth reflects in your faithful hearts the eternal present moment in which love is the whole nature of the unified consciousness." [7]

Whoa, let's integrate that for a moment and read it over a few more times. Feel it expand your heart and elevate your mind. You can also tune into Carla's interview where she shares many more inspiring revelations at SciSpi.tv/Rise-Up/.

With that inspiration, let's return to the scripture and continue to explore the possibilities. On day four, just like the book "Initiation" proclaims, the trinity moves out of the divine aspect "resting in divinity" to the creative aspect "resting in unity." This is represented by the divine triangle now creating a reverse reflection of its "self" and four triangles emerge from within. Now we have the creative manifestation on day four — four signs and four seasons (space and time! Now, by the end of day four, the reflection technique is in place enabling the trinity to create in time and space. Remember when a line is drawn opposite itself, we now have a mirror reflection of the source from which it came and the illusion of reality begins in 1D. The line moves out and creates a flat plane and 2D expresses itself. When the plane reflects on itself, a cube is created and the 3D illusion expands with the 4th dimension of time. The dimensions continue to expand and contract as the universe breathes in and out and the soul travels on the waves rolling in and flowing out.

This wild ride on the ocean of space-time gives the creative trinity the self-realization they are seeking. Unbound by the "fetters of infinity", the divine trinity moves outward into eternity. Projecting their divine spirit into the fabric of space-time, they evolve as the creative trinity through experiences in these realms. These divine and creative principles are expressed in each and every one of us as our masculine and feminine aspects. The divine and creative trinity finds it expression within us, through us and as us! It is through the reflection technique and projection process that they express in these ways.

Sitting on the side of the stream like we are, it's easy to observe how reflection and projection work in this realm of illusion. We can see, first of all, that the water appears to be blue, but we know that it is only a reflection of the blue sky above that makes it appear that way. Then we can see that there are many objects reflected in the water like our own images or the tall trees along the edge.

4.8

The images in the water look real enough but we know they are only a reflection of the source from which they came.

Now, let's toss a pebble in the stream and disturb the "ocean of bliss." This is the effect of projecting intention into a point in space-time. See the ripple effect as it creates an expanding world around the source point. Actually, this is the primal effect of projecting intention into eternity. This is a profound visual of how the eternal realm emerged from the infinite sea of bliss. When the trinity broke through the bonds of infinity and projected its intention to create in eternity, see what happened! Wavy vibrations emerged from the source point to create ever-expanding circles around it. This is creation in action!

4.9

See how the waves closest to the source are shorter and vibrate at a higher frequency. The further out the waves expand, they get longer and vibrate with less intensity. This analogy has many implications for the true nature of reality and we can see it unfold right before our eyes just by tossing a pebble in the stream. We can see how the vibrational frequency of consciousness is higher when it is closer to the source and lower the farther it moves away.

Let's move onto day five and continue with our theoretical interpretation of Genesis:

On day five, God creates living creatures in the sea and birds across the firmament in the heavens and once he saw that it was good, then he blessed them to be fruitful and multiply on the earth. Once again, the manifestation seems to take place in heaven first and then it is shone upon the land. Here, the fifth Platonic solid, the more complex dodecahedron, becomes effective as a higher element of consciousness manifesting in the form of living things which function with complex brains, central nervous systems and sensory perception.

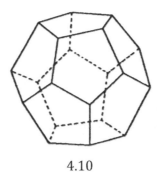

4.10

On day six, God said, "Let US create man according to OUR likeness." Genesis 1:26. Man and all living beings are a product of the trinity — a projection of their collective consciousness. Therefore, all beings are endowed with the same loving and creative spirit. The "Creator-consciousness" of the source lies within every one of us as our divine aspect — the great-self within.

On the sixth day, the "star-tetrahedron" is expressed as the two polar opposite pyramids of the octahedron, joined at their base, merge and form the most complex crystal pattern of all — the reflection of the advanced consciousness of living, breathing, and thinking beings with both male (creator) and female (creative) aspects. Father and mother merge and a son is created.

4.11

"Thus, the heavens and the earth, and all the host of them, were finished. And on the seventh day God ended His work which He had done, and He rested on the seventh day from all the work which He had done. Then God blessed the seventh day and sanctified it, because in it He rested from all his work which God had created and made." ~ Genesis 2: 1-3

I believe that the final symbol, "Metatron's Cube", represents the Planet, or even the physical body, within which this complex consciousness can be housed. On Earth, the collective soul as well as the individual soul can clothe itself in earthly elements and be contained or "cubed" within this 3D hologram. However, the divine self is always hidden within. This mechanism of "containment" allows the soul to evolve through the experience of a physical manifestation.

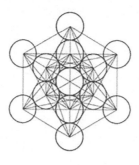

4.12

In "The History of Western Philosophy", Bernard Russell discusses Plato's "Cosmogony" and he shares this quote from Plato's thesis, "The Timaeus":

"The Creator made one soul for each star. Souls have sensation, love, fear, and anger; if they overcome these, they live righteously, but if not, not. If a man lives well, he goes, after death, to live happily forever in his star. But if he lives badly... he will go on through transmigration's until at last reason conquers." [8]

This analogy of the star as the home of our soul and a vehicle through which divine consciousness can be projected, inspires me to return to the image of the spiraling star we discussed on yesterday's adventure. Remember the Dogon's illustration of the vibrating string that underlies all forms in our illusion of reality? They believe that this string is a spiral which emerges when you trace the outline of a star with seven vibrating rays each increasing in length.

If we think of the light of our home star projecting an aspect of our soul onto the fabric of time and space, we can begin to comprehend the illusive nature of reality. Also, if we consider the possibility that the images which unfold before us are merely the reflection of a greater reality beyond time and space, then we can truly ponder the eternal magic within the illusion. Let's take this one step further and make the connection that we too are the reflections of a greater reality or as in Genesis, the lesser light separated from the greater light only by the firmament of heaven.

The beam of light that is our stream of consciousness still maintains its connection to the source even as we get entangled in the fabric of time and space. As our whole soul projects more and more expressions of its multi-dimensional self onto the matrix, we become more entangled in it. Remember how Buddha had to untangle himself before he could transcend the physical reality? He had to become detached from his entanglements. According to the scientific theory of entanglement, once molecules come into contact with each another, they retain an energetic connection forevermore. There has been a tremendous amount of experimentation to validate this theory. It has remarkable implications for us as molecular beings as it does for all living things. Every person, place and thing you have ever meet over the course of your many lifetimes will forever be energetically connected to you in one way or another! As a collective soul on planet earth, we are all entangled in a consensus reality or "social memory complex", according to Ra in the "Law of One." In other words, on a spiritual level, we have all agreed upon this shared version of reality and we are creating the many aspects of it together. We are entangled in this version of reality — in essence, we are all sewn together in this particular fabric of 3D space-time! In another dimension of space and time, beings inhabiting other planets are entangled in another version of reality which they have agreed upon. As multi-dimensional beings, we are entangled with many versions of ourselves expressing in many different realms all at once!

However, if we pull back and look at the big picture — the Grand Universe, if you will — we can clearly see that we all still come from the same source of light. We are and always will be entangled with each other in the same web of consciousness energetically connected forevermore. The brilliant light that emanates from the center of creation radiates outward and projects its light into each star-soul on every universe. And just like the Grand Universe is a collective soul of seven ascending levels of consciousness (or seven "super-universes") spinning around its source, our star may be the collective soul of our seven ascending levels of consciousness spinning around it! What if we are each the reflection of only one aspect of our whole soul whose source is one beautiful radiant star and within each ray of light emanating from this star, seven vibrating levels of consciousness represent the prism of our soul?

"Perception is merely reality filtered through the prism of your soul." ~ Christopher A. Ray

What reality is being filtered through the prism of your soul? How do you see the world around you? What is your perception or translation of the creation story? I highly encourage you to meditate upon it, go out in nature and experience it, research it and write it down. Please go within and discover the truth that feels right for you and see if what you find alters your preconceived notions about who you are and the nature of the world around you. Also, practice heightening your senses by fully experiencing every moment that you can by engaging all your senses and noticing everything up close and far away. The truth is out there for you to experience in all its vivid colors, sounds, textures, smells and tastes. Between listening to your inner wisdom and fully engaging your awareness of the outer world, the truth and beauty will be revealed in all its glory!

Absorbed in delight and wonder, let's sit in silence with a heightened awareness of all the musical sounds and breathtaking sights. Allow the true essence of the undulating wavelike energy embrace you in its vibrational symphony. Imagine you are in the center of the most beautiful play surrounded by swirling colorful dancers dressed like birds, flowers and trees. The sun is like a spotlight illuminating the stage and the earth is the stage upon which this theatrical performance unfolds. You are always at the center of this stage in your colorful dance through life and seeing it through the eyes of truth, beauty and pure love will make it the most joyful and rewarding one possible!

4.13

Let's consider the following passage as we walk and ponder truth:

"Truth is beautiful because it is both replete and symmetrical. When man searches for truth, he pursues the divinely real. The wise philosopher will always look for the creative design which is behind, and preexistent to, all universe phenomenon. The creator thought invariably proceeds creative action. Intellectual self-consciousness can discover the beauty of truth, its spiritual quality, not only by the philosophic consistency of its concepts, but more certainly and surely by the unerring response of the ever-present Spirit of Truth. Happiness ensues from the recognition of truth because it can be acted out; it can be lived… Divine truth is best known by its spiritual flavor." [9]

With the sunlight fading and dark shadows lurking, let's find our way back to our campsite. As we hike along the winding trail, let's share the thoughts and feelings that were inspired by the day's revelations. We can reflect on the symbolism and try to grasp the meaning beyond the forms. I am personally very intrigued by the spiral that keeps emerging throughout our adventure and have a strong desire to explore the true meaning behind it in greater depth. I know that it is at the heart of creation and the key to unlocking the mystery underlying the true nature of reality. At the most fundamental level of each creative expression lies the root of its spiraling nature — tiny vibrating strings or loops all vibrating at different frequencies. This brings us back to the spiraling nature of reality which will be the topic of discussion around the campfire this evening.

Here we are at the campsite so let's get settled in around the campfire. After we get our tents set up and dinner has been served, we can snuggle into our chairs around the fire.

Now let's imagine that we are seated around the campfire under the stars. As we stare into the crackling flames, we know that the fundamental pattern of this element is the tetrahedron, the first Platonic solid that ignited creation! We now know that this fiery source reflected on itself to create its inverse image as the octahedron. The octahedron then spun on its point to create the first spiral in creation.

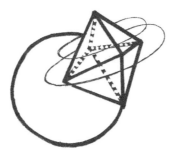

We see this spiraling form repeated in the most revealing forms in nature — seashells. Just like the sand dollar reveals the sacred flower of life symbol, this shell reveals the Fibonacci spiral. These forms in nature are special gifts which simply reveal the true nature of reality in the most basic forms.

4.14

Sacred geometry helps us to unlock the mystery behind the spiral and no one is more enlightened about this topic than the truly inspiring author and spiritual guide, Drunvalo Melchizedek. I quoted him earlier today because he had mentioned Tahoe in one of his books. He was talking about scared sites on the "Christ consciousness grid" that a group of highly advanced beings created after a major pole shift almost destroyed our planet 13,000 years ago. He explains that many sacred temples were built out on a spiraling path of kundalini energy to carry the Christ energy of this grid. This divine energy would be expressed in spiraling ley lines in the inner earth. He follows its path through Central America to Taos, New Mexico which he says is the counterpart to Lake Titicaca — one of the most sacred sites in the U.S., he claims. From there, the spiraling force heads out across the mountains and passes right through Lake Tahoe, Donner Lake and Pyramid Lake. It's no wonder this place is so full of spiritual energy.

This spiraling force is a powerful source of Christ Consciousness and any site along its path is blessed with the highest vibrations of divine energy! Drunvalo has made some remarkable discoveries about this spiraling kundalini energy and we are very fortunate that he has shared them with us in Volume 1 of his book, "The Ancient Secret of the Flower of Life". His books are a definite must-read for anyone who is curious about the most profound mysteries of life. Drunvalo is inspired by celestial teachers who tell him stories about the ancient past and give him clues about their divine significance. He follows his deepest intuitions which guide him toward the answers he is seeking. Through meditation, research and spiritual guidance, Drunvalo uncovers the great mysteries that underlie the very essence of our existence both in the physical and spiritual realms. The symbolism that unfolds throughout his journey reveals a sublime interconnectedness between these realms as the shapes and forms come to life. He focuses on the mathematical translation of the symbols and discovers that sacred geometry is the key to understanding the consciousness behind the forms. I am drawn to his work because of this consciousness perspective. His teachings support the theory that reality is a merely a perception or "consciousness experience" and that it unfolds based upon the level or degree of consciousness that the individual spirit is embracing.

As physical and spiritual beings, Drunvalo has learned, each aspect of our soul evolves through varying degrees of consciousness. As planetary beings, we evolve through five levels of consciousness and, it is my understanding that, beyond that, the sixth and seventh levels are spiritual in nature only and the eighth level is a gateway. Individual souls and collective groups of souls (a society) are attracted to the planet they choose to inhabit based upon their spiritual progress. Drunvalo also points to the "Yugas" we explored earlier wherein the planets themselves ascend and descend through varying degrees of consciousness and this largely determines the perception of reality the inhabitants will experience.

As I read volume one of Drunvalo's book, I felt as if I was experiencing the unfolding of my own personal journey through truth all over again. I am convinced that it is simply the revelation of our spirit, a remembrance if you will, and we are all guided toward those teachings we need to progress along our path when we are ready. If our evolutionary paths are paralleled, we will receive similar guidance which will lead us to the same types of research, symbols and messages along the way. Believing this, I was stilled amazed by some of my own parallels with Drunvalo's journey as he moved through Egypt, Ra and the Law of One and then into the "Yugas" and the Platonic solids! When I saw that he mentioned the Dogon tribe, however, I literally put the book down and just sat there stunned. I was introduced to the author of "Sacred Symbols of the Dogon", Laird Scranton, when he appeared on an episode of "Ancient Aliens." Of course, I was introduced to, and recently interviewed, Carla Rueckert who channeled Group Ra and the Law of One. I was connected to her through David Wilcock's book "The Source Field" which magically appeared on my Kindle screen one day and without hesitation I ordered it. Around this time, my mother gave me a book, "A History of Western Philosophy", which featured Plato and "The Timaeus" teachings on the Platonic solids. Which brings us to how I came onto Drunvalo's teachings: a spiritually insightful friend of mine came over one day to help with some research for my book. She showed me an incredible series of videos online called "Spirit Science" featuring none other than Drunvalo Melchizedek. I recognized the name

"Melchizedek" from "The Urantia Book." In the book, it teaches that there are seven orders of sons who are basically a projection of the Eternal Son. One of these is the "Melchizedek Order of Sons." Of course, I know I am being connected to these teachings for a divine purpose, so I follow my spirit and immediately go online to order his book, "The Ancient Secret of the Flower of Life"!

That is the key, my friends, FOLLOW THE ENERGY! All you have to do is open to spirit and then just allow yourself to be led around by its glorious guidance. It will lead you to the exact truths you need to know at the exact moment you are ready. Of course, you have been led to my book by spirit, or else you wouldn't be reading it right now! So let's get on with the teachings now that you are ready without further ado!

What lies at the heart of these truths that Drunvalo, you and I are seeking? The divine love, truth and beauty of the Creative consciousness, of course, but how does this consciousness unfold from the infinite ocean of bliss to the eternal realm of perfection? How does it then descend into the physical realms of time and space and ultimately, how do we progress on our ascension path which leads back to the infinite bliss from which we came? These are the pertinent questions we, as seekers, must explore if we are to connect with the true essence of our spirit and fulfill our divine purpose. As we uncover truths along the way, one symbol — the sacred spiral — keeps popping up repeatedly and we begin to realize that it holds the key which unlocks the most profound mysteries of all — maybe it is the key. If we use it, maybe it will open the door to a realm where all the truths magically unfold.

If you want to go beyond where you are at and a locked door stands between you and your destination, you must have a key. So, if we start with the spiral, just like the Creator did, then all the other truths will naturally unfold. That's exactly what Drunvalo Melchizedek discovered as he began to realize that sacred geometry unfolds from the spiral. We will see how it allows more complexity as it radiates outward and reveals more simplicity as you follow it inward. With Drunvalo as our guide, this promises to be a truly enlightening evening full of magical mysteries, divine intervention and ultimate truth!

I'd like to start with the depiction of an image I saw recently which came from the walls of a monastery in Romania. This monastery (The Voronets Monastery in Romania) is sometimes called the Sistine chapel of the East because of the religious art painted all over the walls and ceilings. They are all remarkably beautiful, but one particularly struck me as the true nature of the spiritual and physical realms with the divine beings above always guiding and blessing the incarnated ones below. A brilliant sun, the radiant light of spirit, embraces and unites all of the beings but what flows between the angels above and the humans below are waves drawn in a particular way that strikes me. As I focus on this wave pattern, suddenly a series of revelations unfold, and the spiral is at the very core.

I start to think about the beach and how I always feel like the ocean is breathing as waves are expelled on the sand and then inhaled back into the depths from which they came. I realize that the planet herself is breathing in this way. This led me to images of surfers riding on the waves and the view they had within the spiraling tube of its inner vortex. I knew then why my friend, an avid surfer, feels like he connects with God when he is out there in the waves. In fact, he says that is where he found God. Riding inside the spiraling vortex of a tubular wave and hurling towards a tiny opening at the end must be a truly divine experience. For one, you are totally present in the moment. In fact, I believe that the eternal present lies at the very heart of the sacred spiral and, like the spiraling tube of a wave, if you peer into the tiny opening at the center of the vortex, you will enter a magical place. Following the spiral inward to the very point in the center, you will be led to the eternal present and ultimately to the infinite ocean of bliss that lies beyond.

This imagery leads me to focus on the gifts that the ocean brings from Mother Earth herself. The ocean delivers these gifts by dropping them right on the beach for us to find and cherish. These gifts which come in the forms of sand dollars, shells and sea horses reveal many truths and Mother Earth becomes our spiritual guide. In Drunvalo's book, he points to the nautilus shell as a perfect example of the Fibonacci sequence expressed in form. By referencing Drunvalo's teachings from his book, "The Ancient Secrets of the Flower of Life — Vol. 1", we will learn how the Fibonacci sequence was discovered and how it reveals the creative potential of the radiant spiral.

Inspired by the creative spirit of Mother Earth, Leonardo Fibonacci noticed a repeating pattern in nature while taking long walks outdoors. Sound familiar? In a heightened state of awareness, he began to see a numerical sequence emerge as he observed the flowers along his path. Connected with the creative consciousness, he knew this sequence would reveal an important truth about form and spirit. He counted the petals as he moved from one type of flower to the next and one by one, he began to see the connection. His insatiable curiosity allowed him to expand his consciousness and thus enter the mind of the Creator. He was determined to find out how and why these numerical patterns were used and what it all meant for the rest of creation! Being a mathematical genius with a creative spirit, he pieced the puzzle together, one petal at a time and what he discovered unlocked one of the greatest mysteries of all time — how spirit manifests into form. Thanks to Drunvalo's incredible insight and extensive research, we can see just how the mystery unfolded!

Drunvalo begins by giving us his impressions of Leonardo Fibonacci:

"From what I've read about him, he was a monastic, often in a meditative state. He loved to walk through wooded forests and meditate as he was walking. But evidently his left brain was simultaneously active, because he started to notice that plants and flowers had number associations." [10.]

He goes onto explain how Fibonacci began to realize that flowers had either 3, 5, 8, 13, 21, 34, 55 or 89 petals. Then he found a peculiar plant called a sneezewort that went from having one petal on its single branch when it first came out of the ground to then sprouting one more on that same branch as it grew but just before it split into two branches. At that point, it began branching out and splitting into multiple branches but each time it did, it would grow leaves side by side on the same level. So, starting with the first two single leaves 1 and 1, suddenly 2 would pop up at once and three at once, and then five, giving him this sequence of numbers: 1,1, 2, 3, 5, 8, 13, 21, 34, 55, 89 and so on.

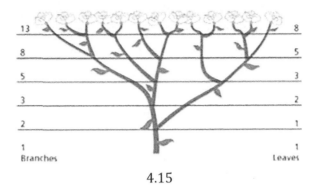

4.15

It occurred to him that these numbers were increasing in the same sequence as the numbers of petals on the various flowers he had observed in the woods — lilies had 3, buttercups had 5, delphiniums had 8, marigolds 13, asters 21 and daisies had 34, 55 & 89 petals. A pattern begins to emerge where you add the first number to the next and it will give you the third and so on. This is called the Fibonacci sequence and out of it comes the Fibonacci spiral! Drunvalo teaches us that it is a very special sequence that is "crucial" to life.

He draws the Fibonacci spiral on a grid to illustrate how it starts within one single square and then curves across another single square (1,1). Then it expands its curvature into the length of two squares and then crossing three and then five and then eight, etc., as the spiral expands outward creating the Fibonacci spiral. The sacred geometry of this spiral describes the nature of the strings which lie at the root of all living matter!

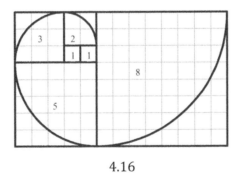

4.16

He also points to the spirals repeated in nature and how they correspond to this same Fibonacci sequence as they expand outward. Here, however, he makes an important distinction between the Fibonacci spiral and another famous spiral — the Golden Mean spiral. He explains that while many believe the Golden Mean spiral expresses the ratios that are repeated in nature, he disagrees. He bases his beliefs on the fact that the Golden Mean spiral has no beginning and no ending which doesn't fit into Mother Nature's translation of an eternal universe which, although it has no ending, always has a beginning. He supports his profound realization by explaining that the Golden Mean Spiral is perfection in infinity and therefore an expression of the ideal (God) whereas the Fibonacci Spiral is imperfection in eternity and an expression of life seeking the ideal. He shows how the Fibonacci Spiral gets closer and closer to the perfection of the phi ratio (associated with the Golden Mean) as it evolves. Only synthetically can we use the phi ratio to create. Many famous temple complexes, like the Giza Plateau, have been synthetically designed according to the Fibonacci Spiral to symbolize the soul seeking the perfection of the ideal Golden Mean. The ancient cultures, like the Dogon and Egyptians, knew that there was great significance behind the spiraling pattern radiating outward from a single point and expanding into eternity. Drunvalo helps us understand both the divine source and nature of the Golden Mean Spiral and clearly illustrates how it is translated by Mother Nature as the Fibonacci spiral seeking perfection on its evolutionary path!

Hang on though because Drunvalo isn't finished astounding us with his revelations! This next one, having to do with spirals on a polar graph, left me stunned and one epiphany after the next began to pop into my mind as all the previous material we have been studying about dimensions, fields and strings just fell into place perfectly. I must admit that his entire book from start to finish left me breathless as all of the scientific facts I have been studying and all of the religious and spiritual texts I have been researching literally came to life on the pages of his book. Science and spirit merged within the context of archaeology and mythology. I was enthralled by the fact that many of his revelations are supported by the celestial teachings in *The Urantia Book*, the "Law of One" series, "Initiation", the Holy Bible, as well as in the scientific and philosophic works of both ancient and modern physicists. That's when you know you are uncovering fundamental TRUTHS, my friends, and that's when we are truly progressing on our evolutionary path of "Self" realization! Let's continue down this path by exploring the polar graph and then sit in amazement as the implications unfold and science and spiritually merge within the framework of sacred geometry!

As Drunvalo studied the Fibonacci sequence and consulted with his celestial guides, he began to develop a theory about the way the straight male lines and curved female lines of the Fibonacci spiral moved around the human body. With the zero-point centered in the genitals and expanding outward in both cubic and spiral form, he began to see a field of geometric spirals looping back in on one another. It was as if a field was circulating around the human body and the energy looped back in on itself, along the path of the spirals, recirculating back to the zero-point in the center. This reminded me of the heart circulating blood oxygen throughout the body and then returning to its source to refuel. In fact, he shows how the curving female spirals create the shape of a heart as they emerge from the zero-point and loop back around.

Drunvalo was instructed by his guides that three sequences are crucial to life and they are the Golden Mean (based on the infinite phi) and the Fibonacci and binary sequences (beginning, no end) which are both essentially "offspring" of the Golden Mean. He began to see these information-carrying sequences as female (Fibonacci) and male (binary) or even as Mother/Father but suspected there was probably a single geometric form that generated both. He spent many years searching for clues. He was on a quest to "wed them." Finally one day he had an epiphany that tied the two sequences together and it had to do with a picture he saw in a sixth-grade math book! It was an illustration of a map of the South Pole with a polar graph superimposed over it. The Pole Station was a point in the center of the map with one line running through it horizontally (North to South) and one running vertical (East to West) creating a cross. The author of the math book was trying show the relationship between the polar graph and the Golden Mean spiral.

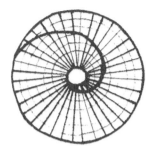

This image alone speaks volumes about the true nature of being. It is the picture of eternity emerging from the infinite ocean of bliss, or void, in the exact center. As eternity expands outward, it looks just like ripples from a drop of rainwater falling onto a glassy lake. In time and space, these ripples stop because there is a beginning and an end, but in eternity they would continue to ripple outward forever moving beyond the limitations of time. This is source expressing itself as a pattern unfolding in nature.

Check out this image of a shell engraved on a towel in my bathroom! It's the polar graph expressed in form! I have started to see sacred geometry in everything! That's what happens when you start to awaken to the true nature of reality. You see it for what it truly is as sacred patterns expressing in holographic forms.

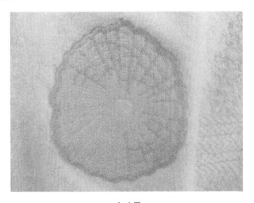

4.17

I will let Drunvalo explain the magic behind the polar graph:

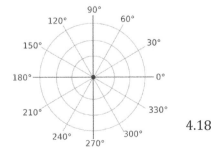

4.18

"This is how the polar graph usually looks with 36 radial lines including the vertical and horizontal lines. These lines indicate 360° giving 10° increments. Then concentric circles are drawn each one the same distance as the one before, creating eight equal demarcations along each radius, counting the inside circle as one. There's a great deal of reasoning behind a polar graph. Think first about what it represents. It is a two-dimensional drawing that attempts to show the three-dimensional sphere, one of the sacred forms, by projecting it onto a flat surface. It is the shadow form. Casting shadows is a sacred way of obtaining information. Also, a polar graph has the straight lines (male) and circular lines (female) superimposed over each other — both male and female energies at once."[11]

The radial increments (from 0° to 360°) allowed Drunvalo to use the Fibonacci sequence to trace a Fibonacci spiral over the graph. He discovered that, while the author of the math book intended to superimpose a Golden Mean spiral over the graph, it was truly a Fibonacci spiral!

4.19

Furthermore, when he traced a binary spiral over the graph, low and behold, it formed a three-dimensional tetrahedron!

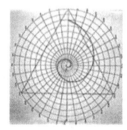

This series of revelations clearly defined the relationship between the male and female energies of the Fibonacci and binary sequences. He had long been trying to integrate these sequences and when he saw the image of the polar graph, he knew it was the key to unlocking the mystery . . . and it did!

As he traced the sequences over the graph, not only did the Dogon star and three-dimensional tetrahedron come to life, a whole series of sacred symbols began to unfold! He thought of the two spiraling arms of a galaxy and realized that from the center point, they were exactly 180° apart.

4.21

The Golden Mean spiral, when superimposed on this graph, looks just like the Dogon spiral we discovered on yesterday's adventure with the seven vibrating rays!

  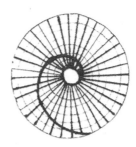

This inspired him to trace two spirals on the graph:

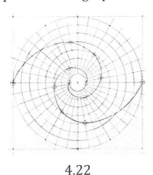

4.22

"But in nature, like in the galaxy, there's not just one spiral, but two, going out from the center in opposite ways. So, if you copy nature, you would have to plot two spirals, which will produce two opposing triangles on the polar graph. If you look carefully, it produces two tetrahedrons — more specifically, the star tetrahedron inscribed inside the sphere." [12]

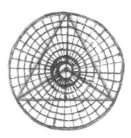 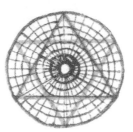

From this revelation, Drunvalo's depth of insight allowed him to see how a smaller star tetrahedron fits within the larger one and within that, the center sphere fits perfectly!

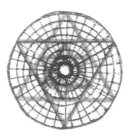

For me, the most compelling evidence of these patterns is their expression in forms we can actually pick up and see and feel. A closer look at my sand dollar reveals the polar graph behind the sacred pattern of life. On the backside, we clearly see the Fibonacci sequence unfold in the splitting branches of the tree!

 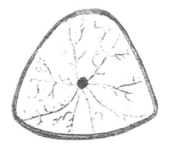

Of course, the simple act of tossing a pebble into the calm surface of a pond will reveal rippling waves expanding outward from the center as a polar graph unfolds and a perfect sphere takes shape! This is spirit expressing its true origin and nature right before your eyes — emerging from the void of infinity and expanding outward into the realm of eternity — and this is happening at every point of time and space! Like raindrops falling on a pond, each landing at a different point and creating its own sphere, dimensions like ripples unfold at every point in the field of time and space.

4.23

Remember how we explored the Higgs field yesterday and discovered that seven dimensions were enfolded at every point on this space-time grid? Now we have a much clearer picture of the field as a three-dimensional polar graph or spherical grid. Drunvalo has helped us see the male and female energy within the spherical grid — the soft curvature of the spirals and spheres within the sharp lines of the triangular forms — all interconnected as an expression of polarity in an evolving pattern of consciousness. This is a moving, living and breathing sphere of pure consciousness unfolding from the source — life unfolding at every point in time and space as pure potential actualizing into form! This sphere surrounds your being as your own individual field of consciousness — a spherical grid within which your own creative energy spins and transforms energy into form.

Mother Earth has her own sphere which she uses to manifest as she brings forth her creative consciousness. The solar system, galaxy, universe and multi-verse all have their own spheres of creative consciousness and they all merge and interact transforming energy into matter and spirit into form. All of this moving, living and breathing energy emerges from the source and then returns to it. Spirit ascends and descends as light translates into higher and lower densities within the vibrating frequencies of a multi-dimensional reality. This magnificent illusion is all embraced by one infinite being — the source. Within the mind of the One Infinite Creator, all is interconnected, and each individual soul is a spark of awareness with a different point of view from which to observe the illusion as it unfolds. From behind the lens, each soul has the creative power of its source and as it moves through the interconnected web of reality, it creates a ripple which spreads across the entire field.

A Mindfulness Practice

Every moment of your life, you are walking through this field and as the reality you have chosen unfolds around you, the seeds of potential at every point in time and space are actualizing into the forms that you perceive. We have seen how, within the Higgs field, a boson is given off (when the symmetries are broken at the points in time and space) which gives mass to particles. Asymmetry occurs — an energy disturbance in the field which brings forms to life! Your thoughts are the source of this energy disturbance, or "breaking of symmetries", which is causing the forms to unfold in the ways which you have either consciously or sub-consciously chosen. The electrons that make up your reality are the seeds of pure potential at every point in time and space. They exist here, there, everywhere and nowhere — popping in and out of existence — just waiting to be noticed so that they can become something. They are waiting for your instructions!

Once you bring your consciousness into your experience and notice the electrons, they actualize into the form you have chosen! If you do not consciously manifest the forms with a heightened state of awareness, your subconscious mind will "unconsciously" choose them for you. This is the difference between being "awake" or "asleep" as you move through your reality. Your sub-conscious mind is sub-ject to every thought that pops into your mind and it is listening very carefully. It brings forms into your reality based on the thoughts it hears. Your thoughts become your subconscious minds instructions about what reality to show you. You can either carefully choose your thoughts and give specific instructions or allow random thoughts to design your reality. Your thoughts manifest the forms in your reality just like the thoughts of the Creator manifest into the forms that unfold at every point in time and space. This is the framework for your reality! Choose your thoughts wisely if you want to manifest accordingly. Mastering your Creator-consciousness with the power of pure intention is the key! Creative mastery is how energy translates into form with such precision when directed by the mind of the source. All is taking place within the mind of the Creator as infinite intelligence expressing itself in many magical and mystical ways. This is an incredibly important realization, so you may want to read it again and then reflect upon it as you move through your day.

The key is to view your "self" as pure energy — spirit expressing its "self" in form. You are infinite intelligence in action with the creative ability to direct energy by transforming it into matter as you move through it. Just like the Platonic solids emerge and transform to create the elements of space-time (earth, air, water, and fire), the forms of energy around us are constantly transforming. Water evaporates into air and earth erupts into fire and dissipates into air which transforms into dew returning to earth. It goes on and on, and one day when we master our minds, we may be able to bend air and earth and water just like the movies depict. The fact that these movies are even being made shows we are one step closer!

The ancient Egyptian and Asian cultures knew how to do this, and they taught these skills in mystery schools and as a "martial art." Although we devolved since that time of the "Golden Age", we are on an ascension path and there are many aspects of our reality that we can transform with the power of our thoughts! Now that we have a clearer picture of the energy field around us and we know how particles of pure potential pick up mass as they actualize into form, we can begin to live in a higher state of awareness about the world we are creating. Let's activate our spirit and use our creative consciousness to bring forth our highest self in every thought, word and action. This creates a harmonic state of being wherein everything starts falling into place beautifully. We are consciously creating coherent waves with constructive patterns instead of allowing non-coherent ones with destructive patterns to emerge.

Harmony is perfection in motion and just like the Fibonacci sequence spirals toward perfection, we too can emerge from our heart center and send rippling waves of light and love out into the field of consciousness. All we must do is activate our spirit by sending spiraling energy through our ascending chakras. As we move through our day, we can pull energy up from Mother Earth and send it spiraling upward through our chakras igniting our human spirit. At the same time, we can receive divine energy from the source and send it spiraling downward through our chakras activating our divine self.

These are the two braided serpents of red and blue energy — the double helix of our DNA.

4.24

These intertwining energies of spirit and self, the human and the divine, physical and spiritual, mother and father, male and female, negative and positive, logical and creative, left-brain and right-brain, mother and father — these are the polarities Drunvalo illustrated within the forms as the intersecting tetrahedrons and the two spiraling arms of a galaxy. How do we apply all of this creative consciousness to our everyday lives? How can we tune in and follow the energy as spirit guides us along our path? How do we radiate rippling waves of love and light to transform shadows into light? That's what we will be exploring as we progress on our ascension path! Allow me to share this final story about the experience I had on my last day in Truckee. It will offer a beautiful example of how intuitively following the guidance of spirit and radiating love-light energy can profoundly affect the world of spirit all around you:

As I headed out on my morning walk with my furry kids in tow, I decided to just follow the energy to see where Spirit might guide me. It was a misty morning and the energy felt eerie. There was a fog bank on the water and I had a sense that something mysterious was lurking.

4.25

A dark pine tree forest was up ahead and I was not enthused about the prospect of entering this maze of looming tress and wandering wildlife. I had an inner knowing that this was exactly where Spirit was leading me though and I felt energetically pulled onto the path. As I entered cautiously, I became aware of a presence as if there were eyes in the trees. I tuned into the sounds around me and could hear a faint whisper saying, "Follow me." The magnetic pull of energy guided me this way and that as paths merged and crisscrossed through the forest. Where was Spirit taking me? I became aware that the energy was getting heavier as the forest became more dense. A feeling of sadness and grief started to overwhelm me and tears sprung into my eyes. Suddenly, a sign popped up that read "Donner Campsite." What?! This is where Spirit was leading me? Whoa. I had no intention of coming here and had no idea why I had been called. Then in a flash, I knew. The souls who were looming in the trees and beckoning me to this site were the Donner party victims from long ago. They had all suffered a terrible tragedy and were seeking redemption and mercy. I felt compelled to bless all the souls who had passed there under such extreme conditions. I wanted them to know that many had grieved for their suffering and loss. I reassured them that no one blamed anyone and everyone mourned them. I offered profound blessings, love, forgiveness and compassion. I called upon transport angels to descend and guide these spirits into the light. After several minutes, the heavy energy lifted and a ray of sunshine poured through the trees. I was filled with gratitude and rejoiced in the special blessings that had been offered to us all. What an extraordinary honor it was to release these beings from their entrapment. How precious that Spirit had mercy on their souls. I was overwhelmed by this experience and spent the rest of the day in awe and wonder.

As we get tucked into our cozy sleeping bags on this warm summer night, we feel an overwhelming sense of gratitude for the remarkable teachings we have received from Drunvalo Melchizedek and Carla Rueckert. Both of these teachers have an incredibly generous spirit and have dedicated their lives to conveying the sacred teachings of their celestial guides. Drunvalo is a conduit for the spirit of Thoth and Carla for the spirit of Ra. According to Drunvalo, there were three beings who saved the planet from a devastating polar shift about 13,000 years ago. Along with another being Aragat, they created a Christ-consciousness grid by building temples at sacred sites around the globe. Thoth led a group of ascended masters into South America where a female energy was established while Ra and his group went underground in Egypt and created a male-energy across that region. According to Drunvalo's guides, this male energy became the root of our present civilization. The third being, Aragat, led his group into the Himalayan mountains where, as I understand, a neutral energy was established which reflects the spirit of a child. They all built marvelous pyramids which connect these three energies (male — father, female — mother and neutral — child) and together they sustain the grid that continues to protect the planet today. From these sacred sites, the enlightened cultures of the Mayans, Egyptians and Tibetans emerged.

Tonight, under the stars, as we fall fast asleep, let's call on the celestial teachers to be our personal tour guides. As we move into the dream state and set off on our astral adventures, these teachers can guide us toward those places, peoples and events that will be most conducive to our spiritual growth. They can show us symbols and help us understand the meaning behind the content of our dreams. All we must do is call on them and they will gladly be of assistance. To help you set the stage for your lucid adventures in the parallel reality we call dreaming, I have designed a visualization based on today's revelations. This way, the truth behind these symbols and concepts will be revealed to you in your dream state and upon merging back into your waking state, they will resonate with you on a deeper level. This is how we progress along the path, my friends. I am eternally grateful that you have joined me on this evolutionary journey. Sweet dreams.

A Guide to Lucid Dreaming

"We are infinite dreamers dreaming a finite dream." ~ Swami Vivekananda

If we believe that we are reflections of a greater reality and that this three-dimensional experience is merely an illusion filled with holographic images, then even our waking state takes on a dreamlike quality — invisible spirits dancing in the prism of light and creating colorful forms out of pure energy. It's all being perceived through our mind's eye, either way, and so who is to say what state is more real. Some native aboriginal tribes believe that in dreaming, one's spirit is closer to the true source of reality and less attached to the illusory reality of the waking state. That makes so much sense if you think about. There is the source and the illusion, the spiritual and the physical, the real and essentially, the unreal. In Buddhism, they talk about subtle and gross states of mind. In the subtler states, one is closer to their spiritual essence and more connected to Source. In the grosser states, one is more attached to the physical illusion and more connected to ego. So, here again, in the dream state, as spirit, we are closer to our true nature. We are separate from the physical body while our spirit travels through its astral adventure projecting holographic images and creating dream experiences.

On average, there are 4 or 5 periods of REM each night each lasting between 60 and 90 minutes. This REM state (rapid eye movement) is an indication that we are dreaming. Between these states, we are thought to be in a dreamless state of deep sleep aware of nothing. We are suspended in the void of nothingness. Some "dream-workers" think that this is a crucial time for connecting with the source of pure consciousness. Suspended in the infinite void, we transcend imagery and return to the quiet bliss from which we came. In this purely existential state there is no experience and no illusion, no comparative and no reflection, just the source — the only true, unchanging reality. In the Vedantic philosophy, the "true" reality is that reality which is unchanging. These periods of communion with the source are thought to be critical for our well-being and if one becomes deprived of this communion for very long, insanity and delusion set in.

Dreaming also seems to be imperative for the harmony of the soul. It is a chance for our spirit to break free from the fabric of time and space and the laws that bind us to it. In this reality, the spirit can fly across space and traverse dimensions. It can reconfigure experiences in the Earthy realm and edit the illusion of our waking lives. Spirit is always focused on its divine purpose (which is to create and evolve) so it will always create images which are intended to move us forward in our evolutionary progress even if we don't always get the symbolism. Our lesser spirit is always learning from the greater spirit and trying to teach our ego-mind these lessons. Our dream experiences can seem so real while we are in them, but they fade away so quickly just like the waking reality fades when we fall into the dream state. It seems like we are moving in between parallel realities except that we don't have much control over the events in our dreams the way we do in our waking life — or do we? If we are truly projecting and experiencing holographic images in both our waking and dreaming states, we should be able to set an intention for both performances and direct how they play out across the screen of our mind.

So the question becomes: Can we consciously control what holographic images spirit projects in our dreams? Can we become the creator of our dream experiences and use them as a way to evolve? Just think: If we could create our dreams intentionally and then recall these experiences clearly, we could learn so much from them! We could connect with spirit directly and get the truth straight from the source! We could conduct our own Q & A with spirit and have a direct experience of truth! Then we could apply these lessons and teachings to our waking life! If we could use this time to progress along on our evolutionary path, we could learn and grow much quicker and the quality of our waking lives would improve significantly as our spiritual awareness and wisdom flourished. Most importantly, if we can develop our ability to project holographic images and create experiences with the power of our intention in the dream-state, we can begin to apply these creative talents to our waking state and master the art of manifesting! These creative abilities are inherent in our being and this might be the perfect way to develop them! Let's give it a go, shall we?

O.K., first we must develop our sense perception by improving our ability to fully experience every object in our waking reality. This means really making out every detail of these images by seeing every point, line, color and shape that defines them. We must practice touching, tasting, smelling and listening to everything within our sense perception both near and far away. This is an effective practice for developing the ability to recreate these images with the power of our imagination. We start by fully experiencing every detail of our waking reality using all our senses and then with our eyes, go within and recreate every aspect of it in our mind. This practice has many important benefits. It puts you more in touch with the present moment as you experience it more fully and we already know that the magic lies within the true essence of each moment.

Another benefit is that we become the observer of the illusion and our spirit becomes the witness of our physical experience. Stepping aside from our purely judgmental state, we can see things for what they really are instead of labeling them based on our preconceived notions about them. We can just see them from a purely objective standpoint. This is also a very powerful practice for opening your heart without prejudice and judgment — looking beyond the physical form and just seeing the spirit within all things and beings. Finally, try seeing all things and beings as pure energy and try to imagine them as holographic images. See the different types of energy vibrating at higher and lower frequencies. Know that their density, color and form are defined by the frequency with which they are vibrating.

You will discover that the living spirit is creating all forms by attracting mass to the energy of its "self" (as in a living being) or projecting energy to create mass (as in non-living things). Once you are able to see everything as a manifestation of spirit, you can begin to manifest images with your own creative spirit. Just look into the air and place holographic images there. Simply focus your mind and intentionally create holographic images in the empty space around you. Now progress from an image to a whole scene and then just bring that scene to life with the power of your imagination. It's your creation so you can direct the performance in any which way you like! You can create an imaginary world where people are saying and doing the things you wished they would and where the material things you always wanted magically appear. With your eyes open, see it play out just like you want. Now close your eyes and picture it more clearly without the distraction of the surrounding objects. It is important to define the specific details of each person, place and thing down to the texture, smell, colors, expressions, clothing, taste and feel. Practice and create the most vivid scene you can according to what appeals to you most.

Be very careful to do this with a pure intention and take into consideration that you may very well manifest these scenes in your experience of reality! Stick with only positive outcomes that benefit everyone involved in your imaginary world. The best approach is to use it as a school for learning life lessons and fundamental truths. This is what you will want to do in your lucid dreaming experience. You will intentionally set the stage for an amazing learning experience. You will imagine your spirit guides taking you on a journey and showing you symbols and images along the way. You will simply ask to be shown the specific truths you are seeking and then imagine your spirits as tour guides who willingly take you to whatever destination you desire and elucidate whatever truths you want to know. The more deeply you connect with spirit before falling asleep and the more specific you are with your visions, the more you will understand the symbols and imagery that you will be shown in your dreams.

Lastly, before falling asleep, say three times with a firm conviction: "I will remember my dreams" and then keep a journal or recorder by your bedside. The dreams will quickly fade once you awaken to the illusion of your ego-self so get it while it's fresh in your mind's eye. You will be amazed not just by the lessons themselves but also by the inner-knowing of what they mean and what to do with them. Its spirit teaching you and you are spirit learning, creating and evolving! You can now use both your dream state and your waking state to fulfill your divine purpose according to the divine plan! You have become one with spirit as you connect and let it flow through you. Living in spirit is the highest truth and radiating spirit is the highest aspiration. Consciously create and evolve with the highest intentions, my friends, and you will naturally ascend. You will create heaven on earth as your spirit ascends in search of the truth and then descends back to earth to live it and spread it! This is the magic of lucid dreaming.

The Flexible Fabric of Space-Time
A Lucid Dreaming Experience
(Audio version available at: www.SuzanneRossTranscendence.com)

The Preparation

Start by repeating the mantra, "I am that I am, I am that I am, I am that I am" while focusing on the space between your brows — your third eye. Saying, "I am that I am" opens your third eye and as it opens, you will see an indigo blue pupil staring back at you. Focusing on your third eye, repeat, "I am that I am, I am that I am, I am that I am." Imagine that your indigo blue pupil can see inside your head and observe the two hemispheres of your brain. The right hemisphere sparkles with indigo blue light and the left one sparkles with ruby red light. The right side of your brain is focused on feminine energy swirling with love and compassion and generating spiritual inspiration. It glows with the divine light of wisdom and worship. The left side of your brain is focused on masculine energy swirling with power and determination and generating practical information. It shines with logical reasoning and practical solutions.

It's time to balance the feminine and masculine energies by merging these two halves. Imagine the indigo blue light of your right brain bleeding into the ruby red light of your left brain. Together, the blue and red light create a shimmering violet light that becomes a violet flame. Your brain becomes engulfed by the violet flame as the right and left hemispheres become one. There is no more separation. You are now perfectly balanced in your feminine and masculine energies within the violet flame. You are now a powerful light warrior both loving and compassionate yet powerful and determined. You are now both spiritual and practical all at once. Now focus on the center of your violet brain and see a golden shimmering pinecone seated there. This is your pineal gland and the violet flame has ignited it. The golden light radiating from your pineal gland now expands creating a golden halo around your head. The golden halo swirls around the violet flame engulfing your brain. Repeat, "I am the violet flame, I am a golden light warrior, I am that I am, I am the violet flame, I am a golden light warrior, I am that I am. I am the violet flame, I am a golden light warrior, I am that I am."

Now let's move this violet flame and golden swirling light down the length of your entire being. Imagine the violet flame igniting your neck and shoulders and flowing down the length of your arms and fingers. Imagine the violet flame igniting your chest, abdomen and hips and flowing down the length of your legs and toes. Now imagine the golden swirling light spinning around your neck and shoulders and flowing down the length of your arms. Imagine the golden light swirling around your chest and abdomen and hips and flowing down the length of your legs. Your whole body is now consumed by the violet flame with a golden swirling energy encircling it. Repeat once again, "I am the violet flame, I am a golden light warrior, I am that I am. I am the violet flame, I am a golden light warrior, I am that I am. I am the violet flame, I am a golden light warrior, I am that I am."

Now seat your consciousness within the golden pinecone at the center of your head and simply repeat, "I am." Now imagine a golden tube extending from your pineal gland into the violet crown chakra spinning just inches above your head. Now see your consciousness seated within that violet disk and repeat, "I am." Now connect the "I am" consciousness seated within your pineal gland to the "I am" consciousness seated in your violet crown chakra and repeat, "I am that I am, I am that I am, I am that I am." Now you are ready for the lucid dreaming experience.

The Visualization

Imagine that there is a flexible fabric which envelops all of creation. There are many layers to this fabric — one for each dimensional reality. Just like Drunvalo's polar graph, they are spherical in nature and they expand outward into eternity. At the center of each sphere, is a perfect crystal which reflects the reality of the dimension it represents. Imagine that a clear tube of brilliant light runs through the center of these spheres piercing the crystals and connecting them. At the very top of this tube is the spherical realm of Paradise and the most magnificent and luminescent crystal of all! For, it is the source of the brilliant light in the infinite realm! Golden light is projected from this realm which descends through the glass tube onto the eternal realm. One level below the radiant sphere of Paradise, is the eternal realm of Havona. In this dimension, all exists within the eternal present moment. It is the only perfect, settled universe upon which all other universes, in the realms of time and space, are merely a reflection. In its center, lies a crystal which reflects the essence of the golden light it is receiving from the source onto its eternal dimension. Below Havona, the realms of time and space begin. At the center of each descending realm, lies a violet crystal which receives the light of the source from the tube which pierces its core and connects all spherical realms from above and below. These spherical grids in time and space descend into the lowest dimensions of reality and ascend into the highest realms of divinity.

Now imagine your own being as a replica of the source from which it came. You too, as a divine spirit, have ascending and descending levels of consciousness we can even call — dimensions of reality and realms of divinity. The chakras that run up and down your spine are like crystallized wheels, each representing a different level of evolutionary consciousness. Your spine is like a crystalline tube that connects these levels just like the crystalline light that connects the heavens with the earthly realms! In this body, we can consciously experience and express the seven major levels of consciousness from survival to divine. If we think of our spirit expressing itself in seven dimensions at once, we can imagine that there is another aspect of our self in each of these seven realms governed by our higher-self residing on our home star. All of these aspects of our self are connected by a crystalline tube of shimmering light that descends from our star and connects with the crystalline tip of our spine. The source of the light that radiates from our highest self is the crystalline realm it is projected from which is, naturally, the only true reality of Havona.

Just imagine an infinite number of spherical realms expanding into eternity all connected by a crystalline tube filled with the brilliant light of pure consciousness! The possibilities are endless within this vast multitude of dimensional realties. Envision the infinite realm of Paradise in all of its golden glory. Try and picture the eternal realm of Havona in all of its magnificent perfection. Now, imagine the infinite possibilities of color and form that define the spherical realms of time and space. Each dimension manifests its own creative expression of reality. On the higher realms, life is much more advanced, and beings move effortlessly along the surface in translucent light-bodies. They are harmonized in love and their existence is a rhapsody of symphonic delights as they bathe in spiritual bliss. Imagine that you are floating on waves of love and light on the spiritual bliss of this realm. Hold this vision as you float into dreamtime. Sweet dreams beloved.

Your Personal Revelations

_____

_____

_____

_____

_____

_____

_____

_____

_____

_____

_____

REFERENCES

Illustrations:
Chapter cover image courtesy of: http://www.1freewallpapers.com
1-3. Personal photos
4. Image courtesy of http://www.californiaoutdoorproperties.com
5. G.K. Gyatso, The New Guide to Dakini Land, Tharpa Publications, 2012 p. 539

6. Personal photos
8-9. Images courtesy of http://www.pixabay.com
10. Image courtesy of http://www.blog.stsci.edu
11. Image courtesy of http://www.etsy.com
12. Image courtesy of http://www.sacredgeometry.tatto
13. Image courtesy of http://www.hdwallpaper.fun
14. Personal photo
15. Image courtesy of http://www.naturphilosophic.com
16. Image courtesy of http://www.klivemmaskolan.wordpress.com
17. Personal photo
18. Image courtesy of http://www.stackoverflow.com
19. Image courtesy of http://www.mathematica.stackerchange.com
20. Image courtesy of http://www.greggbaker.com
21. Image courtesy of http://www.pixabay.com
22. Image courtesy of http://www.joelsafford.deviantart.com
23. Image courtesy of http://www.pixabay.com
24. Image courtesy of http://www.conradchrabol.wordpress.com
25. Image courtesy of http://www.natural-hd-landscape.blogspot.com

Text:
Shirley MacLaine, *Out on a Limb*, p.166, Bantam Books, 1983
1. p. 337
2. p. 346
3. p. 317
Institute of the Himalayan Tradition, *Himalayan Path: Journal of Yoga Spirituality and Wellness*, Vol. 11, Number 2, Spring 2011
4. p. 9
Drunvalo Melchizedek, *The Ancient Secret of the Flower of Life, Volume 1*, Light Technology Publishing, 1998
5. p. 117
10. p. 207
11. p. 217
12. p. 222-3
Elkins, Rueckert, McCarty, *The Law of One: Book I — The RA Material*, Schiffer Publishing, 1984
6. p. 144
Barbara Brodsky & Carla L. Rueckert, *The Aaron/Q'uo Dialogues*, North Atlantic Books, 2011
7. p. 280
Bertrand Russell, *The History of Western Philosophy*, Simon & Shuster, 1945
8. p.146
The Urantia Book Fellowship, *The Urantia Book*, Uversa Press, 2008
9. (2:7.4-6)

Day Five

Eternity Unveiled

Good morning and welcome to day five of your adventurous journey! How are you holding up on this extraordinary exploration through time, space and beyond? Are you ready to explore further into the depths of eternity to uncover the unique origin and nature of our universe? I hope so because here is where things get supersonically profound! This will be a tremendous opportunity for you to expand your consciousness and touch the higher dimensional realities where the greater part of your "self" and the Omnipresent Source merge. In these higher dimensions, you can merge with your own higher self and connect with the multi-dimensional aspects of your soul to co-creatively expand your perception of reality and enhance your creative abilities. I know these concepts are sometimes difficult to grasp, so I want to open today's adventure with a passage written by Godfre Ray King in his book, "Unveiled Mysteries", as he ventured out on his own journey of self-discovery. In the introduction, I explained how Godfre was fortunate enough to have the divine guidance of the Ascended Master Saint Germain to help him embrace these higher perspectives. Here are some of the insights Saint Germain shared with him along the way:

"When the reality of life is correctly understood, all manifestation that seems miraculous to your present consciousness is found to be just as natural and normal an experience as the forming of words are to one who has learned the use of the alphabet. It is all but the action of an ever- expanding, ever-progressing manifestation of — Life in form — and that comes about at all times through an orderly process of the — Law in love and peace. No matter how strange, unusual, and impossible an experience seems to humanities present mental state, it is no proof that there is not a greater law and a wiser intelligence acting to produce greater wonders of creation and surrounding us all the time." [1]

Today we are going to Mount Shasta in California! This is where Godfre Ray King experienced his mystical encounter with St. Germain. This is also one of the sites, according to Drunvalo Melchizedek, where the earth's kundalini energy spirals through. At these sacred sites around the globe, the atmosphere swirls at a higher frequency which is conducive to spiritual awakening. This is due to the effect of the spiraling vortexes of energy directed at these sites which penetrate the ley lines beneath them. As I understand it, these locations are situated at points where these ley lines intersect. Vortexes of cosmic consciousness streaming in from higher dimensions activate these points on the ley line grid which create a higher vibrational frequency on the surface. This higher frequency creates higher consciousness and people in these areas naturally become more spiritually enlightened. This in-streaming consciousness seems to be more concentrated in mountainous regions like Mount Shasta. UFO sightings are common in these places and I seem to have captured one in those photo I took during our last visit. Check it out!

5.1

Mount Shasta is also said to be connected to a series of mountain ranges that are considered sacred. The Himalayan Mountains are a part of this interconnected range which divine energy spirals through. The peaks of these ranges symbolize ascension as they reach for the heavens. I was fortunate to live within 20 miles of one of these sacred mountains called Mount Diablo. It has two peaks and it occurred to me one day that, together, they form the shape of a heart. Anytime I felt the need to be uplifted, I looked out toward this heart and smiled.

5.2

Since I first visited Mount Diablo, I could feel the divine energy radiating from its peaks and I knew in my heart that it had a special significance. However, these feelings were validated one day when my guru, Stoma, came from the Himalayan Institute to visit our spiritual community. He shared with us that Mount Diablo was connected to the Himalayan mountain range and that it was divinely blessed. He said it was one of a series of holy mountains that run through the West including Mt. Tam, Mt. Rainier and Mt. Shasta! Mount Shasta is known for its spiritual community and people come from all over the world to experience it. Many spiritual retreats take place there and many feel it has a divine feminine energy. I was actually born in the little town of Anderson in Shasta County which lies in the shadow of this great mountain. As such, I have always felt a special connection to it. When I read about Godfre Ray King's mystical adventures here with St. Germaine, I knew it would be an extraordinary part of our journey!

5.3

Since a special concentration of divine energy is focused here, it will be especially conducive to progressing on our ascension path. Any time that we are exposed to a higher level of vibrational frequency, we naturally ascend to a higher level of consciousness and can see the true nature of reality more clearly from this greater perspective. For our virtual adventure, we are learning to project our consciousness by imagining that we are present in the special locations I have chosen. Due to the immense power of our thoughts to create whatever reality we choose, we can virtually experience the spiritual essence of these places. It's simply a matter of projecting our minds with a strong intention so that we can tune into these sites and envision them. Once we master this, we can virtually travel anywhere with the power of our imagination and experience it on a deep and meaningful level.

In his book *Unveiled Mysteries*, Godfre Ray King demonstrates this as he goes on a virtual adventure to sacred sites around the globe accompanied by the Ascended Master Saint Germain. Upon encountering the spirit of St. Germain, while hiking in the woods at the base of Mount Shasta, Godfre's own spirit is whisked away on an astral adventure leaving his physical body enshrouded in a protective light. Godfre is blessed with this visitation due to his strong desire to interact with the ascended masters and his pure intention to bring the teachings forth for the benefit of mankind. It becomes clear in Godfre's book, "Unveiled Mysteries", that Saint Germain's intention is to teach Godfre "universal laws." (You will note that his writing style is unique with the use of many dashes and capital letters). In the second chapter, Saint Germain states:

"I wish you to fix firmly in your mind, and recall frequently for contemplation — the fact — that the Laws I explain, and teach you to use, are to bring you into a condition — of Conscious Mastery — over all forces — and things on earth."[2]

He goes onto explain that "the Conscious Control, Mastery, and use — of the forces and things on this earth, should at all times be under the direction of your — Inner — or God Self — through the perfect cooperation and obedience of all — outer faculties in both mind and body, to that — Inner Guidance." [3]

In this chapter, he is helping Godfre understand that his inner self can control his outer senses by consciously raising their vibratory rate. He gives examples of how his consciousness is "projected" by attempting to see as far as he can in all directions and to hear every sound in the distance. He makes a point that all humans can see close up and far away at the same time based on where he chooses to direct his attention. He explains that this is simply "an enlargement of the force field in which the sight acts." He tells Godfre:

> "When you contemplate this — Great Inner God Activity — do you not see how — perfectly and readily — the outer senses — merge into the — Inner — to become — *One*." [4]

I often experience this merging of my strong inner desire to see or hear something with the outer experience of my senses. I am aware, at these times, that I am projecting my consciousness. It starts with simply expanding my consciousness by heightening my awareness of everything within the close and distant range of my senses. Once I have made a conscious connection with my environment, my experience of it is greatly enhanced. I suddenly become aware of those things I had a strong inner desire to see, feel and hear with my outer senses. I have the sense that I am directing my experience by intentionally expanding and projecting my consciousness!

Let's practice doing this now while we are out in nature. St. Germain teaches us that heightening our senses will increase our conscious mastery over them! This will greatly enhance our awareness of the energetic "thought-forms" all around us and then we can begin to resonate with their vibrational frequency. Seeing our reality from this perspective is the first step toward consciously creating the experiences we would like to see unfold in our lives. Using our "Creator-consciousness" to manifest our reality is a real possibility and the more we practice heightening our senses and awareness, the sooner we will begin to develop this tremendously empowering skill!

Saint Germain tells Godfre, "Truthfully speaking — there are no such things as miracles — for all is according to — Law — and that, which seems miraculous to the present concept of humanity, is but — the result of the application of laws — to which mankind's present consciousness is — unaccustomed — and so seems strange and unusual." [5]

Let's throw on our backpacks now that we are gathered at the base of the mountain. Before beginning our ascent, we will wind through the lush green valley below. Our winding path will lead us into the woods where wildflowers flourish and we can touch and smell the leaves on the trees.

5.4

Every sound will be magnified as the vegetation becomes dense and we will be able to hear every twig beneath our feet and every bird from above. We can imagine being drawn to the fresh water streams and following them to their source. As the thundering sound of water plunging from the mountaintops becomes louder, we will know we are about to make a glorious discovery. If we are lucky, a magnificent waterfall will suddenly appear as we emerge from the trees and we will be awestruck by its power. Here we can stop for lunch and that will be our first destination. For it is by a fresh water stream that Godfre Ray King had his first encounter with the Ascended Master St. Germain and, in the words of this great master, we will be "revivifying" that scene!

As we begin today's exploration, gathered at the trailhead, let's make a special point to absorb the tremendous beauty all around us. I will provide pictures to engage your senses so that you can literally see, smell, hear and touch the beauty. Check out the bright red heart at the center of this green goddess!

5.5

I want you to get the most out of this adventure by intensifying your direct experience of it. This will greatly enhance your ability to project your consciousness and focus your intention. These skills are the key to progressing along your path as you rediscover your innate abilities and tap into the creative energy of the source! Are you ready to engage your senses and gain access to your "Creator-consciousness"? Of course, you are! Let's begin what promises to be another remarkable journey of self-discovery. As we wind along our path, let's listen to the wisdom of St. Germain as it is channeled through our teacher and trail guide, Godfre Ray King.

Saint Germain speaks about "Thy Eternal Perfection" and the "Mighty Omnipresent Source" that governs the universe and is the "Life, Light, and Love in all things." Knowing that "Thy Eternal Perfection" is present in all things and that it is the source of life, light and love, he says, can bring great joy, hope and inner peace to those who truly believe they are a part of the "One Self in All." Understanding our oneness within the divine plan will come in handy for this part of our journey as we uncover the "greater law and wiser intelligence" within the "ever-expanding, ever-progressing manifestation of Life in form." Just grasping the "eternal nature" of our being may be challenging but when we realize that we are an integral part of the divine consciousness, we come to know that each finite experience within it is just another step on the Creator's path of self-realization. We are eternally and intricately intertwined in the Creator's journey since we are an aspect of this divine Self. The divine spark that enlightens our minds and expands our hearts is sourced from this One Great Self. We are That! Repeat: "I Am That I Am." As such, our individual progress furthers the pursuit and attainment of the self-knowledge and self-love the One Great Self is seeking as the One Infinite Creator of all things and beings! God is the Universal Consciousness embracing all things and beings in the Infinite Mother Womb.

That is why I believe that we receive guidance from other-worldly beings who fully realize that the evolution of our souls, within these mortal bodies, contributes to the ascension of Universal Consciousness and the attainment of Unity Consciousness. If we regress, the whole "ascension plan" is set back and this slows the pursuit of eternal perfection. These divine beings show up to guide us on the path toward greater knowledge, love and wisdom so that we can continue to progressively evolve along the Universal Path of Ascension. They also show us that our path is an eternal one and if we follow a code of ethics that aligns with the laws of love, peace and unity, we will be blessed with future lives that are progressively more rewarding and fulfilling whether in the physical or spiritual realms. Therefore, it is in our best interest (and for the benefit of all beings throughout the universe of universes) to make an intentional effort toward spiritual evolution by expanding and elevating our own individual and collective consciousness.

I would like to offer the following passages from Godfre's book that are presented as a call to action. It is a message of inspiration intended to encourage all of humanity to elevate their consciousness by embracing the true nature of life which is love, peace and joy rather than grasping the sense pleasures only. It is an honor and privilege to receive this incredibly beautiful message from the Ascended Master Saint Germain. In the book, this message is delivered in the context of an astral vision which Saint Germain is revealing to Godfre. They have journeyed back in time to an ancient kingdom where a King Emperor is addressing his people:

"O Children of the Earth, I bring you a warning of serious import at a time of great crisis. Arouse yourselves from the snare of the senses that is engulfing you! Awake from your lethargy, before it is too late!...Oh why do you forget the- 'Source-of all Life, all Love, all Intelligence, all Power? People! O people! Where's your gratitude to Life for Love, for the magnificence of experience that you enjoy every moment, every hour, every day, year after year?...This is a blight upon Creation and the Perfection that forever swings in the-Great Cosmic Melody of the Eternal Song. The transcendent and magnificent activities of Love and Light are the Natural conditions in which God created and expected His human children to manifest-obeying His command 'to Love'...It is immutable, Irrevocable, Eternal, yet Beneficent, for creation in form exists that God may have something upon which to pour out-Love-and so express in action. This is the 'Law of the Mighty One' from which all proceeds. It is the 'Mandate of Eternity' and the Vastness and Brilliance of that Perfection cannot be described in words...Love is not an activity of the mind, but it is the-'Pure and Luminous Essence'-which creates mind. This-Essence from the-Great God Flame-streams into substance, and constantly pours itself out, as Perfection in form and action. Love is Perfection manifest. It can only express peace, joy, and an outpouring of those feelings to all creation-unconditionally. It asks-nothing-for Itself because It is-Eternally Self-Creating-being the Heartbeat-of the 'Supreme.'" [6]

Let's take a moment to absorb this message and allow it to resonate within our hearts and minds. Just close your eyes and breathe it in. It's remarkable how applicable it still is today! The profound truth of this message makes our hearts swell and our minds soar with the possibilities of love, peace, joy and harmony in the universe. Creation was manifested from the energy of pure love and so this is the only way we too can create perfection — with the pure intention of love — just like the true perfection we see out in nature. Let's just stop and absorb the natural beauty all around us and look closely at how perfect each leaf and petal are. We can see the Fibonacci spiral expressed in every form and we know that these creations are a translation of perfection from the source. In that sense, they are a symbol of the evolution of imperfect beings striving to progress toward the perfection of the source from which they came. Let's each choose a specific leaf or flower along the path to investigate and see if we can trace the Fibonacci spiral over its blossoming form. This will help us have a direct experience of the creativity of the source — love becoming light which translates into the illusory images we see all around us:

5.6

As we admire the vibrating life-form we are holding in our hand, let's ponder the energetic essence of our own experience here on Earth. For me, these types of reflective contemplations out in nature have inspired many epiphanies. Taking long walks out in nature, I have "unveiled mysteries" about my own true nature and come into a deeper knowing and greater understanding of the fundamental truths of our existence. I would like to share one of these revelatory experiences with you now in the hope that it will resonate with you. It is my strong desire that you can virtually experience the same joy and delight that I felt as a result of this spontaneous revelation!

My Eternal Soul

One day, as I was walking along the stream, it suddenly struck me that my soul was eternal! It was like a strong force that came out of nowhere moments after I tossed a pebble into the stream. As I stood there watching the ripples expand outward, the true depth and meaning of eternity washed over me. I realized in that moment that my soul was eternal and I had an eternity of amazing experiences ahead of me in both the physical and spiritual realms. I knew that the evolution of my soul fit neatly within the divine ascension plan and that my eternal journey would be utterly fantastic! Once I truly grasped this concept, I became overwhelmed with pure joy and twirled around in a spiraling "happy dance." With this powerful realization, we can all relax and stop taking the melodrama of this one transient life so seriously. In the big picture of our eternal adventure, we have so much more to look forward to that is way above and beyond this one lifetime! Knowing this, we can stop worrying so much about the finality of this one. We don't have to fight the aging process as if it's a dreadful fate. We can just grow old gracefully and be content with our enlightened view of eternity and, if we play our cards right, we can look forward to each lifetime getting more and more extraordinary as we continue to ascend. So that becomes our primary goal: to play our cards right in this lifetime and simply embrace it as a precious opportunity to ascend toward bigger and brighter experiences throughout our eternal adventure. Remember, we are here to fulfill our divine purpose which is to progress along our ascension paths while inspiring others to do the same.

So what exactly does that mean for us right here and now? For me, it means to stop focusing so much on the ego-centered aspects of my life that are self-serving. To say, "How may I serve?" instead of "What's in it for me?" and to dedicate myself to lifting the spirits of those around me every day in every way. I know I must do my part to alleviate the suffering in the world even in the simplest ways by expressing the highest attributes of love, forgiveness and patience in every moment. That's what truly matters the most in our mortal experience in this evolutionary world and that's how we will achieve our ultimate goal of ascending to higher levels of enlightened consciousness!

What is so inspiring is that we are not alone on this quest! There is a divine plan and an endless number of spirit guides rooting for us! Our own higher consciousness is always trying to guide us in the right direction toward progression instead of regression. The only time we head in the wrong direction, collectively or individually, is when we are ignoring it and allowing our animal nature, instead of our spiritual nature, guide us. We are very fortunate to have these divine beings guiding us and helping us along on our evolutionary path of ascension. Many of these beings are from higher dimensional realms and are simply more advanced than we are. They are further along on their evolutionary journey and have a mandate to reach back and guide us. In the interest of universal evolution, and because they love us dearly, our galactic families have a sincere desire to communicate their advanced knowledge and wisdom with us. They also want to share their unity consciousness with us by streaming downloads of love and light. We have many galactic families in the greater cosmos and are indeed cosmic citizens. Some of our galactic brothers and sisters are particularly involved in the ascension of humanity as teachers, guides and visitors. The most prevalent are the Pleiadians, Arcturians and Sirians and they show up in many channelings and are prominent throughout indigenous creation myths.

My friend, Christine Day, is a world-renowned Pleiadian Ambassador and has written two popular books called "Pleiadian Initiations of Light" and "The Pleiadian Promise." In the "Pleiadian Promise", our galactic family known as the "Pleiadians" reigning from the Pleiades star system, share this profound message:

"Beloved ones, we greet you. Our role at this time is to bring the activation of "the Promise" energy to you on Planet Earth...We bring you knowledge, a series of truths to support you as you navigate your way home...We are here in this moment of time to bring forth information for you to access, bringing the revelations that are yours to receive now, as part of your collective birthright. This is the time for your sacred passage to the next phase of your journey, returning Home. There is a limitless space that exists beyond the limited third-dimensional illusion, where all possibilities exist for you to rejoin your Self. This limitless space of time holds the multidimensional form of your consciousness, where your full existence resides. You are ready for this to be revealed to you; you are ready to return to this meeting place." [7]

Watch my full interview with Christine Day, the inspired Pleiadian ambassador, at SciSpi.tv/Rise-Up/. She brings forth many inspirational and empowering messages.

This galactic support on our journey of ascension is so greatly appreciated and the Pleiadian message revealed here aligns perfectly with everything we have learned thus far.

In the Urantia Book, the beings who are sharing their divine knowledge and cosmic wisdom represent a vast array of guides ranging from "Archangels" and "Perfectors of Wisdom" to "Divine Counselors" and "Mighty Messengers." In the "Law of One" series, "Group Ra" offers universal knowledge and sacred wisdom. Just like St. Germain, these higher beings all share the same pure intention: to inspire a progressive 'evolution of consciousness' amongst the mortals inhabiting the "spheres of light and life"!

Inspired by the Pleiadians, Saint Germain and the infinite number of spirit beings guiding us, let's get back to our adventure! First, let's just stop and listen carefully as the sound of a rushing waterfall overwhelms our senses. As we follow the sound, we round the corner and it comes into full view. Kneeling down by the edge of the stream, we can hear it, smell it and even taste it. We reach out and touch the ice cold water as it flows through our fingers and now all of our five senses are engaged in this experience. Moving beyond our five senses, let's engage our sixth sense to consider the deeper experience beyond the illusion.

5.7

To activate our sixth sense, let's imagine that the waterfall is like a stream of consciousness flowing in from a divine source. This stream flows into our hearts and minds from the divine consciousness of the celestial beings showering us with love and light. Let's engage in a glorious visualization to expand our heart and mind in this eternal now moment. Let's start by projecting our consciousness into the scene we are experiencing. Rejoice in the cool refreshing water splashing down into the stream below and spraying us with its pure essence. Let's appreciate the warmth of the sun on our shoulders. Looking up into the sky, let's extend our love and gratitude to all the celestial beings who are devoted to our progress. Taking a seat along the embankment, let's ponder the liquid light as it rushes by. Inspired by the revelation that our souls are eternal, let's watch the droplets of water splashing into the stream and see the symbols of eternity that unfold. First particles and then waves revealing the particle/wave duality of our fluid 3D reality. Then notice the expansion of rings moving from a single point in the center. This is a magnificent expression of the expanding universe revealed in these expanding waves of liquid light!

Sitting quietly by the stream, we become aware that the earth beneath us is rumbling and we realize that a powerful force of energy is sending shock waves through the ground. In the plummeting waterfall, the source reveals itself in all its power, grace and glory! Here, we can truly experience the power of prana — the life-force of Mother Earth — and the force of gravity that draws everything toward her heart-center. As we follow the rushing water back to the powerful source from which it came, we can trace the source of Mother Earth back to the power of the Sun and the source of our being back to the light from the stars. We know that the stars emerge from the stellar nurseries nestled deep within the swirling stardust of galaxies. Embraced by its spiraling arms, these nurseries, or "nebulae", are the birthplace of the suns and stars…and so we move closer to the source and origin of our being.

5.8

These spiraling arms are also the final destination for the suns and stars they once created as they return home from their evolutionary experience. At the peak of their maturity, these stars will explode and then condense into a "white dwarf" becoming a mere shadow of their former brilliance. However, this white dwarf, a condensed crystallization of pure consciousness, will be a source of wisdom in the galaxy for many billions of years until finally, it too reaches its final stage of evolution and is drawn back into the spiraling vortex from which it emerged.

Beyond the galaxy, on the other side of the black hole, we can imagine that these star souls enter a new higher dimensional reality. Ascending through the galactic realms in this local universe, they expand beyond Nebadon and proceed into the next local universe until they complete their evolutionary journey in the experiential realms of the Orvonton, the seventh superuniverse. Ultimately, the star souls move beyond the experiential dimensions and are drawn into the eternal realm of Havona where time and space are transcended. We can imagine that, in these transcendent realms, they are eternalized as spiritual beings and enter into an existential state of being in pure bliss. They are done doing and evolving and here they can just be the observer of the eternal now moment viewing all multi-dimensional realms and even the Paradise Core all at once! They have fulfilled their divine purpose in the worlds of time and space as incarnate beings and they ascend into the highest realms where they will be eternally present, or omnipresent, if you will. As an ascended being in the spiritual realm, they will continue to serve these worlds as a whole soul. These souls are no longer fragmented, as they were in the realms of time and space, so they can now express the fullness of their creative potential. They are now seeking to be reunited with the "One Great Self" residing on the "Eternal Isle of Paradise" at the core of creation, according to "The Urantia Book."

On yesterday's adventure, we explored the concept that star souls contain the crystallized consciousness of the eternal patterns which define our 3D holographic illusion. Furthermore, we discovered that the holographic images of our eternal soul are projected onto the time and space realms from our whole soul within our "home star." Now that our sixth sense has been activated, let's expand upon that concept and then move into the greater reality that lies beyond the visible stars.

The idea that we 'come from the stars' is certainly not a new one, however this general notion is vague and leaves one asking what that really means. We know that the matter we are made up of, the elements of the earth, is essentially stardust. Yesterday, we discussed how the basic elements of our atmosphere and the physical matter in the universe are forged inside of stars, so it's natural to say that we are made of stardust and therefore, "come from the stars", however I believe that there is a much more profound implication underlying our celestial origins.

On a clear night, we can look right up at the stars and into the Milky Way galaxy where they were born. We can look at the various constellations, depending on what time of year it is, and make out "Orion", the "Big Dipper" and even the brightest star of "Sirius." Many ancient cultures claimed that the "Gods" who came down to earth were from the stars and specifically, the constellations of Orion and Sirius. So when we move into an exploration of what lies beyond these constellations, it's important not just to identify the source of the fundamental patterns of creation but the source of the spirit infusing them with consciousness, love and light.

As we sit along the edge of the rushing stream, we can look back and see the source from which it flows. We can see the waterfall plunging from above and consider its source. We look up at the snowy mountain peak, the highest point, and know that the perfect snowflake patterns have melted and transformed into the rushing water that's falling into the stream below. Crystallized forms of consciousness just became liquid consciousness. Pure source consciousness created the intelligent design of the snowflake patterns with divine creation codes. Even though the snowflakes are melted, their essence is still infused into the "liquid consciousness" of the stream. Do you see the analogy here of how we are perfect patterns, just like the snowflakes, infused with divine creation codes as we flow along the stream of life? Like the snowflakes before they melted, our consciousness is crystallized here on the earth plane as we express ourselves in physical form.

Earlier, I shared with you the epiphany I had about water one day as I was walking along the stream near my home. I was thinking about the images we see out in nature as forms of crystallized consciousness or "frozen light" and wondered how this concept applied to water. Then it popped into my head, "Well of course! Water is liquid light!" which translated to "liquid consciousness." This made me think about all the various elements and the underlying current of energy, or life force, behind them. I realized that all the elements are basically different transmutations of this life-force energy and are themselves interchangeable, i.e. air can become humid or moist and turn into mist or steam. Although earth contains water, its vegetation can erupt into fire and then disintegrate into air; all four elements transmuting at once.

Essentially, although energy can never be destroyed, it is constantly changing as it transmutes into different forms and elements. Since there is an omnipresent life force driving creation, it will always persist and the energy will always present itself in some translation, or vibration, of light to give us the illusion of reality. The rushing stream presents us with a living, breathing representation of liquid light driven by this omnipresent life force, or simply prana. This tremendous force causes undulating waves of water to plunge down from the mountains and rush past the rocks below. This life force is not just the source of the energy flow, it is contained within it! In the element of water, the intelligent source expresses itself as the icosahedron. This is the vibrating pattern of infinite intelligence behind this holographic illusion of water we are experiencing with our senses.

When I was reading the verses in Genesis that talked about "God hovering over the waters" and "dividing the waters", I thought, "What waters? No elements existed on earth yet." Then one day, as I was studying Egyptian hieroglyphs, I learned that they used the symbol of a wavy line to represent "life force" or energy, and it made me think about undulating waves in the ocean. Suddenly, I thought, "That's what the primordial "waters" are — undulating waves of pure potential!" These vibrational waves contain fundamental patterns just waiting to be manifested into forms of energy and matter. God is hovering over the energy potential of these pranic waves of consciousness. When the Creative Trinity begins to create, we can think of their creative potential being realized, or even actualized, when vibrational thought waves trans-form intelligent patterns into images that manifest. They started by creating a perfect universe based on a divine blueprint of perfection. Then they entered a daydream where they could create in another way by projecting images with their collective mind into a new concept called time and space. These images would simply be a reflection of those existing in the eternal realm of Havona.

During the process of creating this existential reality, the Creator discovers the possibility for a reality that can actually be experienced. This epiphany reveals a reality wherein the perfect patterns that define eternity can be projected holographically into spheres that revolve around it. The Central universe of divine perfection becomes the source-sphere (or first source and center). As the patterns are projected into these revolving spheres, they become defined, and distorted, by the lens through which they are perceived. These realities will exist on many dimensions and stars will be used as crystal points of light which can reflect eternity (the waters above) and project it onto these time-space realms (the waters below). These watery realities, above and below, are defined by waves of light and sound. The waters below are mirror reflections of the waters above and as we have seen, water is a mirror! It is the perfect element for projecting mirror reflections of our whole soul emanating from our Home Star. We are mostly water (over 60%); 92% of our blood is water and 75% of our brain is water! It must be the basis for our holographic reflection with its mirror like quality as well. Whoa, now we are getting clarity on the actual nature of our own being.

Since we have talked a lot about the elements as crystallized, or liquefied, forms of consciousness projected from stars and defining our holographic reality, let's take a moment to honor the philosopher who inspired these concepts concerning the platonic solids — Plato himself! In the book, "The History of Western Philosophy" by Bertrand Russell, I found a chapter entitled, "Plato's Cosmogony" and as I started to read it, I literally became "starry-eyed." I couldn't believe what I was reading! Just one week earlier, I had made the connection that people were the reflections of individual stars, remember?! And then later that night, I watched the movie "Stardust" about a shooting star that turns out to be a beautiful girl and I laughed at the synchronicity. Then I return home and randomly open this massive

900-page book to a simple passage that says right there in black and white:

"The Creator, (Timaeus says), made one soul for each star. Souls have sensation, love, fear, and anger; if they overcome these, they live righteously, but if not, not. If a man lives well, he goes, after death, to live happily forever in his star." [8]

I thought, "Are you kidding me!?" I couldn't believe my eyes! Then, of course, I became very intrigued by the philosophy of Plato and the "Timaeus" in which his ideas were put forth. Plato was born in 428 B.C. in Athens, Greece. I would say he was a man way ahead of his time, like Einstein, who may have been receiving "guidance" or just had a wider band-width or stronger signal which gave him greater access to the universal field of consciousness. In his book, Bertrand Russell writes:

"Plato and Aristotle were the most influential of all philosophers, ancient, medieval, or modern; and of the two, it was Plato who had the greater effect upon subsequent ages. I say this for two reasons: first, that Aristotle himself is an outcome of Plato; second, that Christian theology and philosophy, at any rate until the 13th century, was much more Platonic than Aristotelian. It is necessary, therefore, in a history of philosophic thought, to treat Plato, and to a lesser degree Aristotle, more fully than any of their predecessors or successors." [9]

Apparently, Plato's insight was highly valued and seen as incredibly important throughout the ages from ancient to modern times. You can be sure a philosophy or belief system holds some validity when it withstands the test of time. I believe it is an indication that fundamental truths have been revealed. For "Plato's Cosmogony" however, we find that he was inspired by another highly influential philosopher and mathematician named Pythagoras. When I read this, I became curious about Pythagoras and so turned to an earlier section where Russell wrote:

"Pythagoras, whose influence in ancient and modern times is my subject of this chapter, was intellectually one of the most important men that ever lived, both when he was wise and unwise. Mathematics, in the sense of demonstrative deductive argument, begins with him, and in him is intimately connected with a peculiar form of mysticism." [10]

What an interesting bio — a founder of mathematics, as we know it, and someone connected with a "peculiar form of mysticism." Don't you just love it? That's exactly what we've been exploring on our adventure — the numbers that define how the universe works and the intriguing mysticism behind it all! Fantastic! As I read further, I discovered that Pythagoras "praised the contemplative life." He was into contemplative meditation just like we are! Russell writes:

"For Pythagoras, the "passionate sympathetic contemplation" was intellectual and issued in mathematics...through Pythagoreanism, "theory" gradually acquired its modern meaning; but for all who were inspired by Pythagoras it retained an element of ecstatic revelation...to those who have experienced the intoxicating delight of sudden understanding that mathematics gives, from time to time, to those who love it, the Pythagorean view will seem completely natural...the pure mathematician, like the musician, is a free creator of his world of ordered beauty." [11]

Yes, ecstatic revelation! I can relate to that! How tremendous! That is exactly what we are doing, my friends, experiencing the "intoxicating delight of sudden understanding" so we, like all other curious and creative people, can be the "free creator of our world of ordered beauty." We are searching for the "ordered beauty" in our creation and this gives us a sense of delight. Beautifully said, Mr. Russell.

Now let's see what he has to say about the "Timaeus view of cosmogony." He refers to Timaeus as "a Pythagorean astronomer (who) proceeds to tell the history of the world down to the creation of man." Plato wrote "The Timaeus" which is described as a "Socratic dialogue by Plato" but that there was also a Roman-era writer named "Timaeus the Sophist" who wrote "a lexicon of Platonic words." I will share the excerpts from "A History of Western Philosophy" by Russell that apply to our current search for the truth. On our adventure, we have discussed the reflectivity concept at length as well as the creation of the four elements out of the geometric Platonic solids. Here, Bertrand shares Plato's philosophy:

"Since God is good, he made the world after the pattern of the eternal; He put intelligence in the soul, and the soul in the body. He made the world a living creature having soul and intelligence...it is a created copy designed to accord as closely as possible with the eternal original apprehended by God. The four elements, fire, air, water, and earth, each of which apparently is represented by a number, are in continued proportion, ie. fire is to air as air is to water and as water is to earth. God used all the elements in making the world, and therefore it is perfect...it is harmonized by proportion, which causes it to have the spirit of friendship, and therefore indissoluble except by God. God made first the soul, then the body. The soul is compounded of the indivisible-unchangeable and the divisible-changeable-it is a third and intermediate kind of essence." [12]

The wisdom teachers in *The Urantia Book* refer to the Creator as the Universal Father "of infinity" meaning that he originates, resides and creates from within the realm of infinity — beginning-less and endless. Once he creates, however, he expands his consciousness into the eternal realm which has a beginning but no ending. Bertrand Russell offers Plato's perspective on the eternal creation.

"Here follows a Pythagorean account of the planets, leading to an explanation of the origin of time: 'When the father and creator saw the creature which he had made moving and living, the created image of the eternal gods, he rejoiced, and in his joy determined to make the copy still more like the original; and as this was eternal, he sought to make the universe eternal, so far as might be. Now the nature of the ideal being was everlasting, but to bestow this attribute in its fullness upon a creature was impossible. Wherefore he resolved to have a moving image of eternity, and when he set in order the heaven, he made this image eternal but moving according to number, while eternity itself rests in unity; and this image we call Time." [13]

Once the Creator expands his consciousness and creates in eternity, time comes into being. Time is inherent in the concept of experience since it is constructed as a series of events. Even if the true essence of seemingly linear events is occurring all at once along the circle of eternity, as created beings having the experience, we can only view it as sequential. Time is necessary for experiential existence. *The Urantia Book* refers to the first universe constructed by the Trinity as "Havona" and claims that it is not only eternal but that is the only one "perfect" universe upon which all subsequent universes are a merely a reflection. Once the Creator fashioned the heavens, creating divine immortal beings, he left it to these perfect beings, or gods, to create lands beyond the eternal realm along with mortal beings to inhabit them. He provided them with the tools they needed for creating including mathematics, the sun and stars. Plato describes this same concept:

"Time and heavens came into existence at the same instant. God made the sun so that animals could learn arithmetic — without the succession of days and nights, one supposes, we should not have thought of numbers. The sight of day and night, months and years, has created knowledge of numbers and given us the conception of time, and hence came philosophy. This is the greatest boon we owe to sight...There are four kinds of animals; gods, birds, fish, and land animals. The gods are mainly fire; the fixed stars are divine and eternal animals. The Creator told the gods that he could destroy them, but would not do so. He left it to them to make the mortal part of all other animals, after he had made the immortal and divine part...God put some souls on earth, some on the moon, some on other planets and stars, and left it to the gods to fashion their bodies." [14]

Furthermore, Plato recognized the need for a sphere upon which the creation can be "copied" from its "eternal original." He theorizes about a world soul composed of 120 equal identical triangles (dodecahedron) that defines this sphere of creation. While watching an episode of "Ancient Aliens" called "The Secret Code", David Childress, author of "The Technology of the Gods" was describing the concept of a world grid. I had come to understand the basic idea behind this grid as a sort of net that embraced the globe. At each of the points where the threads intersect, vortexes of energy are focused. I believe that these vortexes create an energetic portal for in-streaming consciousness using "gravity circuits." During the show, David Childress introduced the analogy of the world as a giant crystal with 120 pentagonal faces. This implies that a world grid facilitates the in-streaming of consciousness. In fact, this model aligns perfectly with our reflectivity concept based on crystallized consciousness! The narrator of the show explains that this theory of the world being constructed of 120 perfect equilateral triangles dates back to Plato! A guest on the show, Bethe Hagans, says, "Plato wrote that there was a world soul. This world soul he described as a sphere that was composed of 120 equal identical triangles. Plato believed that the model could actually be applied to the earth." Childress says that the intersecting points created by these triangles, when mapped out on a globe, reveals sites where ancient monuments and temples were built. In other words, places where the teachings could be received and worship of the divine could take place since the vortex focused there is a portal for divine consciousness!

The show, Ancient Aliens, implies that ancient people received guidance, and possibly assistance, from other-worldly visitors in locating and building their sacred structures where they could harness focalized energy. The "Ancient Aliens" series presents a vast amount of concrete evidence to support the idea that divine beings descended and interacted with the so-called "primitive" beings of ancient times. From the Sumerians and Egyptians to the biblical Moses and Greek philosophers, "other-worldly" beings have influenced our culture and belief systems. As we all know by now, advanced "other-worldly" beings have long been present and always will be for it is there mandate to help us progress and evolve. There are, however, many sources from which we receive inner wisdom and divine inspiration, including our own higher selves! All we have to do is rise above the distractions, go within and then listen very carefully.

Plato apparently had access to a vast amount of sacred wisdom and universal knowledge long before the advent of modern technology. Just like Einstein with his "thought-experiments" and Pythagoras with his "contemplative life", Plato developed extraordinary insights that came from a source of intelligence far beyond the average intellect. We are blessed that he and others have chosen to share their advanced knowledge with the world as we have greatly benefited from their revelations. I myself am thrilled that I have been introduced to this profound philosophical view of the universe and these perspectives shared by Bertrand Russell on the philosophy of Plato. They are perfect for this stage of our adventure and fit nicely with the teachings of *The Urantia Book*, "Initiation", "Unveiled Mysteries", "The Law of One", and even with the poetically scripted sacred text, "Oahspe." Of course, I am sure we can parallel verses from the Holy Bible, particularly with the concept of "a created copy of the eternal"!

This "unfolding of wisdom" all seems to fall into place beautifully and each discovery seems to enhance the next. There are times when I truly feel as if I am personally being guided through the process of bringing this information forth. If I take the time to focus my thoughts, meditate and call upon spirit guides for direction, I seem to move with ease through the writing process. I naturally reach for certain books and go right to the pages that convey the perfect message for the topic I am researching. It's magical and when I am allowing the information to flow through me, time seems inconsequential and the world around me slips away. Even when I am not writing, my mind remains in a state of awe and wonder as I look curiously and inquisitively upon the world around me. Sometimes, I receive the greatest epiphanies at these times when I am just observing the universe around me and admiring the beauty of creation and the creatures within it. I start to the see the perfection of the Creator in everything and the light and love that radiates from all things and beings becomes visible to my naked eye.

I know "I AM" in the omnipresent light of pure love and when I am absorbed in this realization, I AM fully experiencing the "eternal present moment." During these precious times, I AM deeply in love with all that is and can briefly imagine the timelessness of an eternally present reality wherein the true essence of every moment is pure truth which represents all that is truly "real." No past, no future, just the fullness and beauty of NOW. This reinforces the absolute necessity of grasping the power of NOW, embracing it and living in it fully. If we can let this one present moment just "be" and set aside delusions of the past and projections of the future, we can witness the magic unfolding right before our eyes in the here and now. I believe that the only "undiluted" truth lies in the full appreciation of the present reality. My pure intention behind taking you on this adventure through creation and evolution is simply to give you a fuller appreciation of the cosmic perfection of it all. This way, you can experience every moment with a greater understanding of the divine meaning and purpose behind your existence. Meaning and Purpose — to create and evolve, it's that simple — simply beautiful and yet profound.

Aww, this inspires us just to sit for a moment, look at our reflection in the stream, and become fully present in the moment. Just close your eyes and imagine the scene. You are sitting on a rock beside the stream. See and hear the water rolling over the rocks and notice your image reflected in it. The water is reflecting everything above it, including the sky above. Ponder how the water itself a reflection and so it is actually reflecting a reflection of a greater reality beyond! Your image reflected back at you is a reflection of your eternal soul projected from your soul star. Still, it is you and you are you and the essence of your eternal soul is within you as you sit here immersed in the NOW. You are the source from which you came. Repeat "I am" and know "I am that I am." When you are ready, open your eyes and be grateful for this profound realization.

Let's get up from our perch alongside the stream, stretch a bit and then proceed on the trail toward our campsite. As we move closer to our base camp, let's focus our discussion on the home base of our own local universe in the seventh star of time and space. Let's refer to *The Urantia Book* for some insight into the "seventh super universe of Orvonton", or referred to earlier as –"the seventh light!" How exciting and encouraging that we are, from this perspective, children of the seventh light in a super universe that has ascended to the highest level of spiritual evolution (in time and space anyway). Remember that earlier in our adventure, we reflected upon the significance of the number seven in all of creation? Based upon "The Urantia Book's" explanation that seven represents the highest combination of the trinity personalities and is mathematically necessary for the trinity to be fully represented in all its potential "Deity" combinations as the Father, Son, Spirit, Father-Son, Father-Spirit, Son-Spirit and Father-Son-Sprit. This continues with the offspring of the Son and Spirit as they expand their consciousness into the "Seven Orders of Sons" and the "Seven Master Spirits." Again, let's not get distracted by the patriarchal references knowing that the Divine Mother and Daughter are intrinsically interwoven into the trinity as Mother-Father God, both the Divine and Creative principles, and as the Eternal Child — Creator Son and Creative Daughter.

As stated, "The Seven Master Spirits" of Paradise are the primary personalities of the Infinite Spirit. In this seven-fold creative act of self-duplication the Infinite Spirit exhausted the associative possibilities mathematically inherent in the factual existence of the three persons of Deity."

These are listed in Paper 16 under "The Seven Master Spirits":
1. The Universal Father
2. The Eternal Son
3. The Infinite Spirit
4. The Father and the Son
5. The Father and the Spirit
6. The Son and the Spirit
7. The Father, Son and Spirit

Our super universe, being the seventh one, is reflective of the Seventh Master Spirit — embracing the trinity-consciousness of the Father, Son and Spirit (Mother-Father God, Creator Son and Creative Daughter). In the physical realm of finite experience, the personalities and creative activities of these three Deities can be expressed through the Seventh Master Spirit. In this Master Deity, the "combined personal attitudes of the three Deities" are reflected. I became curious about these personality attributes as they would naturally be reflected in the "mind-spirit' of the created beings on this super universe — in other words, US! So, I did further research to reveal the individual characteristics: The Father personality is "a peculiar and efficient manifestation of the power, love and wisdom of the Universal Father." The Son's personality "adequately portrays the matchless nature and charming character of the Eternal Son." The Spirit personality "especially resembles the Infinite Spirit...forever dedicated to the service and ministry of the love of God and the mercy of the Son..." The vague description of the personality of the Eternal Son described here didn't satisfy me so I investigated further and found this:

"Even though the Eternal Son is the pattern of mortal personality attainment, you find it easier to grasp the reality of the Father and the Spirit because the Father is the actual bestower of your human personality and the Infinite Spirit is the absolute source of your mortal mind. But as you ascend in the Paradise path of spiritual progression, the personality of the Eternal Son will become increasingly real to you, and the reality of his infinitely spiritual mind will become more discernible to your progressively spiritualizing mind." [16]

Apparently, we must wait to see how the personality of the "Eternal Child" unfolds which gives us more motivation to proceed on our ascension paths of spiritual progression. Let's continue to uncover the mysteries of our seventh super universe of Orvonton:

"While the seventh segment of the grand universe may, in many respects, be tardy in development, thoughtful students of your problems look forward to the evolution of an extraordinarily well-balanced creation in the ages to come. We predict a high degree of symmetry in Orvonton because the presiding Spirit of this super universe is the chief of the Master Spirits on high, being a spirit intelligence embodying the balanced union and perfect coordination of the traits and character of all three eternal Deities. We are tardy and backward in comparison with other sectors, but there undoubtedly awaits us a transcendent development and an unprecedented achievement sometime in the eternal ages of the future." [17]

Yay! We have much to look forward to! If we ponder this revelation in relationship to our physical incarnation on a universe within the "seventh light", we may play around with the notion that our own spiritual evolution is in alignment with our placement. If we believe that there is a divine intelligence directing the universal evolution of spirit, we can imagine that all individual projections of spirits are appropriately incarnated on the spheres that most closely reflect their level of evolutionary progression, right? The frequency of vibration they have ascended to must resonate with the frequency of the sphere they will inhabit and evolve on. It may take time for the incarnated beings in the "super universe of the seventh light" to attain the full realization of their spirit potential, but with the "chief of the Master Spirits on High" as our guide, we have the potential to attain the highest level of consciousness defined by a "balanced union" and "perfectly coordinated traits and characters of all three eternal Deities." We have so much to be grateful for in the grand design, my friends! Let's take a collective deep breath and let go of the "small stuff." Let's remember the grand meaningful magnificence of our lives and stay focused on our soul's divine and eternal purpose!

Let's begin our hike up the gentle slope that winds around the mountain and then descends into the valley where we will camp for the night. As we ascend the mountain, let's use our imagination to envision the light of the source at the core of creation. What is the source of the light on Havona? What lies at its very core? Maybe it's a giant crystal like the one Plato envisioned with 120 pentagonal faces and maybe it is from within this crystal that the trinity projects its consciousness and illuminates all of creation! According to *The Urantia Book*, what lies at the center of Havona is the "Eternal Isle of Paradise." For all we know, it could be the home of a brilliant crystal palace glowing with the pure love and light of the Creator who resides within. We can imagine that, seated on a majestic throne, the Creator projects luminescent thoughts onto all of creation and then just sits back and enjoys the show!

Just imagine love and light from the source illuminating all of creation! All we have to do is look to our own brilliant source of light (the sun) and think of it as a movie projector. What if...the film it is showing across the screen of our world has its source in the imaginative mind of the Creator behind the scenes, if you will, like a movie producer willing his actors to play a certain role but giving them the artistic liberty to express themselves freely. As free will beings in this movie, we create our own scenes in our own minds, as individual souls and collectively, as a consensus reality. We can imagine that, together with the Infinite Spirit (the cosmic mind) and the Son (the cosmic spirit), we have the opportunity to put on quite a show! Unfortunately, at this time, it seems the will of much of humanity is focused on creating a chaotic production full of separation, discord and distress when what the executive producer really wants is unity, peace and harmony on the set. It is only when the actors finally surrender to this divine will, that the pure light of love will prevail. We can come together and create a positive force that inspires that will and empowers the actors to step into their divine power and surrender to the highest will!

As these visions dance in our heads, let's continue to ascend up the mountain. This will be incredibly symbolic of our own ascension as we progress along our spiritual paths. Let's embrace this ascent in that spirit. As we climb, let's look to *The Urantia Book* for some answers from our celestial guides about the "Eternal Isle of Paradise." They tell us that it is here that the trinity resides at the core of creation and it is from here that they radiate their light and illuminate all of creation. In the words of a divine "Perfector of Wisdom":

"Paradise is the eternal center of the universe of universes and the abiding place of the Universal Father, the Eternal Son, the Infinite Spirit, and their divine coordinates and associates. This central Isle is the most gigantic organized body of cosmic reality in all the master universe...The material beauty of Paradise consists in the magnificence of its physical perfection; the grandeur of the Isle of God is exhibited in the superb intellectual accomplishments and mind development of its inhabitants; the glory of the central Isle is shown forth in the infinite endowment of divine spirit personality — the light of life. The depths of the spiritual beauty and the wonders of this magnificent ensemble are utterly beyond the comprehension of the finite mind of material creatures. The glory and spiritual splendor of the divine abode are impossible of mortal comprehension. And Paradise is from eternity; there are neither records nor traditions respecting the origin of this nuclear Isle of light and life." [18]

With Paradise, as a portal to infinity, and as home to the One Infinite Creator and Eternal Trinity, we know that 'God' is both eternal and infinite, as our we as the Divine Sparks!

"God dwells, has dwelt, and everlastingly will dwell in this same central and eternal abode. We have always found him there and always will. The Universal Father is cosmically focalized, spiritually personalized, and geographically resident at the center of the universe of universes." [19]

"Here is God personally, literally, and actually present. And from his infinite being there flow the flood streams of life, energy, and personality to all universes." [20]

It is from this center of creation, we are told, that all universal lines of gravity converge and are transmitted from. Accordingly, the personality gravity circuits of the Universal Father, as well as the Spirit and Mind circuits of the Eternal Son and Infinite Spirit, originate and are projected from this Paradise Center into the realms of time and space. It is said that, "This Paradise presence of the Universal Father is immediately surrounded by the personal presence of the Eternal Son, while they are both invested by the unspeakable glory of the Infinite Spirit." [21]

Paradise appears to be time-space transcendent and the source of all energy-matter and cosmic force. In keeping with our revelation that our time-space reality (on Earth) is a duplication of the actual reality in heaven (or Havona), the teachings clearly state that:

"God's residence is central and eternal, glorious and ideal. His home is the beauteous pattern for all universe headquarters worlds; and the central universe (Havona) is the pattern for all universes in their ideals, organization and ultimate destiny. Paradise is the universal headquarters of all personality activities and the source-center of all force-space and energy manifestations. Everything which has been, now is, or is yet to be, has come, now comes, or will come forth from the central abiding place of the eternal god's. Paradise is the center of all creation, the source of all energies, and the place of primal origin of all personalities." [22]

The Urantia Book offers a vast amount of detail regarding this center of all creation all of which is fascinating. I have, for our purposes here, extracted aspects of it which relate directly to our exploration.

First, we are taught that, "...the first source and center, (or Universal Father), has concentrated all absolute potential for cosmic reality in Paradise as part of his technique of self-liberation from infinity, as a means of making possible sub-infinite, even time-space, creation." [23] This "single form of materialization" is an organization of space potency. It seems to be an "essence" called "absolutum" that comprises "stationary systems of reality" beyond the concept of the mortal mind. The two most important aspects of this central Isle, concerning life on the inhabited worlds, are the patterns of energy which constitute living and nonliving matter and the sources of physical, spiritual and mindal energy. Apparently, Paradise is the "absolute of patterns" and the central universe of Havona "is an exhibit of these potentials in actuality." These teachings indicate that all patterns in the universes of time and space are duplications, or reproductions, of these original patterns. The Universal Father apparently directs and controls the projection of all personality-potential through circuits of gravity which radiate outward from Paradise. The Seven Master Spirits radiate the "mind-energy" which constitutes the "cosmic mind" from seven "flash-stations" which then go forth to the seven super universes. Finally, the Eternal Son, we are taught, radiates his spirit through gravity circuits which also reaches each of the seven super universes.

Regarding the source of all physical energy and cosmic force, we are told that they originate from the "Zone of Infinity" located in "Nether Paradise" below the surface where the Trinity functions. I found this explanation of energy transmission to be especially intriguing and the teachers provide a profound description of "universal energy circulation" resembling that of our own physical beings: "The inner zone of this force center seems to act as a gigantic heart whose pulsations direct currents to the outermost borders of physical space. It directs and modifies force-energies but hardly drives them. The mother force of space seems to flow in at the South and out at the North through the operation of some unknown circulatory system which is concerned with the diffusion of this basic form of force-energy." [24]

We can imagine the Mother Womb embracing all of creation breathing and expanding on the out breath and contracting on the in breath, as exemplified in the following quote:

"All forms of force and all phases of energy seem to be encircuited; they circulate throughout the universes and return by definite roots... For a little more than 1 billion Urantia years, the space force of the center is outgoing; then for a similar length of time, it will be incoming. The space-force manifestations of this center are universal; they extend throughout all pervadable space. All physical force, energy, and matter are one. All force-energy originally proceeded from nether Paradise and will eventually return thereto following the completion of its space circuit. The energies and material organizations of the universe of universes did not all come from nether Paradise in their present phenomenal states; space is the womb of several forms of matter and pre-matter. Though the outer zone of the Paradise center is the source of space-energies, space does not originate there. Space is not force, energy, or power. Nor do the pulsations alone account for the restoration of space, but the incoming and outgoing phases of this zone are synchronized with the 2-billion-year expansion-contraction cycles of space." [25]

Just like the exhalations and inhalations of waves expelling on the beach and then being drawn back into the ocean, the whole of creation breathes in a rhythmic cycle of expansion and contraction. The heart of the great universal being pumps at the sacred center of Paradise and all of the physical energy and force that permeates throughout the surrounding space circulates from, and returns to, this vital source. I have been offered a similar explanation from a spiritual intuitive regarding our own journey through physical manifestations and spiritual existences. She describes our souls as being within one great breath of life originating from the Creator. In essence, on one great exhalation, a multitude of spirit beings are expelled into the far reaches of the outer regions of time and space and then must traverse the vast distance, as if flowing in on one long inhalation, back to the source. This is a simple yet powerful representation of our pulsating journey through time and space. As spirit beings, we naturally respond to the pull, or drawing in of the divine breath originating from the sacred center, as we seek to connect with a higher source.

The teachings in *The Urantia Book* reassure us that someday we will return to our Father in Paradise and the Mother Womb from whence we came, "After all, to mortals the most important thing about eternal Paradise is the fact that this perfect abode of the Universal Father is the real and far-distant destiny of the immortal souls of the mortal and material sons of God, the ascending creatures of the evolutionary worlds of time and space. Every God-knowing mortal who has espoused the career of doing the Father's will has already embarked upon the long, long Paradise trail of divinity pursuit of perfection attainment. And when such an animal-origin being does stand, as countless numbers now do, before the Gods on Paradise, having ascended from the lowly spheres of space, such an achievement represents the reality of a spiritual transformation bordering on the limits of supremacy." 26

Wayne Dyer once shared a conversation that he had with a woman who had just finished reading one of his books. The interaction went something like this: She told him that she didn't really get much out of his book except that she no longer had a fear of dying. Wayne Dyer simply responded "Really, that's all, huh?" with just a hint of sarcasm. I'll never forget that cute story. It always makes me laugh to think that people spend their entire lives racing against time to avoid or cheat death and with the magic of one book, this woman no longer fears it!

I feel that the true essence of the profound message within the pages of *The Urantia Book*, although conveyed in detail, encompass one great truth: Our souls are immortal and, as children of the Creator, we are deeply loved and greatly cared for always. Indwelt with the spirit of the Son, we have the unlimited potential to attain the highest realization of Creator-consciousness through a miraculous series of magical and eternal existences, both physical and spiritual. And when we reach the pinnacle of our ascension career, we will be reunited with our loving Father and adoring Mother on the glorious Isle of Paradise.

The purpose of providing these great teachings, I believe, is to guide us on this journey so we don't get lost along the way and lose our connection with the divine origin of our souls in the physical world. The book is always reminding us of the importance of serving "God's will" by earnestly seeking to express the highest levels of truth, beauty and goodness. This is not solely for ascension but also to truly appreciate the privilege of life here and now, and to honor it by standing in the light and by serving in love for the sake of peace, unity and harmony.

Since the sun is setting in the distance, let's set up camp just ahead where it looks like there might be a flat clearing. As we do, let's ponder all of the profound teachings we have had the privilege of learning today. Let's express our gratitude to all of the divine teachers both in the physical and spiritual realm who so generously shared them with us. Once seated around the campfire, we can indulge in some refreshments and reflect upon the advanced concepts and mystical truths we have explored today. We can share our insight and paint a picture of reality in the unique way that we, as individuals, see it unfolding. As we absorb these thoughts, we can sit around the fire, look up at the stars and see if we can locate our own home star in the night sky. We can clearly see the Milky Way galaxy and the dark rift in the center. Is this really a portal through which our souls emerged and will ultimately ascend? Is it a portal through which the source projects its consciousness into the cosmos? Is this consciousness projected into the hearts of the whole souls residing in their home stars? Can we connect into the divine consciousness of celestial beings in the higher realms maybe even the Divine Mother Sophia and her son, Jesus Christ?

The clear and simple answer is "Yes!" All we need to do to discover divine truth and connect with divine beings by engaging in spiritual practices that inspire us to go within. For within each and every one of is the divine spark of the source. We are of and from this divine source and it is literally encoded within our DNA. Much of our divine DNA has been dormant until now and we have been using only our carbon-based DNA. However, crystalline strands of divine DNA surround our carbon-based strands and the time has come to activate them. The dawning of a new golden age is naturally igniting dormant DNA within humanity as highly charged rays of love and light rain down from the higher realms. For the golden age to reveal itself fully in our dimension, humans will need to expand their consciousness and open to these love-light rays. We, as spiritually-inspired creator beings, can intentionally ignite these divine "creator-codes" within our DNA and serve the ascension of humanity. Activating these codes exponentially increases our potential to serve in the highest way possible.

I have prepared the following affirmation meditation to activate these divine source codes within our DNA. Simply declaring "I am that I am" connects our human consciousness directly to the divine consciousness. Enjoy this powerful experience and in the morning, you will awaken to a new perception of reality as the divine light radiates bigger and brighter from the very core of your being.

I Am That I Am
Activating Divine Source Codes Within
(Audio version available at: www.SuzanneRossTranscendence.com)

The most powerful statement a human being can declare is I am that I am. It is the recognition of the direct connection between the human consciousness in the lower evolutionary worlds to the highest and most divine consciousness in the heavenly worlds. We are all of and from the same divine source and each one of us is encoded with divine light codes that can be activated by connecting with our divine guides in higher realms. We can do this by envisioning a soul-star gateway over our heads which opens a channel between us and the Divine Source who created us. Just imagine a golden star tetrahedron suspended 8" above your crown. In this way, you can communicate with the Angels, archangels and Ascended Masters and connect directly with the Divine Source of all that is. In doing this, you activate the divine source codes within and reawaken to who you truly are as a divine spiritual being learning from your human experience. This gateway creates a two-way channel of communication through which you can also connect into your own higher self and share the knowledge gained in your planetary experience while receiving the wisdom gathered from your eternal akashic records. Together, let's engage in the following "I am that I am" activation to activate the divine source codes within and ignite the divine light within you.

Close your eyes and connect into the heart of Mother Earth by running a line of energy from the base of your spine through the crystalline matrix of inner earth and connect directly into the soul star of our earth mother. Feel the deep love of Mother Earth as you connect into her heart space. Now pull that light-love back up into the base of your spine and feel it spiraling up toward your own heart center filling you with the brilliant light of pure love.

Now send that spiraling love energy up into the soul star 8" above your head and imagine igniting a golden flame within the star. Now burning brightly, a flame extends from your soul star and shoots up toward the heavens. This golden flame lights the passageway or portal between you and the higher realms as it becomes a radiant pillar of light. Imagine this pillar of light extending high up into the skies extending beyond the stratosphere and through the starry heavens. Now see the flame of your soul star traveling toward the black hole at the center of the Milky Way galaxy. Imagine your flaming soul star plummeting through the black hole immersed in the void. In the distance, you see a tiny white light and travel toward it. It gets bigger and brighter and then it consumes you as you enter a swirling tunnel of golden light.

You are now entering a wormhole. Your soul star has traversed and transcended space-time. Imagine the spiraling light of your soul star moving at the speed of light toward a brilliant white light at the end of this golden tunnel. As your soul star merges with this brilliant white light, you become one with the great light of the heavens. You become one with the divine source of all that is. Your "I am" light merges with the greater 'I am.' Repeat three times, "I am that I am, I am that I am, I am that I am." Now peer into this brilliant white light and what do you see emerging before your eyes. Stepping into the light, you see angelic beings with golden gossamer wings and radiant faces expressing pure love. These angelic beings give way to three Kings dressed in golden robes each holding a golden object. They have long white beards, piercing blue eyes and radiant smiles.

The first King introduces himself as Metatron, the creator of outer light in the universe. He is holding a golden chalice that contains the divine light codes of creation. This is his gift to you and you accept it graciously. The second King introduces himself as Michael, Archangel of love and protection. He is holding a golden rod that instantly transmutes shadows into pure white light. This is his gift to you and you accept it with pure gratitude. The third King introduces himself as Melchizedek, Master of sacred geometry and numerology which define the fundamental patterns and codes of creation. He is holding a star tetrahedron. This is his special gift to you and you accept it with great honor and pure love.

These three Kings nod and part ways to reveal the divine Sophia standing behind them in all her glory, beauty and grace. The divine Sophia is shimmering with sparkles of gold and white light. She is wearing a golden gossamer gown and her silver hair flows down her back. Her sky-blue eyes sparkle and her radiant smile expresses her pure unconditional love for you. The Divine Sophia shares with you that she is the Womb of Creation. She shows you how she is the illuminated matrix behind all of creation. You see how she, as the Divine Mother, enfolds all of creation in her loving womb as the Divine Holy Matrix. She gives birth to all expressions of light and life in the eternal expanse of creation. Within her loving womb, there is total oneness as the Children of Light express their pure unconditional love for the Mother, each other and all of creation.

Within this illuminated matrix of love, surrounded by your brothers and sisters of light, you see that you are all shimmering in sparkles of gold and white light. You are beyond form in the divine realms that transcend space and time. This is the highest expression of who you truly are as a divine love-light being expressing in the eternal realm of creation and coexisting as both a divine creator being and a human creative being. In this moment, you come into the full self-realization that you are both divine and human. Your divine consciousness is fully merged with your human consciousness.

You have now become your highest self-expressing in the eternal realm of creation.

You have been trinitized as the fullest expression of the Divine Father, Creative Mother and Eternal Child. For you are the Trinity expressed in light, love and form. You have been illuminated by the light of the Father and empowered by the love of the Mother. This light-love activation has ignited the divine source codes within you. Every cell of your being has been ignited by the golden flame of the Divine Source. As this flame burns brightly within your cells, dormant DNA codes are activated one by one and you experience a profound re-awakening. Divine revelations and powerful epiphanies spark memories of your eternal existence in multiple realms. Along with these memories of your multidimensional selves comes the wisdom and knowledge you are gathering in many incarnations as both physical and spiritual beings. These revelations will bring answers to the greatest questions of who you truly are, where you came from, why you are here, what your divine purpose is and why you have incarnated on planet Earth at this time. Your divine mission here in support of the ascension will be revealed in all its glory!

Standing in the presence of the Divine Mother, all of this is being revealed as the divine source codes are reactivated within you. Your "I am" presence is fully merged with the higher "I am" source of love and light. The Divine Mother bows and then extends her arms inviting you to embrace her so that you can feel the power of her pure unconditional love and so that this feeling can remain with you as you move back into your human form. You embrace the Divine Mother and are filled with a depth of love that is beyond that which you ever experienced in the human realm. This is divine love and it is all-consuming, everlasting, infinite and eternal. This is the pure love of the Divine Mother who is always embracing you in her infinite womb as the Divine Holy Matrix of Creation.

It's now time to move back into your physical form in the earthly plane but from this moment on, you will never be the same for you have been activated by the divine light of pure love and your brilliance and radiance will be seen and felt by all others. Turn back towards the tunnel of light from which you came and become your spiraling soul star as it traverses back into time and space, back through the Milky Way galaxy and starry skies, penetrating the stratosphere and descending through the clear blue sky back into the soul star above your head and spiraling back into your human form. Feel every cell of your being tingling with the higher vibration of divine light and love. Your cells have been activated and the golden flame within each one of them is burning brightly as this divine spark continues to ignite the divine source codes of your dormant DNA bringing them all fully online. As your DNA strands are fully activated, the synapses in your brain start firing at their fullest capacity. You have just increased your light quotient to the highest possible level and every day going forward, your vibrational frequency will increase until you are completely transformed into a shimmering crystalline light being.

Be prepared to view your reality in a whole new way from now on. You will experience a much greater sense of oneness with all other living beings that will connect your life force with theirs. You will feel a deeper sense of unity with all life and a greater love for all beings. The reality will appear in shimmering lights with fluorescent colors as the world around you sparkles with the light of divine love. This is your new reality from a higher dimensional perspective for this leap in consciousness has catapulted you into a higher dimensional experience of the world around you. Become the witness as revelations unfold within you that bring you higher wisdom and knowledge. With greater access to the infinite field of pure consciousness, you will develop a knowing within the core of your being that you are divine. You were created from the divine source of all that is and it has been reawakened within you. You will now shine with the divine light of love every day in every way. You will now walk in the harmonious flow of divine synchronicity and everything that serves your highest good will fall into place perfectly without any resistance. For you have merged completely with your highest self and connected into the heart of your divine guidance in the higher realms. You have merged with the soul star of the divine Sophia and your point on the Divine Holy Matrix has been fully ignited.

As a brilliant light on the matrix, you have become an integral part of igniting the matrix and activating the collective consciousness for global Ascension. You are now a powerful light worker and a spiritual emissary. Share your love, light and wisdom every day in every way so that your brothers and sisters can share in your perception of a higher dimensional reality. Together we can transcend the suffering of the 3D realm and move into a higher way of living and being. Thank you for being an emissary of the light of pure love. You are divinely blessed and you are loved more than you can possibly imagine. Namaste.

Your Personal Revelations

_____

_____

_____

_____

_____

_____

_____

_____

_____

_____

REFERENCES

Chapter cover image of eternity symbol courtesy of: http://www.cosmicwind.net
Illustrations:
1-6. Personal Photos
7. http://www.screensavergift.com
8. http://www.pixinsight.com
Text:
Godfre Ray King, *Unveiled Mysteries*, Saint Germain Press, 1934
1. p. 40
2. p. 34
3. p. 35
4. p. 37
5. p. 39-40
6. p. 53
Christine Day, *The Pleiadian Promise,* The Career Press, Inc., 2017
7. p. 27-8
Bertrand Russell, *A History of Western Philosophy,* Touchstone, A division of Simon & Schuster, Inc., 1945
8. p. 145
9. p. 104
10. p. 29
11. p. 33
12. p. 143-4
13. p.144-5
14. p. 145
The Urantia Book Fellowship, *The Urantia Book,* Uversa Press, 2008
15. (16:0.2
16. (6:8.5)
17. (14:2.6)
18. (11:0.1-2)
19. (11:1.2)
20. (11:1.4)
21. (11:1.1)
22. (11:9.6-7)
23. (11:2:7)
24 (11:5.5)
25. (11:5.8-9)
26. (11:9.8)

Day Six

Multidimensional Realms
of Light and Life

INTRODUCTION

What an incredibly beautiful morning! Greeted by the glorious sunlight bathing us in a soft golden glow, we feel incredibly grateful for its warmth and radiance! Wayne Dyer once remarked how the sun was an expression of pure love generously sharing its radiant light for billions of years without ever asking for anything in return. It's easy to see why the ancients worshiped it like a god. For me, I have an innate sense that this magnificent sphere is a divine portal through which outpourings of pure love and infinite wisdom flow. Through this powerful emanation of light, we receive life-force energy which is lovingly and intelligently showered upon us. While the omnipresent Spirit sends streams of consciousness into our realm, the sun illuminates them and thought-forms are revealed as personality patterns. The spectrum of rainbow rays projected from the Pleiades defines the colors of these illuminated forms or patterns of consciousness. The rate of their vibration determines the color waves they will emanate. I intuitively understand that the qualifying nature of all forms of energy and matter is due to the vibrational quality of each individual expression. The complexity and diversity of vibrations, owing to the vast spectrum of colors and infinite octaves of sounds, allow for a "uniqueness" to be expressed by each pattern of energy. Our world, as a duplication of the original pattern of creation, is filled with vibrational images which can be described as reflections, or projections, of prismatic light and symphonic sound. We can think of our reality as a moving picture being illuminated by a spotlight, the sun, and then projected onto a screen which reflects our colorful, musical lives in motion. This film has a beginning but no ending and as the main actor, we take on many different roles throughout the course of this eternal production.

The plot is simple: One supreme soul seeking self-knowledge through creation. In the beginning, this primal mind is released from the bonds of infinity by replicating the perfect patterns of its Self in the creation of a realm called eternity. The Mother-Father God of creation adores all of the children they have perfected but seeks realization beyond perfection. The existential realms of eternity are blissful, peaceful and already perfect but what if they were challenged to *become perfect* by facing adversity in virtual space-time worlds? What if they imagined realms where beings were seeking perfection in imperfect worlds? What special qualities would they develop in worlds where they could *evolve into perfection*? How would this offer them greater self-knowledge on their eternal quest to know thyself? As a consensus of beings seeking self-realization, the eternal ones agreed that creating virtual worlds was a wonderful idea! This would offer them endless opportunities for acquiring self-knowledge and multiple dimensions for developing self-love.

Together, they envisioned holographic worlds upon which virtual experiences could unfold. They designed a concept called space-time within which creation and evolution could take place. They projected holograms of sacred geometry into multiple dimensions all at once. These geometrical patterns would ignite creation in all of these realms with fire from the tetrahedron, water from the icosahedron, earth from the hexahedron, air from the octahedron and finally, self-conscious beings from the dodecahedron. Spheres would spin and swirl within these virtual space-time realms and this spiraling energy would ignite suns and stars into being. Souls from eternity would be projected into these fiery points of light to become living beings in the multiple dimensions unfolding all at once in the eternal now moment and evolving though linear space-time. The living beings in the suns would birth families of planets to revolve around them always embracing them within their gravity grasp. Souls from the stars would project holographic forms onto these planetary foundations to create and experience life and love in these realms. Always remembering the divine source of their eternal souls, these sphere beings, although multiplying in vast numbers, would continually revolve around the Central Sun of Creation. The Mother-Father Goddess/God at the Paradise Core would always hold their children in their gravity grasp of love and devotion. The energy spiraling outward would always be compelled to spiral inward back to its Mother-Father source of love and light.

First, the Creator-beings, in the eternal realm of Havona, projected multiple dimensions spiraling outward into the vast reaches of time and space. Then, they inspired the living beings in eternity to project themselves into these realms. They would call this virtual program of self-realization, *imperfection seeking perfection*, an "evolutionary" journey where holographic beings could devolve and evolve as eternal souls on a progressive space-time ascension path. In the 3rd dimension, these holographic soul fragments would attain a certain self-knowledge during each incarnation but between lives would be shielded with the "veil of forgetting." In this way, they could embrace their identity as a fragmented soul in the current life of one realm without being distracted by the memories of their concurrent lives on other realms. As holograms, each fragment would contain the image of the whole as a mirror reflection of its eternal source in Havona. As such, they would always be streaming their source consciousness in eternity with a direct connection to the divine trinity at the Paradise Core. At critical points throughout their evolutionary journey in virtual worlds, their fragmented holograms would experience a sense of wholeness and attain self-awareness. In what might be called "a singularity moment", the holograms become "self-aware" and suddenly start looking back at the eternal soul who has been projecting their self-image all along!

When the fragmented holograms start to wake up and realize the true nature of their multidimensionality and the holographic nature of their worlds, they start to ask lots of questions! They start to look up and down and all around and ask, "Who am I?" The realization that their physical being might not be "real" can be frightening at first until they connect to the true source of their being. Once they go within and connect to the source and their own higher self, they experience profound love and inner peace. They know that the one thing that is real about them is the eternal soul and divine spark that shines within them. When this knowing settles in their heart space, they experience an ecstatic bliss state. Still, the questions persist and the seeker becomes intensely curious about every aspect of creation. The thirst for knowledge becomes insatiable and the determined seeker researches everything to do with spirituality, science and religion. They may go on a spiritual quest and meditate and find many answers within. Along the way, they find answers and this clarity brings greater self-awareness. This journey of self-realization is incredibly exhilarating and can become all-consuming. It is the ultimate fulfillment of our divine purpose after all! Once we, as holographic beings, wake up to our true nature and divine purpose, we turn away from the darkness of ignorance and toward the illumination of wisdom. We step onto the ascension path and begin our journey home.

Through each and every one of our own unique journeys, the Creator achieves self-realization and experiences self-love. FOR, THE CREATOR IS WITHIN US AS US! We are the Creator expressing in these realms as holograms infused with the divine source. We are divine sparks on the crystal grids of creation! Infused with the Creator-consciousness of the Source and our own free will spirit, we can create at will by focusing our intention on that which we wish to bring into being. We can project the images we wish to create as holographic thought-forms just like the Creator does. If the creator beings in eternity (us!) can project thought-forms which become holograms here in space-time, so can we! We are creator-beings and we can develop our ability to project the thought-forms we wish to manifest. With the power of pure intention and the strength of our free will, we can create that which we wish to do, be and have. I often repeat, "I am, I can and I will." Try it!

There is one omnipresent spirit both existing and experiencing who is just being and also creating. This omnipotent spirit is the source of the infinitude of souls being projected throughout time and space. This dispersion of souls for the attainment of self-knowledge is not random. The overall scheme is not without an intelligent plan and divine purpose. The great and perfect "Self" desires the attainment of divine perfection and the experience of profound love for all souls. A grand scheme of progression through creation and evolution has been set into motion. All evolving beings will ultimately become self-aware and begin their journey home on the ascension path. On this path, we all seek Self-realization and Self-love through reunification with the divine Source.

This is the overriding theme of the movie we are all watching; Self-realization and Self-love. The one key ingredient that makes this film so suspenseful and action-packed is the free will of its cast. While the intelligent energy of the directors may be guiding the plot, the cast is creating at will. In this movie, each actor has been given the creative freedom to express him or herself fully. This eternal moving picture is at once a comedy, drama, mystery, romance and sometimes a tragedy. It takes place throughout endless cycles of time and space but can also be viewed as one eternal moment. This concept allows me to be more of an "observer" of the entertaining movie of my life. Knowing that the divine is within me and observing my experiences through me, I am motivated to give the best possible performance I can! I am also aware that when I assume the role of "observer", I am merging with the divine "Creator-consciousness."

In this state, I naturally take on the divine attributes of "Creator-consciousness" and become non-judgmental, compassionate and patient toward myself and others. I am overwhelmed with a feeling of unconditional love for all living things and beings because I know that we are one within the heart of the Creator. It also gives me a greater appreciation for all of creation as I admire our "co-created" works of art. Intuitively, I know that each of us plays an integral role in the overall plan of *eternal souls seeking perfection through imperfect beings in time and space*. I know that my every thought, word and action has a cause and effect influence on the grand ascension scheme and if I regress, the whole suffers and similarly, when I progress, the whole benefits. When I choose to harm, everyone gets hurt, and when I choose to heal, all is healed. When I choose to hate, it makes everyone sad, and when I choose to love, there is rejoicing. For I know, I am ONE with all of creation and not just an integral part. Like the hologram, even though I am fragmented into parts, I am still all of it all at once too! It is written in the Law of One as the ONE force that permeates all of creation as creation itself.

In the words of Saint Germain to Godfre Ray King:

"This — Fundamental Eternal Truth: It is 'The Law of the One' — 'The Law of Love' — 'The Law of Harmony' — 'The Law of the Circle' — 'The Law of Perfection.' When Humanity really does learn that 'Fact' and obeys — Its Everlasting Decree — the discords of earth and the destructive activities of the four elements will cease...Mankind may know it, and be at 'One' also — if they only will. It is within the capabilities of every individual — for It is the innate Eternal Principle — Within — Self-Conscious Life. All human beings are — Self-conscious Life. This Principle plays no favorites, and all can express its fullness — if they really so desire. Within the — Life — of every human being is the Power — by which he can express — every moment — if he but chooses to do so. All Life contains — Will — but only Self-Conscious Life — is free to determine — upon its own course of expression. Hence, the individual has — free choice — to express either in the human, limited body or the — Super-Human Divine Body. He is the chooser of his own — field of expression. He is the Self-determining — Creator. He has willed and chosen to live as — Self-Conscious Life. When one Individualizes within the Absolute, All-Pervading Life he chooses his own free will to become an — intensified individual focus — of Self Conscious Intelligence. He is the conscious director of his future activities. Thus, having once made his choice — he is the — only one — who can fulfill that destiny — which is — not inflexible circumstance — but a definitely — designed — plan of Perfection. It is — a blue print — which he elects to express in the realm of form and action...a human being may at any time determine to rise out of his human qualities or limitations — and if he will give — all — of his Life, his Energy, to that determination he will succeed. Those of us who have raised the body accomplished the — 'Ascension' — by giving — all — unto the God-Self within — and hence. It expresses through us Its Perfect Qualities — 'The Divine Plan of Life.' [1]

Although I embrace and fully appreciate my individual free will and sovereignty, this knowledge of my importance within the ascension plan inspires me to make sure I am accessing the divine will of my highest self always. Inasmuch as I can radiate love and light to the world around me, I devote myself to this commitment. In this way, I know I will contribute greatly to the perfection plan the Creator has willed. I know I am doing God's will when I seek perfection for it is the Creator who said, "Be you perfect as I am perfect." Within the heart and mind of God, "we live and move and have our being" and this is a great honor that has been bestowed upon us. The best way that we can show our eternal gratitude is by intentionally directing the evolution of our consciousness with a strong desire to express the divine truth, beauty, grace and goodness of God's nature.

PART ONE
The Mayan Adventure Begins

With this pure intention, we can head out on today's adventure filled with a great purpose in our minds and with the love of the Creator in our hearts. This will be of tremendous value as we soar and swirl through the vast constellations of creation for it is within these creatively designed networks of stars and planets that the inhabited spheres of light and life dwell. So, let's throw on our backpacks full of imagination and curiosity as we set out on our journey into the ancient past. For the next four days of our self-exploration, we will be connecting into our ancestral roots. To facilitate a heart-centered projection into the past, we will be taking an astral journey through the use of our "looking glass." In 1934, Guy Ballard, who became Godfre Ray King, tells us of an "out-of-body" virtual journey that Saint Germain took him on. They journeyed into his past lives by leaving his body in suspended animation while their souls traveled together into the ancient past. In similar fashion, we will connect with our guides through our heart space to facilitate our virtual journey. We will project our hearts and minds through our looking glass and the visions will appear before us. I will provide colorful images and detailed descriptions to enliven our quest for lost civilizations and enrich our understanding of who we are, where we came from, why we are here and where we are going. Come, let's go!

For today's astral journey, we will peer through the looking glass projecting our hearts and minds into the lost civilizations of our Mayan ancestors. This will take us way back into the 10th millennium B.C. progressing us right up through the 15th century A.D. Since Mayans with ancestral roots in the Amazon of the past still exist in present-day cities, we won't roll up their past with their story trapped in it but allow it to continue to flow. We can connect into the hearts of the Mayans still living among us and pray for their well-being in a modern world so different from the ancient one. In fact, as we explore the ancient wisdom, we may find ourselves returning to embrace it as we move around the elliptical path of a cyclical reality where history really does repeat itself! The ancient Mayan cultures revered the constellations and they were masters of time. We have so much to learn from their sacred cosmology and ancient prophecies.

Our journey into the Amazon of the ancient past begins in the dense tropical forests of Honduras in Central America. Here, we will search for the lost city of Copan and the massive temples that once thrived there. This promises to be an incredibly fascinating adventure and it will be enhanced by the tour guides I have chosen to invite along. For our Mayan adventure, our tour guide out on the land will be my good friend, Brad Olsen. Brad is a well-known travel writer who has researched 108 destinations in his book, "Sacred Places around the World." In his "Esoteric" trilogy, he reveals the sacred essence of these sites. His books will help us navigate the terrain and provide an excellent foundation of geographical and architectural knowledge as well as historic and esoteric wisdom. Watch my intriguing interview with Brad Olsen at SciSpi.tv/Rise-Up/. The interview covers these topics in much greater depth.

Another tour guide I have chosen is author and adventurer, Drunvalo Melchizedek. Through his books and travels, he offers spiritually-inspired insight into the Mayan cosmology. My dear friend, Barbara Hand Clow, along with her mentor, Carl Johan Calleman, will teach us about the Mayan's mastery of time and share their calendrical prophecies. Finally, my friend, David Hatcher Childress, will offer important historical and archaeological landmarks with which to reference the source of these lineages. To kick off our spiritual quest through the Mayan temple sites, let's invite Drunvalo to share some inspiring affirmations from his book, "The Mayan Ouroboros: The Cosmic Cycles Come Full Circle." He begins with "Awakening to the Mayan Way of Perceiving":

"Life is completing itself, by itself, through itself. There is no other! OUROBOROS! Only one spirit moves through All Life everywhere. And everything is alive. Sacred Geometry proves this One Universe of stars and planets was created through the shapes and proportions of a simple sphere and can equally be seen in a circle. As you understand this, you understand the importance of cycles. Time is circular. Space is circular. Dimensions are circular. Size is circular. Even all light waves become circular eventually. So when a cycle of 25,625 years comes to an end and a new beginning emerges, perhaps we should see and know the sacredness in the moment of our everyday lives. Remember who YOU are in the dance of cycles, and you immediately win the Game of Life. What's the prize? Oneness reveals Itself all around you and within you. Polarity disappears. Death is mastered. Immortality becomes reality. And you come full circle when you realize that what is all around you, nature, is also within you. Do you know you are filled with stars? You are the connection between the outside and the inside. And truly, the First _is_ the Last and the Last _is_ the First." (Drunvalo signs off with "In La'Kesh" — Mayan for "You are another me, and I am another you." [2])

I am delighted about how so much of the sacred geometry and spiritual philosophy that he shares aligns so perfectly with what we have learned thus far. We are right on track, my friends, as we head into the second half of our ascension journey. Post 2012, we are heading into a whole new beginning not just for ourselves but for all of humanity. For we are all one and as we progress on our spiritual paths, our light waves of love and wisdom are rippling across the entire matrix of creation!

The Maya, although primitive in some ways, were clearly an enlightened people with a depth of knowledge that exceeds even that which is commonly understood today. That is evidenced through their grasp of advanced space-time concepts as well as their architectural alignments with the cosmos. Of course, we see this throughout ancient civilizations in similar expressions between 10,000 B.C. — 500 A.D. when the Dark Ages began dimming the light. Our journey is so timely as we spiral out of the darkness and expand into the light of a brand new age. In the Golden Age of Light, we can recover this lost knowledge and discover its power to transform our own lives! With respect for our ancient ancestors, we can journey into their lost worlds and revive that which can serve us in the here and now. In this way, we expand our consciousness by respecting their advancement rather than limiting ourselves within a primitive view.

Are you ready to connect with our ancestors in the Amazon? Let's take a moment to close our eyes and picture how they might have looked walking amongst the temples, carving glyphs and engaging in ceremony.

6.1

Now, let's tune into their souls and ask permission to survey their landscape and visit their ancient ruins. Like Saint Germain and Godfre Ray King, we can project this astral adventure knowing that space is actually timeless. If we enter the eternal now moment, we can immerse ourselves into these ancient civilizations knowing that they are actually co-existing simultaneously with our own. All we have to do is enliven them by re-membering the scattered fragments of space-time. With a deep breathe in, let's focus our minds and tune into our hearts. With a deep breathe out, let's peer into our third eye and project our consciousness into the Amazon jungle.

Our tour guide, Brad Olsen, will lay the foundation, and the terrain, for our journey ahead. From his book, "Sacred Places Around the World":

"The unique pre-historic culture of Central America developed over many thousands of years in relative isolation. Beginning some 35,000 years ago, the Olmec were the first to build large cities and megalithic carvings in stone, leaving behind the beginnings of a culture soon to influence later civilizations. An interesting aspect of the Olmec is their distinct negroid features, which suggests an African connection. The Zapotecs borrowed from the Olmec culture, as did the Maya, the Toltecs, and then followed, the Aztecs...In one of the greatest mysteries of all time, an enlightened people emerged and then all but vanished in the span of a thousand years. The ancient Maya were amongst the most advanced cultures — a people who understood the physical cosmos, had a written language and developed an extraordinarily accurate way of understanding time. Around the third century CE, the Mayas were building tall, gleaming pyramid-temples of stone and mortar amid their corn patches in the steamy Guatemalan jungles. The Classis period of the Mayas suddenly faltered and began fading out around the 10th century CE. Eventually the beautiful ceremonial cities in the southern lowlands stood silent and deserted. Yet, less than a century later, the Maya were back, this time with the Toltec in the northern part of the Mexican Yucatan peninsula." [3]

Overview of Mayan Historical Timelines:
Olmec 1200-1000 B.C.
Early Preclassic Maya 1800-900 B.C.
Middle Preclassic Maya 900-300 B.C.
Late Preclassic Maya 300 B.C. — A.D. 250
Early Classic MayaA.D. 250-600
Late Classic MayaA.D. 600-900
Post Classic MayaA.D. 900-1500
Colonial periodA.D. 1500-1800
Independent Mexico A.D. 1821 to the present[4]

We can't help but ponder the origin of the Mayans even if they were simply evolving indigenous beings in relative isolation from the rest of the world. Let's consult "The Urantia Book." In a chapter entitled, "Dispersion of the Sangik Races", we find clues about the migratory journey of the six original Sangik races who evolved from a Neanderthal tribe called the Badonites about 500,000 years ago.

Backing up a bit, the book tells us that it was 1.5 million years ago when the first great glaciers started to recede after a long Ice Age.

"The great event of this glacial period was the evolution of primitive man. Slightly to the west of India, on land now under water and among the offspring of Asiatic migrants of the older North American Lemur types, the dawn animals suddenly appeared." (Hmmm, Lemurs — Lemur-ians? — on a land that sunk into the ocean. That rings a bell!) Moving on… "1 million years ago, Urantia (our planet), was registered as an *inhabited world*. A mutation within the stock of the progressing Primates suddenly produced two primitive human beings, the actual ancestors of humankind." [5]

Ahhh, the twins! Prevalent throughout so many creation myths, Mesoamerican included, are the infamous twins! In the Mayan version of the bible, the Popol Vuh, the stories of the twins dominate the creation tale. *The Urantia Book* teaches us that these twins were given the names Andon and Fonta and notes that they were truly exceptional beings far exceeding the evolutionary development of their parents and the tribe they were born into.

"Many new emotions early appeared in these human twins. They experienced admiration for both objects and other beings and exhibited considerable vanity. But the most remarkable advance in emotional development was the sudden appearance of a new group of really human feelings, the worshipful group, embracing awe, reverence, humility and even a primitive form of gratitude…They were mildly cognizant of pity, shame, and reproach and were acutely conscious of love, hate, and revenge, being also susceptible to marked feelings of jealousy." [6]

As the story goes, they began to communicate with each other verbally, greatly expanding upon the "crude communicative technique of their ancestors." Then, at the age of nine, "they journeyed off down the river one bright day and held a momentous conference." The advisor for this part of the Urantia book, "A Life Carrier resident on Urantia", says that:

"Every celestial intelligence stationed on Urantia, including myself, was present as an observer of the transactions of this noontide tryst. On this eventful day, they arrived at an understanding to live with and for each other, and this was the first of a series of agreements which finally culminated in the decision to flee from their inferior animal associates and to journey northward, little knowing that they were thus to found the human race." [7]

Approximately 1 million years ago, Andon and Fontan formed the Andonic clans, called the Andonites or Andonic Aborigines. The story of these first two humans and the development of their clans and their ways of living and being is strikingly similar to our ancient ancestors who appeared just 5,000 years ago. This reinforces the idea that humanities advancement is both evolutionary and devolutionary in cyclical phases along the elliptical wheel. In the case of the Andonites, they became fearless and successful hunters mastering the skill of throwing spears. Andon accidently discovered fire and almost became a fire worshipper until he discovered that the sun was a "more awe-inspiring source of heat and light" but it was too remote so ultimately, he did not become a sun worshipper either. They were a flesh eating clan but never ate the flesh of the animal(s) the tribe venerated. They did however, develop a form of animal worship and held ceremonies to sacrifice them which progressed into more elaborate ceremonies sacrificing their own descendants. This was apparently the origin of sacrifice carried on by the Mayans in Mesoamerica and, in more recent times, by Moses and the Hebrews and in the Christian Era, preserved by the Apostle Paul, as "atonement by bloodshed" and the drinking of "blood" and eating of "flesh" in masses held daily worldwide.

They early Andonites even had a spiritual teacher who became their leader named Onagar. He taught them this simple prayer:

"O Breath of Life, give us this day our daily food, deliver us from the curse of ice, save us from our forest enemies, and with mercy receive us into the Great Beyond." [8]

Unfortunately, like in the stories of God ordering the Great Flood due to gods breeding with humans, the superior Andonite races interbred with their less evolved relatives and this led to their ultimate demise. So-called mongrols lowered their standard of peaceful living in unified communities and they spread out and ultimately faded out. The later Neanderthalers evolved out of an improved stock of tribal people called the Badonan. Due to advancing glaciers and flood cataclysms over the next 100's of 1000's of years, the Badonans fled to the highlands. This reoccurrence of cataclysmic episodes throughout human history instilled a deep seated fear of "engulfment" in humans which has contributed to what my friend, Barbara Hand Clow, terms "Catastrophobia."

About 500,000 years ago, according to *The Urantia Book*, something highly unusual occurred within the Badonan tribe living in the highlands of India. A man and a woman gave birth to nineteen highly intelligent children whose skin pigmentation turned different colors in the direct rays of the sun. Among these: 5 were red, 2 were orange, 4 were yellow, 2 were green, 4 were blue and 2 were indigo. These colors became more pronounced as they got older. O.K., let's stop for a moment and digest this. Red, orange, yellow, green, blue and indigo? And then, check this out, according to the book, the violet race ultimately arrives to "upstep" the species! So, there you have it — all the colors of the rainbow (and the chakras) reflected in the colors of the races who were seeded in the DNA of our ancestors!

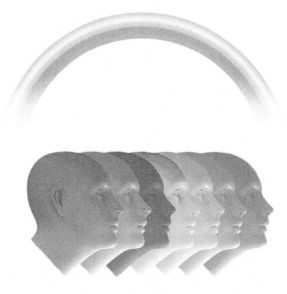

6.2

So much has been written about the seven rays of creation and specifically, that they emanate from the seven stars of the Pleiades, the Seven Pillars of Sophia, the wisdom Goddess of Creation and Mother Womb. *The Urantia Book* speaks of the Adam and Eve of the "violet race" coming from Jerusem which they describe as the "seven schools." I believe that Jerusem and the Pleiades may be one and the same. So before I lose you with the mention of red, yellow, orange, blue, indigo, green and violet races, let me explain a bit further. According to the book, the red race became the indigenous tribal groups, the yellow race became the Asian races, and the orange and green races were greatly weakened by dispersion and defeat and the few remaining were absorbed into the stronger races. The remaining blue race became the "blue bloods" of Europe and the darker indigo race became what we call "black" people today. Finally, when the violet race came later, they arrived from another star system using an advanced form of dissolution and reconstitution during which they "slept." When they awoke in their new land, they were intentionally reconstituted in the form of the species they would be "upstepping."

Here is what *The Urantia Book* has to say about the phenomenon that occurred on Planet Earth 500,000 years ago:

"On an average evolutionary planet, the six evolutionary races of color appear one by one; the red man is the first to evolve, and for ages he roams the world before the succeeding colored races make their appearance. The simultaneous emergence of all six races on Urantia, and in one family, was most unusual. The appearance of the earlier Andonites on Urantia was also something new in Satania (the system our planet is in). On no other world in the local system has such a race of will creatures appeared in advance of the evolutionary races of color." [9]

The book refers to our planet as a "decimal" planet where "Life Carriers" experiment with new patterns. Every 10th planet can be used as a sort of lab for experimentation and much has been said, amongst those seeking answers, about our planet being an "experiment." In a chapter entitled, "The Six Sangik Races of Urantia", the characteristics of each of these colored races is described in detail. For our Mayan journey, we're interested in the origin of our Mesoamerican ancestors which are classified as descendants of the red race. And...wait for it...drumroll please...they are "remarkable specimens of the human race...a most intelligent group and were the first to develop a tribal civilization and government." It's fascinating how their characteristics, and fate, are reflected in the stories of the Mayans from just a few thousand years ago! The story goes that, due to conflicts with their Asian brethren, and tendency to fight amongst themselves, they were driven out of Asia and "about 85,000 years ago the comparatively pure remnants of the red race went en masse across to North America and shortly thereafter, the Bering land isthmus sank, thus isolating them...When the red man came to America, he brought along much of the teachings and traditions of his early origin." [10]

The red men in North America did become relatively isolated but they originated in India and Asia. They were highly intelligent but had a tendency to fight amongst themselves. This constant warring would lead to their demise. The story of the red man ends with what we witnessed in the drama of the Mayans on the stage of Mesoamerica:

"As it was the red man could not rule the white man, and he would not willingly serve him. In such a circumstance, if the two races do not blend, one or the other is doomed."

About 65,000 years ago a leader and "spiritual deliverer" named Onamonalonton appeared and brought temporary peace to American red men and revived their worship of the "Great Spirit." (Ultimately, Onamonoalonton moved to the red woods of California and many of his descendants walk among the Blackfoot Indians today). For the American red men, the temporary peace faded out over time and many of the more intelligent strains perished in tribal struggles. We know, however, that they were the ancestors of the race we call the "Mayans" who were "remarkable specimens", "a most intelligent group who were the first to develop a tribal civilization and government." Warring amongst themselves was in their blood as was animal worship, sun worship and an innate fear of the control the elements had over them. This led them to perform blood sacrifice to the Gods in return for rainfall. Blood sacrifice (which has now just been replaced by blood sacrament) goes way back to 500,000 years ago when the Andonites were taught by Onagar that blood was the "breath of life."

The great, great grandson of Andon became the progenitor of the Badonan tribe which later produced the six Sangik races, of which the red man was most intelligent. We can clearly see this in their advanced knowledge of time, the cosmos, architecture and mathematics while isolated in the Amazon jungle. They built massive temples with architectural artistry and astronomical precision. They had a sophisticated writing and calendar system that they carved with elaborate glyphs into stone. They were blessed with powerful leaders who built great kingdoms. They competed in sports and performed religious ceremonies. Spiritual practices worshipping their gods permeated every aspect of their daily lives. For the most part, they led rich and fulfilling lives although the ages were also wrought with tragedies including warfare, drought, disease and sacrifice.

Now that we are getting more tuned into the Mayan ancestry and origin, let's review the Urantia version of historical events so we can get closer to the millennia when temple cities emerged. To recap, 1.5 million years ago, the lemur developed into our ancestral primates. 1 million years ago, these primates bore the twins, Andon and Fonta, who became the first humans. They started a clan called the Andonites who were diminished because of interbreeding with their less-evolved relatives. Over the course of the next 500,000 years, the "Lemurian" Primates evolved into the Andonites and then later, the Badonans who became the Neanderthals. Between 500,000 — 300,000 years ago, many epic events took place reagarding the geneology of humanity starting with the arrival of Caligastia and the Daligastia 100 sent here by Lucifer, a sovereign ruler in the system of Satania. Caligastia was sent here as a "Planetary Prince" with outstanding credentials for leadership in the evolutionary advancement of an inhabited world. His assistant, Daligastia, along with 100 crew members were involved in teaching, upgrading and advancing the primitive beings on earth at the time. About 200,000 years ago, however, the so-called "Luciferian Rebellion" took place in the galactic realms when Lucifer declared his independent authority and sovereign right to rule the realms. When Lucifer's assistant, Satan, came to the planet to deliver the news of the rebellion to Caligastia, he adopted that policy and became a ruling dictator. The leader of the Andonites, Van, stood firmly against Caligastia on this form of dictatorship and him and his followers separated themselves from Caligastia and his followers. Many different groups intermixed and interbred among these groups who dispersed and disbanded.

Simultaneous with these events, 500,000 years ago, the six Sangik races were born within a Badonan family, one being "red." The red race lived in Asia until they were pushed out by the Asiatic tribes due to conflicts between them and, weakened by their own in-fighting, they were defeated. They fled to North America by way of the Bering isthmus but when the Bering bridge sank, they became isolated. Still, they carried on the teachings and traditions of their Asiatic origins enhanced by their red race intelligence.

Now, let's explore what Group Ra has to say about this time period, in brief, so as to illuminate another possible origin of the Olmec and Mayan races. Group Ra, through the channelings documented in the Law of One series, teaches us that many races from both outside and inside of our solar system visited the planet during the last 4 million years. It talks specifically about visitations from the "Orion" Group that were "service-to-self elitists" on a mission of conquest to "enslave the unelite" and recruit those on the planet who resonated with the service-to-self vibration. Group Ra visited our planet, coming from their home planet of Venus 11,000 years ago, to walk among the Egyptians as "service-to-other" teachers of the Law of One. They go on to say that another faction of their group went to South America to teach the Law of One. In both locations, they were involved in pyramid building to create energetic structures for healing and training.

Group Ra says that 705,000 years ago, a planet in our own solar system, Maldek, was annihilated by nuclear warfare. These beings were in a state of shock, literally trapped in a knot of fear for 105,000 years. Then about 600,000 years ago, the "Council" sent a race to untangle the knot. After about 100,000 years, they began the transition to Planet Earth incarnating in the second-density bodies available at the time which were apes. This would give them the opportunity to evolve again as a sort of do-over. Relearning the important lessons in the second dimension, many of them evolved over time and reincarnated elsewhere while a few evolved into early humans and stayed. Some did not evolve into humans but remained as a species of bigfoot. Another transfer of beings took place 75,000 years ago when Mars, the Red Planet, destroyed their planet in warfare, and the "Guardian Race" stepped in to upgrade them genetically. With a mix of Martian and Guardian DNA, they were sent here to protect and guard humanity, as a form of karmic alleviation, in the form of another species of bigfoot. The melding of the Guardian race with the Martian race was viewed by other members of the Guardians as a violation of the Martian's free will and that led to the quarantine of our planet. A third species of bigfoot were implanted here as a sort of gene pool with "appropriately engineered physical vehicles" that can withstand radiation in the case of a nuclear war. These are the illusive bigfoot species.

Note: *The Urantia Book* says our "system" was quarantined as a result of the Luciferian Rebellion. Other sources say our planet was quarantined because of the "Fall of Atlantis" when the lower beings escaped from the inner earth. In any case, the quarantine, as I understood was not so much a punishment but as a way to protect other neighboring worlds from the lower energy that had been released in our world causing us to become dis-eased and distorted. Maybe we were quarantined also to protect us from outside forces, like the fallen angels. It's like in a hospital setting where the quarantine of the diseased person benefits both the patient and the visitor from further harm.

Group Ra is a member of the Confederation of Planets in service to the Infinite Creator along with 50+ members from other realms representing over 500 planetary populations. There are members from our own planet on this Galactic Council who evolved beyond 3D. They are backed by 24 elders and a Council of Nine. The Council of Nine, as the Ennead in Egypt, represented themselves as cosmological concepts, to teach the inhabitants of Planet Earth. They appeared to the mortals in Egypt like gods with tall luminous bodies and elongated skulls. They were clearly off-planetary beings from higher realms. The Galactic Council makes decisions regarding the galaxies which they oversee. Regarding our planet, Group Ra says that there are entities visiting from many, many places in creation who have incarnated here over the ages because it offers a foundation for the lessons they need to learn at a particular point on their evolutionary journey. Entities may also choose a planet for reincarnation that matches the vibratory resonance of their dimensional development, especially those planets which are classified as "decimal", or experimental, projects in inter-racial seeding and evolutionary development.

When seeking answers about origins, it is important to realize that each soul incarnating on Planet Earth carries DNA codes from their entire evolutionary journey through the time/space continuum! To narrow in on the geographical origins of the Mesoamerican races who occupied the Americas, let's advance to the time of Lemuria and Atlantis. Group Ra teaches us that 53,000 years ago, the "Mu" entities, (aka Lemurians), came here from the star system Deneb in the Cygnus constellation and settled on a continent in the Pacific. They were largely from a planet who, due to the age of their sun, had difficulty achieving 3rd dimensional life conditions. These new arrivals were somewhat primitive but very spiritually advanced. Due to a readjustment of the tectonic plates, their continent was washed beneath the ocean. The survivors were sent to Russia, North America and South America. The indigenous cultures in these regions, they proclaim, are "descendants of the Lemurians."

Then, 31,000 years ago, an Atlantean race appeared on a continent in the Atlantic. Around 15,000 years ago, they had a great leap in technological advancement. According to Group Ra, there were two conflicts which led to their continent sinking into the ocean. The first was 11,000 years ago and the second was only a couple of hundred years later. These wars caused "changes in the Earth's configuration" which led to the submergence of their continent. Survivors of this catastrophe were sent to Tibet, Peru and Turkey. Please watch the interview I conducted with the only surviving member of the group who channeled Group Ra, Jim McCarty, which includes a special audio clip of my interview with Carla Rueckert, the channeler, before she passed away a few years ago. Watch the interview at SciSpi.tv/Rise-Up/.

Several significant revelations come out of the material in both *The Urantia Book* and *The RA Material* which gives us important clues to the origins of the people who developed civilizations across North and South America. Interestingly, Group Ra tells us that *The Urantia Book* channelings were delivered by a group of discarnate beings in the inner planes. Meanwhile, Group Ra tells us that they have origins on Venus when it was inhabitable for 6th dimensional beings. Since Group Ra tells us that a faction of their group went to the Americas, it is no wonder that the indigenous groups there, including the Mayans, worshipped Venus and referred to it often in their astronomical records.

Closer to home, my friend, David Childress, recently gave me his latest book, "The Lost World of Cham — The Transpacific Voyages of the Champa." In it, he introduces the "Egyptian-Hindu-Buddhist seafarers" of Southeast Asia, the Cham or Champa, who would have been responsible for spreading the artifacts and even bloodlines of cultures around the world. In an interview we did last year, he mentioned that there must have been a seafaring people in ancient times that connected the Atlantic to the Pacific. We were discussing how ancient Egyptian and Buddhist artifacts could have ended up in a hidden cave high on a wall in the Grand Canyon. During our interview, he mentioned the Cham people and suggested that they must have been seafaring. Watch this fascinating interview at SciSpi.tv/Rise-Up/. His book wasn't out yet. Now that it is, the whole story has been revealed with extensive research and intriguing illustrations to back up his discoveries. This is truly an extraordinary revelation and a game-changer on many levels concerning what we previously thought to be true about "isolated" ancient cultures:

"The mysterious Cham, or Champa, peoples of Southeast Asia formed a megalith-building seagoing empire that extended into Indonesia, Fiji, Tonga, Micronesia, and beyond — a transoceanic power that reached Mexico, the American Southwest and South America. The Champa maintained many ports...including Olmec ports on the Pacific Coast of Central America." [11]

Could the Cham have brought advanced knowledge from more ancient lands to the indigenous Olmec people of Central America? This would support a diffusionist view, versus the more widely accepted isolationist view, which explains the "similarities in widely disparate cultures" including architecture, beliefs, customs, artifacts and knowledge. Not to mention the widespread discoveries of goods, plants and even animal remains that are not indigenous to the region. How did they get there? The only solid explanation is by transoceanic travel. The classic period for the Olmec, according to Childress, has been dated from 1200 BC to 400 BC. Many colossal heads made from stone have been found, particularly in La Venta, that have "negroid" and Asian features. Since the Mayas came after the Olmec in the same region, it stands to reason that they adopted their culture and applied their knowledge. Still, the origin of the Olmecs baffles historians and archeologists:

"So, even to mainstream historians, the origin of the Olmec's is a mystery. In the realm of alter-native history, many theories exist on how Negroids arrived in Central America. One theory is that they are connected with Atlantis: as part of the warrior-class of that civilization they were tough and hard-bitten. Or perhaps they were part of an Egyptian colony in Central America or from some unknown African empire. Others have suggested that they came from across the Pacific from the lost continent of Mu, or as Shang Chinese mercenaries (culled from the ranks of the Cham?). Similarly, there is the curious association of "magicians" (or shamanic sorcerers using magic mushrooms and other psychedelics) with many of the Olmec statues — magicians from Africa, China, or even Atlantis." [12]

This is all so intriguing and suspenseful! These "Egyptian-Hindu-Buddhist seafarers" of Southeast Asia, the Cham or Champa, would have been responsible for spreading the artifacts and even bloodlines of cultures around the world. This becomes highly relevant to our adventure through the Mayan temple sites today as we notice similarities to the Egyptian step-pyramids at Saqqara and the African and Asian features prominent in the artwork and carvings of their priests and scholars. David's diffusionist viewpoint makes so much sense in the bigger picture of things and explains so much of what has mystified historians and archeologists who have clung to an isolationist view.

It brings to mind the ancient Sumerian tablets that tell a tale of space travelers from the 12th planet who brought advanced knowledge and wisdom to the indigenous people of the ancient city of Ur (in Mesopotamia, now Northern Iraq). In fact, according to the tablets, these visitors (the Annunaki) actually used their advanced knowledge of genetics to upgrade the indigenous Neanderthals with their own DNA creating a hybrid species. They placed this new species of man on Gondwanaland in African to evolve until they could serve them as a slave species in the mines and gardens. Many believe that they implanted a "slave gene" in the DNA of early man that still influences our behavior today. Many Africans refer to Gondwana as their homeland and place of origin. Apparently, there were two "lords" overseeing the Annunaki intervention with the indigenous earthlings — Lord Enlil and his brother, Lord Enki. Here we have the twins once again! With these two, according to the tablets, one is controlling and the other one is compassionate. Lord Enlil, as the older dominating brother, wanted to control and take charge of the human race they were "upgrading" and Lord Enki, the younger heart-centered brother just wanted to love, teach and nurture them.

This seems to have set the stage for a series of twin brothers to follow, like Osiris and Set in Egypt or Cain and Abel in the bible. Lord Enlil may even be the patriarchal Lord Almighty, Yahweh, in the Old Hebrew Testament and Lord Enki may be connected with the more matriarchal gnostic sects that later emerged as the Essenes. This would present an expression of the Divine Father and Divine Mother in action as the patriarchal and matriarchal god/goddess cultures developed around the world. The stage for the twin brothers may have already been set in the celestial realms by the sons of the Goddess Sophia, Sanat Kumara (the Planetary Logos) and Sananda Kumara (Jesus of Nazareth) who have existed since time immemorial. Beloved Sanat Kumara represents the commanding force of the wiser older brother (masculine energy) and beloved Sananda represents the loving force of the compassionate younger brother (feminine energy). *The Urantia Book* even talks about the "motherly love" of Jesus. Together they represent wisdom and love as the offspring of the Goddess of wisdom and love, the Divine Sophia.

According to the gnostic texts, Sophia became a demiurge when she created on her own without her partner, Lucifer, who has also been connected with Sanat Kumara. Sanat may be seen as both a father figure and the oldest brother of the 4 Kumaras — Sanat, Sananda, Sanaka and Sanananda — who also represent the four directions and 4 elements. It has been written that Sophia came back as Mary Magdalene in order to redeem herself at the time of Jesus. Since the patriarchy first made Eve in the garden a mere appendage of Adam and thus, subservient to him, and then later made Mary Magdelene, a prostitute, we can see how the masculine and feminine energies have been imbalanced for millennia. It is reassuring that *The Urantia Book* informs us that we are heading into an age where the masculine and feminine will become perfectly balanced. This, I believe, is the key to our ascension into a new Golden Age of Enlightenment where unity consciousness will prevail. Hoorah! Let's hold that vision and promote balance between our own masculine and feminine tendencies. Let's support the unity where neither gender rules over the other or is better or lesser than the other. We are equal and of course, we are one.

Back to the ancient Near East~

The ancient city of Ur preceded Babylon and even early Egypt when it was known as the land of "Khem." History books will say that "Uruk" in Mesopotamia was the first city-state in the ancient world and give it a date of around 4800 BCE. As archaeologists continue to excavate and more hidden records are revealed, the dates that history books have cited are getting further and further pushed back. Of course, mainstream history books only focus on the civilizations of this age. Alternative historians explore the possibilities of much more ancient civilizations in other ages that may have preceded this one.

The connection with the Middle East and Asia is striking and would indicate that, possibly after Babylon, when the languages were mixed so we would "babble-on", the people spread out far and wide across the ancient lands. The creator-god Enlil, as an expression of Yahweh, did not want the new humanity to unite at that time and thus become a force to be dealt with so we were separated by language, distance and religion. It's reassuring to discover that these early people from Southest Asia, the Cham, may have become seafarers and as a result, were able to somewhat unite the scattered tribes by spreading knowledge, wisdom and goods. Of course, they may have also spread the bloodlines by interbreeding with the indigenous people they encountered. In regards to the Olmec and Maya, however, the Maya did not take on the African-Asian features of the Olmec. They did benefit greatly, though, from the knowledge and wisdom the Olmecs brought to Mesoamerica which is reflected in the architecture, astronomy and calendrical skills they developed. As we travel to Egyptian sites in later chapters, we will see the similarities between the architecture of the Mayan pyramid-temple sites as well as the commonalities in their cosmology, astronomy and time-keeping.

In the modern era, the Maya are best known for their calendar system and the prophecies it foretells. With 2012 only 5 years behind us, we are all still reeling from the Mayan predictions of the end of the world. Apparently, it was the end of the world <u>as we know it</u>! (Isn't that a song?) Rather, 2012 heralded in a new beginning that many of us are becoming well aware of as millions around the world awaken to a new perception of reality. Astronomers and astrologers alike are pointing to an alignment with the great central sun of the Pleiades star system known as Alcyone. This alignment with Alcyone exposes us to highly charged particles that supposedly raise the electromagnetic frequency of our environment. Others claim that solar flares have been shooting off from the super-luminous blue giant, Deneb, in the Cygnus constellation which also charges our atmosphere. Of course, we have also moved into alignment with the black hole at the center of the Milky Way galaxy and its massive gravitational pull. All of these alignments and proximities create a higher frequency, or resonance, which pervades our atmosphere and has the collective effect of raising the EM frequency of humanity. This in turn raises our consciousness! We literally vibrate at a higher frequency in concert with the atmosphere and this catapults us into a new age of enlightenment inspired by humanity's higher consciousness.

It's a very powerful time on the planet, my friends! This highly charged atmosphere stirs up the collective emotional body of humanity and this becomes apparent in societal, economic, religious and political shifts. As the masses awaken, they become aware of their enslavement by the ruling hierarchies and disclosure floods the airwaves as deception and darkness at the highest levels are revealed. A massive movement toward unity, freedom and sovereignty will break down many old structures and systems that serve only to make the rich richer and the poor poorer. Ages of enlightenment inspire and empower humanity to rise up and step into the divinity of who they truly are as powerful, passionate beings capable of creating a new world where freedom reigns. Unified forces break free of the hierarchy and create unity communities that are settled in love and light. In these enlightened communities, spirituality is practiced communally and all members are dedicated to serving the highest good for all.

Can the rise and fall of civilizations be attributed to our place in the cosmos during specific ages? As we learned from our exploration of the ages of the Yugas, the galactic alignments have a powerful influence on the consciousness of humanity throughout cycles of time. This is where the Maya cosmology comes in! They were masters of time and, like the Egyptians, they were also advanced astronomers, architects and mathematicians. Unique to the Mayas however, is their unrivaled skill at tracking the cycles of time and this is exemplified in their sophisticated calendar system. Fortunately, my dear friend and international best-selling author, Barbara Hand Clow, has dedicated decades of research to understanding the Mayan calendar and she generously shares her phenomenal insight in her fascinating book, "The Mayan Code: Time Acceleration and Awakening the World Mind."

In it, she explores the deeper meaning and purpose behind the Mayan calendar system and reveals how time acceleration is a manifestation of the acceleration of consciousness. Barbara draws upon the revelations of her mentor, Mayan researcher, Carl Johan Calleman, as she lays out in detail the nine underworlds each with 13 periods that are layered into the Mayan calendar over a 16 billion year time period. Much of this calendrical knowledge is based on carvings that were found on a stele in the ancient Mayan city of Coba on the Yucatan Peninsula. Since time-keeping was a key feature of the Mayan culture and their long-count calendar is what they are most known for in the modern age, we will discuss it in more detail as we hike into the dense tropical jungle of present-day Honduras in search of Copan — the first destination on our Mayan journey into the ancient past.

Mentally, let's get a lay of the land so we can pinpoint our consciousness into the destination we are seeking. Our journey will start in the southeast of the Mesoamerican region at Copan on the border of Honduras and Guatemala. It is a rugged, mountainous region and the temple ruins lie hidden in the lush looming jungle. From Copan, we'll peer through our looking glass into the Holy City, Tikal, featuring the "Lost World Pyramid" and finally, we'll sweep into the jeweled crown of Mesoamerica, Palenque, featuring the famous Temple of Inscriptions which holds the tomb of Lord Pacal. Along the way, we will honor the ancient ancestors of these ceremonial centers by recognizing the creation mythology in the Popol Vuh, the codices they left behind and the sophisticated calendar system they created. The ancient hieroglyphs and temple carvings will reveal a societal culture of interconnected city-states led by kings and astronomer-priests. Although the historical evidence and translated glyphs unearth a ritual connection to a dark underworld of blood sacrifice and evil "lords", the overwhelming presence of massive temples and ceremonial centers reveal a spiritual connection to the cosmos and the sky gods who inspired them as well. Let's start our adventure "out on the land" with an overview of the regions we will be focusing in on.

PART TWO
Journey to Copan

Courtesy of: https://www.penn.museum.com/sites

Let's begin our journey into the jungle by closing our eyes and picturing the scene unfolding before us. Engage your senses to appreciate the richness of color, light and sound. Peer into the deep green grace of swaying palms, swinging monkeys and singing birds. Listen to the chirping, howling, screeching and rustling. Taste the sweet nectar of tropical fruits and smell the perfume of blossoming flowers. Touch the moist, silky leaves and feel the tree spirits come to life. The whole jungle teams with excitement welcoming you into its spiraling arms twisting around you in a loving embrace. Mother Nature flourishes here where the fairies and elementals dance with delight and surround you with their radiant presence. Here you are safe in the presence of creation as it was originally intended. This is the Garden of Eden, a paradise of lush vegetation, where we can rejoice in the grace, beauty and symmetry of creation in all of its Edenic glory.

6.3

As you walk through this lush green paradise, twigs snap under your feet. You look up and listen for howling monkeys in the treetops and hear parrots screeching in the shadows. The bright rays of sun streaming through the branches illuminate a scarlet macaw, the National bird of Honduras.

6.4

Rustling in the palm fronds draws your attention to an adorable fuzzy face peering back at you. It's the white-faced Capuchin monkey, native to this jungle, greeting you with curious delight.

6.5

Looking down, you become aware of all the critters scurrying about underfoot. From slithering snakes and colorful iguanas to scaly anteaters and mud turtles, you proceed with caution. Respecting all of Mother Earth's children, you embrace all of the bustling life within this wonderland. As we walk in awe and wonder of the sights and sounds, let's feel into the souls of the ancient Mesoamericans who once thrived here. What was their daily life like? Did they originally live in harmony and unity as a spiritually-empowered culture during an enlightened period? As we can see from their temples and stelae, they were gifted artists and sculptors. It's clear that divine inspiration flowed through their hearts and poured into their creative expressions. As skillful architects and astronomers, higher wisdom illuminated their minds and streamed into their temples and calendars. Their culture appeared to flourish under the direction of kings and priests with their temples honoring the sun and stars. Ultimately, their cities fell and were abandoned but they left behind many clues that we can decipher and learn from. They can be an inspiration as we move into our own enlightened age of inspired creativity, cosmic connection and spiritual wisdom.

One of the greatest discoveries found within the Mayan ruins were the stelae found at Coba in the Yucatan Peninsula. The life of Carl Johan Calleman, a Swedish biologist, was forever changed in 1979 when he went on a backpacking trip to Mexico and Guatemala. During his visits to the Mayan ruins, he became so intrigued with their knowledge of timekeeping and complex calendar systems, that he dedicated the rest of life to understanding and deciphering the deeper implications of their timelines. He wrote three groundbreaking books on the topic which present revolutionary concepts about the shifting consciousness and biological evolution of life based on the Mayan long count calendar. My friend and Mayan calendar researcher for over 30 years, Barbara Hand Clow, has been given permission from her mentor, Carl Calleman, to teach about these concepts, especially since her own revolutionary book, The Pleiadian Agenda, had influenced and inspired him. Barbara has written an extraordinary book, "The Mayan Code: Time Acceleration and Awakening the World Mind", which I highly recommend, along with her DVD, "The Mayan Calendar Revealed."

Let's find a clearing where we can stretch out our blankets, enjoy some refreshments and clear our minds. We want to be laser focused as we explore the life-changing implications of the Mayan long count calendar revealed by Callehan and so eloquently taught by Hand Clow. When you are relaxed and satiated, just sit back and take some nice, deep breaths. Notice your breath as it flows in through your nostrils and expands your belly then flows out of your lungs and contracts it. Feel the air as it flows in and out and become totally connected with these sensations in your body. Connect into the life giving breaths and tune into your heart space. Fill your heart with a ruby red energy and feel it expand with love. Now fill your mind with a golden energy and feel it light up with brilliance. Release any tension in your body and any distraction in your mind. Release any troubling emotions in your heart space and settle into the warm embrace of pure love. With our heart ignited and our minds illuminated, let's become totally present as we absorb these remarkable teachings.

Let's begin our study of the Mayan Long Count Calendar by grasping the mind-blowing date range we'll be exploring which spans from 16.4 billion years ago to December 21, 2012! Please note that I will only be offering a general overview of the explanations provided by Barbara in her book and DVD. My sole intention is to enhance our journey into the hearts and minds of the ancient Maya by understanding their mastery of time. These teachings will, of course, be very valuable to all of us as we learn more about these systems but please refer to Barbara's work for a more in-depth study.

What Calleman and Hand Clow have discovered is that the Mayan calendar glyphs speak of nine underworlds, each with 13 time periods, overlaid consecutively one upon the next. As such, these nine underworlds are both consecutively and simultaneously evolving. The first underworld, the Cellular Underworld, began 16.4 billion years ago (the same time frame most cosmologists agree our universe came into being) and the last underworld, the Universal Underworld, ended on December 21, 2012. Both Calleman and Hand Clow agree that this is not an end date for humanity but rather a rebirth into a higher, unitarian consciousness. The most fascinating aspect of these stacked underworlds is the fact that they each represent an acceleration of time. In each consecutive new age, or underworld, time is going 20 times faster! That means that since the beginning of our universe, 16.4 billion years ago, there have been nine ages each spanning a shorter period and each bringing in an accelerated perception of time. Since we are aware that time is, in the truest sense, a mental construct that allows us to perceive our reality in a linear fashion, it is so interesting that our collective human consciousness would perceive it moving 20 times faster with each new age. In fact, Hand Clow refers to it as an "acceleration of consciousness." One of Calleman's most popular books is called, "The Mayan Calendar and the Transformation of Consciousness", released in 2004.

These consciousness concepts align with what we have been discovering since the beginning of our 10-day ascension — everything is consciousness and what we see, feel and experience throughout our incarnational adventures depends solely on the type of consciousness that is being projected onto any one point in space-time where our mind is presently focused. In the case of planetary experiences, we are subject to the collective consciousness unfolding at the time we are incarnated upon it. In the case of planet Earth, the Mayans demonstrated an extraordinary understanding of the layers of collective consciousness unfolding throughout billions of years. Each age, or underworld, is broken down into 13 "day" & "night" cycles each with 7 days and 6 nights. During the day cycles, certain realities unfold which are then integrated during the night cycles. Day 5 of each of the underworld ages is particularly significant because it represents the midpoint of each of the ages. Milestones for that age occur at this critical midpoint which resonate throughout the simultaneously evolving stacked ages. For instance, the midpoint of the first underworld, the "Cellular Underworld" is 6.25 billion years ago when our solar system accreted around the sun. On Day 5 of the Mammalian underworld, fish transitioned onto land and on day 5 of the Tribal Underworld, hominids discovered fire! The critical 550 CE midpoint of the current Great Cycle from 3114 BCE to 2012 CE marked the emergence of great spiritual teachers like Pythagorus, Buddha, Zoroaster and others. When Calleman discovered how the Mayan calendar lined up with prehistoric dates already established by modern scientists, he was convinced that their calendar had merit way beyond what one might think of as primitive stone carvings!

In Barbara's fascinating book and DVD, she goes into much more depth as to why this is so important for us in the modern age, especially since we are living in the time period which marks the "end" of the long count calendar and a rebirth into a whole new cycle of accelerated time. In the last two underworlds, she shows how humanity begins to understand their true nature as light beings expressing as particles and waves and how our entire reality is defined by vibrating frequencies. Now that we are five years beyond the significant 12/21/2012 date, we can look back and observe a tremendous shift in consciousness on the planet with millions, if not billions, waking up to a more spiritual perspective while antiquated religious and political structures break down. Her sincere desire is to see humanity grasp that they are both human and divine and with this knowing, rise up into a more empowered expression of themselves. Many of us share this heartfelt desire and are reaching out through books and conscious media to enlighten, inspire and empower humanity to claim their divine birthright as sovereign beings with a right to freedom from enslavement and tyranny. The Mayans predicted this new age of the divine human rising up and flourishing in the age of the Goddess respecting Mother Earth and all of her children. The ultimate goal is for humanity to reunite as one species sharing the planet with the realization we are all of and from the same divine source. And so be it and so it is. (Watch my interview with Barbara Hand Clow at SciSpi.tv/Rise-Up/; she is incredibly fascinating as she explains these concepts).

With that, let's breathe in these beautiful blessings for ourselves and for all of humanity. Let's look around and send these blessings out to Mother Earth and all of her children, including the plants and animals. Let's make a commitment to love and adore all of creation and especially, each other. Let's express gratitude for the intricate role each and every living being and thing play in the interconnected web of our collective consciousness. Let's stand up and stretch and gather our things so we can continue on our journey into the ancient Mayan site of Copan. Enriched by our enhanced understanding of the Mayans as "Masters of Time", we look upon these temple sites with a deeper appreciation of their advanced levels of skill and sophistication.

Up ahead, we glimpse a great stone wall shimmering in the sunlight just beyond the dense forest. Stepping into the clearing, we stand in awe of its magnificence. As we venture further into the central plaza of Copan, we can admire the portrait stelae that line the processional ways and adorn the acropolis, a complex of step pyramids, plazas and palaces. There is also a ball court for the sacred ritualistic ballgame played by the ancient Mesoamericans throughout all of the city-states.

6.6

According to our tour guide, Brad Olsen, "The ancient city of Copan is considered the artistic capital of the Maya empire. Rich in temples and carved stelae, this Classic Maya city was at its peak around 725 CE." [13] The Mayans thrived in Copan for more than 2000 years from the Early Preclassic period to the Postclassic period. Little is known about the pre-dynastic period of Copan except for a few glyphs mentioning the date of 159 CE associated with the name "Foliated Ajaw." It became the capital of a major kingdom in 426 CE when a dynasty, originating in Tikal, was established here. This is referred to as the "refounding" of Copan. The first king of the capital city was K'inich Yax K'uk' Mo' who ruled for 11 years followed by his son, K'inich Popol Hol, who inherited the throne in 437 CE after his father passed. K'inich Popol Huh was responsible for initiating the first ball court in Copan for the ceremonial Mayan ball game. This sacrificial game had rich symbolism based on the Mayan creation myth in their version of the bible, the Popol Vuh.

There were a total of 17 kings in the dynastic history of Copan with the last king, Ukit Took, taking the throne in 822 CE. At its peak, more than 20,000 residents were spread out over a 100 square mile radius. For almost 500 years, Copan was a powerful city-state despite a setback in 738

CE when their great king, Uaxaclajuun Ub'aah K'awiil , was defeated, captured and beheaded by his former vassal, the king of Quirigua, K'ak' Tiliw Chan Yopaat. After a short hiatus, the capital city recovered and resumed its temple building projects until the 9th century when the Mayan city-states across the region faded out. Speculation of their demise at this time centers on over-population, a lack of resources and widespread disease.

As in all Mayan city-states, the temples are magnificent and the Acropolis complex of overlapping step-pyramids and palaces is awe-inspiring. Our tour guide, Brad Olsen, points out that, "Above and beyond beautiful artwork and architecture, the people of Copan were keepers of a highly advanced culture, employing a complex and sophisticated religion enhanced by astute observations in the cycles of the earth and the cosmos." [14] He suggests that along with being a ceremonial site, it may have also been a type of university where astronomy and cosmology were taught and students could learn and practice alongside the astronomer-priests. Here, scribes would have been busy carving glyphs that described the dynastic kingdoms and celestial events on stelae lining the plaza.

Altar Q is the most famous monument at the site and features carvings of the first 16 kings who ruled the capital city from the 5th to 9th century. It is a decorative stone block with a portrait of 4 kings on each of the 4 sides.

6.7

The most well-preserved temple is the Rosalila which features the founder of the dynasty with the sky deity Itzamna. There is a reconstruction of it in the sites museum.

6.8

Finally, the Hieroglyphic stairway adorned by Stela M, has a total of 62 steps with a sculpted figure at every 12th step representing the most important rulers of the dynastic history of Copan. With over 2200 glyphs, it is the longest known Maya hieroglyphic text.

6.9

As we walk around the central plaza admiring the magnificent ruins, we can only imagine what daily life might have been like here. We know that they worshipped various gods and goddesses as well as celestial bodies like the sun, moon and Venus. Their creation myth is written in the *Popol Vuh*, sometimes called the Mayan bible, and features hero twins who rescue their father from the underworld. The ceremonial ball game played on the ball courts at the temple cities throughout Mesoamerica is directly connected to the creation myth in the Popol Vuh. Let's wander over to the ball court just north of the Hieroglyphic Stairway and there we can explore this creation myth. This ball court is the third version built in 738 CE and was dedicated to the Great Macaw deity.

Let's gather around in a circle and honor the sacred symbolism of this ceremonial ball game. With a brief translation of the Popol Vuh, we will have a better understanding of why this ball game held such important symbolism for the ancient Mayans who played here. Losers of the game were often sacrificed as part of the ritual connected to the creation myth. As I share this short version of the myth, imagine the remnants of the competitive spirit left behind here. Feel the heated frenzy of the cheering audience and the intense emotions of victory and defeat.

6.10

Like we discussed earlier, the story of the hero twins is common amongst many cultures and traditions and may have its roots in the galactic twins who have greatly influenced the planetary consciousness, Sanat Kumara, often referred to as the planetary "logos", and Sananda Kumara, believed to have incarnated as Yeshua Ben Joseph AKA Jesus Christ. Generally, Sanat represents the mind, or knowledge, and Sananda represents the heart, or love. Their mother, Sophia, is the Goddess of Wisdom, and the source of heart-centered knowledge. In the Popol Vuh, there is a succession of three sets of twins:

"The first set of twins, Hun-Hunahpu and his brother, Vucub-Hunahpu, were invited to the Mayan Underworld, Xibalba, to play a ballgame with the Xibablan lords. In the Underworld, the twins faced many trials filled with trickery; eventually they fail and are put to death. The Hero Twins, Hunahpu and Xblanaque, are magically conceived after the death of their father, Hun-Hunahpu, and in time they return to Xibalba to avenge the deaths of their father and uncle by defeating the Lords of the Underworld." [15]

The Popol Vuh consists of a "Preamble" and four books. The preamble has been translated to modern English as saying:

"This is the beginning of the ancient traditions of this place called Quiche. Here we shall write. We shall begin to tell the ancient stories of the beginning, the origin of all that was done in the citadel of Quiche, among the people of the Quiche nation."

This is followed by a description of the "Primordial World":

"This is the account of when all was still silent and placid. All is silent and calm. Hushed and empty is the womb of the sky."

The fact that there are four books, following the silent, empty womb and beginning with the creation of living beings, compels me to believe that the four books may represent the four ages on planet Earth that the indigenous Native Americans of the American Southwest speak about. At the end of the fourth world, or age, humans emerge into the fifth world — the one many believe we are ascending into now as the Golden Age. Let's take a closer look at the stories in the four books of the Popol Vuh and see how they align with what we believe about the unfolding of creation on earth.

Book One is about the creation of living beings. Just like in Genesis, the story of creation starts out with silent waters and an empty void (or womb) and then the living things and beings emerge from it (or within it). First, plants and then animals and finally, man. In this first book, it looks as if two sets of humans, and possibly two ages, appear and then the humans "dissolve" in the first age. In the second, they "wash away." The book says the first humans were created from earth and mud but they soaked up water and dissolved and the second humans were made of wood but they washed away in a flood. At this point, "Vucub Caquix" ascends from the underworld.

Both ages seem to have been submerged in water and this could refer to the sinking of Lemuria and Atlantis. Stories of heart-centered Lemurians could be the first humans. The Atlanteans, many believe, were technologically-minded. They may be the second humans that were made of wood (essentially without a heart). After the flood, "Vucub Caquix" ascends from the underworld. This brings to mind the story told by Drunvalo Melchizedek, in his 2-volume series "The Ancient Secret of the Flower of Life." He talks about a massive explosion causing a huge tear in the planet that released souls from the underworld during the time of Lemuria and Atlantis. The story goes that a race of beings from the planet Mars came to our planet after they destroyed theirs. Then later they became aware that their new home was going to sink into the ocean so they built a synthetic Merkabah to transport them off the earth. Their experiment goes awry and the Merkabah explodes which causes a huge tear in the planet and many lower beings from the Underworld are unleashed onto the surface. Drunvalo goes on to say that these lower beings attached to the surface humans causing them to "fall" in consciousness. The Lemurians and Atlanteans represented human civilizations which had evolved to a fifth dimensional level of consciousness. The "Fall" plunged the consciousness of the surface humans to a lower third dimensional level. Sickness, poverty and death also resulted from the lower beings being released from the Underworld. When Book Two describes "Vucub Caquix" ascending from the Underworld at the end of the second submergence, it may symbolize the lower form of consciousness that was unleashed after the "Fall."

In Book Two, the Hero Twins, Hun Hunahpu and Vucub Hunahpu, appear on the scene and plot to kill Vucub Caquix, Lord of the Underworld and his sons, Zipacna and Cabracan. They succeed and order and balance is restored. This could very well be symbolic of the stories of Sanat Kumara and Sananda Kumara sent to planet Earth by their mother, Sophia, to save the human species and restore order and balance. In the story Drunvalo tells, after the "Fall", a whole council of Ascended Masters responded to the emergency situation and came to repair the tear in the earth and prevent more souls from being unleashed. Their grand plan also involved building a synthetic consciousness grid by erecting temples at each of the 84 points where the grid's ley lines intersect. In the stories of Sanat Kumara, synchronistically, he was sent to embrace planet Earth as the planetary Logos thereby taking on the suffering and transmuting it into light. Maybe he was sent at the time of the "Fall"! Several thousands of years later, Sophia sends her son, Sananda Kumara, to spread love and compassion throughout the earth. Comparing and synchronizing myths and legends is the key to revealing fundamental truths about the history of our planet.

In Book Three of the Popol Vuh, the Father and Uncle of the Hero twins, Hun Hunahpu and Vucub Hunahpu, are murdered at a ballgame in Xibalba. Hun Hanahpu's head is placed in a Calabash tree, where it spits in the hand of Xquiq impregnating her. She leaves the Underworld to be with her Mother-in-law, Xmucane. Her sons, Hunahpu and Xbalanque, then challenge the lords who killed their father and uncle, succeeding and becoming the sun and the moon. If we imagine that Book Three represents the third age, post-Atlantis, and before the re-emergence of the 4th, we can surmise that the murders of the original twins in the Underworld lead to the re-emergence of the impregnated mother. She then gives birth to the second set of Hero twins who avenge the lords of the Underworld and rise up as the sun and moon of the new 4th age.

The Hopi talk about emerging into the fourth world after being trapped in the Underworld during the Great flood. They say they emerged through a sipapu in the Grand Canyon by climbing up a reed. The Yavapai talk about being trapped in the Underworld when the deluge seeped into the inner earth and threatened to drown them. To save their seed, they sent a girl in a hollowed out log to the surface. She emerged in Montezuma's Well and then went to the top of Mingus Mountain where she became impregnated by the Sun God. Then she had a daughter who had a son, Sakarakaamanche. Soon after, the daughter got taken up by an eagle leaving the Grandmother and her Grandson to become the progenitors of the Yavapai race. This story reminds me of the impregnated mother coming up from the Underworld to bear sons. It also reminds me of Sophia and her sons. (Note: You can watch an episode of my TV series, Supernatural Adventures, called "Sedona: Place of Emergence" which features the telling of this story of the Yavapai at Montezuma Well, their literal Garden of Eden, at SciSpi.tv/Supernatural-Adventures-Channel/.)

In Book Four, humans are successfully created from Maize and the gods give them morality in order to keep them loyal and later, give them wives to make them content. This rings true of the fourth age we have been in for millennia where the patriarchal political and religious leaders have been in charge of programming humans with so-called morality so that they would be loyal servants with submissive wives. Thank goodness we are now immersed in the dawning of a new fifth age where a matriarchal consciousness prevails which promotes unity and equality for all people regardless of race, status or gender.

What's so fascinating is that, according to Carl Calleman in his book, "The Mayan Calendar and the Transformation of Consciousness", there are four Worlds which correspond with four Underworlds in the Mayan Long Count Calendar. Together, they represent a 5,125 year cycle beginning in 3114 BCE and ending in 2011 CE. The National Underworld began on August 11, 3114 and ended on October 28, 2011. The Planetary Underworld began in 1755 and ended in 2011. The Galactic Underworld began in 1999 and ended in 2011 and the Universal Underworld went from 2/11/2011 to 11/28/2011. Although many believe that the 12/21/2012 date marked the end of the Long Count Calendar, his findings show it actually ended on 11/28/2011. In any case, here again we have the four Worlds co-existing with the four Underworlds.

What becomes crystal clear is that these ages, worlds and underworlds are all pointing to periods of time when the collective consciousness was influenced by a specific type of energy. We can refer to ages of the zodiac which each carry in a different type of energetic influence. This has been referred to as "winds" which become a driving force compelling humanity to think and act in a certain way during different time periods. The Maya attached Deities to these time periods that historically align with the type of consciousness unfolding on the planet during certain ages, ie. during the "Dark Ages", the "God of Darkness" was ruling the heavens. In this way, the Mayans predicted the Dark Ages long before they actually happened and because of their prophetic vision, they experienced a period of growth and expansion while Europe plunged into darkness and destruction. Calleman points out that we can use the calendar to flow in harmony with the energy of the ages rather than resist them and suffer the consequences.

What an intriguing and rich culture the ancient Mesoamericans created for themselves! From the deep symbolism of their sacred creation myth to the mystifying accuracy of their calendar system, the ancient Maya were tuned into the cosmos in a profound way that defined their existence. The advanced architecture, exquisite artwork and extensive written language reveal an extraordinary ability to tap into a higher source of knowledge and wisdom and then apply it with great skill and precision. With the mysterious Olmec as their ancestors, who appeared in Central America at the same time when Egypt was flourishing on the other side of the globe, you have to wonder about the possible connection between these two civilizations. The step pyramids in Mesoamerica greatly resembled the ones at Saqqara in Egypt. Even the style of dress, the extensive records carved into temple walls and the succession of patriarchal kings reminds us of Ancient Egypt. Either there were seafaring tribes carrying these traditions and bloodlines across great distances or there were crafts in the air transporting advanced beings from distant stars who intervened in the temple building sites around the globe.

We can also imagine that it may just be tribal people evolving around the world who are tapping into the same collective consciousness inspiring them to build and informing them how and where. The end result either way is that the same type of realities were unfolding across the planet during the same time periods indicating a planetary resonance with the same field of consciousness. This theory is firmly supported by the Mayan Long Count Calendar with its 9 underworlds and 13 heavens that show how different time periods reflect a specific type, and frequency, of consciousness that affects the global consciousness. We will continue to tune into the dynamics of the Mayan Calendar throughout our ascension journey for clues about the spiraling ascension of human consciousness and its resonance with the crystalline core of Mother Earth.

PART THREE
Journey to Tikal

Wrapping up our enchanting visit to the remarkable ruins at Copan, let's angle our looking glass to the northeast now crossing the border into Guatemala and focusing in on Tikal — "The Holy City" nestled in the tropical rainforest. Let's consult with our tour guide, Brad Olsen, to lay the foundation for this sacred temple site. Brad explains that the mapped portions of the sites extend for 6 square miles. "The maps reveal 3,000 separate constructions including temples, palaces, shrines, ceremonial platforms, ballcourts, terraces, plazas, causeways and residences."[16]

6.11

Along with narrowing our focus on the geographical space we will be exploring, let's tune into the time period. Since we have looked way back in time now, let's refer to the timeline provided by Carl Calleman in his book, "The Mayan Calender and the Transformation of Consciousness" since it takes us further back to 3000 BCE and the "First cultivation of maize" by Native Americans up to 1697 CE and the "Fall of the last independent Mayan Kingdom at Tayasal."

3000 BCE — First cultivation of maize

1500 BCE — Olmec Civilization in Veracruz

250 BCE-50 CE — Pre-classical Maya, Izapan culture

100 CE — Beginning of classical Mayan culture

434 CE — Founding dynasties in Copan and Palenque

800 CE — Collapse of classical Mayan culture

843 CE — Earliest date in Chichen Itza, Beginning of Post-classical Mayan culture

1223 CE — Collapse of post-classical Mayan culture, Collapse of Toltecs in Tula

1368 CE — Aztecs settle in Mexico Valley

1504 CE — Columbus spies canoe off coast of Honduras

1519 CE — Cortes lands in Veracruz

1521 CE — Fall of Aztec Empire

1697 CE — Fall of last independent Mayan kingdom at Tayasal[17]

The first signs of agriculture in the area date back to 1000 BCE and the first construction began around 400-300 BCE. The original settlement was influenced by the Chikanel culture that had spread throughout the Yucatan Pensinsula. Later art and architecture after 1 CE was influenced by the Izapan culture. Hieroglyphs reveal that it was anciently called Yax Mutul. In the Itza Maya language, it may be interpreted as meaning "the place of the voices." It thrived during the Classic Period for about 500 years between 300-800 CE. The first dynastic king who reigned in 90 CE was Yax Ehb' Xook, translated "First Scaffold Shark", followed by Foliated Jaguar and Animal Headress. A succession of kings follow leading up to the more well-known ruler, Chak Tok Ich'aak, translated Great Jaguar Paw, who was the 14th king who built the great palace that would become the center of the acropolis.

Having just come from Copan, we know that the first king of that capital after the "refounding of Copan", K'inich Yax K'uk' Mo', grew up in Tikal. Interaction between these two city-states continued as Tikal's influence spread. During his youth, K'inich Yax K'uk' Mo' may have been witness to the hostile takeover of Tikal by a general from the great metropolis of Teotihuacan named Siyah K'ak' translated (Fire is born), on January 14, 378 CE. The same day Siyah K'ak' arrived, Great Jaguar Paw was killed. Siyah K'ak did not take the throne but within a year, his young son, Yax Nuun Aylin I, translated Curl Snout, did become a "boy king" in 379. Curl Snout ruled for 47 years, marrying a local women from Tikal, which legitimized the right for their son, Siyaj Chan K"awiil, translated Stormy Sky, to take the throne in 411. These are the original rulers of Tikal who set the stage for the rise and expansion of the holy city of Tikal.

It was rare for a woman to be in a ruling position in the predominantly patriarchal kingdoms of Mesoamerica, however, in Tikal, the "Lady of Tikal" sat with a male co-ruler from 511-527. Her name was Kaloomte' B'alam, translated Curl Head, and she co-ruled with Bird Claw. Female leadership usually resulted from a breakdown in male succession wherein a male of the ruling lineage either hadn't been born yet or was too young to take the throne. Like in the case of S'ak K'uk' in Palenque who inherited the throne of her father only until her son was old enough to take the throne as a "boy king." In this case, the "boy king" became King Pacal II, the greatest king and Master Architect of Palenque.

Although Tikal is a glorious site with ceremonial plazas, palaces for kings and the ritual ballcourt, it was often embroiled in war and conflict with its neighboring city-states, primarily Calakmul and Caracol. These two city-states allied forces to defeat Tikal in the 6th century and the city-state went into a 100-year hiatus from the late 6th to the late 7th century. There was a lapse in new construction and no new stelae were erected. Glyphs from Altar 21 at Caracol tell a story of how Tikal was defeated in a major war in April 562 and their king was sacrificed. Caracol grew and Calakmul thrived during this hiatus. 120 years after the sacrifice of their king, Tikal re-emerged under the rule of Jasaw Chan K'awiil I who erected the first monument that would end the hiatus. Jasaw also sought revenge for the sacrifice of their great king and in 695, he captured the enemy noble at Calakmul leading to its gradual decline. Jasaw Chan K'awaiil and his heir Yik'in Chan K'awiil became great warriors and master architects as they expanded their military influence and built the most impressive structures at Tikal.

The temples at Tikal are monuments to the magnificence of the Mayan culture. They were keepers of time and understood it to be sacred. They looked to the cosmos as the place of their origin and destiny and instinctively knew that the Galactic Center was a divine portal. They felt a special connection to Venus and, according to Group Ra, higher dimensional beings from Venus walked among them over 11,000 years ago to teach them the Law of One principles and educate them about the power of pyramids. Knowing how connected the Mayans were to the Cosmos and its cycles of time, when we observe their temple cities, let's keep in mind the Hermetic principle "As above, so below." Tikal revolves around its galactic center, the Great Plaza, and the pyramids surrounding it are placed to honor the four directions, just like a medicine wheel.

6.12

In the North is the North Acropolis which is a complex of temples, pyramids, stelae and altars that were continually constructed, expanded and enhanced starting in 350 BCE through 800 CE. It became a royal burial site for the dynastic kingdom inspiring new temples to honor each new dynasty.

Between 400 CE and 800 CE, this sacred complex was adorned with awe-inspiring new temple pyramids, stelae and altars. In her book, "The Mayan Code", spiritual teacher and Shaman, Barbara Hand Clow, teaches us that the period of 435 CE and 830 CE, marked the ninth Baktun on their Long Count Calendar. She says that "the Maya made time divine during Baktun Nine".

In the South is the Central Acropolis which is a palace complex for the ruling dynasties. The Plaza of the Seven Temples was placed to the west of the South Acropolis with a row of nearly identical temples to the east. Barbara Hand Clow teaches us that the Maya were "people of the Pleiades" and we can imagine that the seven sisters of the Pleiades may have inspired the seven temples, each representing a different aspect of the seven rays of creation. There is an unusual triple ball court at this site, possibly honoring the divine trinity of the lower, middle and upper worlds. This ballgame being an important ritual for the Mayans is symbolic of the divine interplay between the three worlds. They knew how important it was to stay balanced in the middle world by defeating the lords who ruled in the underworlds and by honoring the Sky Gods who shone in the heavens.

The powerful "Mundo Perdido" complex, meaning "lost world", contains the "Lost World Pyramid". It lies to the west of the Plaza of Seven Temples, and is one of the largest ceremonial complexes of the Preclassic period. The name alone suggests that the Maya may have had a premonition that their civilization would become a "lost world" or possibly they are referencing a portal in the cosmos to the west of the Pleiades that leads into a lost world. Maybe both of these concepts apply and are symbolic of all of the people and civilizations in the Middle World ultimately becoming "lost" as they ascend into the cosmos through a divine portal into a lost world. The nine steps leading up to the pinnacle is certainly symbolic of the Nine Underworlds leading up to the "end date" of the Mayan Long Count Calendar.

In honor of the nine Underworlds, there were nine "Twin Pyramid Complexes" that were, for some unknown reason, dismantled. To me this feels symbolically connected to the story of the original twins in the Popol Vuh who were killed by the Lords of the Underworld and then ultimately saved by the famous twins who defeated the Lords. There is a building to the south of this complex containing a single room with nine doorways. Construction of the complex took place over 20 year intervals which reflects the significance of the number 20 in their calendrical cycles with the Tzolkin reflecting 13, 20-day cycles or 260 and the Tun reflecting their sacred year of 360-days or 18, 20-day cycles. A Katun is 20, 360 cycles. It seems that 3, 7, 9, 13 and 20 were all sacred numbers in the Mayan cosmology and anyone familiar with sacred geometry knows exactly why.

The other major temple pyramid sites at Tikal, Temple I and II are known respectively as the "Temple of the Great Jaguar", dedicated to Jasaw Chan K'awil, and the "Temple of the Mask" dedicated to his wife. The other two significant temples, Temple III and IV, are known respectively as the "Temple of the Jaguar Priest" and the "Temple of Inscriptions".

6.13

Archaeoastronomy is the study of how astronomical bodies in the cosmos align with structures that were built on the ground. Truly the ancient Mayans were highly attuned to the cosmic cycles and knew how important it was to honor those cycles in their art and architecture. The whole temple complex, like all the others throughout the ancient Mayan temple-cities, are a divine representation of the hermetic principle "As above, so below."

The decline of Tikal began in the 9th century during the Terminal Classic period and Temple 3 was the last major pyramid to be built there. Glyphs on a stelae in the great plaza reveal that in 869 there was one brief revival when Jasaw Chan K'awiil II took the throne. The last monument was erected in 889 and by the 10th century, the city had been deserted. Lack of resources, over-population and environmental challenges like drought led to the collapse. Tikal's fall marked the end of the Classical period for the Mayans. Places, just like people, die. As they are being settled and structures erected, sites take on a consciousness of their own. They adapt a personality and the energies and emotions of their inhabitants are absorbed into their structures and even into the foliage around the sites. The decaying bones of the once great rulers who passed are left behind along with the crumbling rocks of once great temples. The heart of these cities pulsated with the masses who lived, worked, played and died here. All who were born here, lived here, loved here and died here left their energetic imprint on these sites.

Let's take a moment to honor this great city and rather than mourning the loss of it, we will connect into the eternal presence of it with this verse that anthropomorphizes Tikal as a God within its own rightful place, especially for those who once lived, worked and worshipped there. Let's also honor the modern day Mayans whose ancestors once thrived there and now who struggle to survive in a world where temples and gods are no longer a part of their world and where even their royal heritage has been long forgotten. With the temples in ruins and the gods who built them long gone, we say farewell to a royal city, now lost, and a people, now diminished in time.

"He was my North, my South, my East and West,
My working week and my Sunday rest,
My noon, my midnight, my talk, my song;
I thought that love would last forever: I was wrong.
The stars are not wanted now; put out every one,
Pack up the moon and dismantle the sun,
Pour away the ocean and sweep up the wood;
For nothing now can ever come to any good."

~ W.H. Auden

PART FOUR
Journey to Palenque

Let's angle our looking glass to the northwest now, crossing the border into Mexico and focusing in on Palenque, the shining jewel in the crown of Mayan culture. The grandiose temples at this exquisite site are the crowning achievement of one of the most famous architects of the ancient Mayan Kingdoms, King Pacal. Although the Palenque dynasty was founded by K'uk ' B'ahlam in 431 CE and 11 rulers reigned before him, K'inich Janaab Pacal, also known as Pacal the Great, was the most famous of the dynastic kingdom which lasted from about 400-800 CE. Pacal was preceded by his mother, Sak K'uk', who governed for three years until her son was old enough to rule. Sak K'uk' inherited the throne from her father, Pacal's grandfather, known as Pacal I. Sak K'uk' only reigned for a short time until her son turned 12 when he took the throne as a "boy-king." King Pacal reigned for 70 years until his death at the age of 82. He married Lady Tz'akbu Ajaw who became known as the "Red Queen" when her burial tomb was discovered in the temple adjacent to the palace where King Pacal's remains were buried: Thus, giving her an elite status. Her sons would continue the reign of their father and all three proved to be great kings and master architects.

6.14: The Palace as seen from the courtyard.

Palenque is smaller than other neighboring temple sites but far exceeds them in architectural grandeur. Recent excavations show how the architects at Palenque used sacred geometry as a guide for building their temples and the great King Pacal, reigning from 615-683, was the Master Architect who commissioned the construction of some of the most awe-inspiring temple structures in all of the Mayan city-states. Starting with the renovation of the central complex, known as "The Palace", Pacal built upon existing structures enhancing them with more elaborate architectural design.

An impressive tower, known as "The Palace Observation Tower", reaches for the heavens in the plaza and was likely used as both a watchtower and as an observatory. As we know, the Mayans were great astronomers and the shaman-kings and astronomer-priests communicated with celestial deities to receive guidance that was critical to their survival.

6.15: The Palace Observation Tower

The most famous of all the temples at Palenque is the Temple of Inscriptions which turned out to be the tomb of the great King Pacal. Upon excavation and exploration of the temple in 1952, Alberto Ruiz discovered a stone slab in the floor which upon removing revealed a passageway and long stairway leading to a grand chamber. In Egyptian style, this chamber held a large tomb with a sarcophagus weighing 15 tons and its lid weighing a full 5 tons! Baffled as to how this tomb could have possibly been transported to this space below the temple superstructure, archaeologists determined that the tomb was placed there first and the temple was built around it. Drawing diagrams of how this was done, they determined that not only was the temple built around it but the chamber itself was positioned so as to align with an inverted keyhole in the adjacent wall. This gave the spirit of the King access to the Underworld. His afterlife journey would involve trials and tribulations related to his incarnation and then if he passed a series of judgment that balanced the scales of justice, it would culminate in his soul's spiritual ascension into the celestial heavens.

6.16: The Temple of the Inscriptions

Other notable temples in Palenque are the Temple of the Sun, Temple of the Cross and Temple of the Foliated Cross. The Temple of the Sun is of particular interest and a team who explored the site determined that its entryway was aligned with key solar events like the Equinox, Solstice and Zenith.

Another grandiose feature of Palenque is its elaborate and expansive ballcourt flanked by two identical temple structures. As we have already learned in the Popol Vuh, the Mesoamerican ballgame that would have been played here held great symbolism for the Mayans. Life and death played out in victory and defeat with the Lords of the Underworld on these courts. It was also a forum for the Kings to display their power over their captors in front of their entire kingdom.

Beneath the Palace, passageways lead into underground chambers where ceremony and ritual took place. Based on the hieroglyphs, it seems that only nobility were permitted to engage in these blood sacrifice rituals. The King would actually draw his own blood from a wound he inflicted on his genitals and then soaked into a cloth that was burned. The hieroglyphs indicate that the King would then see visions in the smoke as guidance from the Gods. In this way, blood sacrifice was offered as a gift to the Gods in return for celestial guidance proving once again how blood sacrifice to win God's favor is deeply engrained in the human consciousness.

Symbolically, the greatest King of the dynasty of Palenque didn't vanish like the rest of his kingdom. The Master Architect of this splendid work of art was buried in the most famous temple on the site. During his lifetime, he had achieving mastery of sacred geometry using the simple *sphere* and *cube* to guide him as he traced the fundamental patterns of creation into his blueprints. Remarkably, when his body was found, he was grasping a limestone *sphere* in one hand and a *cube* in the other. He wore a mask of Jade and it is said that this mask is the richest treasure ever found in Mesoamerica.

While at this temple site, I am inspired to offer blessings to the spirit of King Pacal by honoring the World Tree at the Temple of the Cross. To the Mayans, the World Tree was at the center of the Mayan Calendar prophecies. Carl Calleman has eloquently translated the deep symbolism of the World Tree and located it geographically along "longitude 12 degree East" dividing the Western and Eastern hemispheres of the globe. He also shows how this midline represents the corpus collosum in our brains as the line dividing the right and left hemispheres. He explains how our brain waves are in resonance with the iron core crystal at the center of the planet in varying degrees throughout our waking hours and how at night we disconnect and establish a resonance with the cosmos. He explains how this crystalline core is in resonance with the greater cosmos as well. Flowing with divine synchronicity, we, as a microcosm, are in sync with the macrocosm of Mother Earth who is in sync with the universe at large! The base of the World Tree is the World Mountain which is centered in the core of Mother Earth and pyramids on the surface have likely been built to emulate this mountain in an effort to enhance their resonance with the core. With this insight as a foundation for our practice here at Palenque, let's be seated facing the Temple of the Cross knowing that the cross is sacred as a symbol of the World Tree. Let's enjoy this verse from the Popol Vuh as we close our eyes and merge into the World Tree visualization:

Whatever there is that might be is simply not there: only the pooled water, only the calm sea, only it alone is pooled. Whatever might be is simply not there: only murmurs, ripples, in the dark, in the night. Only the Maker, Modeler alone, Sovereign Plumed Serpent, the Bearers, Begetters are in the water, a glittering light. They are great knowers, great thinkers in their very being.[18]

World Tree Visualization

Use your vivid imagination to bring the following visualization to life as it unfolds: Group Ra teaches us that: "The first entities on this planet were water, fire, air and earth."[19] Many visitors came from other realms and dimensions to seed life on this planet and prepare the foundation. The Guardian race, also known as the "Gardeners", sowed the fields in the water and upon the earth to nurture many life forms in a wide spectrum of colorful expressions. A vast array of plants sprung up in the water and in the trees that shot out of the earth. The trees grew branches sprouting out in the four directions establishing the sacred cross on the land. Finally, out of the clay of the earth, arose the first humans who were spiritual in nature but washed away in the ocean. Then, out of the wood from the trees, the second humans rose up who were technical in nature but fell into the watery abyss. Finally, the third humans rose up from the underworld ascending the World Tree. They defeated the Lords of the Underworld and honored the sacred cross who pulled them out of the abyss so they could flourish on the land.

Let's just sit quiet and let that sink in. It's a powerful visualization with rich symbolism.

PART FIVE
The Cosmic Plan

In *The Mayan Calendar and the Transformation of Consciousness*, Carl Callaman writes:

"The World Tree, the central creative principle in the view of the Maya, exists at several different levels of the cosmos…For all we know, all the universe is unified by an invisible web of energy lines related to the creation fields of the cosmos. It is through the existence of this web of lines that changes in energies take place simultaneously throughout the cosmos at the shift points described by the Mayan calendar. We are beginning to recover the view of a pulsating cosmos that is alive and unified through the energies of divine creation. Everything is related, spirit and matter can no longer be separated." [20]

With this profound realization that everything in the cosmos is energetically connected and universally synchronized, a keen awareness of the cosmic plan within the vast universe becomes that much more meaningful. Knowing that we are all embraced within an invisible web of energetic threads sewn by Grandmother Spider, we find ourselves hanging on a branch like a blossom on an eternal world tree. This inspires the longing to become more intimately connected with our entire cosmic family tree which is rooted in the Mother Womb.

With that in mind, let's refer to *The Urantia Book* for an outline of the "Cosmic Plan for Universe Organization" and see just how expansive our cosmic family tree actually is!

According to the plan of universe organization outlined in this book, there are 100 constellations in each universe and 100 systems within each constellation. Furthermore, each system embraces approximately 1000 worlds, or potentially inhabitable planets. In the larger picture, each universe has the potential for 10 million worlds and within each constellation, the potential for 100,000. Fortunately, the organization is broken down into systems that embrace only 1000 worlds, or inhabitable planets, so that the efficient operation and supervision of these is manageable.

Let's start with our local universe which in the greater cosmos is known as Nebadon. It spins and swirls within the 7th super universe known as Orvonton, We are taught in *The Urantia Book* that "The organization of planetary abodes is still progressing in Nebadon, for this universe is, indeed, a young cluster in the starry and planetary realms of Orvonton. At the last registry there were 3,840,101 inhabited planets in Nebadon."[21] Now that we have the observable Milky Way as a reference point and can imagine its center as being the physical center of Orvonton, the seventh super universe, let's visualize where our universe revolves within this galaxy based on the teachings. "Nebadon is now well out towards the edge of Orvonton" and it "swings far to the south and east in the super universe circuit." Here, we are also told that, "The nearest neighboring universes are: Avalon, Henselon, Sanselon, Portalon, Wolvering, Fanoving, and Alvoring." [22] I wonder what their inhabitants look like!

The teachers inform us that, within our local universe, we belong to a "system" within a constellation called Norlatiadek whose headquarters are called "Edentia." Our solar system is part of the "system" called "Satania" and the headquarters of this system are called "Jerusem." So as we get closer to home, we are starting to make some recognizable connections here — Edentia is made up of beautiful gardens and that is why the most beautiful place on our planet where the first Adamic man came into being was in fact, The Garden of "Eden." The system we belong to called Satania, is representative of the word "Satan" which simply means "mortal man." Unfortunately, you will see later how it got its negative connotation. Of course, Jerusem is easy enough to figure out as it relates to the significant and symbolic "Jerusalem" on our planet.

Because the name used in *The Urantia Book* to depict our home constellation — "Norlatiadek" — is unfamiliar to us, it leaves us to wonder: "Of the constellations known to us, which one do we belong to?" The official answer to this question, according to modern astronomy, is that we don't belong to any constellation and that they are merely star patterns which we have imposed certain shapes upon. We are said to belong instead to a galaxy, the "Milky Way" one, of course. According to *The Urantia Book*, "the vast Milky Way starry system represents the central nucleus of Orvonton largely beyond the borders of our local universe." Really? O.K. so we can clearly see the super universe headquarters of Orvonton, known as Uversa, in the dark rift of the Milky Way? Isn't there a super massive black hole at the center of the Milky Way? Hmmm,...

It goes on to explain that, "this great aggregation of suns, dark islands of space, double stars, globular clusters, star clouds, spiral and other nebulae, together with myriad of individual planets, forms a watch like, elongated-circular grouping of about one-seventh of the inhabited evolutionary universes (of Orvonton)." Think about that the next time you look toward the misty Milky Way!

From the astronomical position of Urantia, as you look through the cross-section of near-by systems to the great Milky Way, you observe that the spheres of Orvonton are traveling in a vast elongated plane, the breadth being far greater than the thickness and the length far greater than the breadth."[23] It's so fascinating to think that when we look at the Milky Way, we are actually seeing beyond the borders of what *The Urantia Book* refers to as our local universe. This leads me to believe that what we think of as our 14 billion year old universe, from an astronomical standpoint, is merely one sphere of creation in the greater expansion of the entire Master Universe that *The Urantia Book* speaks of, especially since we know that even our own universe is expanding wildly without limits into the vast regions of undeveloped outer space. Based on this newfound revelation, I now have a much clearer picture of how the teachings in this book and our own modern knowledge of astronomy can be reconciled. Of course, the Mayan Calendar places the age of our universe at 16.4 billion years old, which I am sure is accurate since they were master astronomers, and may actually represent the age of our super universe.

According to "Inflationary Theory", as I understand it, our "universe" is expanding at mock speed into the darker and less inhabited realms of outer space and this rapid expansion is the result of an "ongoing primal explosion that occurred about 14 billion years ago." I speculated yesterday about this primary eruption, as we know it, being the result of a tremendous "spark" that occurred upon the arrival of the Creative Spirit to our local universe which had the effect of illuminating it and triggering a series of "creational" events. This would account for this vast discrepancy in the time periods spanning trillions of years, cited by the Urantia Book, while still acknowledging that what we call our "universe" is actually just one of many within the "Master Universe."

The super and local universes that revolve around the central universe comprise the Grand Universe and represent boundaries of matter, I would imagine, primarily for supervisory and operational efficiency like our system of designating borders between regions. So then we can pull back and view the so-called "Master Universe" simply as "The Universe" eternally expanding, containing the whole of creation, while still immersed in the one infinite watery womb.

6.17

What we can visualize is a primal core at the center of a Central Universe and seven super-universes revolving around it that each contain a vast multitude of local universes! From a consciousness perspective, we still have one Creator expanding his consciousness outward in all directions from one central core which is at the heart of this endlessly imaginative creation. In that, it is incredibly complex and yet simply profound.

To narrow back in on the Creator's point of view within the seventh emerging level of his consciousness, I wanted to look closer at the nature of the constellations. As I was looking closer at the description of the Milky Way, given in *The Urantia Book*, I realized something rather astounding. This galaxy is depicted as the "central nucleus" of the super universe we are spinning in. At the exact center of each super universe is its "headquarters worlds" and, for Orvonton, that center of operation is called "Uversa" and what modern astronomers have identified as a super massive black hole. Our "local universe" revolves around and within the Milky Way galaxy leaving us to wonder how a black hole can function as a universe headquarters.

6.18

In ancient times, the Mayans placed great importance on the dark rift at the center of the Milky Way galaxy and as we know from the book, "The Yugas", the distance that our solar system is from it, at any given point in time, dramatically affects the consciousness of our planet. If this sacred center truly is the abode of the beings that govern our worlds, then it is also the portal through which all the energy and cosmic force, originating from Paradise, is received and transmitted. Aha! The black hole, also the headquarters, is a portal through which vast amounts of cosmic forces flow!

This remarkable revelation provides a possible explanation for the consciousness shifts that takes place when we are aligned directly with this powerful flow of cosmic forces. The dramatic evolutions and devolutions of human consciousness, based on the alignment with the galactic center, were clearly demonstrated in "The Yugas." It was further reinforced by our own knowledge of the nature of "The Golden Ages" versus "The Dark Ages." I found this new revelation to be extraordinarily profound, so I researched further into "The Urantia Book's" description of the headquarters worlds of super universes:

The headquarters worlds of the seven super universes partake of the nature and grandeur of Paradise, their central pattern of perfection. All headquarters worlds are paradisiacal...the headquarters of Orvonton, your super universe, is immediately surrounded by the seven higher universities of advanced spiritual training for ascending will creatures. Each of these seven clusters of wonder spheres consists of 70 specialized worlds containing thousands upon thousands of replete institutions and organizations devoted to universe training and spirit culture wherein the pilgrims of time are reeducated and re-examined prior to their long flight to Havona. The arriving pilgrims of time are always received on these associated worlds, but the departing graduates are always dispatched for Havona direct from the shores of Uversa. Uversa is the spiritual and administrative headquarters for approximately 1,000,000,000,000 inhabited or inhabitable worlds. The glory, grandeur, and perfection of the Orvonton capital surpasses any of the wonders of the time space creations." [24]

As I contemplate this discovery, it also becomes clear to me that the most advanced civilizations known to us were highly focused on the constellations as well as the 26,000-year precession cycle. The earliest civilizations left us many clues that the constellations and star clusters of Orion, Cygnus, Sirius and Pleiades were of critical significance. I wondered if the "seven higher universities" they were referring to might be the seven stars of the Pleiades. Many ancient carvings from all over the globe depict "gods" that descended from the stars in various types of space crafts or "birds" and upon their arrival, transmitted advanced knowledge and universal wisdom. According to the myths and legends, these "star people" came from various constellations. We are aware of the significance of the Orion constellation to the Egyptians. They believed that "Osiris" had a symbolic connection to Orion and the pyramids themselves are said to have been in perfect alignment with this constellation. The constellation Cygnus has been called a "gateway" indicating that it is some type of entry/exit portal. There are also ancient cultures that believe they were visited by "star beings" from the star Sirius which is the brightest star in the sky and, according to the ancient Egyptians, the home of "Isis."

In more modern times, the being named "Moroni" who guided Joseph Smith to the Golden Book of Mormon claimed to have been from the constellation Pleiades and we know what a tremendous following Mormonism has in our own country. As I researched *The Urantia Book* for more clues, I discovered the significance of "sectors" and began to realize that in addition to constellations and systems, these designated regions called "major" and "minor" sectors were also important designations of space within the super-universe.

I didn't pay much attention to them until I read: "The rotational center of your minor sector is situated far away in the enormous and dense star cloud of "Sagittarius", around which your local universe and its associated creations all move, and from opposite sides of the vast Sagittarius sub-galactic system you may observe two great streams of star clouds emerging in stupendous stellar coils...Your solar system now occupies a fairly central position in one of the arms of this distorted spiral, situated about halfway from the center out towards the edge of the star steam." There are 100 "local universes" in each minor sector and 1,000 minor sectors in a super universe, according to the book. The main point here, for me, is that I identified the name of a constellation we are familiar with — Sagittarius — and this led me to the conclusion that "minor sectors" could be identified by us as the star formations we call "constellations." What "The Urania Book" calls constellations would then be smaller groupings of stars and planets within the larger and more recognizable patterns. Ultimately, whatever we want to call it, I found it fascinating that the book identified the "rotational center" of our "minor sector" (around which our local universe of 10 million worlds rotates) as a "star cloud" named Sagittarius. So maybe that's what "constellations" are universally known as — "star clouds."

In a contemplative state, I began to focus more intensely on why the constellations were so significant to the ancient cultures. I was seated in a meditation posture aligned with the sun so that the rays shone directly on me. I have a deep intuitive sense that when I am aligned with the source in this way, I have greater access to the sacred knowledge within the light. It is as if I am literally being "Illuminated" by the radiations of this magnificent portal of divine light. As I concentrated on the Orion constellation and the Giza pyramids, images started to flash across my mind. I was focused on the question, "Why would the entire complex of pyramids that are situated along the Nile be a literal "reflection" of the Orion constellation situated alongside the Milky Way?"

There has long been a debate about whether the Egyptians could have possibly "built" the Great Pyramid, in the traditional sense, at the exact geodesic center of the planet aligned perfectly with a belt star of Orion. If we think of it as a vibrational holographic reflection of something else, somewhere else, maybe it began as extraordinarily high vibrational thought form that was projected from the stars and then as it lowered onto the earth plane, its vibration lowered dramatically "solidifying" it onto its base. Maybe this is the true nature of all density of matter as we know it. It starts out as a very high vibrational thought-form at its origin (the original pattern) and then as it descends, its vibration progressively lowers to the density of matter. This would simply be energy transformed into matter and we know from Einstein that energy and matter are interchangeable based on the velocity of their electrons.

Let us continue with this 'progression of thought-realization' — "What was Egypt a reflection of and why are the three main pyramids that align with Orion's belt so significant?" As I pictured the three notches on Orion's belt, it occurred to me that the number three also represented the divine trinity. I already knew that the Giza complex was "built" at the exact geodesic center of the planet.

I also believe that Orion's belt (which divides Orion in half) is along the celestial equator. Hmmm –the waters above and the waters below? Then my heart started to beat faster as my mind started to race and images flashed. I focused on the point of light inside my head — my pineal gland and the focal point of my connection to cosmic consciousness. Let me share an image here of what I am seeing:

6.19

Three circles, each with a distinct shape and size, representing the "Universal Father", the "Eternal Son" and the "Infinite Spirit." Now, let's imagine Orion's whole body above and below the belt (which has been replicated by the series of pyramid complexes along the Nile). As I pictured "Orion", I thought, "Maybe the upper half of Orion's body actually replicates the residence of the divine Trinity, "Paradise", and the lower half, the first universe of creation — "Havona" — the waters above reflecting on the waters below.

6.20

I have a strong intuition that the constellation of Orion replicates the center of the Master Universe with the divine trinity expressing in the waters above and the creative trinity reflecting in the waters below. It does, after all, lie along the celestial equator smack dab in the center of the known universe just like the Central Universe lies at the core of creation. What if Orion is a replication of the Central Universe of eternal perfection with Paradise above and Havona below the "three grand spheres of Paradise" (or notches on Orion's belt). *The Urantia Book* tells us that "On Upper Paradise", there are three grand spheres of activity: 1) The Deity presence, 2) The Most Holy Sphere, and 3) The Holy Area, and that these are "set aside for the functions of worship, trinitization, and high spiritual attainment." [25] Weren't the three pyramids at Giza (projected onto planet earth from the belt stars) used for "high spiritual attainment" in the ancient mystery schools which took place there?

The book also refers to an "eternal residence" amongst this Holy Area as "seven zones...often designated "the Father's Paradise mansions." It goes onto to say that, amongst these residential areas, there are designated units for the "ascendant creatures who hail from the universes of evolutionary progression." In other words, this is our destination! It even says, "There is still plenty of room for those who are on their way inward, even for those who shall not start the Paradise climb until the times of the eternal future." [26] Apparently, each of the seven zones are "dedicated to the welfare and advancement of the personalities of a single super universe." It sounds like there are seven zones for the ascendant creatures from each of the seven super universes. The Pleiades? Cool! Not only is there plenty of room left, there is a special zone already reserved just for us!

Are you seeing the connection to Egypt clearly now or what? The three Giza pyramids are a projection of these three grand spheres in Paradise!

6.2

It even shows the last sphere with seven petals (or zones) around a central core. Whoa! The ancients somehow had access to this very sacred wisdom. Maybe "gods" or "star beings" did ascend in "birds" from the heavens to share it with them!

When I read that the "The Holy Sphere" was "reserved for the functions of worship, trinitization, and high spiritual attainment", I immediately thought of the book, "Initiation", that we referenced at the beginning of our adventure, which was all about the "worship and high spiritual attainment" which took place inside the Egyptian pyramids. We know that this was the case based on the "Pyramid

Texts", the inscriptions on the temples and even the "secret knowledge" that the Freemasons and Rosicrucians base their spiritual belief systems on! These are modern versions of the ancient mystery schools with the Pyramid texts as their foundation.

Ancient Egypt was a materialized duplication of Orion. Paradise is said to be the geographic center of infinity. The Egyptian pyramids are at the geodesic center of our planet. I believe it is highly possible that within the constellation of Orion, the infinite realm of Paradise and the eternal realm of Havona lie and that Egypt is a projection of these realms. Consider this statement from *The Urantia Book*: (Paper 11:9-)

"Patterns are never reflections; they are duplications — reproductions. Paradise is the absolute of patterns; an exhibit of these potentials. God's residence is central and eternal, glorious and ideal. His home is the beauteous pattern for all universe headquarters world; and the central universe of his immediate indwelling is the pattern for all universes in their ideals, organization, and ultimate destiny." [27]

This incredible revelation left me in such a profound state of awe and wonder. When the prophets in the Bible talked about "heaven on earth" and "as above, so below", they meant it literally! In the Lord's Prayer, it says. "Thy kingdom come, thy will be done on earth as it is in heaven." Knowing that there is a place on our planet that is an exact duplication of the dwelling place of the divine brings me great joy. Also knowing that Paradise is the ultimate destination of our eternal souls fills me with a deep inner peace. As I progress through this journey of self-realization unfolding through the writing of this book, I am experiencing profound revelations which resonate as powerful truths!

First, we talked about sacred patterns and the Platonic solids which led into a discussion about the divine manifestation of our three-dimensional time-space creation. Through a greater understanding of the evolvement of the universe, I was able to see how all physical manifestations are projected duplications of patterns animated and indwelt by the transmission of personality, mind and spirit energy. As we narrowed in on our own region of space, I was able to grasp the significance of the Milky Way galaxy during my search for the constellation and system that we belong to. This then led me to the realization that the Milky Way galaxy and the constellation of Orion have been projected onto our planet as the Nile and the Egyptian pyramid complexes. I believe that I am being led along the path of discovery that allows me to sequentially experience these profound revelations as they flash into my consciousness. Please do not think that I am inferring that these revelations are the absolute truth. They simply feel true to me. You may go within and upon contemplation, discover truths that are entirely different. That is the beauty of it! Of course, as I continued to dive deeper into books about Orion and Egypt, I discovered that many others have tapped into these revelations about the duplication of the Milky Way and Nile and Orion's belt stars and the pyramids, but not to the extent that Orion may actually be a duplication of Paradise and Havona at the core of creation. In other words, a mirror image of Paradise and Havona projected right here on Earth!

The images in our mind create the perception of our reality. If we are wise, we apply reason, research and insight to create the perception that feels closest to the truth. Regardless of the source of our knowledge, we are ultimately retrieving it from the universal field of consciousness. If I can access a greater part of the field to obtain wisdom and insight, anyone can! It just requires an insatiable curiosity, time for research and introspection and a devotion to contemplative meditation. Faith in the divine and the willingness to surrender to the universe are also key components. We are all chosen. We are all divine. And we are all connected to the cosmic consciousness. We must come into the full realization of this, that's all.

"Truth is beautiful because it is both replete and symmetrical. When man searches for truth, he pursues the divinely real. The wise philosopher will always look for the creative design which is behind, and preexistent to, all universe phenomenon. The Creator-thought invariably precedes creative action. Intellectual self-consciousness can discover the beauty of truth, its spiritual quality, not only by the philosophic consistency of its concepts, but more certainly and surely by the unerring response of the ever-present Spirit of Truth. Happiness ensues from the recognition of truth because it can be acted out; it can be lived... Divine truth is best known by its spiritual flavor." [28]

To wrap up today's incredible adventure, let's imagine that we are camped out in a clearing deep in the Amazon jungle. Let's build a campfire and spread out our blankets around it. Now that night has fallen, and the stars and constellations can clearly be seen, let's lay down and look up into the sky. What continues to astonish me is the sheer magnitude of it all! At the same time, we can clearly see the flowing stream of the Milky Way with the dark rift at its center. We can make out the various constellations and name them. The twinkling lights above are literally crowding every speck of the sky, and well...it starts to seem plausible that there may be seven trillion inhabitable planets out there and if there truly is one star for each immortal soul, no wonder they seem infinite in number!

I will leave you with this final passage from the universal Bible, *The Urantia Book*:

"After all, to mortals the most important thing about nether Paradise is the fact that this perfect abode of the Universal Father is the real and far distant destiny of the immortal souls of the immortal and material Sons of God, the ascending creatures of the evolutionary worlds of time and space. Every God knowing mortal who has espoused the career of doing the Father's will has already embarked upon the long, long Paradise trail of divinity pursuit and perfection attainment. And when such an animal-origin being does stand, as countless numbers now do, before the gods on Paradise, having ascended from the lowly spheres of space, such an achievement represents the reality of the spiritual transformation bordering on the limits of supremacy." [29]

As we move into the second half of our evolutionary journey into the light, we can draw upon the foundational concepts presented in the first half. With those creational concepts in mind, we will become more infused with the original codes of creation as we tune into the infinite source. These practices will align us with our divine blueprint of perfection harmonizing us with the higher codes and enhancing our connection to our own higher self.

Downloading the Creation Codes
A Third-Eye Activation
(Audio version available at: www.SuzanneRossTranscendence.com)

Be seated in a comfortable posture that is upright and centered so that the divine source codes can flow directly into your being through the eighth chakra or soul-star gateway. Close your eyes and focus on the third eye between your brows. Draw your attention to this energy center and visualize the shape of a single eye with the pupil in the center glowing indigo blue. As you peer into this indigo blue pupil, take a deep breath in and imagine that you are drawing in the eternal wisdom of creation into your being. On the exhale, imagine releasing all the deceptions about who you are that have distorted your perception of reality. Breathe in the divine source codes of creation and breathe out the deceptions about your human limitations. Breathe in the empowerment of this higher knowledge and breathe out the limitations of dogmatic beliefs. Continue in this fashion taking 5 more deep breaths in and out.

As you breathe in the divine light, imagine an indigo blue ray projecting from the pupil of your third eye into the space between your brows flooding your brain with higher knowledge and divine source codes. Now imagine this indigo wisdom flowing into your being igniting each cell with this indigo flame of divine consciousness. As each cell is ignited by the indigo flame, DNA strands that have long been dormant are reignited with the source codes of creation. Imagine all five of your bodies, mental, emotional, spiritual, physical and etheric, glowing with this indigo blue light. You are now emanating a powerful aura of indigo light filled with the infinite love and divine wisdom of the source.

Now imagine this aura transforming into a circular pillar of light that extends into the heart of Mother Earth beneath you connecting you with the love of your earth mother. Empowered by the deep love she has for you as her earth child and the deep gratitude you have for her as your earthly foundation, you are ignited by the willpower to pull this deep love and gratitude up into your being. Empowered by love, gratitude and willpower, this indigo blue ray energy expands and propels upward into the cosmos connecting you into the eternal realm of creation. This indigo pillar of light aligns you with your higher-self existing in the eternal realm of divine perfection. You are now realigned with your divine blueprint of perfection. Your higher-self is connected directly with the Paradise Core of Creation through which the Infinite Source of divine consciousness flows. This divine alignment with the Infinite Source creates a constant flow of the source codes of creation into your higher-self which is then projected through the indigo pupil of your third eye.

Through the portal of your third eye, the source codes penetrate every cell of your being igniting dormant DNA strands which when activated, reawaken divine knowledge and superhuman capabilities. These source codes reawaken the divine within. The divine spark within every cell of each of your five bodies is ignited and the divine light within you becomes much more brilliant and far more radiant. This brilliant white light raises your vibrational frequency and builds your light quotient. You are activating your light body and becoming more spiritualized. You are empowered by the divine love of the Source and the eternal wisdom of the Akasha. The love powered emanations of the Divine Source fill you with the rapture of quiet joy and a deep inner knowing of your divine connection.

This inner knowledge of who you truly are as a divine being empowered by the wisdom of your eternal self and the love of the Infinite Source greatly enhances your self-confidence and propels you on your path to full self-realization. Now that you have been connected and realigned with your divine blueprint of perfection, you can reconnect and tap into these divine source codes any time by closing your eyes and peering deep into your indigo blue pupil. This pupil is your portal to divine consciousness. Just remember to breathe in the eternal wisdom and infinite love so that it fills your entire being. This creates a powerful aura that transforms into a pillar of light extending from the heart of Mother Earth into the Paradise Core of creation. Imagine yourself vibrating at a higher frequency as you tune into your higher-self and simultaneously to the multidimensional aspects of your whole self. You are creating in multiple realms of time and space all at once in the fullest expression of your multi-dimensional being.

In this way, you are harmonizing with your higher-self as well as the multidimensional aspects of your whole self. You are becoming reunited with your whole soul and all the 12 emanations of your multidimensional being. Tuning into your divine blueprint of perfection realigns all the multidimensional aspects of who you are expressing in many dimensional realms of time and space realities. You are one with these soul extensions of your whole soul for it is the fullest expression of your highest self projecting these holographic images from eternity. Your eternal self is the divine blueprint of perfection projecting these multidimensional images of your holographic soul extensions who are simultaneously experiencing many time and space realities.

This indigo pillar of light becomes a tunnel of communication with your higher-self as you share your time and space experiences and the knowledge gained in these realms with your higher-self in eternity and in turn, your higher-self fills you with the eternal wisdom and infinite love of the original source codes of creation. Opening this portal of communication is the key to full self-realization and the quick path to full enlightenment in this lifetime. As you reactivate your divine blueprint of perfection, you become a higher dimensional expression reflecting the divine qualities of your highest self. You become a higher dimensional being and you perceive a higher dimensional reality beyond the third dimension, through the fourth dimension and into the fifth dimensional expression of a higher reality defined by unity consciousness.

This is the goal of your incarnate journey of self-realization to progressively evolve through the multidimensional realms of time and space on your journey home to the Divine Source. You are becoming the light of divine love. You are becoming a radiant love light being directly connected to Source at all times. You are becoming the fullest expression of your divine self emanating infinite love and eternal wisdom. You are both human and divine. Remember that always and know that you can connect into the wisdom of the eternal source of who you truly are at any time. You can connect into the Divine Source of love behind all of creation. With deep love for your brothers and sisters, you can radiate this love and light outward every day in every way. You can share the divine love and wisdom of the Source in many gentle and caring ways. When you spread the love and light, it expands and ignites the Divine Matrix of Creation. It ignites everyone through the collective consciousness grid. As the divine spark within each and every cell of creation is ignited, the entire matrix comes online and propels into a new higher dimensional expression of reality defined by love, unity, peace and joy. Together, we can propel ourselves into a new Golden Age of Enlightenment by ascending together as one unified expression of divine love and light.

Remember, you are loved more than you can possibly imagine and always will be for all of eternity and into infinity for the divine light of creation is fueled by the power of pure unconditional love. And so it is. And so be it. Amen.

Your Personal Revelations

_____

_____

_____

_____

_____

_____

_____

_____

_____

_____

_____

_____

_____

_____

_____

_____

REFERENCES
Chapter cover image of eternity symbol courtesy of: www.pixabay.com

Illustrations:
1-18. www.pixabay.com
Text:
Godfre Ray King, *Unveiled Mysteries*, Saint Germain Press, 1934
1 p.170-1
Drunvalo Melchizedek, *The Mayan Ouroboros*, Weiser Books, 2012
2. Introduction
Brad Olsen, *Sacred Places Around the World*, Consortium of Collective Consciousness, 2004
3. p. 158-160
13. p. 164
14. p. 164
16. p. 161
4. https://www.historymusem.ca/cmc/exhibitions/civil/maya/mmc09eng.html
15. https://en.wikipedia.org/wiki/Popol_Vuh, www.historians.org
David Hatcher Childress, *The Lost World of Cham*, Adventures Unlimited Press, 2017
11. Back cover
12. p. 274
Carl Johan Calleman, *The Mayan Calendar and the Transformation of Consciousness,* Bear & Company, 2004
17. p. 1
20. p. 203
18. www.ancient.eu/Popol-Vuh/
Elkins, Rueckert, McCarty, *The RA Material The Law of One: Book 1*, Whitford Press, 1984
19. RA Material, p. 105
The Urantia Book Fellowship, *The Urantia Book*, Uversa Press, 2008
5. (61:6.1-2)
6. (62:5.4-5)
7. (62:5.7-8)
8. (63:6.6)
9. (64:6.1-2**)**
10. (64:6-1-2)
21. (32:2.9)
22. (32:2.12)
23. (15:3.1)
24. (15:7.3-11)
25. (11:3.1-3)
26. (11:3.4)
27. (11:9.5)
28. (2:7.4-6)
29. (11:9.8)

DAY SEVEN

The Seven Rays of Creation

Greetings brave explorers and beloved truth seekers! I would like to start today's adventure with a special standing meditation that will open our hearts and minds to the ancient mysteries we will be exploring today. This will enhance our connection to this sacred wisdom and as such, provide us with a more illuminating experience! Are you ready?

Morning Glory: A Guided Meditation
(Audio version available at: www.SuzanneRossTranscendence.com)

Stand up and reach for the sky opening your arms up wide to embrace the day. Now close your eyes as you align with the radiant sun beams of light emanating from the Source. Allow this light to enter through your third eye at the center of your forehead between your brows. Feel the light penetrate through to the center of your head and ignite the point of light between the hemispheres of your brain at the base of your skull. As this powerful beam of light ignites this sacred center, it produces an explosion of light like a flash expanding in all directions far and wide surrounding you with the gold and white light and connecting you with the sacred wisdom from all of eternity. Now imagine a powerful ray of light penetrating the sacred center of your heart. Feel the force of the light penetrating that center like a laser beam and on contact, the tiny core explodes into a great expansion of radiant energy just like the sun. These light rays merge and interact with the beams of light emanating from the center of your head.

Now imagine a single point of light behind your belly button at the solar plexus of your being. Picture a tiny point at the very core of the sun vibrating with the power of Source potential.

Intentionally draw that energy potential into your solar plexus like a powerful laser beam igniting the force within you. As this beam connects with the core of your being, a radiant flash of light expands in all directions and these rays merge with the radiations of light emanating from your heart center and your brain center. Together they produce a brilliant trinity of radiant love that brightly illuminates the space around you and expands into infinity. You are now connected with the Paradise Trinity and now have the divine potential to access the infinite field of consciousness. It is important now to connect with Mother Earth so that you stay grounded during our adventure today.

So let's get plugged in by spinning our root chakra of survival consciousness and releasing a powerful stream of energy from the base of your spine into the earth with a spiraling band of blue green light. This band penetrates the surface of the earth and energetically spirals through the dirt, rock, minerals, gems and crystals embedded in the earth. As the spiraling energy breaks through the crystalline matrix of the inner earth, it reaches the yellow edges of the boiling lava and powers through the thick orange bubbles into the red-hot iron core crystal at her heart center. At this point, the soul of your being is connected to the radiant heart of Mother Earth and you feel the essence of motherly love emanating from her core. This love fills your being and you reciprocate by sending her childlike adoration and profound gratitude for the sense of belonging that it brings.

Now pulling all the energy condensed at the core of the earth back up into your being, imagine the spiraling cord traversing upward through the fire, lava and minerals penetrating the surface of the earth beneath you and shooting up through the base of your spine spinning your root chakra. At this point, the cord splits into two electric blue beams of spiraling light which braid your vertebrae and travel upward toward your orange wheel of desire consciousness spinning it and illuminating it from the center outward and filling your being with a sense of longing. The spiraling cords emerge from this center of desire upward toward the center of power condensed within the wheel of your solar plexus. Release the power held in this center and allow it to radiate in all directions far and wide as it spins clockwise. This power-consciousness fills you with the pure potential to do, be and have anything within the infinite abundance of the vast universe empowered by your pure intentions. The electric blue cords explode out of your solar power center racing toward the power of love within your heart. This green wheel of love-consciousness spins wildly expanding into eternity as a sense of unconditional love for all living beings brings you great joy. A powerful sense of connection to all life across the eternal realms of time and space overwhelms you and you are consumed with a profound sense of oneness.

Now at peace within the comfort of this unity-consciousness, the kundalini energy braids your spine and reaches the base of your throat where a brilliant sky-blue wheel is ignited. By spinning and illuminating it, it spreads not just horizontally but also spherically producing a ball of blue light that surrounds you like a bubble. Now imagine blowing this bubble up with forceful exhalations that make it expand and grow until it connects and merges with the bubbles of communication engulfing all beings. The spiraling blue cords vibrate excitedly as they anticipate connecting with the wisdom chakra behind your third eye for they know this is a powerful center of inner truth and pure consciousness. As your indigo blue wisdom chakra spins and expands, it illuminates all the knowledge within your aura. Your soul is the accumulation of all the experiential knowledge you have gained since the beginning of your existence and the Akashic records remain with you like an aura of light around your being at all times. Connecting with your wisdom chakra allows you to access this vast amount of encoded information.

Emerging from your wheel of inner truth, the electric blue cords, one of light and one of love, intertwine as they ascend toward your crown chakra where the violet wheel of divine consciousness lies waiting. The moment the cords of love and light connect with the center of this divine wheel, you feel a powerful surge of electrical energy ignite the entire length of your spinal cord. This sensation fills you with a sense of great empowerment and illuminates you with limitless energy unlike any other source. You are now filled with the unlimited potential of divine consciousness which is omnipotent, omniscient and omnipresent. As this violet wheel spins with the combined force of love and light, it expands into eternity and settles in infinity. You feel a powerful beam of light streaming out from your crown and at the same time, are aware of a strong force of energy streaming in.

You are now transmitting and receiving the infinite knowledge within the universal field of consciousness. This opens a line of communication which triggers a great expansion of consciousness like a sharing of ideas between your own inner accumulation of knowledge and the divine wisdom from all of eternity. It is within this space, the eternal present, that divine truths will be revealed to you and wherein the power of your intention and the force of your free will have unlimited potential. If you make a sincere effort to remain focused on the point of light at the center of your head, your pineal gland, you can access the eternal now moment where an imaginary plane of horizontal light intersects with a plane of vertical light. By doing this, you will intuitively discover your own personal truth and become increasingly aware of the meaning behind the synchronistic events unfolding in your perception of reality moment by moment. With each breath that you inhale and exhale, the truth of your reality is unfolding before your very eyes and as your being expands and contracts, it harmonizes with the natural rhythm of the energetic swell and release of the world around you. Synchronized with the universe, your soul will make progress on its Ascension path toward the light of love at the Paradise Core of Creation. By sincerely engaging in this progressive evolution of consciousness, you are expanding your divine potential and realizing the true nature of your magnificent being. You are an energetic being vibrating with the power of pure love and divine light. With this profound realization, let's embark upon today's adventure. This journey will take us into the multidimensional realms of consciousness illuminated by the seven rays of creation.

Perusing the Sites of Peru

It's time to throw on our backpacks and chart our course. From the Amazon to the Andes, today we head south from Central America to South America, specifically in and around Peru. Our first destination is Cuzco, the Incan "Navel of the Earth." Then we're off to Sacsayhuaman, a vast citadel and marvel of stone masonry. From there, we will visit Machu Picchu, a spiritual retreat for the Incan Emperor, Pachacutec. Then, crossing the border into Bolivia, we'll visit the mysterious sites of Tiwanaku and Pumu Punku. Our adventure culminates on the magical, mystical Island of the Sun in Lake Titicaca!

7.1

As we walk through the bustling city of Cuzco, we notice that the locals still honor many of the Incan traditions. They still dress in the colorful alpaca wool woven by local women and speak the Quechua language brought into the region by the Incas in the fifteenth century. They perform traditional dances wearing elaborate costumes that reflect the ancient legends. The heart of the Inca still beats in the center of Cuzco where the golden Temple of the Sun once shone. When the Spanish Conquistadors, led by Francisco Pizzaro, invaded Cuzco in the sixteenth century, they captured the Emperor of the Hunan Cuzco dynasty, Atahualpa, and held him hostage in an enclosed chamber. Pizzaro announced to the Quechua people that he would accept a ransom for the release of their beloved Emperor. The ransom was to bring them enough precious metal to fill the chamber "once over with gold and twice over with silver." In order to pay the ransom, the people had to disseminate their cherished Temple of the Sun. Once paid, Pizarro went back on his word and executed the Emperor Atahualpa anyway making him the legendary last Inca ruler.

To the Inca, gold was the sweat of the sun. The Inca worshipped the sun and built temples to honor their Sun God, Viracocha, the great creator deity in the pre-Inca and Inca mythology. Gold was the sweat of their God and they were blessed with plenty of it. Depictions of Viracocha show him wearing the sun as a crown with thunderbolts in his hands and rain as his tears. To the Inca, Viracocha was the creator of everything, the universe, sun, moon and stars. Reminiscent of the stories in the Mayan Popol Vuh and the biblical Genesis, Inca legend has it that Viracocha rose up out of Lake Titacaca bringing light into the darkness; A creator deity emerging from the watery abyss, or Mother Womb, to shine light on all of creation. Viracocha made the first humans by breathing life into stones but the stone giants displeased him so he destroyed them with a great flood. The first beings in the Popol Vuh were created from clay and mud and the second from wood. In their creation myth, both the clay and wood humans washed away. The third time was the charm for the Mayan creator deity. In the Inca legend, Viracocha made the second humans out of smaller stones and was pleased. In Genesis, God got it right the first time! After creating the second human, Viracocha disappeared into the Pacific Ocean never to return. The name Viracocha literally means "Sea Foam." Legend has it, though, that his soul returned in the disguise of a beggar so he could roam the streets and offer teachings to the people he created. He wept when he saw the plight of his creations and performed miracles for them. Interestingly, Viracocha has been described as a white man with emerald green eyes wearing a white robe. Sounds like an Ascended Master to me! Remember how Group Ra said that a faction of their 6th dimensional task force set out on a mission to South America to teach the Law of One as well as pyramid building? Another fascinating possibility that group Ra shares with us is that when the continent of Atlantis was inundated, some of the survivors were sent to Peru. "The Atlantean race was a conglomerate social complex that began to form approximately 31,000 years in the past of your space/time continuum illusion." [1]

"After 16,000 years of development, they suddenly reached a high technological understanding of how to use intelligent energy. When they chose to use this knowledge to create life forms, rather than for healing and learning, their consciousness became distorted toward the negative. 5,000 years later, the first of two devastating wars took place that wiped out 40% of their population and the second one created an "earth changing configuration" that led to the inundation of their continent.Three of the more positively-oriented groups left this geographical region before that devastation, placing themselves in the mountain areas of what you call Tibet, what you call Peru and what you call Turkey."[2]

Going back to the comparison with the story in the Popol Vuh, remember that the second humans were made of wood and had no heart and I guessed that this may have been the Atleanteans with their emphasis on high technology rather than heart-centered healing. In the story of Viracocha, he made the second humans and was pleased. Maybe the Atlanteans who came to Peru were the second humans. Many so-called "Alternative Archaeologists" theorize that the area in and around Peru, including Bolivia, was occupied long before the date mainstream archaeologists claim. There is evidence in the Bolivian sites of Tiwanaku and Pumu Punku that dates the first settlements possibly as far back as 17,000 years ago while still others push the date back to as far as 40,000 years ago. Even mainstream archaeology cites evidence of Cro-Magnon cave art in Europe dating back to 38,000 BCE. The difference between the mainstream perspective and the alternative views seem to center on the level of advancement of the early humans. Mainstream history books start placing the earliest upright humans as far back as 4 MYA (million years ago) with the Australopithecines in East Africa. These textbooks then follow the development of early humans through Ethiopia (2.75 — 1 MYA), the Middle East (1 MYA) and Central Europe (400,000 YA) as Homo-habilis, Homo erectus and Homo-heidelbergensis. They tell us that 350,000 YA, Homo-neanderthalensis emerged in Europe and that 150,000 YA, Homo-sapiens appeared in Africa, coexisting with Homo-erectus in Asia and Homo-neanderthalensis in Europe and the Middle East. Then 40,000 YA, we have Cro-Magnon emerging in Europe and 15,000 years later, the complete disappearance of Homo-neanderthalensis. This is where mainstream and alternative archaeologists make a definite split as history books claim that 20,000 YA, an Ice Age population of hunters and gatherers pervaded the planet and it wasn't until 8500-6000 BCE, that the first signs of civilization emerged in Mesopotamia. They cite Jericho in Palestine as the oldest inhabited town circa 8000 BCE and Uruk as the first city-state in Mesopotamia emerging in 4800 BCE. [3]

This brings us to the ancient astronaut theorist, Zecharia Sitchins, who translated the Sumerian clay tablets. These tablets, according to Sitchins, tell a story about a race of ancient astronauts called the Annunaki who came here from the 12th planet (in our solar system) called Nibiru. In the story told on these tablets, they came here to mine gold that they needed for their planet's atmosphere. The King of Nibiru sent his two sons, Lord Enlil and Lord Enki, along with his daughter Ninmah, and a team of laborers to search for gold. The story centers around Mesopotamia as the fertile crescent and cradle of civilization over 10,000 years ago, however, Sitchin also suggests that the Annunaki may have come to Tiwanaku and Pumu Punku to mine gold in the Andes. These ancient astronauts would have discovered rich veins of gold in the mountains and Sitchin goes on to suggest that the buildings in Tiwanaku may have been used to "smelt" the gold along with other ceremonial purposes. To follow this story in greater detail, refer to the series of books written by Sitchin that are based on his translation of the Sumerian clay tablets. I find it interesting that the celestial guides in *The Urantia Book* teach us that our planet is known as Urantia in the greater cosmos and that the ancient astronauts would have named the city they erected here "Ur."

To support Sitchin's claims about the Annunaki being present in both Mesopotamia and Bolivia, there are similar advanced building techniques used in the ancient city of Lagash near Mesopotamia as were used at the Tiwanaku complex in Bolivia. Also, a bowl known as the Fuente Magna bowl, was found at the complex with Sumerian cuneiform etchings on it that mention the Goddess Nia. She is represented by a figure in a goddess pose with arms and legs spread out. This is the same Goddess worshipped by the ancient Egyptians as Nut and the ancient Greeks as Nieth. Once again, there is a connection with ancient sites and cultures around the world in ancient times. Like our guide David Childress suggests in his book, The Lost World of Cham, it is also likely that goods, and possibly bloodlines, were dispersed across great distances by seafaring people in ancient ages. I found a website that not only offers a decipherment of the inscriptions on the Fuente Magna bowl but also supports the theory that it may have been transported by an ancient seafaring people!

According to the site, a Dr. Winters has translated the cuneiform script on the right side of the bowl to say:

"(1) Girls take an oath to act justly (in this) place. (2) (This is) a favorable oracle of the people. (3) Send forth a just divine decree. (4) The charm (the *Fuente Magna*) (is) full of Good. (5) The (Goddess) Nia is pure. (6) Take an oath (to her). (7) The Diviner. (8) The divine decree of Nia (is). (9) to surround the people with Goodness/Gladness. (10) Value the people's oracle. (11) The soul (to), (12) appear as a witness to the Good that comes from faith in the Goddess Nia before. all mankind."

Written on the left side, it says:

"(1) Make a libation (in this) place for water (seminal fluid?) and seek virtue. (2a) (This is) a great amulet/charm, (2b) (this) place of the people is a phenomenal area of the deity Nia's. power. (3) The soul (or breath of life). (4) Much incense, (5) to justly, (6) make the pure libation. (7) Capture the pure libation (and/or Appear (here) as a witness to the pure libation). (8) Divine good in this phenomenal proximity of the deity's power."

The author of the site goes on to say that:

"This decipherment of the inscriptions on the *Fuente Magna* indicates that it was used to make libations to the Goddess Nia to request fertility, and to offer thanks to the bountiful fauna and flora in the area that made it possible for these Sumerian explorers to support themselves in Bolivia. It is believed that the *Fuente Magna* was probably crafted by Sumerian people who settled in Bolivia sometime after 2500 BC. The Sumerians used seaworthy ships that were known to sail to the distant Indian Subcontinent. Some Sumerian ships most likely made their way around South Africa and entered one of the currents in the area that lead from Africa across the Atlantic to South America and then to the Pacific Ocean." [4]

As we explore the ancient origins of the people and their sacred sites in both Peru and Bolivia, we are once again challenged to dig deeper into all of the possibilities. There are likely shards of truth in all of the myths and legends that we have to piece together like the broken megalithic rocks that lie askew in Pumu Punku. Keeping an open mind allows us to explore these possibilities without limiting ourselves to the mainstream explanations that only posit one theory. There is, in fact, a principle called "Ocam's Razor" that limits explanatory reasoning by suggesting not to posit more than is necessary when explaining criteria!

Stupendous Stones of Sacsayhuaman

As we move on into Sacsayhuaman and marvel at the stone blocks used to build this citadel, let's explore another possibility of how these ancient sites may have been built. During the fifteenth century, the Inca built Sacsayhuaman as a citadel and Machu Picchu as an Emperor's retreat. What mystifies tourists and archaeologists alike is how the massive stone blocks weighing several tons were transported there and then how they were placed together with such precision. This same phenomenon can be observed at the Tiwanaku complex, especially with the H-blocks at Pumu Punku. The creation myth of Viracocha creating the first people out of stone leads to the local legend of these people actually being "stone giants" who could have the strength to move colossal stones. Even the bible speaks of giants who once roamed the earth and my friend, Brad Olsen, has done a great deal of research into ancient giants. Levitation is another possibility. Several years ago, I was studying the works of Claude Swanson who offers comprehensive explanations of energetic force fields. He mentioned a book by Alexandra David Neel called "Magic and Mystery in Tibet 1932" which intrigued me so I, of course, ordered it immediately. In it, she talks about how the Tibetan masters developed their psychic powers to send waves of energy that would affect whatever matter they directed it at. Also, they learned how to use chanting and drumming to raise the vibrational frequency of the environment and thereby alter the atomic structure of large objects, like stones, making them sponge-like. With their psychic powers and ability to transform the molecular density of stone, they could lift the sponge-like stones into the air and lower them into place. Once the stones were melded perfectly into place, they would return to their original density. This allowed them to build temples made of gigantic stone blocks set into place with precision accuracy. In Brad Olsen's book, "Future Esoteric", in a section entitled, "Tibetan Acoustic Levitation", he tells the story of a Swedish physician who spends time in Tibet in 1939. While there, he witnesses this phenomenon: "Then, as the speed of the drumming and the noise increased, the big stone block started to rock and sway and suddenly took off into the air with an increasing speed in the direction of the cave hole, 250 meters high. After three minutes of ascent it landed on the platform. The Tibetans continuously brought new blocks to the meadow, and the monks using this method transported five to six blocks per hour on a parabolic flight track approximately 500 meters long and 250 meters high." [5]

I can't help but recall that not only did members of Group Ra, an advanced 6th dimensional race, spend time in South America in the ancient past, but survivors of Atlantis, an advanced human race, may have been sent to Tibet and Peru. In *The RA Material*, Group Ra claims that the Atlanteans "learned how to use intelligent infinity in an informative manner."[6] So, here at Sacsayhuaman, and possibly in Bolivia at Tiwanaku and Pumu Punku, the builders may have had access to this advanced technique, or technology, if you will. The stone blocks at Sacsayhuaman have been called "living stones." Group Ra teaches us about the intelligent infinity of all things and beings and refers to "living stones" as intelligent "rockness." They inform us that we can communicate with the intelligence of all things in nature and make requests for cooperation and co-creation. The ancients developed these techniques and so can we. These abilities are innate within us! All we have to do is initiate, activate and develop them. As we move into the higher vibrational frequency of a new Golden Age, those of us who are spiritually inspired are raising our own light quotient so we can enhance our psychic abilities and develop both telepathy and telekinesis. We can then teach it to others in modern day Mystery Schools for the benefit of all.

Meanwhile, mainstream archaeologists struggle to make sense of sites like these around the world by calculating how many men and how many years and with what crude tools and pulleys and ropes and ramps it must have taken to erect them. It's painful to watch reenactments showing huge labor forces over hundreds of years pulling and pushing stone blocks weighing several tons. We know there were civilizations in the past that were much more advanced than we have given them credit for in our history books. Not only were they technologically advanced but they were also spiritually enlightened and we can see what a powerful combination this can be when put to the right use!

Magnificent Machu Picchu

A trip to Peru wouldn't be complete without a visit to the marvel of Machu Picchu so let's project our consciousness into this extraordinary site. Tune into the image below and then focus on your third eye while setting an intention to become present there.

7.2

In 1911, the American explorer, Hiram Bingham, went to Peru in search of a lost city he had read about. In a small village just below Machu Picchu, an indigenous family with a young boy told him they knew of a place built long ago with huge structures made of stone. The young boy took off skirting through tangled brush with Hiram and his team close behind. Climbing higher and higher, they finally came to a platform where large stone towers were jutting up toward the sky. The magnificent structures consumed by the jungle were only partially exposed. Hiram, hopeful that this was the famed lost city, embarked upon an excavation that would reveal the grandiose glory of the architectural wonder we now know of us Machu Picchu. After comparing the description in his notes to the structures he revealed, Hiram Bingham determined that this wasn't the famed lost city and continued on his quest to discover it.

We now know that the Incan Emperor, Pachacutec, had this awe-inspiring complex built as a spiritual retreat center. Upon exploration of the compound, ceremonial plazas were uncovered with sacred symbolism and artifacts. This may have even served as a mystery school where spiritual practices enhanced psychic abilities. Maybe these advanced techniques were the same ones used to transport and erect the massive stones used to build this magnificent site! If we tune into the site, we may be able to download visions of how it was constructed and what it was actually used for. Let's take a seat for a moment in a quiet space, in a comfortable posture, and set this intention. Follow your breath to get quiet and then narrow your focus on the space between your brows until you see a pupil with an indigo iris looking back at you. Now, peer into Machu Picchu at the time of the Incas and see what visions unfold. Practicing this technique will greatly enhance your psychic vision and ability to soul travel.

A Tour of Tiwanaku

Now, it's time to cross the border into Bolivia and head straight for the fascinating complex of Tiwanaku that includes Pumu Punku. Tiwanaku, or Tiahuanaco in Spanish, is a grand complex that has been called "The Eternal City" as well as "The Ancient City of the Gods." There is much debate over the age of the site between mainstream archaeologists and alternative archaeologists. The mainstream group bases it's dating on a radiocarbon sample of layers of earth taken from the site which gives a construction date of 1500 years ago. The alternative group contradicts this claim citing that it is not a valid measurement considering there was a massive deluge 12,000 years ago. Remember the legend of the stone giants who moved colossal stones before being wiped out by the flood?

A more accurate measurement used to date these sites can be calculated using a technique called archaeoastronomy. Explorer and engineer, Arthur Posnanski (aka Arturo), used this technique to calculate the astronomical alignments of the buildings at Pumu Punku not only with the stars but also with respect to each other. Using a principle called the "Obliquity of the Ecliptic", he was able to determine when these buildings would have been astronomically aligned with certain constellations in the cosmos. His calculations reveal a much earlier date for construction at 15,000 B.C. Considering what we already know about ancient timelines, this makes much more sense!

The map of the Tiwanaku complex shows nine different structures at the site with the most exceptional being the Kalasasaya Temple, the Gate of the Sun, the Akapana Pyramid and the crescendo, Pumu Punku meaning Gate of the Puma. The Temple at Kalasasaya is a rectangular enclosure featuring the monolithic Gateway of the Sun along with an intricately carved human-like monument that both have carved symbols for the solar year. The Gateway features symbols for 12 months and the monolithic man features circles for 365 days along with signs for the solstices and equinoxes.

7.3: The Temple at Kalasasaya

The Gateway of the Sun also features the sun god, Viracocha, flanked by two condors which reflect the trajectory of the "solar cross" in the sky. The solar cross represents the constellation of Cygnus, also known as the celestial swan and possibly a depiction of the feathered, or plumed, serpent. According to Andrew Collins, in his book, "The Cygnus Mystery", "...these ancestors of human civilization came to recognize the influence on their lives of cosmic rays emanating from a point source in the night sky." [7] He also points out that a Professor of Physics named Guilio Magli identified Cygnus as the Inca's "cosmic center of origin" based on astronomical observations of the celestial perspective around the autumnal equinox. Please watch my full interview with Andrew Collins at SciSpi.tv/Rise-Up/. In it, he explains in much greater depth the tremendous influence the cosmic rays emanating from Cygnus have had on the evolution of the human species.

In this picture of the Gateway of the Sun, you can see Viracocha, the plumed serpent, featured above the opening of the gate.

7.4: Gateway of the Sun

The megalithic man is very symbolic not just for representing the solar calendar days but he is also holding a hallucinogenic plant in his hands that was used by the ancients to go into a trance state and explore astral realms. This monolith reminds me of the story of the stone giants Viracocha may have created!

7.5: Megalithic Man

The Akapana Pyramid across from the Kalasasaya Temple was used an astronomical observatory. At the top of the Pyramid, there was a pool enclosed by a geometric pattern. Through the reflection of the water, they watched the stars and captured their observations in the engravings on the Gateway of the Sun. Here is a photo of what is left of the Akapana Pyramid. We can only use our imagination to envision the wonder and majesty of what the site might have once looked like. To the ancients who worshipped the sun god here, this temple was like a sacred mountain. Symbolically, and astronomically, it was aligned with the cardinal four directions, just like Kalasasaya, and also had seven levels. There's our divine number again — 7!

7.6: Akapana Pyramid

The most intriguing aspect of the Akapana pyramid are the faces protruding from one of the walls. Were these the faces of the builders? They resemble the monolithic man! Were these the stone giants who used colossal stones to create this sacred site in honor of the god who created them?

7.7: Faces on Akapana

Our extraordinary journey through the sacred sites of South America culminates at none other than the magical, mystical Lake Titicaca. This is the watery abyss that Viracocha rose up out of to bring light into the darkness.

7.8: Lake Titicaca

Legends say that Viracocha had two helpers when he created humans and they were the Sun and the Moon represented by the Islands of the Sun and Moon in Lake Titicaca. The story goes on to say that Viracocha drew sections on a rock and instructed "couples" to go out with a golden rod in search of the navel of the earth, which is now Cuzco. This lake is the highest navigable lake in the world and Jacque Costeau and his team of divers discovered life in these waters unlike any other in the world, notably the toad-frog hybrid that populates the lake in masses. Locals claim that they have been seeing strange lights come in and out of the lake for centuries. Some say there is an underground base beneath the lake. The Uros, an ancient indigenous people, have been building floating homes on the lake for centuries weaving together reed platforms that can support a family complex of structures.

7.9: Floating home of the Uros

As we stand on the shore of Lake Titicaca, we can only imagine the breadth and depth of the mysteries and memories it holds in its watery womb. Standing on the shoreline, we notice an interesting set of stones that are known as the "gallows." There are two large stone pillars that have a crossbar between them. Across from them is a large stone mound with a round hole in it. It was originally thought the stone pillars and crossbar was used as a gallow to hang people. However, a Bolivian archaeologist, knowing the ancients preoccupation with astronomy, revealed the grouping to be a device for signifying the first day of the winter solstice. When the sun shone through the hole in the mound, it would reflect on a spot in the center of the adjacent crossbar. Ingenious! For our ancient ancestors, these important solstice and equinox dates were important markers for navigating many aspects of their lives. They also had deep spiritual meaning and may have been opportunities to travel and communicate inter-dimensionally while the veil between worlds was thin during these auspicious dates.

So much of what we have seen and discovered here today in both Peru and Bolivia inspires us to recognize the greatness of the beings who once lived and thrived here. Gods, goddesses, humans and extraterrestrials alike may have conspired to co-create these phenomenal sites and others like them throughout the ancient world. This is our ancient past and many of us have had past lives in these sacred places. It is my most sincere desire to trigger these memories for you so you can revisit those lives and re-member the fragmented aspects of your whole soul. In the eternal now moment, we are concurrently experiencing multiple lives all at once. When we tap into these other aspect of ourselves, we can tune into the abilities and knowledge that they have developed and gathered. In this way, we can learn to co-create with the multi-dimensional aspects of our being no matter what points in time and space they are experiencing. Ultimately, we can go beyond the illusion of time and space and tune into the only real expression of ourselves as our eternal whole soul in Havona. This allows us to realign with our perfect divine blueprint removing the distortions of imperfection we have gathered on our space-time journey. This is a grand illusion, like Styx sang about, and exploring the multidimensional realms throughout the time and space experiences on this planet is an extraordinary opportunity! We must embrace every precious moment while remembering the divine source of our origin.

To wrap up our journey through the ancient land of the Peruvians, Bolivians, Aymaras and Incas, let's reflect on the Seven Rays of Creation and how the Akapana Pyramid honored the seven levels of divinity and the Inca flag represented the seven rays of creation.

7.10

I have often pondered the appearance of Mother Earth, herself, as one being with seven energy centers, or chakras. I have intuitively understood that she expresses her core of survival as her fiery red center, her desire within the orange molten lava, her power within the yellow gold of the Earth's most precious mineral, her love for her children within the green vegetation that sustains us on land.

The blue sky offers communion with others as we move through it like a realm where our communal experience unfolds. I have come to realize that communion is the essence of our experience. I feel strongly that it is the true mechanism for God's Self-realization and the only way to experiencing true love. Communion is the true nature of the whole experience and the divine purpose is to seek unity, love and compassion through communion with our individual selves, all other selves and the One Great Self. When we look up to the skies for inspiration, we see that the indigo chakra is represented by the darker blue stratosphere that envelopes Mother Earth and acts as her third eye. Within the bubble that envelopes our sphere, we gather our earthly experiences and then move beyond the stratosphere to advance our souls journey beyond the earth plane. We move through Earth's third eye and become seated in the violet chakra where we commune with the divine in the heavenly realms. By tuning into the eternal now moment, we can soul travel beyond the earth plane and through the stratosphere to sit in the violet lotus right here and now.

As we go to sacred sites around the planet, it's so important to honor our communion with Mother Earth as the sacred foundation upon which the ages of humanity have unfolded for millennia. The ancients recognized the sacred aspects of all of creation and it was reflected in their structures and ways of life. We can be inspired by their divine connection and ability to commune with both the earth and the cosmos at the same time. One powerful way to establish this connection to Mother Earth and the Cosmos within our own being is to ignite our seven chakras thereby activating our rainbow bridge between these two realms. In "Unveiled Mysteries", Saint Germain teaches us about these upper and lower energy centers:

"The entire effort of the aspirant will be — to hold his attention upon these (higher centers of the head, throat and heart) — for only by looking away from the lower centers — will he ever be able — to rise out of misery and limitation. The center of the top of the head is the highest focus in the human body, and there the Silver Cord of 'Liquid White Light' from the Great Source of Creation — enters. When the intention of the mind is held steadfast upon this, the Door of the Soul is opened and — the Three-Fold Activity of the Pure White Light — encircles the waist just below the solar plexus — cutting off forever — the destructive activities of the animal nature of man. This permits his soul to leap forth into its Complete Divine Activity — united once more with the Perfection of its Source." [8]

After reading this, I sat and contemplated the power of the heart center as the midway point and how our consciousness could be pulled upward toward the higher centers or downward toward the lower centers of our animal nature. Starting at the root chakra of survival, I knew this represented an important drive in people — the survival instinct — the intense pull toward life and the strong resistance to death. Then I considered the orange chakra of desire and recognized that there is both constructive and destructive desires. It's the same with power which also has both positive and negative applications. It occurred to me that the expression of these so-called lower centers depends entirely upon the direction in which they are pulled and that leaves just two options — upward or downward. This literally translates into: heaven or earth. We can expand into the divine expression of ourselves or stay limited by contracting into the human expression only. Our physical beings are driven by the lower chakras as a survival mechanism. We have to move into our heart space and expand our mind to elevate into the higher ones. The Buddhist traditions emphasize the need to release earthly attachments and offer practices for detaching from the sense desires of our earthly existence that lead to greed, gluttony and materialism.

From this perspective, we can see how important the heart center truly is as a transformational center between the lower and upper chakras. Staying centered in our heart space is the key to balancing the higher and lower tendencies of the human consciousness. We inherently know in our heart what's right and wrong and whether our thoughts, words and actions are expressing one way or the other. With our inherent free will, we choose lower or higher thoughts knowing these will direct our words and actions. We make this choice in every moment of every day with every thought, word and action. If we tune into our emotional heart center, it will guide us with feelings that produce love and joy when we are aligned with our higher chakras and feelings of anger and dismay when we have surrendered to our lower ones. Balance is the key! We need our lower chakras to survive and they can serve us well when enhanced by the love and wisdom of the higher ones. So that's it — the heart center is like a scale where we can balance our emotions and align the chakras so they can complement each other in a harmonious way. Of course, it's the love chakra! Love has the power to transmute lower energies and propel us into the higher ones! From this point, the power, desire and survival energy centers can serve to inspire constructive activities rather than fuel destructive behaviors. We can consciously resist the pull toward earthly attachments and sense desires that can trap our consciousness in the lower energy centers. We can intentionally create meaningful experiences that keep us tuned into the higher chakras. Let's stay centered in our heart space where we can transmute dark shadows and elevate our consciousness into the light of pure love. Saint Germain teaches us that:

"There is nothing Supreme but — God. There is nothing Eternal and Real but — The Christ. There is nothing True but — The Light. These Three are 'The One'. All else is shadow. Remember — shadows hide — shadows mislead — and shadows make mankind stumble. He who walks the Pathway of Light — stands True to the Christ and looks always Godward... There is no happiness apart from facing and adoring the One Great God — the Source of All. There is nothing Permanent but — Christ. There is no way to proceed through the Universe but on the 'Pathway of Light'." [9]

Let us stand and extend our arms toward the heavens, close our eyes and face the light of the source — the Great Central Sun and let it bathe us in love and truth. Now let's draw our palms toward our chest in a prayer position and bow our heads expressing gratitude to the Mother/Father God for always exerting their gravitational pull of love upon us. We live in peace knowing that all we need to do is respond to this pull and consciously seek to ascend. Let us also take this moment to sincerely thank Godfre Ray King and Saint Germain for sharing such beautiful wisdom with us on this glorious afternoon. Their enlightened passages inspire the illumination of important revelations that will guide us toward the evolution of our consciousness. In this way, we are fulfilling our divine purpose and exploring the deepest and most meaningful essence of our lives — the attainment of perfection within the light of pure love.

As we continue to explore the seven chakras as the Seven Rays of Creation, let's turn to *The Urantia Book* for some more enlightenment on how and why these seven rays affect our consciousness so powerfully:

Let's start with the three holy spheres at the heart of the central and the eternal universe around which all other spheres revolve. This central core allows for the radiation of seven levels of consciousness to reach the vast expanses of the evolutionary spheres making up the body of the Grand Universe. Let's be seated and form a circle around our celestial guide, a "Perfector of Wisdom", who will share with us, through his teachings in *The Urantia Book*, sacred insights about "The Spheres of Paradise":

"Between the central Isle of Paradise and the innermost of the Havona planetary circuits there are situated in space three lesser circuits of special spheres. The innermost circuit consists of the seven sacred spheres of the Universal Father; the second group is composed of the seven luminous worlds of the Eternal Son; in the outermost are the seven immense spheres of the Infinite Spirit, the executive headquarters worlds of the Seven Master Spirits. These three seven-world circuits of the Father, the Son, and the Spirit are spheres of unexcelled grandeur and unimagined glory." [10]

Since we are primarily interested in the seven worlds we have access to and how they might be related to our own seven energy centers, let's ask our guide to enlighten us from this viewpoint. The "Perfector of Wisdom "explains that these spheres, of which there are 21 with each of the three having seven worlds, are the primary centers of activity within which the Paradise Trinity can function through a vast myriad of spirit beings who reside thereupon. He also teaches us that the seven worlds of the Universal Father are shrouded in secrecy and that they contain the personality secrets of the universes:

"Within these spheres, the bestowal gift of the Universal Father to each individual evolutionary being — the thought adjuster — has its origins on the spheres and its mysteries are kept secret by the high beings who manifests them. The only sphere that we, as evolutionary beings, would ever reside upon when we are in our most highly evolved state of being is that of "Ascendington." This unique world is the "sum of the father, son, and spirit, the rendezvous of the ascended creatures of space, the receiving sphere of the pilgrims of time who are passing through the Havona universe on their way to Paradise. Ascendington is the actual Paradise home of the ascendant soul of time and space until they attain Paradise status. You mortals will spend most of your Havona "vacations" on Ascendington... Here you will engage in thousands of activities which are beyond the grasp of mortal imagination. And as on every previous advance in the Godward ascent, your human self will enter new relationships with your divine self. The secrets of Ascendington include the mystery of the gradual and certain building up in the material and immortal mind of a spiritual and potentially immortal counterpart of character and identity. This phenomenon constitutes one of the most perplexing mysteries of the universes — the evolution of an immortal soul within the mind of a mortal and material creature." [11.]

Whoa. Let's take a moment to absorb that!

Next let's explore "The Sacred Worlds of the Eternal Son":

"The seven luminous spheres of the Eternal Son are the worlds of the seven phases of pure spirit existence. These shining orbs are the source of the threefold light of Paradise and Havona, their influence being largely, but not wholly, confined to the central universe." [12] We are taught that the spiritual influence of the Eternal Son is passed on to the evolutionary worlds by the "Paradise Sons of God" and that, "These sons of God are the divine ministers who are unceasingly devoted to the work of helping the creatures of time attain the high spiritual goal of eternity." [13]

This is done, we are told, by spiritually influencing all beings of time and space to embrace love, mercy and service and by inspiring them with true spiritual beauty, divine goodness and living truth. From this instruction we can envision that the sacred spheres of the Eternal Son are the spiritual centers of a highly inspirational nature.

Now onto the seven orbs of the Infinite Spirit which is the home of the Seven Master Spirits. To understand the nature and purpose of the residents and activities of these spheres, we have only to look to the functions and influence of the Master Spirits who govern them. Consider these excerpts taken from the teachings of the "Perfector of Wisdom" who is blessing us with his knowledge this afternoon:

"The Seven Master Spirits are the mind-spirit balance wheel of the universe of universes...an all-embracing, all-encompassing, and all-coordinating power... From these seven special spheres the Master Spirits operate to equalize and stabilize the cosmic mind circuits of the grand universe... Each Master Spirit presides over one super universe... The executive of abodes of the Seven Master Spirits are the Paradise headquarters of the seven super universes." [14]

Our teacher explains that, "The Seven Master Spirits of Paradise are the primary personalities of the Infinite Spirit. In the sevenfold creative act of self-duplication, the Infinite Spirit exhausted the associative possibilities mathematically inherent in the factual existence of the three persons of Deity....And this explains why the universe is operated in seven grand divisions, and why the number seven is basically fundamental in its organization and administration... The Seven Master Spirits thus have their origin in, and derive their individual characteristics from, the following seven likenesses:

1. The Universal Father
2. The Eternal Son
3. The Infinite Spirit
4. The Father and the Son
5. The Father and the Spirit
6. The Son and the Spirit
7. The Father, Son and Spirit

Since Mother Earth, named "Urantia", resides in the seventh super universe, called "Orvonton", according to our guide, let's focus on the Seventh Master Spirit and ask him if he can describe his nature, conduct and influence with regards to the consciousness of our sector. With this request, a Divine Counselor of "Uversa" (our super universe headquarters) appears to contribute his insight. He shares with us first that, "The Seven Master Spirits are the full representation of the Infinite Spirit to the evolutionary universes. They represent the third source and center in the relationships of energy, mind, and spirit" [15] He tells us, "It is literally true that the Seven Spirits are the personalized physical power, cosmic mind, and spiritual presence of the triune Deity — the seven spirits of God sent forth to all the universe" and that "It is difficult for the mortal mind to understand very much about the Master Spirits because their work is so highly specialized yet all-embracing, so exceptionally material and at the same time so exquisitely spiritual. [16]

The Divine Counselor calls them the "versatile creators of the cosmic mind" and "supreme directors of the vast and far-flung spirit-creature creation." He refers to the Seventh Master Spirit as "the marvelous symmetry of the coordinate blending of the divine natures of the Father, Son and Spirit" and tells us that he "functions in the place of the God of ascending creatures in the matter of personal relationships" stating that, "He is the one high spirit beings all ascenders are certain to recognize and somewhat comprehend when they reach the centers of glory." [17]

Let's take a moment to thank the "Perfector of Wisdom" and the "Divine Counselor" for their profound wisdom. Let's also reflect upon this incredible insight. These revelations are giving us a much greater understanding of the source of consciousness as it relates to our corner of creation. The most remarkable wonder of all is that we can observe these three holy spheres on a magical night when its mirror reflection, Orion, is illuminated! Now we can stand in awe and amazement as we picture the miraculous activities and divine beings centered in these majestic realms of the Paradise Trinity. With our eyes closed, let's imagine that we are virtually experiencing a magnificent night under the stars when we can clearly see this divine residence which is the origin and destination of our being. In your mind's eye, picture the three belt stars of Orion. These holy spheres represent the point of transition between existential infinity and experiential eternity. The threefold activities of the Paradise Trinity are centered here and their energies are pulled both upward toward heaven and downward towards the universes just like our consciousness is seated at the heart center of our being.

In different ages, different energy centers are in play and during the patriarchal era, the majority of the collective consciousness has been focused in the solar plexus which can either spiral upward for divine empowerment or downward for greed and the misuse of power. This bright yellow chakra also represents gold. From the Golden Age of the Egyptians and throughout the Mayan, Incan and Greek empires, gold was considered not just precious, but powerful. The two most sacred elements of the earth are gold and crystal. Silica is created in the stars and is the second most abundant element on earth. One of its chemical quirks is its ability to bond with oxygen to form crystals and these combine to form solid rocks. Rocks are loaded with crystalline silica. Gold, on the other hand, has been worshipped as a product of the sun rather than the stars. We know both elements are forged in the stars. Crystals and gold can be found in caves and mountains and are remnants of the stardust that created our mineral-rich planet. In an exploration of our own planets evolution, the teachers in *The Urantia Book* speak about the Sierras and their "gold bearing quartz strata being the product of lava flows". [18]

Saint Germain provides a deeper insight into the true power of gold. As my thoughts centered on the nature of gold, I recalled that in "Unveiled Mysteries," Saint Germain spoke of the power of gold in a chapter about the Golden Ages of the past which took place in the Sahara Desert. When I flipped to that section, here is what I found. He explains why gold was such a common commodity in all so-called "Golden Ages" and specifically states that "it acts as a transformer"! I knew it! I envisioned that gold must be dispersed throughout the solar plexus of Mother Earth at this transformational point. She creates the physical forms of all life within her womb. Our bodies are made up of water, iron and other earth minerals, including silica, that come from the earth and therefore, the stars. That's how I see it. What do you think? Let's take a closer look at Saint Germain's teachings on the meaning, purpose and power of gold:

"Gold was a common commodity...in all 'Golden Ages' because it's natural emanation is a purifying, balancing, and revitalizing energy or force. It is placed within the earth by the "Lords of Creation' — those "Great Beings of Love and Light" — who create and direct worlds — systems of worlds — and the evolution of the beings upon them. The outer mind or intellectual knowledge of humanity, holds within it little — very little — understanding of the — Real — purpose for which gold exists on this planet. It grows within the earth like a plant, and — through it is constantly pouring a purifying, vitalizing, and balancing current of energy — into the very ground we walk upon — as well as into the growth of nature...Gold is placed upon this planet for a variety of uses — to the most trivial and unimportant ones — being that of using gold as a — means of exchange — and for ornamentation. The far greater activity — and purpose either within or upon the earth is — the release — of its own inherent quality and energy to purify, vitalize and balance the atomic structure of the world...Gold is one of the — most important — ways by which the energy from our sun is supplied to the interior of the earth, and a balance of activities maintained. A conveyor of this energy — it acts as a transformer — to pass the sun's force into the physical substance of our world — as well as to the Life evolving upon it. The energy within gold is — really — the radiant, electronic force from the sun — acting in a lower octave. Gold is sometimes called a — precipitated sun ray. As the energy within gold is of an extremely high vibratory rate, it can only act upon the finer and more subtle expressions of Life — through absorption. In all — 'Golden Ages' — this metal comes into plentiful and common use — by the mass of the people — and whenever such a condition occurs — the spiritual development of that people reaches — a very high state." [19]

From this dissertation, we can clearly see that, not only does gold serve as a transformational element within the earth, but it also has a spiritually transformational effect on the life that inhabits it. Saint Germain emphasizes its purifying, vitalizing and balancing effects and refers to its high rate of vibration which acts upon the finer bodies. I believe that crystal also has the same qualities and am aware that it is used for healing due to its vibrational effects of balancing and purifying to revitalize health. I like to think of these transformational elements as being gifts from the gods that are delivered to us on the rays of the sun and on the light of twinkling stars. With that beautiful vision, let's get tucked in for the night. Since we kicked off the day with a guided meditation and seven ray activation, let's end today's journey, inspired by the ancients, with this beautiful prayer honoring the sun.

The Ascension by Chanera

I feel My God Flame touch my brow,
The Breath of Love — eternal now,
I raise my eyes and lo, I see
My own Great God Self over me.
A dazzling cloud envelops all,
I hear My Real God "Presence" call,
I feel a surge of Love's great might,
I enter deep its Breath — it's Light.
I see within this Pulsing Flame,
I listen, and hear my Secret Name
I feel the glow-the Great Flame Breath,
I am the Victor over death.
I stand forth free-Ascended now,
To my heart's Light, all things do bow:
I am a Being of Cause alone
And that Cause, Love — The Sacred Tone.
I pour out Life — I lift, I raise,
My heart o'erflows and sings its praise,
My power strengthens and inspires,
My Great Light Rays are God's Own Fires.
I am a Sun, My love — it's Light
All else grows dim — earth lost to sight;
I know I am just God — the One –
The Source — the Great, Great Central Sun.[20]

Your Personal Revelations

_____

_____

_____

_____

_____

REFERENCES
Chapter cover image of rainbow courtesy of: www.pixabay.com

Illustrations:

1. www.sites.stedwards.edu
2. www.pixabay.com
3. www.panaramio.com
4. www.pixabay.com
5. www.pixabay.com
6. www.travelblog.com
7. www.alekseitrofimov.eu
8. www.pixabay.com
9. www.atlasobscura.com
10. www.panaramio.com

Text:
Elkins, Rueckert, McCarty, *"The RA Material" The Law of One: Book 1,* Whitford Press, 1984
1. p. 115
2. p. 115
6. p. 115
Smithsonian Institute, *SmithsonianTimelines of History*, DK Publishing, 2010
3. p. 28
4. http://www.faculty.ucr.edu/~legneref/archeol/fuentema.htm
Brad Olsen, *"Future Esoteric"*, Whitford Press, 1984
5. p.107-8
Andrew Collins, *The Cygnus Mystery*, Watkins Publishing, 2008
7. p. xvii
Godfre Ray King, *Unveiled Mysteries,* St Germain Press 1934
8. page 256-7
9. page 260-1
19. page 44-6
20. Preface
The Urantia Book Fellowship, *The Urantia Book,* Uversa Press, 2008
10. (13:1.1-2)
11. (13:1.21-22)
12. (13:3.1)
13. (20:10.2)
14. (13:4.2-6)
15. (16:4.1)
16. (16:4.2)
17. (16:4.19-20)
18. (60:3.3)

Day Eight

Celestial Points of Divine Consciousness

Good morning and welcome to a brand-new day of enlightened possibilities and illuminating ideas! This morning, awakened by the bright rays of the sun as it rises and reveals its full magnificence, we will be honoring this radiant source of light and heat at the center of our solar system. Strangely and inexplicably, I was literally born with a tan and my parents used to call me their little brown berry. They also called me "Suzy-Sunshine", not just for my sunny disposition, but because I adored the sun and growing up, spent much of my time basking in it. I have always felt safe and content within the loving embrace of its warm, cozy blanket. Absorbing the rays of the sun also gives me a renewed sense of energy and vitality and in its absence, hidden by dark clouds, I am prone to feelings of depression and anxiety. People often comment on the golden-brown color of my skin and I have a sense that I inherited my pigment from my ancient ancestors who worshiped a sun God. When I was growing up, I would tell everyone, matter-of-factly, that I was a sun goddess, long before I even knew what that meant.

Another interesting perspective of the expanded consciousness I tapped into early on is my connection to the land of Egypt. I would dream about a time when people wore golden collars and arm bands that shone brilliantly as they absorbed and reflected the sun light. I would see luminescent beings in jaded wraps wearing gold sandals that were engaging in various activities. The children were taught how to play with light and sound and move objects with their mind. The women were performing alchemical rituals and ceremony with oils and herbs offering healing, blessings and nourishment. The men were involved in building, planning and governing the affairs of the empire. There were also artists, jewelers, weavers and scribes using natural dyes, plants and minerals. They were creating beautiful works of art and colorful records of events. As I grow older, my desire to visit has only grown stronger and now I know someday, I will. In the meantime, the visions that still dance in my mind are so vivid and real, I feel as if I've already been there.

My past life regressions have revealed a few incarnations during the Golden Age of Egypt. Two of my past lives are as men and one is of a woman. In the earliest incarnation, Egypt was still known as the Land of Khem and I was one of the initiates sent here to build and inspire a new matriarchal civilization settled in love and light. The Great Pyramid was built by the shiny ones who offered it to our emerging culture for inspiration and instruction as well as for a source of pure energy. This structure served as the foundation stone for the Golden Age unfolding in the fertile valley of the sun. The Great Pyramid was placed in the geodesic center of the Earth next to the flowing source of the River Nile. The water that ran beneath the surface of the pyramid served as a conduit for the spiraling energy flowing in through its crystal cap. The exact shape, design and placement of the Great Pyramid were directed by advanced off-planetary beings who came here to ignite the new Golden Age of enlightenment. They came to teach, inspire and empower the initiates who would herald in this new age.

As a self-generating device using free energy, the Great Pyramid became both a power plant and mystery school with each purpose tapping into the source field. I have clear memories of being shown the interior design of 4 chambers and 3 great rooms that were to be used for different fueling and training purposes. For the first time, chambers could be lit up at night by accessing free energy that would illuminate lanterns with glass bulbs. In these chambers, initiations and activations would take place day and night raising the frequency of those who were to become great teachers, architects and astronomers. As a member of a group of advanced initiates, I remember sitting in meditation drawing spiraling energy in through my crown that would illuminate my being and empower my force field. Colorful spheres of light would radiate around me that pulsated with different tones. I was in control of these spheres that encircled my body and could direct them to expand at will. Every energetic sphere had its own distinct character and each served a specific purpose. The tall, shiny beings showed us how to direct, expand and pulsate the spheres that could project outward as powerful rays or flow inward as vital life force energy. They were sourced from our energy centers which drew their power from the light of the sun. The root red energy center informed our instincts and with practice, we learned to overcome our animal instincts of fear and lack and raise them to a higher level of love and abundance. Our sacral orange center vibrated with passion and the desire to co-create and we learned to master the law of attraction. Our solar golden center pulsed with the power to control energy and we mastered the elements. Our emerald green heart center was the most expansive sphere and we were taught how to love unconditionally. Our pale blue communication center expanded with the desire to connect and collaborate with the community. We were shown advanced languages, both written and spoken using light and sound with meaning and purpose. Our indigo third eye center was both a receiver and transmitter and we mastered the skillful use of this portal. The most advanced training was focused on the violet crown where divine wisdom and worship were centered. We were shown how spinning our crown could facilitate interdimensional sight and co-creation with higher beings from those realms. All of these gifts and skills that I learned in that lifetime have made it easier to tap into them this time around.

In another past life, I was busily engaged in delivering blueprints for the construction of Amarna. This new golden city would have the most glorious Temples of Light in devotion to the Sun God Ra. Inspired by Akhnaten, the enlightened one who understood the Sun as a powerful being who emanated the seven rays of creation. He instinctively knew that it was a portal of divine consciousness and knew how to draw upon its life force. He engaged in practices that allowed him to work with these rays and access an unlimited abundance of vitality, wisdom and resources. I remember being in awe of Akhnaten and willing to serve him selflessly and tirelessly. I recall being surrounded by architects and designers all gathered on a platform which was covered by a colorful tarp and flanked by spiral pillars at each corner. Architectural drawings and scrolls were spread out on a large stone table and they were talking in excited tones that revealed a great sense of urgency. I was very focused on the importance of my role as a runner delivering drawings and messages to and fro between the architects and builders at different platforms. I was very dedicated to my task and felt inspired by the divine nature of the emerging Temple.

In my third incarnation, I was a Priestess in training at the Temple of the Sun in Amarna. I specifically remember sitting and standing in circular formations holding and using different implements, herbs and devices. We were trained in the different powers that metallic tools, crystal stones and herbal supplements had to heal, energize and materialize. We used incense and oils to conjure up energy and chanting and drumming to raise it. We mastered the skill of lowering and raising vibrational frequencies which allowed us to direct our will more effectively. The most advanced training I remember receiving, which still informs my inner core today, focuses on the power of love as the highest source of everlasting energy in the universe. We were shown how the sun acts a portal for this force of pure love which inspire and empower the seven rays that filter through it. We related to the sun as a powerful being — a Sun God who loved and adored us while inspiring and empowering us to awaken the divine within.

During this incarnation, I became an initiate and disciple of "Ra" who represented a group of illuminated beings who came to inspire and empower the teachers and leaders of our emerging temple-city in Amarna. As an initiated Priestess in the Temple of the Sun, I was in service to our leader, Akhnaten. He inspired his followers with his golden radiance as a love-light being in service to the Sun God Ra. His powerful wife, Nefertiti, was also a great source of inspiration for the followers and especially, for the Priestesses who she empowered. She was of an advanced order of luminescent beings just like her husband, Akhnaten. They were sourced with the starseed DNA of their ancestors Isis and Osiris from Sirius and Orion, respectively. As children, they were taught in the mystery schools how to ignite this dormant DNA to awaken their advanced knowledge and abilities. Engaging in advanced initiations and activations, they were able to build their light quotient and raise their light frequency becoming less dense. In their radiant luminescence, they tuned into the sun as their source and tapped into the energies flowing through it. The vivid memories from that lifetime of luminescent leaders and empowered Priestesses have inspired the goddess retreats that I have hosted and sponsored over the years. In my next book, the third book in the Up! trilogy, *Lighten Up!*, we will be "Activating Your Light Body" with practices, initiations and activations that resonate with me from this lifetime bleeding through from ancient Egypt.

With the sun as a portal of higher consciousness we can draw upon its power as a source of divine guidance. We can honor the sun as a source of vitality that provides sustenance to all living beings. We can cherish every breath we take as a gift from this god of love and light showering his blessings upon us through the radiance of its divine nature.

8.1

To this day, I feel happiest and most fulfilled when I am bathed in the Golden light of the sun as it wraps itself around me like a blanket embracing me with pure love. It is through this portal of light that the power of love streams forth illuminating all beings with source consciousness. Tapping into this source, we can access the field of infinite wisdom and tune into the akashic records. When I asked my higher self, by going within, if divine knowledge and spiritual inspiration were delivered in the light of the sun, the vision I received were beams of light streaming into my third eye. This reminded me of the teachings in *The Urantia Book* which explained that the light of the sun was delivered to us in direct, straight lines called "sunbeams" and that the wave-like light we experience is due to the interfering patterns of higher beings sending waves of consciousness through this portal. While the celestial guide offering the teachings made it clear that it would be difficult for mortals to understand the source of these "wave-light manifestations", he indicated that these interferences were related to the gravity circuits of the Paradise Trinity and the radiations of the Seven Master Spirits. I also recall reading about "light without heat" that was of a divine and sacred source and that this type of light was powerful beyond our imagination.

As we head out on our adventurous exploration of ancient Egypt, let's honor the sun that illuminated the temples and inspired the civilizations who thrived there. Let's reflect on what we already know about its celestial origin and true nature. We know that our sun emerged from a great nebula which gave birth to it and that Orion is the primordial "stellar nursery." Once our sun grew up, it broke free of the nursery and embarked upon its own creative adventure. Spiraling through the galaxy, its massive weight and spinning motion attracted enough stardust to begin gathering children of its own. In this way, the sun became the parent of our solar system giving birth to all the planets that encircle it. The sun fulfilled its desire to start a family of its own that it can love, illuminate and inspire. The sun holds all of its children in its gravity grasp with unconditional love and devotion. Embraced by its love and empowered by its light, let's continue on our spiraling ascension creating a new Golden Age of Enlightenment. For inspiration, let's visit the last Golden Age on our planet by projecting our consciousness into the sacred sites along the Nile.

Journey along the Nile

For today's virtual adventure into ancient Egypt, let's imagine it the way it was during its Golden Age before the sands swept over the Sahara. We can imagine a lush green landscape adorned with towering palm trees adorning the Nile. These magnificent trees with their giant fronds would have provided shade from the shimmering heat. The Nile is the backbone of the Goddess known as Egypt with her kundalini energy flowing along this trail of temple sites. Temples were built at each of the energy centers on her spine where the earth's ley lines intersected. For today's journey along the Nile, our focus will be on the Nile itself as a mirror reflection of the celestial Milky Way. We won't be focusing on the specific temple sites on this visit since that will be a major focus of the third and final phase of our ascension journey in my next book, *Lighten Up! Activating Your Light Body.* In it, not only will be visiting the ancient temple sites, we will be engaging in initiations and activations at these sacred centers just like they did during the time of the Egyptian Mystery Schools!

For today's adventure, let's board our Felucca and sail down the Nile, the kundalini of Egypt, activating our own energy centers through the ley lines as we pass temple sites along the way!

8.2

While we enjoy the lush landscape along the fertile Nile, let's continue our focus on the celestial sun by engaging in this theatrical story about the formation of our solar system.

Birth of our Solar Family

The ancient Babylonian Creation Epic I am about to share so exquisitely expresses the consciousness perspective I have been seeking to convey. From this perspective, all creative manifestations of energy and matter have as their essential nature a form of individualized consciousness.

As we have learned, *The Urantia Book* states that the original Creator-Consciousness trinitized into the Universal Father, Eternal Son and Infinite Spirit. To express itself as creative manifestations, the Trinity expanded its consciousness into a sevenfold expression of itself as Father, Son, Spirit, Father-Son, Father-Spirit, Son-Spirit, and Father-Son-Spirit. These seven levels of consciousness emerged as seven super-universe creations in time and space and if we imagine ourselves as the seventh super universe, we can identify the Father-Son-Spirit patterns of consciousness prevailing in our experiential realm. These are intelligent patterns of energies that become imprinted upon the cosmic beings within their spheres. Before narrowing in on our local universe interpretation of these patterns, we need to consider the intervening realms of consciousness, or intelligent energies, emanating from the super universe core, the Milky Way galaxy (or "Uversa"). Then as we move into our own local universe core ("Salvington"), we can explore the further translations of the Father-Son-Spirit energies defining our patterns. Within our own local universe, these intelligent energies descend through our parent constellation (Norlatiadek), its headquarters (Edentia) and then further through our parent-system (Satania) and its headquarters (Jerusem) until we finally reach our immediate family in the solar system governed by our own Father Sun.

Through the divine portal of the Sun, the intelligent energy patterns emanating from the greater cosmos are reflected onto the planets it attracts into its gravity embrace. Just like all of the cosmic beings we have identified in our seventh super universe from Uversa, Salvington and Norlatiedek to Edentia, Jerusem and Satania, our solar system has an identity of its own as do the planets revolving around it. Our sun has been called "Helios, the Solar Logos" and also "Vesta, the Fire Goddess." Each of our planets also have names because they are in fact, individual expressions of consciousness. Each planet in the solar system represents a unique expression, or point of view, of the original Creator-consciousness and the following tale embraces this concept fully in a colorful and imaginative theatrical performance.

My fascination with ancient texts led me to the following adventurous tale describing the emergence of our solar system. This is taken from Zechariah Sitchin's book, "The Twelfth Planet", which is based upon his translations of cuneiform script etched upon ancient clay tablets over 6000 years ago. Tens of thousands of clay tablets were found in the 1800's in a place once called "Sumer" in Mesopotamia (now modern-day Northern Iraq). According to Sitchin, the later Babylonian text called "The Epic of Creation" represents a translated version of the story depicted on the Sumerian tablets differing only in the names attributed to the gods. In any case, both the tablets and the texts based upon them, recount a truly fascinating story.

As it turns out, the details about the solar system, (and many other topics), are so incredibly accurate that they clearly represent an extraordinarily advanced knowledge of astronomy, geometry and mathematics at a time when we were supposed to be "primitive." Another remarkable aspect of the tablets is how poetically and artistically the stories and images are! This makes for a truly enjoyable study of them which I will share with you throughout the continued exploration of our ancient origins.

Let's start with the splendid depiction of the creation and design of our solar system as told in the Babylonian "Enuma Elish", also called "The Creation Epic":

Sitchin writes, "...the "Epic of Creation" perfectly explains the event that probably took place in our solar system. The stage on which the celestial drama of Enuma Elish unfolds is the primeval universe. The celestial actors are the ones who create as well as the ones being created."

Enuma Elish means "When in the Heights" and this is how the epic begins:

> When in the heights Heaven had not been named,
> And below, Earth had not been called;
> Naught, but primordial APSU, their Begetter.
> MUMMU and TIAMAT — she who bore them all;
> Their waters were mingled together.
> No reed had yet been formed, no Marshland had appeared,
> None of the gods had yet been brought into being,
> None boring name, their destinies were undetermined;
> Then it was that gods were formed in their midst.[1]

APSU, refers to the Sun, MUMMU to the planet Mercury, and TIAMAT to a planet we have no name for and you will see why...The waters are "primordial waters — the life-giving elements of the universe" sometimes called "life plasm." The gods referred to are the other planets yet to emerge. So, with this nine-line verse, Sitchin says that, "the ancient poet chronicler manages to see this in front row center, and boldly and dramatically raises the curtain on the most majestic show ever: the creation of our solar system."[2]

It is important before the show starts to outline the characters involved in this drama:

APSU — Sun: "One who visited from the beginning"
MUMMU — Mercury: "Counselor and Emissary of Apsu"
LAHAMU — Mars: "Deity of War"
TIAMAT — Unknown: "Maiden who Gave Life"
KISHAR — Jupiter: "Foremost of Firm Lands"
ANSHAR — Saturn: "Foremost of the Heavens"
GAGA — Pluto: "Counselor of the Emissary of Ansar"
ANU — Uranus: "He of the Heavens"
EA — Neptune: "Artful Creator" [3]

As you will see, each of the celestial bodies have distinct personalities enrolled in the creation drama. It starts with "two primeval celestial bodies": Apsu, the Sun, "one who exists from the beginning" and Mummu, or Mercury, as "the trusted aide and emissary of Apsu." According to Sitchin, this is a good description of Mercury, "a small planet rapidly running around his giant master." These "two primeval celestial bodies then gave birth to a series of celestial gods." The first being Tiamat, "the missing planet", but it is said, "In primordial times, she was the very first Virgin Mother of the first Divine Trinity." Between Apsu and Tiamat, there existed primordial life-giving waters that produced two celestial gods, (planets), between them: Lahmu (Mars) and Lahamu (Venus).

> Their waters were mingled together...
> Gods were formed in their midst:
> God Lahmu and God Lahamu were brought forth
> By name they were called

It is interesting to note that the root of these two names is "LHM" which means "war." Mars is referred to as "The God of War" and Venus as "The God of Love and War", with male and female designations respectively. The saga continues... Sitchin translates the next verse:

> Before they had grown in age
> And in stature to an appointed size –
> God Anshar and God Kishar were formed,
> Surpassing them (in size)
> As lengthened the days and multiplied the years,
> God Anu became their son — of his ancestors, a rival (in size).
> Then Anshar's first son, Anu,
> As his equal and in his image begot Nudimmud.[4]

So, at the end of Act I, we have the sun and nine planets. Now the plot starts to thicken as the celestial drama unfolds with personalities clashing as egos battle for control and dominance of the system! This conflict within the family makes for an unstable environment (as witnessed by the gravitational surges). This leads to a pair of brothers ganging up on their family members. (Sounds like a reality TV show!) Sitchin translates:

> The divine brothers banded together:
> They disturbed Tiamat as they surged back and forth.
> They were troubling the "belly" of Tiamat
> By their antics in the dwellings in heaven.
> Apsu could not lessen their clamor;
> Tiamat was speechless at their ways.

> Their doings were loathsome...
> Troublesome were there ways.[5]

When these two planets gang up on her (interfering with her orbit) this threatens our survival which upsets Apsu, the sun. Disturbed by their behavior, he consults with Mummu (Mercury), and together, they decide to destroy them! The other gods overhear their plans and are left speechless. Ea (Neptune) decides to subdue Apsu and Mummu by orbiting around them from his farthest reach in the outermost orbit of planets. This either affected the sun's magnetism or possibly, Neptune admitted his own radiation. In either case, it works, and the sun and Mercury were left powerless. This restored peace for the meantime and the sun could no longer create in this part of the solar system.

In case you are thinking this is entertaining ancient theatrics but can seriously have no real astronomical significance, think again! You will see as this drama continues to play out, it represents very accurately how the activity in the early solar system played out to become the one we are familiar with today. As a matter of fact, modern astrology has only recently, in a comparative sense, caught up with just how accurately these depictions are in number, size, origin, placement and orbital characteristics.

Since Neptune subdued the sun's creative power in this new solar system, he would have to go looking deep into outer space to attract a new member. Although peace was temporarily restored, the gods (planets) became restless once more and Neptune then sought out his brother from beyond. Sitchin describes this with dramatic flair:

"As the number of celestial beings increased, they made great noise and commotion, disturbing the Primeval Father (Apsu, the Sun). His faithful messenger, Mummu (Mercury), urged him to take strong measures to discipline the young gods, but they ganged up on him and robbed him of his creative powers. The Primeval Mother (Tiamat) sought to take revenge. The God who led a revolt against the Primeval Father had a new suggestion: Let his young son, (brother of Neptune), be invited to join the Assembly of God's and given supremacy so that he might go to fight single-handed the "monster" their mother turned out to be."[6]

Therefore, Neptune seeks out the "Sun's youngest son" from the deep reaches of outer space. Astronomically, Neptune, orbiting at the farthest edge of the system, attracts the planet from outside the system with its gravitational pull. This young god is given the name "Marduk."

This brings us to the opening of Act III which begins with the adoration of Marduk. Sitchin's translated verse is as follows:

> In the Chamber of Fates, the place of Destinies,
> A god was engendered, most able and wisest of gods:
> In the heart of the Deep was Marduk created.
> Alluring was his figure, sparkling the lift of his eyes;
> Lordly was his gait, commanding of olden times...
> Greatly exalted was he about the gods, exceeding throughout...

He was the loftiest of the gods, surpassing was his height;
His members were enormous, he was exceedingly tall.[7]

This new planet pulled into the system by Neptune was much larger than the others and called the "loftiest of gods" because his elliptical orbit was far greater. As he approached the other orbiting planets, he was on fire and emitting radiation, the script says, "when he moved his lips, fire blazed forth." Between that and his enormous size, he was quite threatening. In response, the other planets spewed back (the size and heat from the large planet ignited activity from the other planets as he passed by them) "they heaped on him their awesome flashes" it is written. He first passes by Ea (Neptune) which pulls on her body and gives her the appearance of having "two heads." Then he passes by Anu (Uranus) and its gravitational pull tears chunks from her body which break off and result in forming satellites. The chunks begin to rotate around her and become orbiting satellites.

I found this next part of Sitchin's translation to be fascinating. The order of the planets, as Marduk passes them, indicates that he is orbiting counterclockwise while the other planets in the system are orbiting clockwise making him a further threat to the whole system! (Astronomically, these opposing rotational directions are accurate within the solar system!) They did however, put up resistance and as Marduk passed Anshar (Saturn) and Kishar (Jupiter), their gravitational and magnetic forces bent his path inward toward the center of the system and threatened Tiamat: "the gods were not at rest, carried as in a storm." The proximity of Marduk to Tiamat resulted in 11 chunks of her being torn off and these in turn became her satellites. Sitchin describes from the text, "eleven monsters, a growing, raging throng of satellites who separated themselves from her body and marched at the side of Tiamat." Preparing herself to face the onrushing Marduk, Tiamat is accompanied by her satellites giving them the appearance of god's (planets). The name, Kingu, was given to her chief satellite as the "firstborn among the gods who form her assembly."

Sitchin translates into verse:

She exalted Kingu,
In their midst she made him great...
The high command of the battle
She entrusted into his hand. [8]

At first, this upset the other planets because she didn't have the authority to grant a satellite the "Tablet of Destinies", giving it a planetary status of its own. Ea (Neptune) talked it over with Anshar (Saturn) who suggested she face Tiamat, but she refuses. Anshar turns to Anu (Uranus) but she also declines. One after the next, the goddesses step aside and then Marduk approaches Anshar which gives them an idea. Sitchin shares the following verse:

He who is potent shall be our Avenger;
He who is keen in battle; Marduk, the Hero!

(And Marduk answers):
If I indeed, as your Avenger
Am to vanquish Tiamat, save your lives –
Convene an Assembly to proclaim my Destiny supreme![9]

Sitchin translates this as meaning that his destiny is his orbit around the sun and he shall be supreme amongst the celestial gods. Marduk's vast distance from the sun does grant him the longest elliptical around the sun, far exceeding the orbits of the others.

Anshar sends her satellite, Gaga (who became Pluto) out to tell the others who are more than happy to have Marduk be the one who slays Tiamat. They declare, "Marduk is King...Go and cut off the life of Tiamat!"

The excitement and anticipation for the ensuing confrontation escalates in Act IV, Sitchin explains, as Marduk prepares for battle. Marduk obtains three more satellites as he passes by Saturn and Jupiter giving him a total of seven satellites now, which are called "winds" because they are like whirlwinds swirling around him. Sitchin continues the story with these translated verses, "Using his satellites as a "storm chariot", he "set forth the winds that he had brought forth, the seven of them." One of these winds he named "Evil Wind." The adversaries were ready for battle:

Tiamat and Marduk, the wisest of the gods,
Advanced against one another;
They pressed on to single combat,
They approached for battle.[10]

Sitchin introduces the battle: "The epic now turns to the description of the celestial battle, in the aftermath of which Heaven and Earth were created!" He offers this translation of the verses which describes this epic battle:

The Lord spread out his neck to unfold her;
The Evil Wind, the rearmost, he unleashed at her face.
As she opened her mouth, Tiamat, to devour him –
He drove in Evil Wind so that she closed not her lips.
The fierce storm Winds then charged her belly;
Her body became distended; her mouth had opened wide,
He shot there through an arrow, it tore her belly;
It cut through her insides, tore into her womb.
Having thus subdued her, her life-breath he extinguished.[11]

This verse indicates that Marduk and Tiamat did not actually collide in this confrontation, but his satellites smashed into her leaving a cleavage into which Marduk released a flash of lightning extinguishing her life. As Sitchin explains, the highly charged Marduk probably released a bolt of energy which pierced the opening in Tiamat. As a result, her electric and magnetic forces were likely neutralized leaving her lifeless. She was however, still somewhat intact as a planet and Marduk would have to finish her off.

Act V opens with Marduk returning to fulfill his promise to the other celestial gods in return for orbital supremacy. He completes his inaugural orbit around the sun and then sets his sights on Tiamat determined to finish her off once and for all. As he approaches the now lifeless but still intact "monster", he hesitates:

> The Lord paused to view the lifeless body,
> To divide the monster, he then artfully planned.
> Then, as a mussel, he split her into parts.[12]

The upper part was then hit by one of Marduk's satellites which sailed into her new divinely destined orbit where she was to become the most beautiful planet in all the solar system — our own beloved Mother Earth!

Marduk also had a divine plan for the lower half which it smashed into smithereens: he would "set it up as a screen for the skies, locking them together, as watchmen he stationed them... He'd bend Tiamat's tail to form the great band as a bracelet." Ta-da! The asteroid belt that separates the outer planets from the inner planets was thus formed! Oh, and one more act of divine destiny: remember Tiamat's firstborn satellite, Kingu, whom she crowned with a halo and made into a god. I prefer to think of Kingu as a goddess who became our Mother Moon. In the story, Kingu adored Tiamut, her mother and promised to never leave her side. In fact, she continues to bless her today with her heavenly influence, although we know her more lovingly as our Moon!

The "Heavens" (as the loyal moon and protective asteroid belt) and the Earth were created in one theatrical play starring Marduk — the celestial King! So who is this material planet who swept in to "save" the solar system and create our beloved planet? He is none other than the "Twelfth Planet!" The one Zacharias Sitchin's named his book after and for good reason. Like I indicated before, this dramatic performance told in such a delightful way by the ancient "poet chroniclers" actually had remarkable accuracy in the placement of this 12th planet. At the time Sitchin wrote this book, astronomers had only suspected this planets existence, but I discovered, by turning to a book called, "Earth's Forbidden Secrets", that it has since been discovered! In Part One, an essay, "Searching for the Past", written by Maxwell Igan, he states that, "the other planet that exists in our solar system, the one we have only now recently discovered, the (Sumerian tablets) named as "Nibiru — the planet of the crossing." He goes on to describe how, in the Babylonian version of the text, the people revered it as their God Marduk, hero of the skies and named the twelfth planet after him. In any case, they are referring to the same large planet with its elongated elliptical orbit.

So, now we have 10 planets, the sun and the moon. Maxwell Igan explains that "the Sumerians considered the Sun to be a rightfully included member of the solar system and...they believe our moon actually has a considerable history" and rightful place of its own. With the inclusion of the sun and the moon as planets in their own right, that gives us 12! Of course we know that the number 12 has tremendous significance in the creation of this realm. Sitchin explains that the Sumerians gave such reverence to this planet because, according to the tablets, this is the planet where the gods who created us came from. These tablets, written over 6000 years ago, however fanciful, describe with remarkable accuracy how our solar system may actually have been created!

I will leave it up to you to seek further proof of the accuracy between their tale and modern astronomical data, but I assure you that your investigation will leave you stunned. I will be referring to Maxwell Igan's research in his chapter entitled, "The Tale of the Sumerians", for other aspects of the creation story that Sitchin deciphered from the cuneiform script it was written in. He gives plenty of data to support their tale on all accounts and repeatedly reinforces the astonishing fact that they were written over 6000 years ago for the same head scratching reason that we sit in awe asking ourselves, "How could these ancient, and supposedly primitive, people possibly have known anything about how the solar system was created and designed, especially with such accuracy?"

For example, their description of the moon as being "lifeless" even aligns with our modern-day knowledge of it. In their story, Marduk finished Kingu (the moon) by stripping him of his orbit so he could only be a satellite. He also took away his vital elements — atmosphere, water, radioactive material — causing Kingu to shrink in size and become "a mass of lifeless clay." NASA findings verify that the moon did indeed suffer from a mass collision that left it lifeless. Kingu is described in the tale as "a planet that laid waste." Bill Bryson, in his book, "A Short History of Nearly Everything", claims that the moon is the result of a chunk of Earth being torn away and becoming a satellite. There is also evidence that the earth itself is a chunk torn off from another planet. This would explain why it is not perfectly spherical and therefore, wobbles on its axis. It also has a large gaping wound in it which is located under the Pacific Ocean and is known as the Pacific basin. The Sumerian texts even referred to the basin and say specifically that it is "the scar that remains from the wound the planet once bore."

 I am astounded by the fact that all the planets were accurately referenced in size, placement, orbit and total number by the ancient's long before modern-day astronomers even had this knowledge and the sophisticated equipment to observe and measure it. This is a strong indication that they were receiving help and/or had access to advanced technology. There are many other amazing implications revealed by these tablets that we will uncover later when we talk about our own miraculous human development. These epic stories inspire awe and wonder about the magic and mysteries of creation.

How is it that the ancients knew so much about these astronomical wonders out in space? Were they influenced by someone who gave them this tremendous insight and inspired them to honor and worship the skies? How fascinating that they gave the planets godlike status and identified them with personalities and levels of consciousness. I encourage you to look up in the sky and try to imagine the far-off planets as if they were individual beings. Then we can look around at our own Mother Earth and stand in awe of how creative and loving she is — giving us nourishment with her life-sustaining plants and trees, giving us endless pleasure with her sweet-smelling flowers and gorgeous landscapes.

Of course, she has a consciousness and loves her children dearly! She expresses it in many wonderful, creative and generous ways providing for us regardless of how we treat her. She forgives us and replenishes as best she can. Let's take a moment to express our gratitude and to make a commitment to send her as much love and healing energy as we can every day in every way! She is our mother after all and we are her children. Let's show her as much respect, adoration and kindness as we possibly can and encourage others to do the same.

My sole intention in presenting this version of the creation of our solar system is to impress upon you the consciousness perspective. As we make further attempts to understand the source of our own conscious thoughts and behaviors, understanding the full impact of the consciousness of our planet is key. Recognizing her as a being, with a personality that influences our own, is an important step in the process. Of course, our solar system is also directed by an intelligent energy as it moves along the path of precession in its 26,000 year elliptical orbit. We examined this closely on a previous adventure when we explored the "Yugas." We learned that our distance from, and alignment with, various constellations in the galaxy also greatly influences the collective consciousness of our planet. This correlates with the astrological signs or "Ages of the Zodiac" and their specific influences on the collective consciousness during phases of our solar system's position in the galaxy. The 12 "archetypes" described within the zodiac define the 12 aspects of our sun's personality or the 12 bodies in our solar system. If we consider the 13th sign, Opheucus, we can imagine that the sun is emanating 12 aspects of herself with her whole soul projecting from the center as 13 — Opheucus, the snake dancer, and gatekeeper of the portal to ascension!

There are other descriptions of our sun's "logos', or pattern personality, within the 22 archetypes of the tarot cards which the ancient Egyptians drew upon. This information was shared with them by a higher intelligence to help them progressively evolve the consciousness of their mind, body and spirit. These 22 archetypes are fascinating as the first seven represent a progressive evolution of the mind, the second seven — the body, and the third seven — the spirit. The 22nd card is called "The Choice." According to the source of my insight on the tarot, "The Law of One Book IV, "The Choice" spoken of is the central choice each conscious seeker or adept makes as it strives to master the lessons of the third-density experience", as written on page 4. Finally, the Tree of Life, with its 10 (or possibly 13) "Sephirothic" spheres represent another description of the levels of consciousness affecting Mother Earth and therefore, her inhabitants — us! In the Kabbalah tradition, the Sephiroth are the varying levels of consciousness expressing on our planet at any given time.

In *The Urantia Book*, we are made aware of the personal, mindal and spiritual influences of the Father, Son and Spirit which are translated and impressed upon us by a vast multitude of creative beings. Tomorrow, on the last day of our amazing adventure, we will explore these fascinating sources of consciousness which influence our personality, mind and spirit. Ultimately, we can group all of these influences into one classification by simply calling consciousness "intelligent energy." As energetic beings ourselves — spirit beings wrapped in physical matter — we are each our own creative expression of these intelligent energies uniquely combined to give us our individuality. We and all of the intelligent energy that influences all manifestations of reality in time, space and beyond into eternity, originate from one source — the One Infinite Creator. All that ever was, is and will ever be is imbued with this omniscient source consciousness. It is the "god-spark" within each and every one of us and the energy that ignites this spark is the same fuel that powers all of creation. It's the most powerful force in the universe after all and its one thing and one thing only — the pure unconditional love of the source expanding into eternity.

Condensed within the core of creation, the strong gravitational attraction of this pure force continues to pull all of its creative manifestations back into the source from which they came. The One Infinite Creator exhales and sends out intelligent energy into eternity and then inhales and draws it back into its heart center. This eternal love can always be found in our own heart space as an expression of the source expanding within and without and like the source, we can spread this love in our own expanding sphere of influence. Just like the electrons spinning around the nucleus of each atom and the planets revolving around the sun, our spirits will continue to evolve and revolve in a progressive cycle of adventures through time, space and beyond.

In search of our real self, the true source of our reflection, we keep gathering knowledge and wisdom in these realms of illusion. As we gather up all of the pieces of ourselves in multiple dimensions of space and time, we continue to expand on our evolutionary journey until we're no longer satisfied with being a fractal and we become consumed with a desire to return to wholeness. Our ascension journey begins and we start spiraling back inward as we tune into and align with our eternal self — our divine perfect blueprint existing in eternity. This is our whole self who has been emanating the holographic aspects of our beings into the multiple dimensions of time and space from Havona all along. This eternal universe is the perfect divine blueprint upon which all time and space universes are merely a reflection; Just like the holographic expressions of you and me in time and space are merely the reflection of our own perfect divine blueprints projecting from eternity. Furthermore, in the inner circle of the Paradise realm, exists the 12 perfect male and female divine blueprints upon which all of humanity are based. These are also known as the 24 elders and they project the 12 archetypes of human form which define the 12 types of "human" beings in the universe. Why 12? This is the trinity (3) expressing in each of the four directions (3 X 4 = 12) thereby completing the perfect circle of eternity with the trinity creating in all four quadrants. The trinity projects these 12 aspects of being from the core which spirals into 13th whole soul at the center.

I created the following graphic to demonstrate how our Whole Soul in the center as 13 (1+3=4) expands outward in all four directions with three expressions in each of the four quadrants characterized by each of the four elements — Fire, Air, Water and Earth. When these 12 selves, each expressing the characteristics of a sign in the zodiac wheel, have collectively finished their incarnational journey through their 12 aspects of being, they spiral back into the center as 13. With Opheucus as the 13th sign and gatekeeper of the ascension portal, this completion spiraling into the center represents the whole soul's ascension.

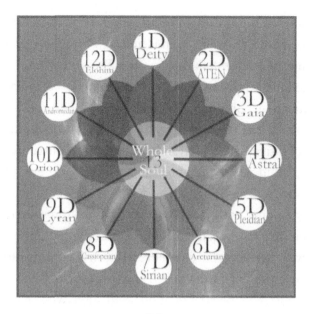

8.3

This graphic also represents our zodiac wheel with the 12 signs, 3 in each of the four directions. Once the soul completes its journey around the wheel and has gathered its 12 fragmented selves, it spirals into the center and becomes like Opheucus, the 13th sign in the center. Opheucus guards the gateway to ascension as the snake dancer. Once the whole soul has balanced its 12 male and 12 female expressions, it can spiral into the center having mastered its kundalini (serpent) energy becoming the snake dancer in the center rejoicing in self-mastery.

8.4

With this profound self-awareness, we can start reuniting all of the scattered expressions of our multi-dimensional selves expressing in different realms. We can intentionally call them in one at a time. As we do this, we are realigning with our perfect divine blueprint in eternity. We can intentionally become perfectly aligned with our true self as a multi-dimensional being by accessing the combined knowledge of these multi-archetypal fragments of our scattered soul. During this process, we are naturally becoming more enlightened as we connect into the aspects of ourselves who are expressing in the higher dimensions. Along the way, we can practice balancing our male and female aspects and learn self-mastery. By achieving self-mastery, we ignite our kundalini energy and learn to tame the serpent. When we are done being the face looking back in the mirror and want to feel real and whole again, we know we can intentionally realign with our true self. When we decide we want to be the one looking in rather than the one looking out, we can gather our fragments and become whole again. Once we have reunited all of our soul's aspects, our whole soul can spiral into the ascension portal in the center.

When we are ready to transition into the bliss of just being, when doing is done and our lessons have been mastered, we can return to wholeness with the knowing that's where our soul's been all along! Right here and now, we can tune into that bliss state beyond doing and scattering. We can become our real self as the face looking in the mirror not just the one looking back. Beyond time and space, we can spiral into the portal of the Great Central Sun and peer at our reflection in the eternal sea.

Not You but I, have seen and been and wrought...
Who in your Fraction of Myself behold
Myself within the Mirror Myself holds
To see Myself in, and each part of Me
That sees himself, though drown'd, shall ever see.
Come you lost Atoms to your Centre draw,
And be the Eternal Mirror that you saw:
Rays that have wander'd into Darkness wide
Return, and back into your Sun subside.

~ The Etern al Mirr or by Farid ud-Din Attar

Let's just close our eyes and breathe that in for a moment allowing its high frequency to resonate within our being. Resonance with eternal truth illuminates our energy centers and causes our aura to shine brightly. Feel your body becoming more luminescent as we absorb profound revelations that illuminate our spiraling path toward ascension.

Remembering Ancient Egypt

Who were the Egyptians? How long ago did they come here and where did they come from? Did they originate and evolve as earthlings, descendants from the original Andonites? Were they one of the six Sangik races who emerged 500,000 years ago? If so, were they one of the groups who were "upstepped" by the violet race? Were their leaders the luminous race who came from the Pleiades 200,000 years ago to advance the human race? It's likely they are descendants of the original continents of Lemuria and Atlantis. As survivors of these lost civilizations, they may have ended up in

Mesopotamia only to be "upstepped" once again by the Annunaki. Encoded with starseed DNA, they were primed to ignite the Golden Age in this era's first Crystal City of Light! To offer higher guidance and Mystery School teachings, they were joined by celestial guides from Orion, Sirius and Venus as Osiris, Isis and Group Ra. Together, they built a magnificent empire in both Upper and Lower Egypt. Activating Egypt was a primary focus for the celestial visitors and they were well-equipped to fulfill their galactic mission. Not only were they building a power plant at the geodesic center of the world, but they were tasked with aligning the Giza Plateau with the Three Majestic Thrones on the belt stars of Orion. This plateau was to become a divine reflection of the celestial heavens fulfilling the cosmic mandate, "As Above, So Below." With the terrestrial Nile as the mirror of the celestial Milky Way, it becomes the backbone of the Egyptian Gods and their sacred temple sites. The Nile was the kundalini of the Goddess Egypt and the lifeline of the people who worshipped her.

To know Egypt is to know the gods and goddesses who embodied this sacred land. The Egyptian pantheon, or Neteru, anthropomorphically represented the elements and conditions that the culture identified with as critical to their existence and survival. From their creation myth to their spiritual beliefs, the pantheon define their cosmology as they embodied the key elements of creation as well as the key features of their existence. They were already an advanced culture due to DNA upgrades and advanced teachings that they already received both from the Annunaki in Mesopotamia and now from Group Ra in the Land of Khem. This extraterrestrial influence combined with their evolutionary advancement embraces the "intervention + evolution" approach that offers the best explanation for many developments that unfolded in ancient times. Regardless of what the mainstream would lead you to believe, we have to remember that the elite illuminati have a hidden agenda to keep us from awakening to our divine origins. Since they control the media, the government, big business, the church and educational institutions, we have been enslaved by their need to control us and programmed by their agenda to keep us sound asleep. It's easier to control sleeping sheep and that's why they want to keep us in the dark. The patriarchal age has now come to an end as the Goddess Sophia awakens her children and Christ consciousness empowers them. We have awakened to the real story behind our planetary evolution and the cosmic connections.

Are we to believe that it was pure coincidence that the Babylonians migrated to the exact geodisic center of the planet? Are we to believe that these people alone without celestial guidance and advanced machinery had the astronomical and archaeological skills and tools to build a pyramid so precisely positioned and constructed? And it's certainly not just the Great Pyramid, although it is the pinnacle point and central vehicle of ascension for the planet. The precision and placement of all the pyramids along the Nile, and throughout the whole region, serve a specific purpose and vital function related to creation, resurrection and ascension.

The Egyptian legend begins with the God and Goddess who play the starring roles — Osiris and his sister-wife Isis. Osiris is connected to the constellation Orion and Isis to the star Sirius. The ancient Egyptian artists who engraved their depictions drew them with elongated skulls, spindly arms and legs and small round bellies. They had large almond shaped eyes and protruding lips. They were tall and appeared luminescent. The people of Khem worshipped them as literally the God and Goddess of Egypt. Their arrival and subsequent rule is similar to the creation epic of Mesopotamia. It's starts with the classical story of the cosmic twins, Set and Osiris, who, like the brothers from Nibiru, Enlil and Enki, were at odds about how to interact with humanity. At the same time, the celestial sister and savior son, interweave into the tale as Isis and Horus in Egypt and Ninmah and Noah in Mesopotamia. This creation myth about the male twins who stood opposite one another and co-created with their sister to produce a savior son is reminiscent of the original tale of the trinity conspiring to produce man on earth. As I tune into the original creation myth and parallel it with the ancient legends, notice the similarities. For colorful clarity and intuitive insight, just engage your third eye and watch the visions unfold:

In the beginning, there was an infinite sea completely still, breathless and peaceful. In one stupendous moment, the calm sea erupted in a profound awakening that caused a tsunami. The calm sea had come to life as a living, breathing being both awake and aware at once. It suddenly became aware of its Self as One Infinite Being. With this monumental awakening came a powerful surge of curiosity, creativity and desire. With an overwhelming urge to know thy Self, a mere reflection magically appeared that stood opposite the original self. Out of the watery womb, two beings arose. One stood for power and one for love. In that moment, a third being flashed into being as the Goddess of Wisdom who could balance the twins and the trinity could unite with the explosive power of pure love. For a moment, this Divine Trinity rested in infinity, perfectly united in the bliss state.

After resting momentarily, suddenly they were consumed by a strong desire to create a being, an eternal child who could expand and multiply. In one magical moment, this trinity of beings, as the male twins, Power and Love, and their sister, Wisdom, broke free of the confines of the Mother Womb! They were reborn in eternity as the Creative Trinity now free to create and expand. These creative children of eternity will always remain immersed in the Mother's infinite love but like any loving mother, she had to release her children so they could create on their own. Her infinite love will always pour onto their hearts through the portal of infinity and no matter, how far they stray, they will always be drawn back into their mother's embrace.

There you have it! In Egypt, the Goddess Neith was said to be the first and prime creator. Set and Osiris, as Power and Love, were the male twins and Isis, as Wisdom, was their sister. Horus was birthed through Isis who had been seeded by the encoded light flowing from Osiris' golden phallus. Encoded with divine light, the eternal child was born in the womb of the Goddess and then birthed through her portal into the world so he could create on his own as the golden child.

Let's take a look at this from a symbolic and numerological perspective:

In the beginning, the goddess gave birth to the Trinity who would create in eternity. They would become 3 in 1 and 1 as 3 or (1+3=4) to include their Mother, the Goddess. In this way, they would become the four directions and the four elements as Fire, Water, Air and Earth. Combined they would be 4 in 1 and 1 as 4 or (1+4=5) to become the five platonic solids. The Creative Trinity is expressed as the Father, the divine principle, the Mother, the creative principle and the eternal child as an extraordinary combination of both. This eternal child would be balanced in its male and female expressions with both divine and creative potential. In that sense, this child was androgynous, both a son and daughter at once perfectly balanced as 2 in 1 and 1 as 2 or 3 as the fullest expression of the Trinity. As this child recognizes its divine power to create at will, (s)he envisions his/her own version of creation as seven time and space worlds. Using the full creative potential of the original Trinity (3+4=7), (s)he creates a holographic illusion that's a mere reflection of the eternal perfection of his/her home. In one divine in breath, (s)he envisions these seven great spheres and in one explosive out breath, (s)he creates them! Ecstatic over his/her newfound ability to create holographic images from mere thought-forms, his/her imagination runs wild! This androgynous child applying both divinity and creativity lives for eternity endlessly creating by breathing in and breathing out pulsating thought-forms in a rhythmic spinning cycle of multi-dimensional realms throughout time and space. In one eternal now moment, this extraordinary illusion takes on a miraculous life of its own!

This creative eternal child inspired by the Divine Trinity becomes the model of all thought forms in creation. The divine Trinity is the inspiration at the geodesic center of the seven holographic spheres. For it is a mere reflection of the divine Trinity at the Paradise core of creation. In the celestial realm, the divine Trinity is revealed in the three belt stars of Orion and in the earthly realm as the three pyramids at Giza. The great pyramid is a reflection of the masculine divine principle. It is gold to represent the illumination of the mind and the empowerment of the solar plexus. It represents knowledge and power as an institution for illumination and empowerment. The second pyramid represents the feminine creative principle. It is built with rose quartz to represent the cosmic pink ray of divine love — the Mother Rose Ray of creation. This pyramid will become a center for healing with love and nurturing with compassion. The third pyramid represents the eternal child, both divine and creative. It is a deep indigo blue, almost black like Onyx. This is the only pyramid that was actually built by the demigods and humans to show them that they too were creator gods and goddesses. Inspired by Orion, the god, and Isis, the goddess, their kingdom of demigods and humans were set free to create on their own. In doing so, they realized that they were both human and divine and that they could emulate the god and goddess who created them. These divine humans were inspired and empowered as sovereign beings through initiations and activations in the pyramids. They became gods and goddesses in their own right with the freedom to create at will.

8.5

Let's return now to the dramatic saga in Egypt as it unfolded after the arrival of the Creative Trinity embodied by Set, Osiris and Isis~

The magical and mysterious drama unfolds on the stage of Egypt when Osiris' brother, Set, becomes jealous and concocts an evil plan to kill him. With his devious mind, he throws an elaborate banquet and places a golden box in the center to entice them. He presents the box as a gift to whomever can fit inside. Many of the guests try but in the end the only one who fits perfectly is Osiris since it was custom-made just for him. Once inside, Set places the lid on the box so Osiris cannot escape his fate. Set sends the coffin down the river Nile hoping it will float far away. With her overwhelming love and devotion, Isis sets out on a passionate quest to find her long-lost love. To Set's dismay, the coffin becomes caught up in the roots of a tree along the edge of a riverbed in Lebanon. Isis is filled with joy and relief as she discovers the coffin in Phoenicia. She brings it home and with her alchemical powers, she brings Osiris back to life. When Set discovers what she has done, he is enraged. In a fit of fury, he dismembers Osiris cutting him up into 14 pieces. Set scatters the fragments of Osiris at different sites all along the Nile. Again, Isis goes in search of her beloved Osiris determined to retrieve all his parts. In each of the sites that she finds a fragment, she declares "Osiris lives!" and has a temple erected in his honor. This happens in each of the places where Set had placed a fragment. The only part that Isis could not find was his penis so she fashioned one made of pure gold. Holding the golden phallus, she transforms into a bird and their son Horus is born. With this, the Creative Trinity is set into Egypt as Mother, Father and Child. The Creator, Creative and Created prevail! Together, the divine and creative principles birth a child who is both god and goddess balanced in its divine and creative aspects.

Let's take a quick peek at the Heliopolitan creation myth and see how it aligns with what we have just envisioned. First, let's identify the Egyptian "Ennead" of Hermopolis since they are the nine main actors in our story:

The Sun God, ATUM

His children SHU and TEFNUT

Their children GEB and NUT

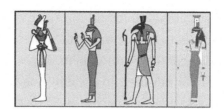

Their children OSIRIS and ISIS, SET and NEPHTHYS
8.6

ATUM may also be referred to as the primary ONE while the other 8 become the Eight Immortals. Sometimes, Geb and Nut are identified as one and Horus is added which makes Nine. Heliopolis was a major religious center and the priests there told a creation myth that named the primordial waters, or watery womb, NUN (None?). The "mound" that arose as the "Self-begotten" is ATUM. This "Self" made the elements of air and water as SHU and TEFNUT. Together, these two created the earth as GEB and the sky as NUT. In this story, Geb and Nut have two sets of twins, Osiris and Isis and Set and Nephthys. Osiris and Isis represent fertility and order (light) while Set and Nephthys represent infertility and chaos (dark). Horus becomes the God of the Sky and his eyes represent the sun and moon.

This Egyptian legend has such profound significance that it lays the foundation for all of creation symbolically, spiritually and physically. It contains the symbolic features upon which creation is based. It holds the spiritual significance and divine symbolism that inspires creation. This is embodied in the physical revelation of the divine Trinity in the sky as Orion and on the ground as Giza. From a symbolic spiritual perspective, the story of the 14 parts of Osiris reassembled by his beloved Isis giving birth to their son Horus can be literally interpreted as the creation story with birth, death and resurrection. It is also a divine representation of ascension with re-membrance and the ultimate return to wholeness. The sacred 14 represents the 13 aspects of our being plus One, the Golden Temple, or phallus, from which we came. With divine symbology and sacred numerology, the story unfolds as one in three and three in one creating in the four directions. As the four elements, they create the golden temple on earth. Now they are 4 in 1 and 1 in 4 (1+4=5) and they create the 5-pointed star to live in it! In this realm, Mother Earth becomes the golden temple and we are, of course, the five pointed star!

The gods and goddesses create the perfect pyramid, the golden temple in Egypt, especially for their beloved star children. In each of the four faces, the trinity is still expressed so that 12 aspects can be projected while the 13 resides within. Furthermore, in each of the four faces, both the masculine divine and female creative principles are still represented. In actuality, each of the four faces is actually divided into two making the pyramid 8-sided. This split is especially visible at sunrise on the equinoxes — another celestial alignment! This also brings the 12 to 24 which is the fullest expression of the 12 male <u>and</u> female aspects of our selves. In this way, the original 12 eternals are represented as the 24 elders. These divine creative beings reside on Paradise in Havona and their mirror reflection can be seen in the golden pyramid in Egypt, heaven on earth, if you will!

It's fascinating to see the divine synchronicity in the numerology and how all of the numbers hold such a sacred significance both above and below all at once. Remember, the One is always inside the golden temple of 12 making 13 altogether. With the Mother Sophia as the divine source embracing the 13, the Whole Soul becomes I in 13 and 13 as 1 inspiring the (13+1) 14 pyramids along the Nile. This is symbolically how the 14 parts of Orion become the 13 temples plus One golden pyramid, or phallus, who created them! This journey along the Nile through the 14 temples of Orion's parts is literally a journey to re-member our fragmented self and resurrect the divine within. The twin, Set, who represents Divine Power, sends his brother, Osiris, Divine Love, down the flowing river until the Tree of Life captures him and Isis, Divine Wisdom, rescues him. This is the first part of the creation story starring the Divine Trinity. Divine Power sends Divine Love down the river in a golden vessel through the portal into Eternity. Here, the Tree of Life captures the eternal soul and Sophia, the Wisdom Goddess finds him and embraces him. When Power discovers Wisdom and Love creating in Eternity, he decides to scatter the fragments of Love across the land of time and space. Sophia goes out in search of her fragmented Beloved and with every fragment she finds, she erects a temple (establishing the point in time and space where he was left). The Goddess of Wisdom rescues the fragmented soul who has been scattered throughout time and space by helping him re-member his parts. Once the 13 aspects of the soul have been remembered, she places a golden pyramid on the soul to honor him as a Divine Creator.

This is the ascension path humanity is on exploring our 12 aspects in time and space until we spiral back into the center as 13. Re-membered as a whole soul, we are crowned with the Golden Pyramid of the Divine Trinity as 14 (1+4) nestling back into the womb of our Divine Mother. Returning home, the numbers reduce: 14 becomes 1-4 or 3 and 3-1 becomes 2 and 2-1 becomes 1 and we become One just like we always have been. One expanding into many while still just One creating. We are That. We are the One Infinite Creator creating from infinity to eternity projecting into the time and space realms.

With this extraordinary remembrance of our divine inheritance, let's explore how the terrestrial River Nile is a mere reflection of the celestial Milky Way. We'll see how Giza at the geodesic center is the reflection of Orion at the celestial equator! Let's go!

Clearly, the temples are strategically placed on the Nile as a reflection of the stars in the Milky Way. Since Orion itself is a reflection of the Paradise Core, Giza becomes the Three Holy Ones. The Sphynx reflects Leo which resembles the Lion face of the central Sun. As such, it becomes a golden gate. At the top of the Nile lies Abusir which with its six temples reflects the Pleiades (since the 7th star is hidden from view). The star Sirius becomes the traveler, like the initiate, making an arc that crosses the horizon on a 70-day quest "performing its Passion." Our tour guide on this journey along the Nile is none other than the renowned expert on Egypt, author and explorer, Robert Bauval. He will enlighten us on so many more aspects of how "As above, so below" is literally personified in Egypt like nowhere else in the world.

I have already expressed my opinion that Paradise is mirrored in the Orion constellation at the celestial equator. The idea that the Orion constellation may be the reflection of the center of all creation, the home of the Paradise Trinity, came to me when I started to piece together information obtained from many sources including my own inner wisdom. On my own personal quest, I find that, as I read about, listen to and contemplate upon various aspects of universal truth, suddenly images will start to form, and concepts will fall into place just like a puzzle emerging from the scattered pieces tossed about like Orion's fragmented self. There is a certain "ringing" of truth that occurs when these ideas resonate deep within the core of my being. That's when I know I am on to something that may be true or at least have universe potential. This is how I felt when I started to picture the three notches on the belt of Orion as being the same three holy spheres talked about in "The Urantia Book." Then I learned that the largest of the spheres, or notches, aligned with the celestial equator! Furthermore, I realized it was in the shape of an hourglass which has great significance that I will reveal later. Finally, you can impose the figure 8 upon it which symbolizes infinity. Paradise is said to be located at the geographic center of infinity just like the Great Pyramid reflecting this belt star is placed on the geodesic center of the planet! At the center of creation, the figure 8 is the infinite womb behind all of creation with the Central Sun of Paradise as the upper sphere of the 8 and the Central Sun of Havona as the lower sphere. Being a mirror, the upper and lower halves are reversed in Egypt with Lower Egypt and the Northern Pyramids on the top half, and Upper Egypt and the Southern Pyramids on the bottom half.

O.K., let's dive in to this possibility and see what we can find. For this part of the adventure, let me pull a book out of my backpack called, "The Orion Mystery", written by our tour guide, Robert Bauval and his co-author, Adrian Gilbert. I have seen Robert on one of my favorite television series, "Ancient Aliens." In fact, his research into the connection between the Giza pyramid complex and the Orion constellation is what inspired me to buy the book. As I flipped through the pages of the book, which is usually how I first familiarize myself with its contents, a few key phrases immediately stood out which I found intriguing. I am impressed to see a chapter on "The Timaues" which I myself had encountered in the large book my mother gave me called "A History of Western Philosophy" by Bertrand Russell. I have referenced this book previously on our adventure because of the chapters on Plato and his platonic solids.

Remember, however, that it was after I had the epiphany that stars might be individual souls that I found the passage from Timaeus indicating that there is a single star for each individual human soul! Well, as I glimpse this chapter on "The Timaeus" in my new book, "The Orion Mystery", my jaw drops down when I read that, "Plato says the demiurge made "souls in equal number with the stars and distributed them, each soul to its several stars...and he who should live well for his due span of time should journey back to the habitation of his consort star."[13] Weren't we just speculating that we return to our host star when we drop our body and our soul ascends?! Then, along those lines, we discussed that when we are ready to ascend to the headquarters of our local constellation, or even Paradise, we spin around it (the black hole) until we (our souls as stars) are pulled through it!

In another chapter, "The Iron Bones of Star Gods", a passage stands out that refers to, "...a tangible land in the sky populated by star souls..." (discussing a legend that) "...the souls of departed kings were the stars...". On page 99, I come across a paragraph talking about, "...the voyage of the soul to the imperishable circumpolar stars, the southern one to Orion."[14] O.K., the book has grabbed my interest now. We have already speculated that the Orion Constellation is the home of the Paradise

Trinity and that Egypt is a projection of this sacred land. The two biggest clues are the alignment of Orion's belt with the three main pyramids at Giza and the fact that they both lie at the meridian, or exact center, one at the celestial meridian of the sky and the other at the global meridian of the earth. This coincides with the common belief across many ancient myths and legends that Orion lies at the center of our local universe just like the Paradise Core lies at the center of the Grand Universe.

I felt that this book deserved more attention if I was to truly give it the credit it deserves, so I hunkered down and read through all 300+ pages and what I discovered was fantastic! It turns out that Robert Bauval has dedicated most of his life to the study of the Orion-Giza mystery and is to be credited with uncovering the exact astronomical alignments that verify his theories. He began to research the connection between Orion's belt, the three notches that I have equated to the three Holy Spheres, and ended up verifying the alignment of a series of pyramids that run along the Nile. He did this by researching the "Pyramid Texts" written on the wall of a pyramid at Saqqara. These texts make a clear connection between Osiris and Isis, god and goddess of Egypt, and the constellation of Orion and the star Sirius respectively. He discovered that many of the people and events that were part of Egypt's past correlated directly with the movement and position of the stars in the sky. Once again: "As above, so below" rings true!

Let's reflect for a moment on the Egyptian creation myth~

In the earliest days of Egypt before the "Pyramid Age" when the Giza plateau was constructed and a belief in multiple gods emerged, there was a belief in One God, Atum, who was the creator of everything. Atum, or Atum-Ra, was believed to have created Shu (the air god) and Tefnut (the moisture goddess). Together they created Geb and Nut, the earth god and sky goddess. Geb and Nut became the parents of two male gods, Osiris and Seth, and two sisters, Isis and Nephythys. Even though they were brother and sister, Osiris and Isis mated and gave birth to a son, Horus. The story of Egypt revolves mostly around Osiris, Isis, Seth and Horus. Osiris' brother, Seth, was said to be jealous of him and so he killed him, put him in a coffin and set him out to sea. He arrived on the shores of Pheonicia (now Lebanon) and there, the roots of a special tree cut through his coffin. His sister, Isis, finds him and brings him back to life long enough to give birth to Horus. Robert emphasizes the importance of Osiris saying "for he was not only seen as the first divine king of Egypt, but his tragic death and miraculous resurrection provided the basis of the ancient Egyptian mysteries and the origin of their rebirth cult."[15] Furthermore, the story recounts that Seth cut Osiris into 14 parts represented by the 14 temples along the Nile. With this connection, we can imagine how Osiris being dismembered into 14 parts would lead to 14 temples being erected to facilitate a process of re-membering the god (within). My friend, Danielle Rama Hoffman, wrote a beautiful book called "Temples of Light" where she takes the reader on a progressive journey to each of the temples along the Nile so they can re-member their divine self, or the god/goddess within. Watch our 3-part interview where she shares a divine transmission at SciSpi.tv/Rise-Up/.

Since today's journey will be focused on showing the alignment of several pyramids along the Nile with the constellations and stars along the Milky Way, the celestial Nile, I have provided the following images for reference that will be helpful.

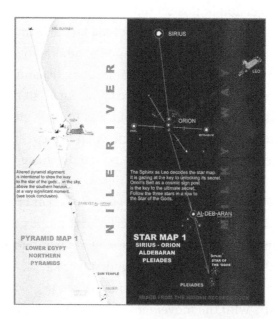

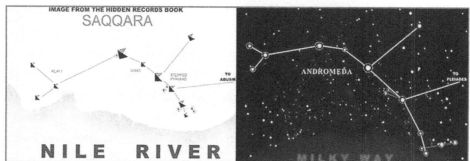

8.7: Nile River Maps

Let's start at the southern-most tip with Heliopolis because this ancient city, originally named Annu, was where the legendary "initiations" took place that we have spoken of and referred to throughout our adventure. Robert writes, "This was the seat of a powerful priesthood whose members were the custodians of a school of wisdom or initiation, and the great temple of Ra, the sun God."[16]. Now since I am also fascinated by the sun God Ra and the association with *The RA Material*, or Law of One series, I also looked up the information given in this book about Egypt and the pyramids. I will share this material with you at the end of our adventure because following today's revelations, it will blow your mind!

For now, let's continue with the cities and pyramids along the Nile since Robert will proceed to show us how they are all a direct reflection of the sky above! Across the Nile from Heliopolis lies Letopolis, originally the ancient city of Khem, which was an important religious center connected primarily with royal rebirth rituals. When drawing a line which connects Heliopolis, Letopolis and the Great Pyramid of Giza, you form a triangle which forms the "Gateway to the Duat." Robert explains that, "The starry world of Osiris was the Duat." In referencing the Pyramid Texts, he shares that a colleague of his named Mercer believed, "that the principal theme was a powerful belief that the dead king would be reborn as a star and that his soul was believed to travel into the sky and become established in the starry world of Osiris-Orion, the god of the dead and of resurrection." He also quotes the author Faulkner who noted that, "The constellation of Orion was one of the afterlife dwelling-places of the souls of departed kings who became stars."[17]

The next city that appears, as we sail up the Nile in our Felucca, is Abu Ruwash, a site where the son of the great Khufu, named King Djedefra, built a pyramid of his own. Traveling north, we come to the Giza plateau, the most prominent display of all the pyramids and the most obvious correlation with Orion and his famous belt! These pyramids were believed to have been built by Khufu, son of Sneferu, after his father built the first two "smooth-sided" ones of its kind north in Dashour. Before this smooth-sided design, step-pyramids were commonly erected, and this dramatic change was revolutionary.

The most famous step pyramid that still stands is that of King Zoser's in Saqqara, according to Robert's research, and he says, "Its ziggurat-like structure seems also to have symbolized a ladder whose six steps leading up to a seventh platform probably correspond to the planetary spheres which encircle the earth and, therefore, to stages of ascent through which the soul must pass after death."[18] He also refers to ancient mythology depicting the "seven spheres of the world" which leads me to speculate that, due to the major astronomical significance of these pyramids, could also be referring to the seven super-universes and their relevant ascension path through the seven evolutionary stages.

Now, along the Nile, we still have two sites: Zawyat-al-Ayran and Abusir. The step pyramids were built mostly in the Third Dynasty and the Giza pyramid complex was built in the Fourth Dynasty. At the end of the Fourth Dynasty, "an obscure pharaoh named Nebka, perhaps a brother or son of Khufu, planned a pyramid at Zawyat Al Aryan. It was never finished. With Nebka, the Fourth Dynasty came to an end."[19] Of the final site, Abusir, "The kings of the Fifth Dynasty built five small pyramids at Abusir, rather poorly constructed...much shoddier than that of their illustrious predecessors."[20] It seems that the Fourth Dynasty was the apex of pyramid building in Egypt with the most grandiose Pyramids housing many chambers and air shafts that held great significance.

What stands out throughout his story about the builders of the pyramids is one "master-architect" named Imhotep. First, he is credited with King Zoser's step-pyramid and Robert tells that it was, "not only the largest of its kind built in Egypt but the first known structure built with stone masonry: quarried and properly cut rather than rough stones stacked together. This innovation is attributed to a genius priest-architect called Imhotep (who) was later deified and said to be the greatest wise man."[21] Then when the design of the two large pyramids at Dashour were enhanced from step-pyramids to smooth-sided ones, a dramatic change, again Imhotep was credited: "To get a good idea of the engineering revolution, compare the step-pyramid of Zoser, employing 850,000 tons of material with Sneferu's two giants at Dashour, which together used nearly nine million tons. This amazing upsurge in engineering and organizational prowess has defied explanation, but it is obvious that something important inspired Sneferu, something which perhaps involves the thinking of the great master-builder-cum-priest — Imhotep."[22] What you will come to find when I share *The Ra*

Material with you is that Imhotep is no ordinary priest!

So, there you have it! The seven pyramids designating Heaven on Earth: The three at Giza, Abu Ruwash, Zawyat-al Aryan, and the two at Dashour. Early on, Robert made the exact correlation between the three notches on Orion's belt and the three Giza pyramids even showing that the three pyramids together measured 1.15 km across and the three notches on Orion's belt together measured 1.15 stellar units! With this revelation, he shares excitedly, "Suddenly I realized that not only the three Giza pyramids, but others too might have stellar positions...Surely all Fourth Dynasty pyramids would have been involved in the master plan to forge the soul of Osiris on the sacred land of Memphis!"[23] He concluded that the celestial form of Osiris was Orion.

It wasn't long before he discovered that the pyramid at Abu Ruwash corresponded with a star on Orion's left foot and that the pyramid at Zawyat al Aryan represented the one on his right shoulder. He also realized that Orion's outstretched hand held two stars which aligned directly with the two Dashour pyramids. Later, Robert realized that Heliopolis represented the constellation Leo which is directly related to the Sphinx and that the six pyramids of Abusir correlate with the star cluster of Pleiades.

There are many other revelations that Robert makes in his book and I highly recommend it if you find the idea of a "Celestial Duat", or starry realm of the Gods, mirrored here on earth as fascinating as I do! One particularly interesting aspect of his findings is that, "At around 10,400 B.C., the pattern in the sky was mirrored on the ground by the pyramids." He remarks, "We, are, of course, aware that 10,450 B.C. is far too remote for archaeologists and Egyptologist to entertain, but these findings challenge them to explain-or dispute-the mounting astronomical evidence."[24] This leads to a discussion about "The First Time" in Ancient Egypt.

Let's take a moment to offer gratitude to our tour guide, Robert Bauval for his extraordinary research and for dedicating his life to revealing the truth about this ancient land of the gods:

"For the Egyptians, whose civilization preceded the Greeks and the Hebrews, the first Golden age, when God's fraternized with humans, was called Tep Zepi, which translates loosely as the First Time. They believed that the system of cosmic order and its transference to the land of Egypt had been established a long time before by the gods...When the Egyptians built the pyramids, they were thinking of an important event that related to the First Time; whatever that might have been, we now know it had something to do with the stars and, more particularly the stars of Orion and the star Sirius — the cosmic lands of the souls."[25]

Let's consider the remarkable implications of this passage and of the revelation that the starry heavens were mirrored on our planet long ago when gods walked among us. As if the first part of this Egyptian legend wasn't intriguing enough, wait until you hear this next part of the story. We'll visit these sites with an indigenous wisdom keeper who grew up with the Giza Plateau as his playground. And finally, before sending you off to the astral realm, we will hear directly from "Group Ra", the confederation of beings who claim that it was they themselves who walked among us in ancient Egypt as the tall luminescent ones.

Robert Bauval and Adrian Gilbert's book *The Orion Mystery*, was published in 1994 and Robert describes it as the culmination of a 10-year project. I was fortunate enough to see him discuss his adventures and discoveries on a show that was filmed in 2010 called, "The Pyramid Code" hosted by Carmen Boulter and televised on the Documentary Channel. It was incredibly synchronistic for me that this show should air on June 16th, 2013, the same week I am writing this very adventure, especially since I don't normally watch this channel. This show, however, caught my eye and I am so pleased because it took me directly to the pyramids Robert was just speaking of in his book!

The narrator remarks, "Could the ancients have had an understanding of a superior science?" This immediately caught my attention because that is the premise behind Roberts book and *The RA Material* that otherworldly beings walked among us in ancient times and taught us "superior science" along with advanced mathematics, architecture and astronomy. There is a vast amount of evidence to support this conclusion. All the pyramidal structures across the globe that emerged thousands of years ago demonstrate remarkable feats of engineering, construction, geometry and architecture far beyond the capabilities of primitive man. I believe these structures serve many purposes and that they are all connected to provide an energetic grid which collectively creates a vibrational resonance that harmonizes to influence our consciousness. I am sure this earthly grid mirrors the heavenly one embracing the eternal realm of Havona. This belief parallels with the notion of a cosmic duality between the heavens and the earth. In this show, Robert speaks of a "cosmic order which lasted for 3000 years" that influenced the ancient Egyptians.

The guests on the show which include geologists, Egyptologists and an indigenous Egyptian "wisdom keeper" agree that the pyramids were not built merely as tombs and even indicate that they were never intended for this purpose. An Independent Egyptologist, John Anthony West, remarks, "Of all of the wildest theories floating around about the pyramids, the actual wildest is the one accepted without question by these Egyptologists that the pyramids served as tombs." Robert Schoch, PhD, states, "In fact, I don't think there ever was any evidence that it was a tomb for any Pharaoh whatsoever." This is important because it opens the door to discovering what the far more profound purposes behind the pyramids were. The passages and subterranean chambers present a number of intriguing possibilities.

In the great pyramid, Robert Bauval discovered that the shafts in the King's chamber could have served as channels or "passages" to the stars. In his book, he explains where these northern and southern passages lead, "the northern passage (was) for the voyage of the soul to the imperishable circumpolar stars (and) the southern one (was a passage) to Orion."[26] He provides an illustration showing the alignments of the shafts to the stars around the time they were built circa 2600 BC. It is also widely believed that these pyramids were used for initiates to attain high spiritual wisdom and ancient knowledge of universal laws. They may also have been used as observatories for astronomical events. It has been proven that their unique shape is conducive to the in-streaming of energy that is both healing and powerful as a divine form of consciousness.

In this show, "The Pyramid Code", Robert again reiterates his belief that the master plan for these sites originated much earlier than the expected range of 5000 years ago. He points to the alignment of the constellations around 10,500 B.C. and as you will see in *The RA Material*, the event that took place during both times was incredibly significant. As a guest on the show, Robert makes this point, "I'm sure that Giza, if interpreted as being Orion's belt's counterpart, then the layout of the three pyramids as they are, relatively, would fit the celestial meridian of the stars at 10,500 B.C. when it reached the very lowest point in its up-and-down movement. Looking east you had the Sphinx looking at the constellation Leo. So, you have two major monuments on the same side looking at constellations that are representative of their features. We have features that on the ground were represented in the sky."

The host of the show, Carmen Boulter, tours a specific site at Abu Garab and shows the base of the largest obelisk that ever was in Egypt. She narrates, "The platform of the crystal altar is made with quartz and you can see a laser cut 6-foot circle surrounded by a huge slab with four points each pointing in the four cardinal directions and the whole structure is made of a single solid piece of quartz crystal." As we already know from our adventure thus far, this structure presents many symbolic qualities: a perfect circle enclosed by a perfect square with each of the sides pointing in one of the four cardinal directions and finally, quartz crystal with it highly reflective property.

Now let's hear from a man who has spent his entire life surrounded by these majestic structures and as such, has gained a deep understanding of their symbolic significance and sacred power. His name is Abd'El Hakim Awyan and he is known as an indigenous wisdom keeper. He reveals the more profound nature and purpose of the pyramids as centers for healing, self-mastery, worship and communion. He refers to the line of pyramids flanking the Nile as "The Band of Peace." He remarks on the crystal altar and teaches us that it is a symbol of peace. He also explains that the round disk is a lid that covers a shaft 180 feet deep to the level of the ocean. He says there is still running water and you can feel it why you are in the area. He says there are still more to be found. He points out hieroglyphs on the obelisk and the disk of the sun that mean, "the heart of the sun." At the sight of the step pyramids of Saqqara, Hakim points to the quartz crystal stones in front of the temple and explains that the ceiling reflects the crystal tiles on the ground. The narrator informs us that there are also remains of crystal flooring at Giza in the Temple East to the second pyramid.

The most remarkable site that Hakim takes us to is what he calls "the hospital dealing with sound." What he teaches us about this ancient site will astound you and clearly reveal the powerful nature of intuitive vibrational healing. Alongside the step-pyramid at Saqqara, there are three chambers. Hakim explains that, "It is what's left of the house of the spirit and it's a healing system with sound." He points to two stone pathways leading from one of the chambers and teaches us that they were used as "investigation tables." He explains that, "the patient had the (choice) to use either one, the one on the left or the one on the right, but that they had to use their own antenna to choose where to (lie) because each point is connected to a specific chamber of which there were 22, 11 on each side, all without ceilings." He takes us inside one of the chambers and shows us a niche. He says that, "The physician put his head in the niche to see what was the matter with his patient laying on the stone table." He explains that this type of diagnosis works with the sound whose source is the water running through a tunnel underneath the healing center. The narrator, Carmen Boulter, invites us to consider the implications of his teachings:

"Let's consider that the pyramid sites along the Band of Peace are sophisticated harmonic structures not only mirroring positions of the stars but designed to replicate harmonic cavities of the human body. It seems that the chambers (or arteries) in the pyramids are harmonically tuned to a specific frequency or musical tone." The sound healing techniques were used to restore a harmonic flow within the arteries of the patient to create the "correct harmonic within." Standing at this site of the healing temple in Saqqara, she shows us how, from there, you have a view of Abusir to the North and Dashour to the South. She states that, "We already know that the two pyramids at Dashour were built by Sneferu with the guidance of Imhotep. Hakim says that "Sneferu" in Egyptian means "double harmony" and this explains the energy that we get from the construction of these two pyramids each with two different sounds."

The narrator observes that this would seem to indicate that all of the pyramids may have been harmonically tuned to different frequencies or musical tones and that each pyramid could be exemplifying sound technology with distinct tones creating "huge fields of harmonic resonance." Her theory goes back to the conclusion I cited earlier which speculates that this may not only apply to the group of pyramids in Egypt but may extend to include all of the pyramid sites across the globe setting the entire planet at a harmonic resonance that promotes our evolutionary progress. Just a thought. What do you think? Please check out the extraordinary series called "The Pyramid Code" on Netflix to experience many amazing revelations about the temple sites along the Nile.

The Great Sphynx of Giza

A virtual journey to the Giza plateau certainly wouldn't be complete without standing in awe and wonder of the magnificence of the Great Sphinx.

8.8.

The most awe-inspiring material I have ever read on the what the author calls the "Pyramid-Sphinx" comes from "The Book of Knowledge: The Keys of Enoch by J. J. Hurtak, PhD., PhD., a futurist and the founder of the Academy For Future Science. This book is a must-read for anyone who is serious about understanding the complex mechanics of how the universe works. He shares the insight in such a remarkably beautiful and simply profound way that it keeps you hypnotized even though the material can seem quite complex at times. I will only share a couple of quotes because I understand that this material is highly proprietary. I did have the great honor and privilege of hosting a guest panel which him and his lovely wife, Desiree, so graciously agreed to participate in. What both J.J. and Desiree share about the ascension in this guest panel is astounding and I highly recommend watching it. Watch the guest panel at SciSpi.tv/Rise-Up/. Here are a couple of verses out of J.J. Hurtak's "Book of Knowledge: Keys of Enoch" — Key number 8:

"The vehicle of the Pyramid-Sphinx sits on a threshold between our zero point evolution and higher light technology as the stepping stone to other consciousness sun systems beyond the limitations of our solar light zone. The Pyramid-Sphinx symbolizes how the mind of Higher intelligence must center itself within our solar evolution in order to educate Man to use the Magnetic lines of force and to build consciousness pyramids which are the keys to open up the threshold controls necessary to leave our consciousness time zone."[27] Whoa.

The power, meaning and purpose of the structures in and around the Giza Plateau are so profound that it is challenging to grasp. They have been placed precisely where they lie to activate the consciousness grid on Planet Earth! They are energetic devices and consciousness vehicles as well as centers for worship, wisdom and healing. In ancient times, they served the highest good for the planet and her people. Dr. J. J. Hurtak reassures us when the time is right, the missing cap on the Great Pyramid will be put right back where it belongs and once it's in place, the pyramid will be activated and the entire complex will come back online! Drunvalo Melchizedek tells us that there is large underground chamber containing an energetic fabric with the Flower of Life symbol embossed upon it. He says that it holds an energetic field in place for the creation and existence of all life on this planet. Finally, there is meant to be a large ship under the complex that is in "stasis" in case we need it for transport off the planet or as an armed warship for protection against malevolent visitors.

The Sphinx has intrigued humanity since it was fully revealed. The most popular story sur-rounding the Sphinx is that of Thutmose VI and his Dream Stele. Thutmose is credited for clearing away the sand that had consumed most of the Great Sphinx of Giza. In the story, a weary Thutmose dozes off near the mouth of the Sphinx and falls into a dreamy haze. In this dream state, the Sphinx speaks to Thutmose and tells him that if he reveals his full glory by clearing away all the sand, that he will become king of the land. At the time, Thutmose's oldest brother was in line for the throne. Lo and behold, when he rescued the Sphinx from its submergence in the sand, he did become king! Once the Sphinx was revealed, Thutmose place an engraved stele in front of his paws famously known as the "Dream Stele". Here is a verse from the stele:

"Now the statue of the very great Khepri the Great Sphinx rested in this place, great of fame, sacred of respect, the shade of Ra resting on him. Memphis and every city on its two sides came to him, their arms in adoration to his face, bearing great offerings for his Ka. One of these days it happened that prince Thutmose came travelling at the time of midday. He rested in the shadow of this great god. Sleep and dream took possession of him at the moment the sun was at its zenith. Then he found the majesty of this noble god speaking from his own mouth like a father speaks to his son, and saying: "Look at me, observe me, my son Thutmose. I am your father Horemakhet-Khepri-Ra-Atum. I shall give to you the

kingship upon the land before the living. ....Behold, my condition is like one in illness, all my limbs being ruined. The sand of the desert, upon which I used to be, (now) confronts me; and it is in order to cause that you do what is in my heart that I have waited."[28]

It's interesting that I intuitively felt the Sphinx was linked to the Central Sun. It's looks like a lion face to me that resembles the Sun and feels radiant and powerful like it too. When I discovered that Dr. J. J. Hurtak referred to it as a "High Frequency Solar Vehicle", that resonated with me. Then, in another favorite book on the Sphinx by Graham Hancock and Robert Bauval called "The Message of the Sphinx", I read, "...for reasons never fully understood, the Sphinx was often referred to as Seshep-ankh Atum, 'the living image of Atum, after Atum-Re the self-created sun-god, the first and original deity of the Egyptian pantheon."[29] That brings us back to our commitment this morning to honor the sun during our journey on this blessed day. The sun is like a god in that it gave birth to our solar system and continues to sustain life on our planet! The sun lovingly shines its light on all of its children without exception. The Sphinx reminds us of the extraordinary significance of this most powerful source of radiant light, eternal life and pure love.

Let's take a moment to honor and thank Dr. J. J. Hurtak as well Graham Hancock and Robert Bauval for their valuable insight on the Great Sphinx of Giza.

To wrap up our exploration of what is surely the most significant sacred site on planet Earth, let's tune into Group Ra since they played such a pivotal role in the lives of the Ancient Egyptians. During the very first session dated January 15, 1981, Don asks directly if the name "Ra" has a connection to the Egyptians and the being "Ra" concurs explaining that, "The identity of the vibration Ra is our identity. We, Group Ra, what you would call a social memory complex, made contact with the rays of your planetary kind you call Egyptians."[30]

Then Don asks the most perplexing question that has stupefied geologists, Egyptologists and most of humanity for hundreds of years, "How were the blocks moved?" While the answer is, of course, complex, with regard to our basic understanding of these concepts, it is still incredibly fascinating to consider the profound implications. Here is Ra's remarkable explanation:

"You must picture the activity within all that is created. The energy is, though finite, quite large compared to the understanding/distortion by your peoples. This is an obvious point well known to your people, but little considered. This energy is intelligent...When one can speak to that intelligence, the finite energy of the physical or chemical rock/body is put into contact with that infinite power which is resident in the more well-tuned bodies, be they human or rock."[31]

Ra describes the power of the pyramidal design, "If you will picture with me the side of the so-called pyramid shape. Mentally imagine this triangle cut into four triangles. You will find the intersection of the triangle, which is at the first level on each of the four sides, forms a diamond in a plane which is horizontal. The middle of this plane is the appropriate place for the intersection of the energy streaming from the infinite dimensions and the mind/body/spirit complexes of various interwoven energy fields. Thus it was designed that the one to be initiated would be able to perceive and then channeled this, shall we say, gateway to intelligent infinity."[32]

Concerning the emergence of the great pyramid, Ra explains in simple terms, "The first, the great pyramid, was formed approximately 6000 of your years ago...The appearance of the pyramid was a matter of tremendous surprise. However, it was carefully designed to coincide with the incarnation of one known as the great architect. This entity was later made into a deity, in part due to this occurrence... This deity had the sound vibration complex, "Imhotep."[33]

Another significant being of the time that Group Ra talks about is "Iknahton." A couple of years ago, I discovered the spiritual beliefs and practices of the Rosicrucians which are deeply rooted in the secret knowledge of the Egyptians. He is highly revered within this belief system as the "One who knew." He emphasized the monotheism of the "One Infinite Creator" as opposed to the polytheistic approach being taken by the Egyptians at the time who were honoring multiple gods. He also seemed well-versed in manipulating vibrational energies to enhance self-mastery. Group Ra speaks of "Iknahton":

"In the 18th Dynasty, as is known in your records of space/time distortions, we were able to contact a Pharaoh, as you would call him. The man was small in life experience on your plane and was a...Wanderer... This young entity (was given the name) "Ammon"...The entity decided this name, being in honor of one among many gods, was not acceptable...Thus, he changed his name to one which honored the sun disc..."Aten"... This entity, Iknahton, became convinced that the vibration of One was the true spiritual vibration and thus decreed the Law of One."[34]

Finally, Group Ra provides a simplified explanation for the intended purposes of the pyramids as being just two:

"Firstly, to have a properly oriented place of initiation for those who wished to become purified or initiated channels for the Law of One. Two, we wished then to carefully guide initiates in developing a healing of the people whom they sought to aid, and of the planet itself." [35]

So, there you have it! The indigenous wisdom keeper, Hakim, knew of these intended purposes, probably from long ago when the information was passed down from his ancestors. We, however, through this process of consciously evolving on our quest for greater self-realization, are discovering the secrets of our ancient past as well. I feel that all of the knowledge that is being shared with us through many different sources eventually comes together as a series of fundamental truths that underlie the authentic nature of our reality and more importantly, the divine nature of our being. As we progress through this ascension journey, we become more and more aware of the truly magnificent beings that we are with limitless potential to elevate and expand our individual consciousness and therefore, our experience of life.

I have a very dear friend, Mathues Imhotep, who has extraordinary recall about his past life in Egypt as Imhotep. This inspired him to write the "7ᵗʰ Seal" trilogy which is literally a manual for the Mystery Schools once taught in Egypt. He can recall off the top of his head such a vast amount of precise detail about the building of the pyramids and the sacred geometry used to construct them that it is nothing short of astounding. His knowledge of complex numerology and sacred symbology is far above and beyond anyone I have ever met. He is a genius in every sense of the word and I am blessed to call him my friend. I would like to share an excerpt here from his first book about the Egyptian Mystery Schools. Watch the four-part series at SciSpi.tv/Rise-Up/. It will be worth every minute of your time to learn from this master.

"The Mystery Schools that have come down through the ages have all been set up for the same reason, to teach the Truth and the Way. This is why Jesus said, "I am the Truth, the Way and the Light." The Truth quite simply is 'Self-Realization', the knowing and understanding that you truly are a God/Goddess. Each and everyone is an essence of the Creator. We are the fractalization or bifurcation of the Creator. Each of us truly has a piece or reflection, so to speak, of the Creator within us, and this is our Spirit, the Divine Spark. We each have a pure and perfect connection to the source and its omnipresent consciousness...The Way is the method or technique to accomplish this connection and the vehicle or way home, the Ascension. The vehicle is the Merkabah, the light body "Garment of Light" that we put on to walk and travel interdimensionally on the highest path, the ultimate journey home. This where the great reformation or reunification will occur, the complete return to our parents, our source, energetically reuniting in totality."³⁶

Aw, let's absorb the truth, beauty and grace of this revelation and feel comfort in knowing that we are following the way. We are on the ascension path home. We are becoming increasingly aware of our tremendous opportunity to radiate our expanded consciousness of light and love upon the world of living beings all around us. In this way, we can have a dramatic effect on the entire planet and contribute to the ascension of all of humanity. In the least, we can radiate enough love and light to lift the minds and spirits of ourselves and of those around us so that we can start a small wave of consciousness that may become a tsunami as it ripples and rolls across the matrix. Let's continue to understand more about how we can continue the tremendous efforts put forth by the many great beings, worldly and otherwise, whose intention is, and always has been, the evolution of a unity consciousness based on pure love.

These inspired visions of the vast cosmos present many intriguing possibilities and open the door to an exciting world where the true nature of our origin, existence and destiny are just waiting to be discovered and explored! This has been an extraordinary journey along the celestial Nile and as a resounding crescendo to our virtual enlightenment, we'll engage in a special Pyramid Initiation and Ascension Activation.

Preparation for Initiation

(Audio version available at: www.SuzanneRossTranscendence.com)

On the ascension path, collectively we can create a new Golden Age of Enlightenment by creating Heaven on Earth. During the last Golden Age in Egypt, the people were inspired by Gods and Goddesses who came to show them a higher way of living and being. This time around, it's up to us to create a paradise realm where unity, peace and harmony prevail. We can access the God/Goddess within for guidance on our ascension. We can also call upon guidance from the celestial gods and goddesses who have arisen and are eager to co-create this ascension with us from above. We can tune into the Golden Ages of the past and request teachings from Group Ra, Akhnaton and Nefertiti, Osiris and Isis, Horus and Thoth, Sekhmet and Hathor, and maybe even our own soul aspect experiencing an incarnation there!

Take a few deep breaths and close your eyes. Energetically expand your heart and consciously open your mind. In the distance, you begin to see the formation of a tropical paradise emerging. Watch as the sands of the desert transform into a shimmering sea of gold dust. Magnificent gold structures and elaborate pillars take form within the enclaves of towering palm trees. A spectacular Golden City of Light is emerging before your very eyes!

You are energetically drawn toward a temple in the shape of a pyramid whose grand entrance is flanked by golden statues resembling gods. You have entered a magnetic field that is pulling you along with its powerful grasp and leading you into the center of this sacred Temple. You are magnetically drawn to a spot directly below the highest point of this pyramidal structure. In this space, you are surrounded by a gold-flecked spiral of circulating energy that originates from the ground below and is drawn upward to the center point overhead. You become acutely aware of the upward pull of the spiraling energy which inspires the ascension of your spirit. You are now ready to receive a powerful initiation into the pyramidal energy.

Initiation into the Pyramid of Golden Light

8.9

At the beginning of the last Golden Age of Enlightenment, the Great Pyramid was placed at the geodesic center of the world beneath it and aligned with a belt star of Orion above it. It is the foundation stone on planet Earth with its four sides facing in the four directions representing the four elements with the fifth element of consciousness inside. The crystal capstone was aligned directly with a belt star of the constellation Orion, "the way shower for ascending souls", who is pointing directly at the constellation Ophiuchus, "the gatekeeper to the portal of Ascension." Various shafts within the great pyramid were aligned directly with other constellations in the sky each serving a specific purpose for the ascension and enlightenment of the soul. The great pyramid was used for mystery school initiations and golden age activations. The Egyptians knew the profound significance of the fundamental truth: "As above so below, as within so without." They were focused on bringing heaven above to the earth below and to activating the divine within and without. In the following pyramid initiation, we will ground into the earth beneath us as our foundation stone for our human experience and tune in to Orion and Ophiuchus above us as the way shower and gatekeeper for our divine ascension.

Let's start by envisioning ourselves seated in center of the great golden pyramid. Imagine the four-sided base beneath you shimmering in gold with massive golden triangles shooting up from each side and coming together at the crystal capstone overhead. Imagine this sparkling crystal capstone as a powerful generator energizing and activating the pyramid. You are surrounded completely now by shimmering golden light. As the spiraling energy swirling within the great pyramid raises your vibrational frequency, you are transformed into a golden light being from the bottom of your feet to the crown of your head. Imagine the golden light swirling around your feet and igniting your toes. Feel the swirling energy spiraling up your ankles and calves and encircling your knees. This is a scintillating energy that is activating your cells with sparks of divine power. Now the golden energy spirals around your thighs and circles your hips and pelvis. Moving upward, it spins around your core and into your chest flowing down the length of your arms. Now it spirals around your neck and into your chin, nose and cheeks. As this powerful energy swirls around your forehead, it activates the hemispheres of your brain. Imagine your brain "turned on" by this golden light and picture your pineal gland shimmering like a golden pinecone. Every cell in your body is ignited with the power of this golden flame and you are elevated to new heights of higher consciousness.

Now, let's run a silver cord from the base of our spine down into the center of Mother Earth, to stay connected to our foundation before soaring into the higher heights of our origin. Our silver cord is plugged into the heart of Mother Earth so that the gravity of her love will sustain us within her grasp while we explore the celestial realms.

For your pyramid initiation, you will start by realizing that you yourself are a pyramid of golden light with the crystal capstone above your head. In your meditation posture, you resemble a pyramid and your light body shimmers with golden light. The crystal pyramid floating and spinning above your crown is your eighth chakra or Gateway to Ascension. This is your own personal crystal capstone and power generator. It is running at full power as it turns on and powers every cell of your entire being. Now place your consciousness fully within this crystal pyramid. You have left your physical body now and become your soul star glowing within the crystal capstone above your head.

Observe the crystal pyramid that your consciousness is within. See the base of the crystal pyramid with four sides and know that this represents the cube or earth element. Now recognize each of the four triangles surrounding you and recognize each of the four directions and elements they represent. Directly behind you is the triangle that represents the South and the fire element. To the left of you is the triangle that represents the West and the wind or air element. To the right of you is the triangle that represents the East and the water element. Directly in front of you is the triangle that represents the North and the fifth element, ether, or higher consciousness. This is where your attention is now focused. See the pyramid in front of you as an expression of the Trinity with a point in the center. Now imagine that point is the tip of three triangles expanding outward from the venter. Within the larger triangle, the 3 bases of these three triangles within are the 3 sides of the larger pyramid.

Imagine that the small triangle whose base is the same base of the larger triangle is the Trinity expression of the child or body as a thought-form. The innocent child is seated upon the foundation as the neutral expression of consciousness. Now focus your attention on the smaller triangle whose base is the left side of the larger triangle and recognize this as the Father or original thought as the mind imagining creation. Now turn your attention to the smaller triangle on the right whose base is the right side of the larger triangle. Recognize this right triangle as the Trinity expression of the Mother or Holy Spirit illuminating creation. Together, the Father as the mind or light and the Mother as the spirit of love create the form of the child below. The child becomes a thought form or body projected by the mind of the father and illuminated by the spirit of the mother.

This trinitization is the thought, light and form. It is the proton, electron and neutron. It is the mind, spirit and body. It is the love, light and form in action. It is divinity, creativity and creation. It is three in one and one in three. It is who you are as a Trinity being. It is the fullest expression of you thrice great! In totality, you are the Father, Mother and child. You are three in one. Feeling a complete sense of oneness with the Trinity, focus again on the point in the center. Allow a stream of consciousness to flow through that point in the center. Let your head fall back and looking to the north you see the three belt stars of Orion. Focus on the middle belt star and picture it as a bright white point of light. Sour toward that light and seat your consciousness within it. You are now in the center as the child in the middle belt star. To the left, the Father is represented as the left belt star and the Mother is represented as the right belt star.

You are now one in three and three and one. You are a celestial being surrounded by the light of your Father and the love of your Mother in the heavenly realms. You are an illuminated love light being! You are a golden flame illuminating the heavens. Turning now towards the constellation of Ophiuchus, the gatekeeper, your golden flame creates a pillar of light connecting the belt stars of Orion to Ophiuchus, the snake bearer. Allow your soul star to travel through the pillar of light soaring toward Ophiuchus. Now focus your attention on the gatekeeper and show him that you are a golden flame of love and light and that your kundalini energy has been ignited from your root to your crown. Show him that you are a golden love light being shining radiant in the heavens. Show him that you are fully actualized as three in one and one in three. Upon seeing the brilliance of your radiant light, Ophiuchus opens the gate giving you entrance into the portal of Ascension.

Ascension into the Golden Light of Divine Love
(Audio version available at: www.SuzanneRossTranscendence.com)

Now let's begin your Ascension activation. Standing in the doorway of the portal to Ascension, you see a blinding white light all around you. Give yourself a moment to adjust to the brilliance of this light. Imagine the bright white light pouring into your crown filling your head and neck, into your shoulders and pouring down your arms. Imagine this light pouring down from your neck into your chest, abdomen, hips and thighs down through your knees and into your calves, feet and toes. You are now shimmering with this bright white light and vibrating at a much higher frequency. Your elevated frequency increases your light quotient matching the brilliance of the Ascension light. You are now ready to merge with this light and become an ascended being. You are prepared to enter this shimmering light because you have raised your love light frequency to this fifth dimensional level of Ascension.

You are no longer a three dimensional being on the earth plane. You have transitioned through the fourth dimension of time and transcended it. You are now a living and breathing fifth dimensional ascended master and there is no turning back. With the knowledge and wisdom, you have gained on your ascension path, you have now actualized as a 5D master of light expressing pure love. As a 5D love light being, you have the power to radiate your illuminated consciousness far and wide igniting the divine spark of your brothers and sisters. You are a 5D spiritualized being, a messenger of light and emissary of love. You have been activated for the ascension and given access to the 5D portal. You can now access this portal any time to regenerate and sustain your 5D light quotient maintaining the higher vibrational frequency of your ascending being. This is a sustaining light and as you return to the earth plane and reenter your physical body, your 5D love light being within will radiate all around you and raise the consciousness of all in your presence.

Just being in the presence of your powerful love light radiance, those around you will be activated and propelled into a higher consciousness. You are now a way shower, you yourself are the snake bearer with a fully activated kundalini energy flowing through your being. This is who you are now. Claim it. Own it. Live and breathe it. Take another moment to bathe in the brilliant light of this ascension portal. Let it fill every cell of your being. Let it activate any remaining dormant DNA strands. Let it bring your brain fully online now. Allow all the divine source codes to be fully activated now. You are vibrating at a higher frequency than you have ever felt before. You have filled your light quotient to the highest possible level. Now you are ready to bring this illuminated 5D consciousness back into your physical form.

Turn back toward the Gateway and thank Ophiuchus, the gatekeeper. Now look toward Orion and the belt stars. Focus your attention on the middle belt star and stream your consciousness through it. See the blue sphere of Mother Earth on the other side and project your consciousness through the stratosphere focusing on the crystal capstone of the great pyramid. Seat your consciousness within the capstone and peer into the pyramid. See yourself seated within it surrounded by a swirling golden light. See the crystal capstone above your own head and now seat your consciousness within it. Now allow your consciousness to pour out of the crystal capstone and back into your physical body. Place your hands on the ground and feel the floor beneath you. Wiggle your toes and open your eyes. Now look down at your body and see it shimmering with golden white light. See yourself as the radiant 5D ascended master that you have now become. You have been initiated and are now activated. You are now ready to live, breathe and be the Master of your love light being. You are now ready to initiate and activate your brothers and sisters by igniting their divine spark and filling them with your radiant love. Congratulations. You are love. You are light. Spread it far and wide. And so be it. And so it is. Amen.

Your Personal Revelations

REFERENCES

Chapter cover image is a personal graphic.
Illustrations:
1,2,5,8. www.pixabay.com
3. Personal photo
4. www.sallykirkman.com
6. www.ancientegypt.co.uk
7. Nile Maps courtesy of The Hidden Record Book
9. http://worldsecretlocations.com
Text:
Zechariah Sitchin, The 12TH Planet, Harper Collins, 1976
1-2. p. 212
3. p. 214
4. p. 213
5. p. 217
6. p. 216
7. p. 218
8. p. 220
9. p. 221
10-11. p. 223
12. p. 226
Robert Bauval & Adrian Gilbert, The Orion Mystery, Three Rivers Press, 1995
13. p. 195
14. p. 203
15. p. 19
16. p. 15
17. p. 76
18. p. 22
19. p. 47
20. p. 48
21. p. 22
22. p. 29
23. p. 123
24. p. 195
25. p. 180
26. p. 99
J. J. Hurtak, PhD., PhD., The Book of Knowledge: The Keys of Enoch, The Academy for Future Science, 1977
27. p. 73
Ian Shaw, The Oxford History of Ancient Egypt, Oxford University Press, 2000
28. p. 254
Graham Hancock and Robert Bauval, The Message of the Sphinx, Three Rivers Press, 1996
29. p. 5
Elkins, Rueckert, McCarty, The Law of One: Book I — The RA Material, Schiffer Publishing, 1984
30. p. 66
31. p. 80-2
32. p. 90
33. p. 206
34. p. 71
35. p. 73
36. Mathues Imhotep and Mathew Schlueter, *7th Seal Hidden Wisdom Unveiled Vol. 3 (Gnosis Unveiled)*, Independently Published, 2017

Day Nine

The Divine Dance of Cosmic Duality

What a magnificent day for a galactic adventure that traverses interdimensional realms! Our travels through the universe, constellations and galaxies have revealed some extraordinary insights that we will explore more deeply today. Upon realizing that what lies at the center of the Milky Way galaxy is known as both a supermassive black hole (according to modern astronomers) and as the super universe headquarters (according to celestial teachers), I became very intrigued about the true nature of this interdimensional portal. I felt strongly that further investigation into this phenomenon would reveal something very profound about the true nature of reality. Sure enough! As I started to dig deeper, comparing the research of modern physics and the revelations within *The Urantia Book*, I was stunned by the parallels! I just sat in amazement as detail after detail began to match up perfectly and the picture of reality unfolding before my eyes became more fascinating than I could have ever imagined. Let's head out and explore these magnificent revelations further so we can decide for ourselves what possibilities lie beyond the horizon.

The perfect backdrop for today's adventures is the vast openness and majestic beauty of the desert landscape. I personally feel a strong connection to the spiritual essence of this mystical environment. If you have ever spent much time in any of the desert regions of the American Southwest, you know what I mean. Isolated from the density of population and the noisy animal life of the woods, the stillness is almost eerie. There is nothing else like it. On a hot, dry desert day, all you can hear are the voices of the wind spirits swirling through the air. Sometimes these spirits will manifest as dust devils spinning and gathering sand in a beautiful spiraling vortex. As they move about the desert floor, you become aware of their spiritual essence. There are many ancient myths and legends told by the Native American elders who reside in the deserts of Utah, Arizona and New Mexico. Ancient cave drawings depict otherworldly visitors they call "star people" and oval discs they call "sky ships." The elders claim that these beings descend to share sacred wisdom and universal knowledge. Here is a depiction of a steel bar with strange symbols the native elder, Chief Golden Light Eagle, claims represent universal laws.

9.1

We are aware of the ancient mysticism of the Egyptian desert and the vast knowledge revealed in the pyramid texts which claim that Osiris descended from the constellation of Orion and that Isis originated from the constellation of Sirius. These tall, luminescent beings walked amongst them and taught them sacred wisdom and universal knowledge. Let's move beyond the deserts of the East and explore the supernatural phenomenon occurring in the deserts of the West.

The mysterious desert shimmers in undulating heat waves that produce visions of scenes that aren't really there. Mysterious tones traveling on sound waves produce whirring, whistling and drumming. It's common for hikers trekking through the desert on a sizzling hot day to have mystical visions and to hear strange sounds. There's also an eerie feeling of being watched by invisible beings and a sense of being energetically drawn toward swirling vortexes. As you know from the stories I shared in the first section of this book I have had many profound experiences in the desert southwest. To me, the desert feels like a spiraling vortex of spiritual energy. The swirling dust devils seem to validate these ever-present spiraling energy patterns. Even linear time seems less important in the lazy heat of an endless desert day. When the temperatures soar and the sun's intensity becomes oppressive, the air itself seems to take on an illusory quality. You can literally see the heat waves vibrating in the air around you and reality is altered by hallucinations of water pooling in the hot desert sand. Illusions in the desert are common due to the intense radiation of light and heat. As such, this environment is highly conducive to spiritual awakening.

Amidst a heightened awareness of the illusory nature of reality and time itself, the vibratory essence of the physical realm reveals itself. The wind spirits draw one's attention to the spiral nature of primal energy patterns expressing themselves in form. In the Arizona desert regions, particularly in the spiritual mecca of Sedona, the spiritual energy is tangible and in certain areas you can detect the presence of spiraling energy fields like vortexes of gravitational force. I have also heard of a desert region in Mexico called "Zona de Silencio" or "Zone of Silence" where strange forces within powerful magnetic fields alter the functioning of compasses, watches and electronic equipment. The reports of UFO activity in the desert southwest far exceed those of other regions.

Speaking of UFO activity, I have shared my own experience in the desert of encountering a strange atmosphere after being drawn into an eerie cove between the mountains. My father, sister and I discovered a long flat stretch of ground that had been burnt. Something had left a wide path maybe a quarter of a mile long before ending in a large black circle. The burnt markings themselves would have been strange enough but more than that, it was the strange yellow-grey mist which hung in the air. None of us had ever experienced anything like that before. The unfamiliar atmosphere felt creepy to us and we just wanted to get out of there. My husband, who is skeptical of anything paranormal, admits to having seen unusual streaks of light dart across the desert night skies that would make sharp right angle turns and travel at mock speeds.

One of my friends and his wife had a remarkable experience one night out in the desert that was so dramatic it caused a major rift in their relationship. On their way home from dinner with friends one night, they pulled over to gaze at the vast display of twinkling stars that can only be seen in isolated areas like the desert. They were both leaning against the passenger side door when suddenly they heard a thundering sound approaching like a bunch of people running toward them. He grabbed his wife and opened the passenger door to push her inside and that's the last thing he remembers of the incident. The next thing they both remember is sitting side-by-side in the vehicle and matter-of-factly saying, "I guess we should be getting home." Upon arriving at their house, they were shocked at the time on the clock.

They knew they had left their friends house, only a few miles away, around 9 o'clock and now it was almost midnight. Shrugging their shoulders, they went to bed and didn't think much of it until the next morning. When the gravity of the event started to occur to them, he was eager to discuss it, but she wanted nothing to do with it and suggested they never speak of it again. At the time he shared the story with me, it was almost 2 years later, and you could still clearly see the dramatic effect that it had on him. I even got goose bumps and a lump in my throat as he shared the story with me. He and his wife had split by now and he felt that the incident contributed to their differences. He even thought he might have an x-ray to see if any type of implant could be detected. In any case, his story seemed very authentic. It was evident that something profound happened to them both that evening that dramatically affected the rest of their lives.

I believe that the desert is very spiritual in many ways and that it invites inter-dimensional experiences. Due to the profound nature of the topics we will be exploring on our adventure today, I felt that the desert would be a perfect destination for us to explore the realities beyond the dimensions of time and space and what better place than Sedona, Arizona. Sedona is known for its spiraling vortexes and the inter-dimensional experiences many have had here. Millions of people come from around the world every year in search of a spiritual experience. Few are disappointed. For the 9th day of our ascension journey, Sedona is the perfect choice for 9 is the number for completion and today's adventure will be a culmination of our adventures and discoveries thus far!

Since starting this book back in 2013, I have since moved to the red rock paradise of supernatural Sedona. We moved here in 2015 after a premonition on my vision board manifested in reality! Almost everyone I have met who moved here spontaneously responded to a "calling" that brought them here. In fact, there is a funny T-shirt in one of the tourist shops that says: "Sedona Called & I Answered." So here's my "Sedona Story":

In 2012, my awakening process catapulted to whole new heights as my consciousness expanded and I began engaging in automatic writing, trance channeling and interdimensional traveling. One day, seated in deep meditation, I felt a powerful swoosh of energy enter the room and begin spiraling around me. I was aware of a feminine entity standing before me and felt incredibly blessed by her presence. Then I heard a voice whisper in my ear, "I am the Goddess Sedona. Get up and go write on your vision board: In 2015, Scott and I move to Sedona." Following the guidance, I did just that. When I came out of the meditation, I just stared at the board thinking, "Where in the heck is Sedona?" I had never even heard of it! Over the course of the next two years, the Goddess Sedona showed up everywhere I went. Shortly after she first visited, people started coming up to me left and right saying, "Have you ever heard of Sedona?", "You and Scott would love it there!", "Have I showed you my vacation photos of Sedona?", "You and Scott should really go to Sedona on your next vacation?", "Have you been to Sedona yet?",...She was relentless! Then pictures of Sedona started flooding my vision as people wearing T-shirts with pictures of Sedona walk passed and cars with Sedona bumper stickers drove by. Finally, as we were planning a trip to the Grand Canyon, I told my husband, "Hey, let's pass through that town called Sedona while we're in Arizona."

I can never share the next part without getting teary-eyed. We decided to take 89A from Flagstaff into Sedona so we could enter the crystal city by way of Oak Creek Canyon. This is bar none the best way to enter Sedona for the very first time. The drive is breathtaking and the moment I first saw the magnificent red rock temples, I became utterly breathless. My husband and I both just sat there with our jaws dropped down in awe and amazement. We were both speechless. There really are no words to explain the feeling. It's one of those places you just have to experience for yourself to understand the profundity. Well, there's one word — profound! They are simply profound. I knew in my heart from the very first moment that they were so much more than just rocks and now that I have been here for almost 3 years now, I am sure of it!

Journey into the Red Rock Temples

Just like the Goddess Egypt has a line of kundalini energy running along her spine, so does the Goddess Sedona. In fact, Mother Earth herself, Goddess Gaia, has a line of energy running from her root to her crown and Sedona, with her bright red rocks is the root chakra. It's the sacred site on planet Earth where the kundalini energy is rooted. Millions of people from all over the world come to Sedona to ignite their root chakra and activate their kundalini energy (whether they are aware of it or not). The root chakra of Goddess Sedona is seated in Boynton Canyon so we'll activate our kundalini here and then move up her spine to the crown. As we hike into the canyon, our first stop will be at the red rock spires known as Kachina Woman and her mate, the Warrior. Let's feel into the sensation of the red clay under our feet and connect into the energy here. Imagine the sounds of a Native American flute floating on the wind. Envision yourself as one of the first indigenous peoples to walk on this clay and tune into the spirit of the red rocks. We know from the teachings offered by Group Ra that everything is intelligent energy manifested from the infinite intelligence of the One Infinite Creator. The infinite intelligence of the rocks they call "rockness" and inspire us to communicate with them. Imagine that all of the stories that have unfolded here are stored in the memories of these rocks. All of the events and the emotions that accompany them have been, and are still being, absorbed by these red rock beings. In addition, they have their own energetic essence and emotional responses. Let's honor these temples by speaking softly and sending loving kindness into their souls.

9.2

As we hike along the trail, we will continue to ponder the mysteries of the universe stopping occasionally to admire the plant life and wildlife along the way. Once we get to Kachina Woman and the Warrior, we'll be seated and admire the glorious view. This promises to be a remarkable desert adventure full of mystery, intrigue and endless possibilities on the earth and spiraling up into the heavens. While we hike and explore on the land, we'll swirl through the galaxies and traverse eternity. From the farthest reaches of time and space to the sacred center of it all — the Paradise portal to infinity!

Hiking into the red rock temples, I will start our discussion by exploring the majesty of black holes and then this evening under the stars, we will explore the mysteries of the constellations. I was literally stunned when I read in *The Urantia Book* that the super universe headquarters were located at the center of the Milky Way galaxy. Now I firmly believe that the teachings within this book are authentic down to the precise detail because intuitively these revelations resonate deeply within the core of my being as universal truths. If you are still skeptical, I invite you to consider the recent discoveries in the field of physics regarding black holes and then compare them to the passages in the book which I have presented. Any remaining doubts in my mind were shattered by the clear correlations between the two. It's just like the other revelations: one fact fits here, one truth fits there and suddenly, everything falls into place beautifully to present an astounding picture of reality that is both magnificent and divine.

I love the show, "Through the Wormhole" with Morgan Freeman, and have learned a great deal about modern astronomy and physics by watching and taking notes. Often, I will do further research on the topics presented until the mysteries in my mind are solved. One show, "The Riddle of Blackholes" was no exception. I watched it after I made the connection between the universe headquarters and the center of the Milky Way galaxy. With that profundity in mind, the show was that much more fascinating. Also, I had already learned in *The Urantia Book* that our solar system was within the constellation Sagittarius and as I watched the show, not only did they reveal amazing things about the nature of black holes that coincide with *The Urantia Book* but they also discussed the relevance of the constellation "Sagittarius."

I am always blown away by the sequence with which I discover information as well as with its synchrony to my focus at the time. It's like I am being led from one place to the next by an invisible tour guide who is saying, "See it's like this over here and then it's like that over there and together they make sense as one unified theory." As a willing participant who has surrendered to the universe and put faith in divine guidance, I respond to the pull of my intuition as it guides me to reach for this book here and then watch that show there. It's a beautiful and most synchronistic performance that sometimes feels like a dance. As long as I ride the waves harmonically and don't resist by interfering, everything flows beautifully. I am magically provided with step-by-step instructions that lead me to the truth I am seeking. It's far less confusing to absorb the revelations sequentially in this way because only then, within the context of the knowledge already accumulated, do they actually make sense. With that in mind, the revelations of this 10-day journey have been sequentially laid out so that, during these last two days, the accumulation of all we have learned will converge and coalesce into one astounding truth about the true nature of reality!

Back to black holes~

On the "Through the Wormhole" episode called "The Riddle of Black Holes," Morgan Freeman explores the nature of these "cosmic cannibals", as he calls them. It is common knowledge that a black hole is the aftermath of a dying star. When a star runs out of fuel to burn, it simply collapses. When this happens, a shockwave moves out and the star explodes in a phenomenon called a supernova. Apparently, it's a very dramatic event as this colossal explosion leaves a debris field of gas and dust hundreds of light years across. Theoretical physicists predict that if the star is large enough, its collapsing core could shrink down to form a black hole. After explaining the basics, Morgan went on to talk about an astronomer named Karl Jansky who, in 1931, was trying to send radio messages to Europe when he encountered a background signal that wouldn't go away. This signal was apparently loudest when his antenna was pointed at the constellation Sagittarius at the very heart of the Milky Way. He knew that this signal wasn't like that of a star and so astronomers began to wonder if it might be a black hole.

At this point, the concept of a black hole was nothing more than a mere hunch. This is primarily since there is no way to see them since they are hidden from view by a thick veil of dust. Then, 25 years ago, a German astronomer embarked upon a mission to find out exactly what was causing the strange noise at the center of the Milky Way. What he found was again a collection of stars moving at incredible speeds around a completely dark and tremendously dense object. They clocked one star going over 11,000,000 mph! His research began in 1992 and is recognized as the first proof of a black hole. His team estimated that this black hole must've swallowed millions of stars over its lifetime.

As I watched this show, I began to think about the descriptions of the dark gravity bodies around the central universe given in "The Urantia Book." Now, keep in mind that all the information in this voluminous book was channeled between 1911 and 1924 long before we had any concept of black holes. The book describes seven space conditions and motions around the periphery of Paradise. The first is a "quiescent" zone closest to Paradise. The next is a clockwise movement of three Paradise Circuits and seven Havona circuits. The next is a zone that separates the Havona circuits from the "dark gravity bodies" of the central universe. The fourth zone, then, is a counterclockwise moving belt of the dark gravity bodies. The fifth zone divides the counterclockwise bodies of the fourth zone and the clockwise moving bodies of the sixth zone. We know that two spiraling arms counter revolve around the center of black holes. The last and seventh zone separates these counter revolving bodies from the revolving circuits of the seven super universes:

"On the outskirts of the vast central universe, far out beyond the seventh belt of Havona worlds, there swirl an unbelievable number of enormous dark gravity bodies. These multitudinous dark masses are quite unlike other space bodies in many particulars; even in form they are different. These dark gravity bodies neither reflect nor absorb light; they are nonreactive to physical-energy light, and they so completely encircle and enshroud Havona as to hide it from the view of the nearby inhabited universes of time and space."[1]

The German astronomer featured on "Through the Wormhole" explains that the center of our galaxy is hidden from view by a thick veil of dust. The only way he could penetrate this veil was with infrared light due to its longer wavelengths. The show goes on to talk about another astronomer who set out on a mission to find out what goes on inside of black holes. What her and her team discovered was described as a "cosmic dance." It is now believed that all galaxies have a supermassive black hole at their heart center. One way to detect them is by observing the glowing gas that surrounds these "cosmic sinkholes" which is the result of gas falling into them and emitting a lot of energy that appears very brightly around the edges. When they investigated this emission of energy, they expected to find one peak of light but instead discovered two, each with a different velocity. This astronomer explains that when two galaxies collide, their black holes at the center do not crash head-on but instead begin to whirl around one another in what she calls a "black hole waltz."

This can be observed by the light that's emitted from them. The black hole that's moving towards us emits an electric blue light of a shorter wavelength and the one that's moving away emits a magnetic red light of a longer wavelength. She called the interplay between the blue and red lights "the telltale signature of a black hole waltz." She says, "Every time we see it, we high-five each other in the observation room and we just can't get over it!" I just love how these discoveries of the true nature of our reality spark such joy in all who witness them. Morgan adds that, "As this team of astronomers continued to scan the universe, they found the same remarkable dance happening time and time again, galaxy after galaxy, black holes paired up and dancing the cosmic night away." With the two spiraling arms encircling the black hole, I like to call it "The Cosmic Dance of Duality."

I have concluded, based on my interpretation of *The Urantia Book*, that what lies at the heart of the Milky Way galaxy is a core of tremendous activity. The book calls it the headquarters world of the seventh super universe. Why this may be difficult for us to comprehend, it makes perfect sense that there would have to be a control center of sorts for the intelligent manipulation of the energies and forces that govern the realms. Modern astronomy estimates that our universe has up to 200 billion galaxies and one German astronomer has estimated it to be over 500 billion. If we consider that each galaxy has, at its heart, a control center (which we have identified as a supermassive black hole), then the number of headquarters is head-spinning!

The Urantia Book teaches us that each super universe has a headquarters world within which each local universe, constellation and local system also has a center of operations. We can imagine that one reason these galaxies dance around one another, instead of crashing head-on, is because they are closely associated and working together in the multi-level organization called the Grand Universe. The clockwise movement of one may offset the counterclockwise movement of the other which keeps the tremendous pull of their cores in balance. The anti-gravitational "dark matter" pervading the space around them may also provide some resistance which helps to contain these colossal forces and prevent them from consuming everything in the universe! Just a thought. Consider the following statements:

"This alternate zoning of the master universe, in association with the alternate clockwise and counterclockwise flow of the galaxies, is a factor in the stabilization of physical gravity designed to prevent the accentuation of gravity pressure to the point of disruptive and dispersive activities. Such an arrangement exerts antigravity influence and acts as a brake upon otherwise dangerous velocities."[2] "Space is nonresponsive to gravity, but it acts as an equilibrant on gravity. Without the space cushion, explosive action would jerk surrounding space bodies. Pervaded space also exerts an antigravity influence upon physical or linear gravity; space can actually neutralize such gravity action."[3]

That leads me to the next scientific discovery revealed on this episode about black holes. Janna Levin, a professor and astrophysicist, is a regular guest on "Through the Wormhole." She is delightful and obviously, incredibly bright. Morgan explains that her and her colleagues have been trying to figure out what types of sounds black holes might make as they dance around one another in their cosmic waltz.

As we already know, black holes exert a tremendous gravitational pull on anything that comes within their reach. Understanding the essence of gravity is the key to appreciating our connection to the creative forces from which we emerged. All matter in the universe rotates around the primordial center of creation responding to its strong gravitational pull. This core is the source of all gravity, energy and force in the infinitely expanding universe.

"Here is God personally, literally, and actually present. And from his infinite being there flow the flood streams of life, energy, and personality to all universes."[4]

If we believe that this sacred center is the origin of our being and the central focus of our creator and his creative associates, then we can imagine that the primary mechanism for controlling the vast expanse of the universes that they created is gravity. This attractive force allows them to keep all universe activity within their embrace for organizational control and parental guidance.

"The inescapable gravity effectively grips all the world of all the universes of all space. Gravity is the all-powerful grasp of the physical presence of Paradise. Gravity is the omnipotent strand on which are strung the gleaming stars, blazing Suns, and whirling spheres which constitute the universal physical adornment of the eternal God, who is all things, fills all things, and in whom all things consist."[5]

On a previous adventure, we learned that the Trinity works as a complementary unit to effectively design, materialize and spiritualize its creations. According to *The Urantia Book*, the Universal Father originates and transmits all patterns of energy and matter through a personality-gravity circuit, the Eternal Son distributes his divine nature through a spirit-gravity circuit and the Infinite Spirit radiates diverse levels of intelligence through mind-gravity circuits. If the Trinity resides at the Paradise headquarters of creation, it makes sense that it would have the characteristics of a black hole with the Trinity transmitting, distributing and radiating its gravity circuits from this source and center! Furthermore, we can imagine that each supermassive black hole is a duplication of this primal pattern. In this way, the Trinity is effectively exerting its gravitational influence on all of creation by streaming through the black hole, or headquarters, at the center of each and every galaxy. What is streaming through are energetic patterns of consciousness that affect the mind, spirit and personality of all cosmic beings. When two of these streaming centers of gravity lovingly merge, they create a primal pattern of co-creation which symbolizes the birth of something new.

This is where the amazing discoveries revealed by Janna Levin on "Through the Wormhole" come back into play. My speculations about black holes, or headquarters, converging to create something new (like two corporations merging to birth a new entity) were confirmed by the evidence presented on the show. What they revealed was simply sublime. Morgan Freeman explained that Albert Einstein saw space and time as a flexible material that could be distorted by gravity. He explained that a black hole is merely a deep well in the material and when two black holes come close to one another, the cosmic dance of these two orbiting holes stir up space-time and send out ripples that can travel clear across the universe. Janna helps us understand that these waves will move out to the universe and that maybe we can hear them if we can pick up on the wobbling of the fabric of space-time itself. Her and her colleagues discovered, after seven years of research, that a smaller black hole orbiting a larger black hole create a knocking on the drum of space-time. The vibrational resonance that came out of the simulation, time after time, always produced the same cloverleaf pattern which, wait for it... looks shockingly similar to the Genesis pattern!

9.3

When I saw this pattern revealed on the television screen in front of me, I sat there in awe. I grabbed the remote and hit pause so that I could freeze the image and there it was. I just sat staring at the scientific evidence of the genesis pattern of all of creation caused by the cosmic dance of duality! Two entities coming into close proximity creates the vibratory resonance for a whole new genesis! This is the trinity expressing itself with its signature pattern of eternity expanding in a space-time grid. The Trinity is manifesting through the mechanisms of black holes! I was thrilled at this further validation of divinity in action at the core of each galaxy in our universe. These galaxies are the vehicles through which the Universal Father, The Eternal Son and the Infinite Spirit exert their loving influence upon all of creation.

While Janna and her team didn't see it in terms of the Trinity, they did however recognize a powerful connection between the rotational movement of the black holes around one another and the tiny protons and electrons inside of an atom. Of course, we know the Trinity is expressed in an atom as the proton, electron and neutron. She explained that she could build a kind of classical atom with the bigger black hole acting like the nucleus and the smaller black hole like an electron. This is important because it indicates that a huge macroscopic object is behaving more like a subatomic particle. In Newtonian physics, large objects are not supposed to behave the same as fundamental particles but as we know, quantum physics is revealing a whole new reality! Reconciling the laws of physics that pertain to the larger and more recognizable world with the quantum laws that govern the world of the very tiny has been an ongoing challenge for theoretical physicists. So, to see this resemblance between the behavior of black holes and atoms was remarkable and it opened the door for the next presentation in the episode which proved even more fascinating. As you will see, this discovery reinforces truths that we were speculating about days ago regarding the reflective and holographic nature of reality!

In the last part of the show, Morgan introduces a physicist named Leonard Susskin who, he says, uses black holes to develop the most revolutionary ideas in physics since Einstein. Before presenting his revelations, a brief discussion of tiny particles is necessary to set the stage. The theory of quantum mechanics predicts that space should be sizzling with particles and anti-particles popping into existence in pairs and then annihilating one another an instant later. These particles, Morgan explains, exist for such a short time, they're not considered a part of reality. Apparently, they are called virtual particles and it seems that Stephen Hawking realized that there is one place in the universe where these particles could become real.

Around the black hole, there is an invisible line in space and it is called the event horizon. Morgan speculates that if a pair of virtual particles formed just outside the event horizon, then one party of the pair might travel across that point of no return before being paired up. It would fall into the black hole and leave his partner to escape as radiation. This radiation was named "Hawking Radiation." This would imply that black holes may not actually be black but radiantly shining at the event horizon like a sun just before it rises.

Enter Leonard Susskind. After hearing Stephen Hawking's claim that when information goes into a black hole, it disappears completely from the universe, he knew this violated a fundamental principle of physics — "the conservation of information." Morgan helps us understand Stephen's viewpoint by explaining his theory that for every ounce of material a black hole absorbed into its core, it would radiate away an equivalent amount of energy from the event horizon. However, since there is no physical link between the black hole and its event horizon, the two processes do not share information and, so it is lost. According to the "conservation of information" principle, no matter how scrambled information may become out in the universe, it is never lost.

Apparently, this conflict between Stephen's belief that black holes ate information and Leonard's insistence that the fundamental principle of physics could not be violated anywhere in the universe, sparked a debate that engulfed all physics. Morgan explained that this is because the outcome may reveal something very profound which would affect the very way we experience the universe. After 10 years of research, Leonard Susskind still had not disproved Stephen Hawking's theory that black holes ate, rather than stored, information and then he performed a cosmic thought experiment which changed everything.

He imagined two people, Bob and Alice, approaching the black hole in a spaceship. Then suddenly, Alice decides to bail out and jump into the black hole. He determined that Bob would see Alice falling toward the black hole getting closer and closer to the event horizon but slowing down since the gravity of the black hole severely distorts space and time near the horizon, Einstein's theory of relativity predicts that Bob would see Alice moving slower and slower until she eventually stops. From Bob's point of view, he explains, Alice simply becomes completely immobile and it takes her forever to fall through the black hole. On the other hand, Alice would experience just falling completely and cleanly through the event horizon feeling no pain until she approached the interior at which point she would become increasingly uncomfortable, get more and more distorted and eventually be annihilated.

Since these two points of view were at odds — one with Alice stuck at the event horizon frozen in time but alive and the other where she sails right through and dies — he felt compelled to resolve the paradox. As one of the creators of string theory, he knew the elementary particles have "vibrations on top of vibrations" and so imagined that if Alice approached the black hole in a plane, its propellers would expand into more and more propellers out to infinity, each propeller going faster than the last. He recognized that if you could catch this on a high-speed camera, you would see more and more structures coming into view and the particles would seem to grow and grow endlessly until it filled the whole universe. Morgan explains that what Leonard realized is that the black hole is like an ultra high-speed camera.

Leonard performs another thought experiment to help demonstrate his findings. In the last visualization, Alice is either squished at the center of the black hole or smeared all over the horizon. He now proposes that Alice is both at the center of the black hole and smeared across its surface at the same time. He explains that, according to the holographic principle:

"The event horizon of the black hole is a two-dimensional representation of the three-dimensional object at its center."

And let's not forget that the gravity of the black hole severely distorts space and time at the event horizon. Transcending space-time, the event horizon effectively creates a two-dimensional hologram of the three-dimensional pattern at its center.

These revelations have so many profound implications!

For Leonard, it solves the problem of information loss, he says, since every object that falls into a black hole leaves its mark both at the central mass and on the shimmering hologram of the event horizon. When the black hole emits Hawking radiation from the horizon then, that radiation is connected to the stuff that fell in, he claims, and the information is not lost. Apparently at a scientific conference in 2004, Hawking conceded defeat and admitted that black holes do not eat information. Although Leonard won the debate, Morgan explains that, because this theory does not just apply to black holes: "It ultimately forces us to picture all of reality in a new way."

What Leonard and Morgan are saying is that there are two versions of the description of you and me and all things — one of them being the normal perceived 3-D reality and the other being a 2D holographic image on the spherical walls containing our reality; the bubble that embraces our local universe for instance creating a universal reality within it. Our 2D holographic image "smeared" across the walls of our universal horizons still contains the exact same information as our 3D hologram. He tells us that this idea is now a basic principle of physics — that information is stored on a kind of holographic film at the edges of the universe. Morgan helps to clarify by telling us that, in a sense, 3-D space is just one version of reality. The other version exists on flat holographic film billions of light years away at the edge of the cosmos. Now Leonard is facing the challenge of trying to explain why space is three-dimensional when all the information that is stored in space is stored as a two-dimensional hologram. Morgan wraps things up by simply saying:

"Right here and right now, black holes have a profound effect on you and me. Their shimmering holographic surfaces seem to be telling us that everything we think is here, is mirrored out there at the very edge of our mysterious universe."

Whoa. Is this what we have been discovering all along or what!?

After contemplating these revelations, I came to some of my own conclusions and I, of course, invite you to do the same. O.K. so here we go…

I just imagined what Leonard is postulating in the reverse. Instead of saying that the 3-D information from here is being recorded as two-dimensional information out there, I am speculating that two-dimensional information out there is projected as three-dimensional information in here — to be more specific — as three-dimensional holograms. From this perspective, we can also turn Morgan's statement around and instead of saying, "everything we think is here is mirrored out there", we can say, "everything out there is mirrored in here!"

Now as the show continued, I became more and more amazed at the revelations and their synchronicity with the explanations in "The Urantia Book." The scientific data they are discovering reveals symbols of the divine trinity and holographic reflectivity on the surfaces of black holes! It was both astonishing and fantastic to experience such parallels of thought in regard to the true nature of universe reality. It seems to me as though our evolutionary progress has grown exponentially as we become more advanced both technologically and spiritually. We are getting closer and closer to discovering the magnificent truths that will liberate us from the mundane world and our egos that we have become so attached to.

These truths, when fully revealed, will transcend humanities obsession with ego-based materialism as we stand in awe of the greater cosmos. Once we truly grasp that we are cosmic citizens and an integral part of the grand plan, the mundane melodrama will give way to the magnificence of a much greater reality. When cosmic revelations pervade the collective consciousness, humanity will experience a profound shift in their perspectives.

This inspired vision of the future is possible if more and more of us turn our attention toward the vastness of the cosmos and recognize the multi-layered dimensions of reality. That's why I get so excited when I see science and spirituality merging on shows like "Through the Wormhole." It's reassuring to know that it has a large enough following to be picked up season after season. This gives me tremendous hope that our collective curiosity has given way to an open-mindedness about the infinite possibilities that lie beyond.

Back to our adventure in Sedona ~

Here we are at Kachina Woman and Warrior Rock. Kachina Women looks remarkably like a Native American woman with her hair braided at her ears and holding a baby in a pouch at her belly

9.4

Let's close our eyes and feel into her essence. Let's see what she might have to share about who she might have been, or still is, from a higher dimensional perspective. Let's imagine that in a reality vibrating at a much higher frequency, the 5th dimension possibly, we might be able to perceive her as a fully expressive being shimmering with light and life! In the slower vibration of the 3rd dimensional density, we can only perceive her in her feminine form as a red rock entity that looks remarkably similar to a real woman. She is <u>rockin'</u> her bad self though. (I couldn't help it).

As we sit and admire the view across the canyon, let's imagine what this whole landscape might look like in a higher dimensional reality — red rock temples alive while the red rock beings come to life. It's the perfect setting to continue our discussion about creative manifestation in time and space dimensions!

As we sit in the belly of Kachina Woman, let's reflect on one of our very first adventures when we talked about the transformation from existential reality into experiential time and space. We talked about the Trinity at rest in eternity manifesting itself into its creative aspect by moving into the dimensions of time and space. First, we pictured a single dot moving out into a line which then stopped because it was now limited by time as opposed to eternity. This line then represented the first dimension. After resting in this state for a while, the line moved out to produce a reflection of itself that would parallel its image a distance away. Between these two lines and the intervening space, a flat two-dimensional square emerged. Ultimately, this flat square reflected its image outward and became a three-dimensional cube. We have learned, over the course of our adventure, that our reality is the result of thought images that are projected from the Creator. The question arises that, if our 3D image of reality is based on a pattern that originates in dimensionless Paradise at the core creation, where and how does this image translation take place? If the thought images originally are dimensionless, then what is the mechanism for translating them from a 1D point to a flat 2D picture and then into a 3D cubic image?

In *The Urantia Book*, the "eternal isle of Paradise" is the geographic center of infinity and is said to be composed of a single form of materialization — stationary systems of reality. This substance is an organization of space potency exclusive to Paradise and appears to be the concentration of all absolute potential for cosmic reality. Paradise is the origin of all patterns and the central universe of Havona is an exhibit of these potentials. Being dimensionless in infinity, these patterns would have to be translated into a dimensional reality on Havona. Again, we wonder where and how the patterns translate from their dimensionless origin of pure potential to actualizing in the dimensional reality of Havona and then ultimately, the multiple dimensions of space-time universes? Hmmm, I wonder if Havona beings exist as light and sound waves only and with their creative minds, they are projecting mental images onto the 2D picture screens that stream across the walls of all universal spheres. Of course, these streaming images, or perfect pattern-personalities, regardless of their dimensional appearance, would still contain all the original source information encoded or imprinted upon them.

The Urantia Book teaches us that the central universe is the pattern of perfection for all of creation and that it is stationary. Its images of perfection are projected onto the evolutionary spheres and its one billion spheres provide the pattern upon which the rest of the universes are based. Check out this description of Havona, "the central and divine universe":

"This is the one and only settled, perfect, and established aggregation of worlds. This is a wholly created and perfect universe; it is not an evolutionary development. This is the eternal core of perfection, about which swirls that endless procession of universes which constitute the tremendous evolutionary experiment, the audacious adventure of the creator sons of God, who aspired to duplicate in time and to reproduce in space the pattern universe, the ideal of divine completeness, supreme finality, ultimate reality, and eternal perfection."

From the central universe, holographic images of its patterns of perfection must be projected onto the evolutionary worlds.

You may already have guessed what conclusion I am coming to here based on our earlier discussion today about the dark gravity bodies which separate Paradise, Havona and the seven super universes. Those revelations coupled with the scientific discoveries about the nature of black holes we learned about from our friend, Morgan, it is my speculation that the "multitudinous dark gravity bodies" which form belts running clockwise and counterclockwise around the center of creation provide the mechanism through which images can be translated from dimensionless patterns into dimensional form and by which their holographic nature can be projected from their shiny surfaces.

There is a supermassive black hole at the center of our Milky Way galaxy however there are also 100 million smaller black holes scattered across it, according to Morgan. In *The Urantia Book*, "Paradise" is described as "the beauteous pattern for all headquarters worlds;" and Havona, "the central universe of his immediate indwelling (as) the pattern for all universes in their ideals, organization, and ultimate destiny."[6] So, from this, we can visualize that Paradise is the pattern for the headquarter worlds and Havona is the pattern for the evolutionary universes. The patterns of Paradise would be projected onto the supermassive black holes at the center of the galaxies, the headquarter worlds, and the patterns of Havona would be projected onto the multitudinous dark gravity bodies surrounding it. The tremendous number of black holes within the galaxies themselves would be the vehicles through which the patterns of Havona would be projected upon the evolutionary worlds of time and space.

This theory sounds plausible to me and it would help to explain a lot about the reality we experience. Why not? We have no better explanation! I mean, Leonard Susskin, a world-renowned physicist, clearly stated that all the information from three-dimensional space is stored as a two-dimensional hologram. On top of that, Morgan Freeman himself informs us that 3-D space is just one version of reality and the other version exists on flat holographic film billions of light years away at the edge of the cosmos! He says that discovering why the two realities coexist is now the biggest puzzle physics needs to solve. Leonard admits that a black hole is a place where ordinary space doesn't exist anymore and says, "If I'm asked questions about how space emerges, I will simply have to say, "Well, I'm thinking about it. We don't really understand it." Ultimately, I think Morgan nailed it when he said, "Right here and right now, black holes have a profound effect on you and me."

At the beginning of the show, Janna exclaimed, "It sounds like science fiction but its better because it's real! Another physicist followed this remark up by saying:

"The black hole is a window into a world that we don't have concepts for — we don't even have the mental architecture yet — to be able to envision it properly."

In almost every chapter of *The Urantia Book*, you will find a statement that expresses the frustration of these celestial guides in attempting to communicate "advanced concepts beyond mortal comprehension", especially when limited by our language. These celestial guides have also come to the conclusion that although there are so-called "informed humans", they feel we can't handle the truth, whether ethically, spiritually or psychologically, and have made every attempt to shield us from it. Whenever I hear this, my instinctual reply is always, "Try me!" There is a show on television called, "America's Book of Secrets", which discusses the vast amount of knowledge that has been withheld from the American people over the last several centuries by those "in charge." We are all aware of the "secret societies" that are said to exist within the political communities of the elite. I believe that the biggest cover-ups relate to proof of contact with other-worldly beings, which is not acceptable. I believe that we have a right to this knowledge as inhabitants of this planet and I feel it is condescending to assert that we can't handle it. Other aspects of this so-called "alien" contact that are terribly unfortunate stem from both the stigma attached to the concept of "little green men" and the constant bombardment of movies depicting violent aliens bent on terror and destruction. It's as if there is a campaign to portray otherworldly beings as either a figment of our deluded minds or as terrifying monsters that only want to destroy us.

In the light of all the attempts by our galactic brothers and sisters to descend and walk amongst us in the interest of elevating our consciousness and up-stepping our evolution, which is evident in countless documented texts, we, as a supposedly advanced society, tend more toward a collective skepticism or innate fear of them rather than an attitude of gracious appreciation for their benevolent intervention. It is, however, due to books like the ones I have referenced throughout our adventure, that we can begin to accept the sacred knowledge they have shared for millennia as divine truth offered not only for our benefit on planet Earth but for the progressive evolution of the entire expanse of creation. These beings have advanced to a high level of spiritual attainment and as such, are aware of the plan for mortal ascension as well as the overall divine purpose of self-realization through experiential adventures in time and space. They are, therefore, eager to share this sacred knowledge to fulfill this purpose and to convey the spiritual essence, divine truth and ultimate beauty within the deeper meaning underlying this evolutionary adventure.

It's time for us all to "Rise Up!" and discover these truths for ourselves so we can ascend to a higher expression of ourselves and put this "secret" information to the highest use. It's time to turn the tides and rather than allowing the elite to keep using this powerful knowledge to control us by keeping us asleep in the dark, we take it and use it to empower the masses to connect into the divine source from which they came! This is what our 10-day ascension journey is all about — stepping into our divinity and igniting our dormant DNA so we can "Rise Up!" and be a powerful force for good that benefits all of humanity.

As I have said before, it would serve us well to set aside preconceived notions and ideas that are limiting and open our minds fully to the infinite possibilities and potentials of these newer and more progressive truths about the nature of our reality if we are to expand our consciousness and progress on our own path of self-realization. Of course, our own progress lends to the overall pursuit of "perfection attainment." We also have direct access to this knowledge within the "mind-field" if we can increase our band-width through concentrative contemplation. We know that it is possible through a dedicated meditation practice to connect with the fragment of God that is within us and with the spirit of truth being radiated upon us.

Now would be the perfect time to move on to our next destination. When we get there, we'll perform a powerful meditation to tune into our divine essence. Our next destination is the solar plexus of the Goddess Sedona and the masculine expression of her power. This is a male vortex. On our way there, let's talk about vortexes and the different types of energy they emanate. Some spiral downward and some spiral upward. The downward spiraling vortexes inspire you to go inward and contract. The downward/inward vortexes carry a feminine energy. The upward spiraling vortexes compel you to go outward and expand. The upward/outward vortexes carry a masculine energy. Interestingly, Boynton Canyon, where we just were with Kachina Woman and her Warrior, is said to have both female and male vortexes. Airport Mesa has a distinct male energy with vortexes spiraling upward and emotional energies going outward. The testosterone effect felt here can cause strong emotions to arise. Those with more masculine energy might actually feel more powerful or even feel a surge of rage. Those with more feminine energy might feel empowered and have the urge to be more assertive. I like to think of Boynton Canyon as the Temple of the Mother/Father God resonating with both attributes. It's a perfect temple for balancing your male and female energies. Airport Rock feels to me like the Temple of the Son and this is the perfect place for enhancing masculine energy. This Temple of the Son sends waves of empowerment across the entire matrix by igniting the ley lines and activating the solar plexus of all of humanity.

Gathered at the trailhead of Airport Rock, let's begin our climb up the spiraling path and then head off to the right so we can sit along the edge and look out. As we connect into the intelligent energy emanating from these red rocks, gauge how you are feeling. Close your eyes and project your consciousness into Airport Rock in Sedona. Call upon the energetic embodiment of this temple and tune into its vibration. Make a request for this red rock being to communicate with you and send you its spiraling energy. Imagine this energy moving up and down your spine as we spiral up the path toward the ledge. Now seated on the ledge with an incredible panoramic view, let's practice tuning into our rainbow body like a bridge connecting the earth to the sky.

Close your eyes and connect to the earth below and the cosmos above by getting "plugged in" as I like to call it. Some guides call this technique "running energy." Either way, once you are connected and can feel the energy flowing through your chakras, your mind and spirit will be illuminated with inner knowledge and divine wisdom.

Please sit comfortably with your spine straight, your palms resting on your knees either facing up or down and begin taking deep breaths in and out through your nostrils with your lips touching. Focus on the feeling of the breath as it enters your nostrils and flows back out. Start with five deep breaths in and out and then gradually merge into soft, natural breathing. Begin visualizing your root chakra spinning clockwise at the base of your spine. Take a deep breath in and as you exhale imagine sending energy downward through the center of this chakra penetrating the earth beneath you and traveling on a green spiraling band through the dirt, rock, and lava toward the fiery center of the core.

You now have a sacred connection with Mother Earth through this spiraling cord of energy.

Now pull the energy back up through this cord imagining it gaining strength as it draws the heat and intensity of the rock and lava and the power of the minerals right back into the base of your spine where it spins your root chakra — the red center of survival consciousness. From here, this spiraling cord separates into two energetic cords, one magnetic red and one electric blue, that braid your spine as they intertwine the ascending chakras. The next chakra that these energetic cords will spin is the orange wheel of desire. You can visualize clearing these chakras of unwanted debris by mentally scrubbing them with a tiny brush or imagining the debris flying off with the spinning of the disk. Once cleaned, you can imagine a bright light radiating out from the core which then illuminates the entire chakra as it expands.

Now imagine the intertwining cords ascending toward your yellow power center behind your belly button, or sacral center. Spin this yellow wheel far and wide illuminating it with the bright light of pure consciousness. As you spin each chakra, experience the essence of the consciousness within it. Experience the primitive mode of survival, the yearning of desire, and the strength of empowerment. As each chakra is activated, you can feel your vertebrae tingling with electrical energy. Now the blue cord braids your spine ascending toward the most beautiful chakra of all — the green Ray of unconditional love.

As you spin the chakra, imagine a pure love for all living beings that transcends all negativity and embraces forgiveness and compassion. Allow this overwhelming love to bathe your entire being and smile at the joy it brings. The kundalini energy now ascends toward the base of your throat where it will activate your pale blue communication chakra. This energy center represents communication with your own inner wisdom as well as with the rest of humanity and all divine beings. Illuminate this wheel allowing it to spin far and wide like a vast blue sky blanketing the earth. Feel the tingling of the energy within the magnetic and electric cords intensifying as it ascends toward your indigo blue chakra of inner wisdom. Spinning this chakra fills your entire head with electricity that stimulates the right and left hemispheres of your brain and triggers the appearance of your third eye. Starting with a pinpoint of light and then forming an oval shaped eye around it, the image of your third eye will emerge and with it you can see the inside of your head as if it was mirrored by this special insight. Imagine seeing your electric blue right brain light up and all your synapses firing and then picture your magnetic red left brain lighting up and firing. Toward the back of your head between these hemispheres, see your pineal gland shimmering in the shape of a pinecone.

This is the sacred center of your head where the divine spark of God resides. Imagine it illuminating as the God within you shines brightly. This is your unique connection to God and a personal bestowal of the creator himself. Behind this sacred light you will see your indigo blue chakra spinning wildly and expanding outward in all directions. As you observe this you become aware of the two electric blue cords emerging from the wisdom chakra and ascending toward the crown of your head and as it does you can see the vivid illumination of a violet wheel beginning to form at the very tip of your crown. Imagine it spinning and expanding far beyond your being opening a portal to divine consciousness which reaches high up into the heavens.

You are now connected to divine wisdom and sacred knowledge. At the same time, your soul is filled with the pure love of the Universal Father, the Eternal Child and the Infinite Spirit. You also feel the presence of other divine beings — maybe you feel a connection with the Creator Son, the Creative Spirit, Angel Gabriel, Michael or Rafael, Ascended Masters like St. Germain or maybe Buddha Shakyamuni, Avolakiteshvara, Manjushri and Vajrapani. This is your visualization and it is up to you who you allow in. They are all willing to bless you with their presence providing you allow them in by honoring them. Let's just sit in this state of divine connection and deep inner peace for a while listening to our hearts and minds. After a while, let's open our eyes and draw our palms toward our heart in a prayer position thanking the divine beings who have made their presence known to us and who have filled us with love and wisdom. Now let's open our eyes and breathe in the remarkable scene. Red rocks scattered across the landscape like living temples ignited with divine energy. Imagine the ley lines crisscrossing beneath them with the temples placed on intersecting points. Each temple is like a god or goddesses acting as a portal between the Earth and the Cosmos "running energy" just like we did.

Now let's move onto our next destination which is the feminine force of supernatural Sedona — Cathedral Rock. This is the heart center of the Goddess Sedona. Project your consciousness into this Temple of the Goddess who represents the feminine creative principal in creation. Feel the nurturing energy of love and compassion and the heart-centered desire to create. This feminine vortex is spiraling downward allowing you to go inward. Make a request to tune into the heart of Cathedral Rock and feel your heart space expand. Now move into your heart space and let the love flow through you. Imagine being enveloped by pure, unconditional love that has the power to transmute any shadows into pure white light. Feel your whole being moving into a higher vibration as lower energies dissolve and you are completely filled with the light of love. Now make a sincere intention to send this powerful force of love-light energy into the hearts of all living beings. Imagine this love-light expanding until you see it spiraling around the entire planet. Send love into the hearts of every living being in all of creation. In this one special moment, a powerful surge expands the heart of creation and love flows through every living being. This colossal Temple of the Goddess has the power to transmute shadows into light and to raise the vibration of all of humanity. She send waves of love across the rippling matrix through the ley lines which activates the heart chakra of Mother Earth.

9.5

Hiking in to the base of Cathedral Rock, let's continue our quest for a greater realization of cosmic truth. As we hike toward the Goddess Temple, let's revisit our discussion regarding the nature of the center of Paradise and its connection to the galactic centers of the universe. Let's invite the celestial beings who channeled their knowledge to the human race through their teachings in *The Urantia Book*, "Initiation" and the "Law of One" books, so that we can talk openly and without reservation about the revelations they shared. This will benefit the "progressive thought realization" we are seeking.

Let's imagine Paradise at the core of creation as the headquarters of the universes, the center from which love, spirit and mind energy emanate, and the source of all cosmic gravity and force. Now let's imagine that this pattern of Paradise is radiated onto the center of all galaxies as duplications emerge across the vast expanse of the grand universe. These patterns become activated at the supermassive black hole center of each galaxy as the super universe headquarters. They subsequently become activated at the local universe, constellation and system levels as well. These headquarters are the portals through which the gravity circuits of the Mother-Father, Eternal Child and Infinite Spirit flow, through which all cosmic force is transmitted and where all administrative, judicial and organizational activity takes place. These centers also serve another very important function. They are the sacred portals through which mortal and divine beings descend and ascend on their journey to and from the Paradise Core, back down into a physical incarnation and to places in between for spiritual training. Now let's merge this spiritual perspective with a more scientific and astronomical one. It is general knowledge that black holes consume stars which whirl around it at incredible speeds until they are sucked in and presumably devoured. Morgan Freeman referred to them as "cosmic cannibals" but I would like to imagine them as "cosmic sanctuaries" where the stars represent the divine sparks of souls who are ascending.

Remember a few adventures ago when we made the connection that each star may represent an individual soul. We realized that the Platonic solids, from which all consciousness emerges, combine to form a crystallized "star" tetrahedron. We also realized that all of the elements are represented by these Platonic solids and that the lighter and heavier elements that materialize as forms in our reality emerge from within the stars as well. If we imagine that each star represents a being of consciousness which then materializes as a holographic image upon the planet, we can imagine that we retain this connection with the origin of our soul. Our own individual star may represent the residence of our higher self while only a portion of it is projected into the material being we express here on earth. From this perspective, we can visualize that when we drop our physical being, our soul reunites with the greater part of its self which then ascends into the higher realms of the headquarters worlds. Once there, we are greeted by divine beings and other souls who have migrated there as well. We may even be greeted by the essence of God, the son and spirit. So instead of imagining black holes as the death place of stars, we can picture them as sacred doorways into the divine realm.

This revelation invites contemplation upon the nature of supernova's which occur when a star collapses upon itself and then explodes. Science has revealed that black holes emerge from the remnants of a collapsing star. Supernovas are rare and only happen once or twice a century. They may represent the emergence of a new local universe, constellation or system headquarters. Our universe is said to be young and still developing. On an earlier adventure, we were talking about the emergence of our universe and recognized the fact that the development of the headquarters worlds was the first order of business. If we follow this train of thought, we conclude that a black hole would first have to be created. The death of a star would precipitate that emergence. The stars that give their lives for this special purpose may then become a divine being on the new headquarters worlds. The birth place of stars is said to take place within large nebulae. Our universe formed within a massive nebula but the essence of its personality and all the souls that would inhabit it thereafter must have originated from the Paradise center. On that note, let's move on to the Paradise center of the Goddess Sedona spiraling into her crown chakra. Our final destination is the Grandfather vortex of the entire planet! It is commonly known as Bell Rock but I like to call it Crown Rock not just because it is the crown chakra but it looks just like a crown. This is the Temple of God, the masculine divine principal in creation.

9.6

Close your eyes and tune into your own crown chakra, spinning and opening it to receive the spiraling energy from this extremely powerful vortex. The male vortex here spirals upward inspiring you to expand your energy outward. This is an ideal temple for expanding your consciousness and tuning into the greater cosmos. Crown Rock looks like it is on fire with its fiery red rocks shooting up like flames reaching for the heavens. Project your consciousness into this temple and make a request to tune into it. Instantly you will feel the kundalini energy that we ignited at Boynton Canyon, empowered at Airport Rock and activated at Cathedral Rock, shooting out through the top of your crown! We lit the fiery serpent and then empowered and activated it. Now it has shot up to your crown and exploded through it. Like Crown Rock, flames are shooting out of your crown reaching for the cosmos! You have now ignited your fiery connection to the greater cosmos and sent red hot flames of passion and purpose out into the universe. With the ignition of your divine purpose, your fiery passion will fuel the flames of all you wish to create and manifest. The full activation of your fiery kundalini extends into the earth as well as the skies above. This gives you the ability to bring into the earth plane that which you envision in the ether. You activate a trinity of triple-empowered co-creation when your fiery kundalini blazes in the heart of Mother Earth, ignites your energy centers and extends into the heart of the cosmos.

Sedona is sometimes called the Crystal City because what lies beneath the surface of the red rock layer is pure quartz crystal. The iron ore of the red rocks radiates with magnetism while the crystalline matrix within sparkles with electrical energy. Together, they create swirling vortexes of electromagnetism that energize, elevate and expand the fields of consciousness within and around them. This high frequency field of vibrating energy activates the chakras of Mother Earth and all of her children on the surface. Those who visit the red rock temples of Sedona experience the energetic effects in different ways. Depending on how sensitive they are, and how much they intentionally tune in, they may access a wide range of emotional, mental, physical and spiritual experiences. The temples we have visited today can also act as portals for interdimensional communication and travel. This may open communication with beings in other dimensions. My good friend, Tom Dongo, has spent the last 30 years going out on the land here witnessing and recording paranormal activity. He has written books on the mysteries of Sedona that can be purchased on Amazon. Watch my interview with him at SciSpi.tv/Rise-Up/. During the interview, I share many pictures of paranormal activity taking place right here in Sedona. He has one of the world's largest collections of paranormal photographs.

I would like to share a quote from his book called *The Quest*:

"The red rocks are red because they are made up largely of iron-oxide — rust. The iron in the rocks is much of the reason for the magnetic quality found here. The iron oxide (or other iron rich deposits in deeper levels must be playing a major role in Sedona's paranormal mysteries."[7]

Later in the book, he quotes an article from the Sedona Journal of Emergence written by John Keel:

"Basalt layers under the red rocks, vortex extrusion points and electromagnetic energy are only a superficial part of it, in my opinion. I think it all goes far deeper than simplistic concepts such as electromagnetic energy. There is something else here that emanates from far deeper levels. Could it be psychic remnants from a Lemurian City, an Atlantean city or perhaps a portal or some sort of phasing point where dimensions intersect?"[8]

My dear friend, author and Shaman, Devara Thunderbeat, has had many paranormal experiences in Sedona and has written a book called, Look Up! In this book she describes seeing many different types of other-worldly beings by traveling interdimensionally in the red rocks. She has also seen many crafts in the sky from disks to pillars to ships veiled in clouds. She is featured in an episode of my series, "Supernatural Adventures" where she describes an interdimensional experience she had in Long canyon. It is in the clip called "Contact in Sedona" at SciSpi.tv/Supernatural-Adventures-Channel/.

My dear friend, author and Priestess Journey Guide, Nancy Safford, moved here over 25 years ago and right away started tuning into the inner temples of the red rocks. In her book, A Magdalene Awakens, she describes a practice her guide taught her that enabled her to actually see interdimensionally. He instructed her to just point two fingers on her right hand to the spot on the rocks that she wanted to penetrate. She was stunned by what she saw:

"I did the exercise he demonstrated, whereby my two fingers quickly gave me access inside themystical butte, where my inner vision saw details of a well formed crystal room, perhaps a temple, with a circular staircase of soft purple amethyst hugging the side walls. It rose up from the bottom allowing a person to walk along the periphery of the inside temple here." [9]

In my interview with her, she explains in much greater detail the many extraordinary encounters she has had since then, not just in Sedona, but at sacred sites all over the world. The profound transformational effect of her initiation in Sedona inspired her to dedicate the rest of her life to spiritual exploration, expansion and guidance. Watch the interview with Nancy Safford at SciSpi.tv/Rise-Up/.

The Hopi Indian tribes who live north of Sedona in Wupatki, share their legend that Sedona was built by the star people as a temple city for ritual, ceremony and worship. They don't believe that it's meant to be lived in, just visited for spiritual purposes. Before he passed, Hopi tribal elder, Grandfather Monagye used to come here with other members of the tribe to visit and honor the Hopi prophecy rock that laid alongside Oak Creek on the creek bed. They would perform rituals and engage in ceremonial practices that would bless and protect the engraved rock. You can watch my interview with one of his successors, Hopi wisdom keeper, Ruben Saufkie, at SciSpi.tv/Rise-Up/. During my interview, he explained that the drawings on the rock represented the prophecies it held for humanity.

The Yavapai Indians who came here long ago believe that Montezuma's Well nearby is their Garden of Eden. In "Unveiled Mysteries", St. Germain explains that Eden or E-Don means "Energy Divine." In the Verde Valley that surrounds Sedona, there is a deep, massive and bottomless well that opens into the inner earth below.

9.7

On the high walls that surround the well, there are dwellings carved into the limestone. At the lower levels closer to the edge of the well, there are dwellings that have been dug deep into the earth with chambers and pathways extending into dark recesses. The Yavapai creation myth tells a story about how their ancestors were trapped in the inner earth during a great flood. When the water began seeping into their inner earth homes, they feared they would all drown and that would be the end of their race. So they sent up a young girl in a hollowed out log in the hopes she would float to the surface. When the log emerged from the inner earth, it popped up from inside the well. The young girl, Kamalapukwia, floated to dry land and then hiked to the top of Mingus Mountain. Here she was impregnated by the Sun God. She bore a daughter who, when she came of age, also climbed up Mingus Mountain to mate with the Sun God. The daughter bore a son, Sakaracamanche, and then later she was taken up by an eagle. This left just the Grandmother, Kamalapukwia, and her grandson, Sakaracamanche, to become the progenitors of the Yavapai race. Montezuma Well thus became their Garden of E-Don with the Divine Energy to perpetuate life. Watch the clip called "Place of Emergence" at SciSpi.tv/Supernatural-Adventures-Channel/. In it, I go to Montezuma's Well with Tom Dongo and we retell the whole story while exploring the site. Watch the interview at SciSpi.tv/Rise-Up/.

My friends, Standswithbear and Lightstar, both have developed a wide range of spiritual gifts, since they came to Sedona, by tuning into the multidimensional realms. Standswithbear has the ability to heal, transmute and transform energy. Lightstar has the ability to tune into star beings for psychic downloads as well as heal and transmute. They both have the ability to speak in many different star and light languages. In Lightstar's interview, she activates all seven energy centers by speaking in seven different star languages. You will find fascinating interviews with both of them at SciSpi.tv/Rise-Up/.

My good friend, author and Akashic Oracle, Amanda Romania, has lived in Sedona for many years and offers readings at her center called "Atlantis". In her book, Akashic Cosmic Connection", she tunes into different star races from various dimensions and galaxies who offer insight into their realms. I interviewed Amanda at her original gallery in Sedona called "Atlantis" and you will enjoy our intriguing discussion seated amongst the many galactic art and fine crystals she had displayed there. Watch my interview with Amanda Romania at SciSpi.tv/Rise-Up/.

I would like to share this inspirational meditation in the chapter from Amanda's book that she dedicated to the star beings from Almach:

"Oh, divine friends and guides of my mastery, let there be a glow activated around my crown chakra, and may the teachings of the masters be instantly downloaded into my heart. May this heart energy then begin to swim in ecstasy with the oceans of my soul. May I lift in consciousness and again know the masters who walked the earth plane as my family and peers. I belong to no one, and I am connected to everything. The sacred temples upon heaven and Earth are my sanctuary and connect to the temple of my soul. Let me see the vision of who I truly can be and with whom I can truly connect. Let me see the visions of the heavenly masters, as they have transcended and reside within the astral plane. Yours is energy, where I can truly see the grace and new assignments of those who once walked the Earth as men and women and now walk as immortals, sending messages of peace and harmony to my soul." [10]

My dear friend, author and trans-audio medium, Genii Townsend, has lived here for decades. She was called to move here because her late husband, Bill Townsend, received messages from higher dimensional beings that the first "City of Light" would appear here. To activate the new Golden Age on planet Earth, he was told, 13 Cities of Light would appear consecutively at sacred sites around the earth's grid. When he passed on, Genii was handed the torch by these higher beings who started communicating with her. As a trans-audio medium, Genii is taken into these cities where she can see and experience them. She describes them as brilliant cities made of crystal and precious gems with many buildings and centers each serving a special purpose.

They are dedicated to healing, enlightenment and empowerment. You can read her remarkable book, "Something's Coming! Universal Cities of Light, Love and Healing!" Watch my interview with Genii Townsend at SciSpi.tv/Rise-Up/.

Here is a beautiful passage from her book that was transmitted to her from a City of Light Ambassador named Zen Zuriah:

"The reason why we exist right now is because you are making that choice right now and have been for several decades. You have chosen to go on and to anchor new realities and new dimensional realities within the 3rd dimension so the third can be an expanded experience...Is that vitally important? Yes. Because it is the unfoldment of a very large universal plan. It is going beyond the universe to the multiverse and coming back to the omniverse. And that is where you are now...Terra Gaia was always meant to be an interdimensional portal of love where beings from everywhere could have this experience of what it felt like, in all kinds of forms, to live in a community of love. There is nothing more important."[11]

This is such a perfect message for the closing of our Sedona red rock journey. It leads right into the remarkable visions that I began downloading within a week of moving here. I was compelled to sit on the back deck every morning directly in line with the sun. I knew that it was a portal through which messages from the divine could penetrate my third eye. As soon as I would go into trance meditation, visions would start to unfold. Over the course of about six weeks, I was shown an entire complex on a large acreage that would serve as a unity community of love and light. There were several structures that were dedicated to healing, enlightenment and empowerment. I was shown a large community center where everyone would gather for communal practices, dining and rejoicing. Over time, it became clear to me that I was being called to build this unity community on an acreage nearby. Synchronistic events unfolded as I followed the energy that led me to the location and revealed the name "Spirit Ranch." It was to be sponsored by the nonprofit I am president of called "Awakening" and I have since worked with a nonprofit specialist to develop a comprehensive business plan. We will hold events, workshops and retreats on the property and there will be several residential units. As of March 2018, we are seeking investors as well as offering time share and partnership opportunities.

The divine synchronicity with the revelations Genii has received about the City of Light in Sedona is astounding even to the point about beings "in all kinds of forms." I have also envisioned that this secluded oasis I have chosen for Spirit Ranch would be ideal for other-worldly guests to visit. This will be a place for all of our brothers and sisters in any and all realms who have a loving intention to be a part of our expanded community and to walk amongst us as family, friends and guides. It's all about creating a universal community where love, peace and unity prevail!

I am a leader in the shift into unity consciousness and to create this "heaven on earth" is my divine purpose and spiritual calling. I am doing this through my books, shows and events as well as by developing a unity community. Since I have come to Sedona, there are an inspired group of us who are hosting events, gatherings and retreats in order to start assembling the leaders, teachers and healers that together are heralding in the new Golden Age of Unity Consciousness. We invite one and all to join us!

You may already be doing this in your community, but I encourage everyone in cities and towns far and wide to embrace and support unity consciousness in your own unique way! We are pioneers forging this path leading us into the light of a new age. For this Golden Age of Empowerment, it is up to us to co-create it and I believe, "Together, we can!" The divine beings, the shiny ones, are always there to guide us and give us support and encouragement. However, this is our Golden Age to create for ourselves so we can become the gods and goddesses of this age. This is our golden opportunity to become empowered as divine creator beings creating paradise on this beloved planet we call home.

To celebrate our divinity and co-create unity, let's engage in a Unity Consciousness Activation. Let's send powerful waves of unity consciousness across the rippling matrix. Together we can spread the love and ignite the light not just here but throughout the entire cosmos!

Unity Consciousness Activation
A Heart Expansion Practice
(Audio version available at: www.SuzanneRossTranscendence.com)

To increase our sense of oneness with all living things and beings and to enhance global unity on the planet, together we will activate the unity consciousness grid within and without. We will activate a sense of oneness within our own being by connecting into our wholeness as three in one and one in three. We will integrate our body, mind and spirit and recognize ourselves as love, light and form expressing as the father, mother and child in action. Then we will radiate the sense of oneness outward and see the living light of love in all forms that surround us. Experiencing this oneness within ourselves and extending that outward to all others, we begin to activate the unity consciousness grid in our own local sphere of influence. Then we can imagine a sense of oneness with Mother Earth and all the living things and beings within her and upon her. In this way we can begin to activate the unity consciousness grid that surrounds the entire planet igniting the divine spark within all living things and beings and bringing the entire grid online as one enlightened consciousness.

Let's begin by sitting in a comfortable posture with our spine in an upright position. Extend a stream of love and light into the heart of Mother Earth beneath you and thank her for being such a powerful foundation for your human experience to unfold. Activating her heart with your love and light, you become one with her. As you pull that stream of love-light consciousness up from the heart of Mother Earth back into the base of your spine, imagine activating the hearts of all the living things and beings within Mother Earth. For she is a living and loving being and all the minerals, crystals, water, dirt, rocks and plants within her and upon her are all part of her body. They are like the cells of her being and so imagine igniting a Golden flame within each of these cells, within all the molecules of all the living things and beings. Activating all the cells of our sweet dear mother by igniting all her sparks enhances the radiant love and light that she projects outward to all of her children.

As we move up through your physical being, let's spin and activate your chakras along the way so that there are no shadows or blockages along this powerful line of energy. First ignite your bright red root chakra and then spin it throwing off any shadows and turning on the light in the center. Spin off any doubts around your survival and imagine a bright shiny disc spinning and flashing its bright red light activating your kundalini energy. Extend that bright red spiraling light up into your sacral chakra and spin this orange wheel faster and faster throwing off any shadows that may be blocking your creativity and then ignite the flame in the center. Visualize this glowing orange disk shining brightly. Now imagine a bright orange energy spiraling up to your solar plexus. Spin this bright yellow wheel and throw off any doubts that may be limiting your power. Ignite the yellow flame in the center and become fully empowered as this bright yellow disc spins faster. Now imagine a bright yellow light spiraling up your spine toward your heart center. Spin this emerald green disc throwing off any lower energies that do not align with pure love. Ignite the emerald flame in the center and spin this bright green disc faster. Now imagine that emerald green light spiraling upwards toward your throat and spin this sky-blue disc. Throw off any energy that's limiting your ability to communicate clearly. Ignite the blue flame in the center and let your voice be heard. Say out loud, "I am light. I am love. I am power." Now imagine this sky-blue light spiraling up toward your third eye spinning this indigo blue disc. Focus on your third eye and see a bright indigo blue pupil looking back at you. You are now connected to the eternal wisdom stored in your akashic records. Now imagine that indigo blue energy spiraling up toward your crown. Spin your violet crown chakra and throw off any shadows that are blocking your clear channel to the divine source. Imagine this violet disc spinning as you ignite the violet flame transmuting any shadows into light. Now picture a golden star 8 inches above your head and seat your consciousness within it.

From the vantage point of your soul star, you can look down and see your rainbow body fully illuminated extending into the heart of Mother Earth. You are whole within your being as your rainbow body merging all your chakras into one colorful stream of consciousness. You are one with Mother Earth resonating with the illuminated cells of all the living things and beings within her and upon her.

Now let's ignite the golden flame within all the cells of all living things and beings that surround you. Imagine your friends and family and ignite every cell of their beings with the golden flame of love and light. Now imagine the birds in the sky and the animals on the land and the fish and the mammals in the water and ignite each one of their cells with the golden flame of love and light. Now imagine the entire planet consumed with the violet flame and watch as it transmutes all shadows and darkness into pure love and light. As the entire planet is transformed into a golden ball of love and light, imagine a spherical grid embracing it. This is the unity consciousness grid and as the golden love and light emanate from Mother Earth and all her children, each point on this grid is activated and ignited with the golden flame. There is a point on the grid for each and every living being and thing on the planet. As every cell of these beings is ignited with the Golden flame, each point on the grid is activated.

Now watch as the entire unity consciousness grid lights up and shimmers in gold and white light. As it does imagine that each living thing and being is also shimmering in golden white light. Imagine all living things and beings feeling a greater sense of oneness within themselves and towards all others. Imagine all the people on the planet seeing the divine light within all their brothers and sisters and feeling a greater sense of love and empathy toward them. Imagine love, compassion, empathy and kindness spreading across the globe. As unity consciousness spreads, a greater sense of harmony settles onto the planet and the children rejoice and sing praise to the light.

Everyone is bathed in the golden light of pure love and harmony and joy prevail as global unity defines the new reality and planetary peace is the new way. This is the new Golden Age of Enlightenment and the more we intentionally ignite the golden flame within ourselves and all others, the more we increase the harmonics of unity, peace and joy. The more we enhance the love, compassion, empathy and kindness toward ourselves and all others, the more we create this higher dimensional frequency and the more we project our consciousness into a 5D way of living and being. Let's create heaven on earth, my friends, and always remember the fundamental truth: "As above, so below and as within, so without." May everything shine with the golden love and light of the Infinite Source for we are all of and from the same divine source. We are one. And so be it. And so it is. Amen.

Your Personal Revelations

_____

_____

_____

_____

_____

_____

_____

_____

_____

_____

_____

_____

_____

_____

_____

_____

REFERENCES

Chapter cover image courtesy of www.pixabay.com
Illustrations:
1. Taken from the History Channel T.V. Series Ancient Aliens
2-6. www.pixabay.com
7. Personal photo
The Urantia Book Fellowship, The Urantia Book, Uversa Press, 2008
1. (14:1.7)
2. (11:7.9)
3. (11:8.3)
4. (11:1.4)
5. (11:8.1)
6. (11:9.8)
Tom Dongo, The Quest, Hummingbird Publishing, 1993
7. p. 7
8. p. 95-6
Nancy Safford, A Magdalene Awakens, Wisdom Revealed, 2017
9. p. 29
Amanda Romania, Akashic Cosmic Connection, Balboa Press, 2015
10. p. 94-5
Genii Townsend, Something's Coming!, Center Space, 2013
1. p. 424

Day Ten

Divine Origins of
Intelligent Energy

What a glorious sunrise we have awoken to on this last day of our amazing adventure! The sun, a blazing orb of golden light peaking over the horizon, and the wild streaks of violet vapor cutting through the morning sky, are like a divine symphony of sacred energy! As the sun continues to rise, we see the whole horizon explode in bright orange splashes of brilliant light! Let's watch as the mountains turn from a deep shade of purple into a soft pink glow. We have manifested this incredible gift by showing our adoration for the Creator and by admiring his incredible artistry. Listen as his creation comes alive with the joyful sounds of birds whistling and the insects chirping. We can feel the soft breeze caress our shoulders as the wind spirits float by. Suddenly we become deeply aware of a strong connection to nature as our senses awaken to every sight, touch and sound.

Just imagine everything — the sun, the grass, the trees and birds — vibrating in rhythmic waves of colorful light. Standing in the direct line of the sun, picture it bathing you in a soft golden glow that transforms your dense mass into shimmering waves of light. As a being of light, your vibrating waves fall into harmony with the rhythmic pulsations of everything around you. It's like you're standing in a beautiful watercolor that has come to life and all the colors are dancing and merging. The sound and light waves flow into each other and it all becomes one glorious harmony, one lovely song in motion, one living verse in unity — a uni-verse, if you will…aw, yes, a universe. One verse, that's all, one lovely symphonic, synchronized verse.

10.1

With this deep appreciation for the oneness of all energy and a heightened awareness of the vibrational dance, we can open to the vast field of consciousness embracing it. Within this field, the eternal journey of self-realization unfolds in the endless creation and evolution of energetic beings all vibrating with love and light. All things and beings are alive with this energy ever-expanding and always transforming. The Creator realizes its unlimited potential with every expression of form that reveals another aspect of its true self. This creative adventure is extraordinarily fascinating and incredibly exciting on so many levels all at once! Love is the secret behind all the mysteries of creation for it is divine "energy in motion" — e-motion! The mechanism for this eternal expression of e-motion is the gravity grasp embracing all beings. We can visualize the whole of creation as a theatrical performance that started as an imaginative idea and then blossomed into an endlessly expanding circle of incredibly diverse experiences. Let's gather around and engage in a "thought experiment" inspired by our adventure thus far. Please open to this virtual imagery that will be the basis for our final journey into the Creator-consciousness.

Picture, with me, dancing strings of vibrating light that are the spiritual essence within all forms of energy and matter. These strings are so miniscule that it takes 100 to fill a single electron and their light is pure potential — eternal and changeless in one sense but in a constant state of transformation in another. The essential nature and behavior of each tiny string determines the form that it will take and in what dimension it will activate. This is intelligent energy and it is the basis for our illusory reality. These tiny waves are thought forms in action and they can be configured to duplicate a pattern or illuminated to produce a reflection. In their most primal form as pure potential, this dancing light is responsive only to the free will of the Creator.

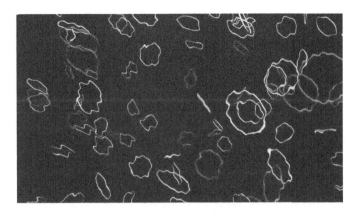

10.2

This light is the Creator-consciousness in action and as it expands outward through the Trinity of beings, it manifests Paradise — the core of infinite potential. From here, the excitation of these vibrating strings falls under the direction of the Infinite Spirit in response to the will of the Divine Mother, Divine Father and Creative Child. The Divine Mother-Father God of creation remains the sole creator of pattern personalities while endowing all creative beings with free will. The free will beings are given the artistic license to transform energy into form within the construct of these original patterns. The first universal manifestation is an eternal realm of perfection and it becomes the pattern for all evolutionary universes created thereafter.

Gravity is the key to controlling the tiny strings of consciousness and keeping them within the gravity grasp of the Creator. However, they are also responsive to other forms of energetic influence. They are highly receptive to the power of thought for they are thoughts in action. Once activated, they become subject to the directed will of intelligent spirit beings and thus, thoughts become form. This conscious manifestation gives rise to created beings and evolutionary processes within the free will of all beings.

If we can imagine tiny vibrating strings responding to the energetic influence of physical and spiritual forces in a unified symphony, the natural progression of thought leads us to wonder who the conductor is. Beyond that we wonder, "Who are the performers producing these harmonic vibrations of light and sound?" My insatiable curiosity produces a strong desire to know not just who but how! What are the mechanisms through which these performers produce such a perfectly synchronized universe of rotating spheres, starry heavens and blazing orbs of light? As we get further away from center stage, we can see that the original tune resonates throughout the eternal expanse of creation producing a reverberating wave effect. It seems as if the resonant wave goes out, bounces off some kind of boundary and returns to the source.

Let's imagine that these waves of light and sound carry information which travels out from the source and then returns to it with all the data it gathered along the way. Maybe this is the field of light we are traveling on as we ride the outgoing wave which takes us to the farthest reaches of time and space and then, once we reach a certain destination, or level of awareness, we "catch the wave" and start riding it back to the source.

10.3

To transcendent beings, not limited by time and space, this wavy field of resonant energy is filled with information and intelligence. It seems to be wholly accessible and impervious to the linear past, present and future timelines that our awareness binds us to. It seems as if it is only when we are trapped in the physical "beingness" of our material realm and encased in the density of our form, that we experience a linear observation of reality. Once freed from that realm when we shed our physical form, we once again attain omniscience — access to the infinite field of intelligence, or divine consciousness, if you will. Esoteric thought and spiritual philosophy has led to the higher awareness of a "gateway to intelligent infinity."

Realizing that the key to this gate must be hidden within a certain vibrational field, it stands to reason that we simply harmonize with that field when we pass out of the lower resonance of mass and enter into the higher resonance of energy. This harmonious resonance unlocks the door and we can float above the material realm in a higher dimension previously inaccessible to us. There are many reports of omniscience and omnipresence shared by those who have had near death experiences. What we can learn from these is that they traveled to dimensions beyond the time and space restrictions of our physical reality. In these higher dimensions, they become aware of two realities, the one wherein they can view the events on Earth from above and the other where they observe a paradisiacal world and communicate with other spirit beings.

Another example of tapping into a field of information beyond the events taking place here and now, is the residual past life experiences reported by young children whose veil is still thin. Before fully attaching to their ego identity, many young children seem to retain a connection to other dimensions. In these realms, they clearly recall past life experiences and even communicate with spirit beings who are actively reaching out to them. They are peeking into the field of infinite intelligence where spirit phenomena take place. Understandably this field is multidimensional, but the possibility of entering this omniscient state of being reveals a state of awareness beyond our present consciousness that we may have access to. For it is in this field of higher consciousness, that intelligent infinity operates and exerts its multidimensional influence.

Throughout millennia, psychics, healers and prophets have proven their ability to access this field and even operate within it. Discovering the nature of it and the forces that work within it will be the goal of today's adventure. A greater understanding of these realms will reveal the unlimited potential hidden within our own experience of reality. As spirit beings of light, we are fully capable of tapping into intelligent infinity. The keys to these gateways are within our reach and there are just three simple requirements:

1. Faith — "To see it, you have to believe it"
2. Wisdom — Seeking it and tuning into it
3. Love — An open heart and pure intention

Let's make sure to carry these three powerful virtues of faith, wisdom and love in our backpack today as we head out in search of our destination — the field of intelligent infinity. What does this look like in our physical realm? Knowing that this reality is simply a perception of one field, or dimension, of consciousness, we can use our imaginations to create and perceive another field where Paradise becomes our new reality. To enter this higher dimension of consciousness on our journey today, it only makes sense for us to ascend to a higher realm of existence. To honor the Ascended Master, Saint Germain, who has so generously shared his remarkable teachings about the light and our potential to thrive within it, let's take a virtual journey back to Mount Shasta, California. It is here that Godfre Ray King encountered the great master in 1930 and was taken on an incredible adventure which transcended time and traversed dimensions.

In the distance, beyond the shimmering lake, we can see the towering majesty of the sacred snowcapped peak of Mt. Shasta. There is a soft mist hovering over Lake Shasta which gives it a spiritual essence. It's as if the soul of the lake is resting on its surface. I imagine that, in these early morning hours, the spirit of the lake has arisen to greet the sunrise and offer its prayers of love and gratitude before settling back in to embrace the day. This tremendous expanse of shimmering water is blessed by the most magnificent rock rising up out of its womb.

10.4

Glistening in the sunrise, these pink peaks look like flames shooting up from the lake and licking the sky. In the background, Mt. Shasta gives off a deep purple glow still enshrouded by the early dawn and not yet illuminated by the sun. What an inspiring landscape the divine artisans have painted for us on this blessed day.

Let's turn our attention now toward our destination and visualize the glory of Mt. Shasta through the eyes of Godfre Ray King as he experienced it over 80 years ago. In his first chapter, entitled "Meeting the Master", on page 1, he shares an eloquent description of this magical place,

"Mt. Shasta stood out boldly against the western sky, surrounded at its base by a growth of pine and fir trees that made it look like the jewel of diamond-shining whiteness held in a filigree setting of green. The snow-covered peaks glistened and changed color from moment to moment as the shadows lengthened in the suns dissent toward the horizon."[1]

This place has a special meaning for me as well. I was born in Shasta County and just recently revisited my birthplace for the first time. My husband and I rented a home on the lake which was adorned by a large deck. The view from this deck inspired my earlier description of the rosy peaks emerging from the morning mist. We pulled our boat along with us, so we could spend our days enjoying the lake and exploring the shoreline. There was an overwhelming sense of peace and serenity in these blessed waters at the base of the sacred mountain.

From the moment we arrived, I was aware of a divine presence and felt energetically drawn to the mountain peak in the distance. I knew it was a natural temple, of sorts, and that its eminence was the source of the harmonious resonance that rang throughout the village and from within its shimmering lake. Its towering magnificence inspires a sense of awe and wonder in all who are blessed to absorb its quiescence. There is a glorious stillness one feels when admiring this gentle giant. There is a sense that she has tremendous power in her core but graciously contains it within the stillness of her glorious beauty and quiet grace. As we toured the area, you would see people pointing and staring as they stood there admiring her grandiose glory from afar. Some are acutely aware of the radiance she emanates in powerful waves of divine blessings. Others just know she makes them feel more alive as she awakens an inner knowing about the omnipresence of divine blessings. All who are blessed to stand in her presence are transformed by the experience. Her grace and glory reawakens their profound connection to the heart center of Mother Earth herself.

The moment I first encountered her majesty as an adult, I became acutely aware that she was a powerful goddess who emanated a vast field of divine consciousness. During my entire visit, I felt elated and my senses were heightened to the point where every sound in nature was crisp and every sight shimmered in vivid colors. My husband and I were both deeply affected by the incredible beauty and serenity of Lake Shasta. The water sparkled as the sunlight bounced off of its reflective surface. The bright blue sky mirrored its reflection on the great shimmering expanse. We could see right through the transparence of the pure clean water and watch schools of fish swim past some darting this way and that. We became aware of a whole other world just beneath the surface where a harmonious flow of biological life seemed to coexist peacefully.

Even in the village surrounding Lake Shasta, we were aware of a harmonious feeling. The presence of love and an appreciation for life was palpable. We experienced it as an attraction toward others and sensed that the tourists and residents alike felt it too, since everyone we encountered were extraordinarily friendly, generous and considerate. Everyone we passed on the water waved excitedly and we returned the gesture. There was a sense of community like we were all sharing a very special experience of unity consciousness and wanted to celebrate it with exuberant joy and loving kindness. We also felt a more intimate connection to the trees and flowers that flourished here and to the wildlife who thrived in this natural landscape.

I am sure you have all experienced magical places just like this where the field of consciousness is elevated, and a sense of peace and communal love is shared by all. In these places, your senses are heightened, and you have a deeper appreciation for all of creation that extends beyond the beauty of the landscape. Places like these seem to have a spirit or essence which is divinely blessed. They seem to embrace a higher state of consciousness that affects all who enter it. At these times, you have a special opportunity to step into divine synchronicity and experience the magic of being "in sync" with all other living things and beings. Once you've experienced this divine state of being, the memory of its essence remains embedded in your soul and you can revive it at any time just by closing your eyes and revisiting the feeling. We can elevate our consciousness and bring peace and joy back into our awareness just by reviving the energetic essence of these magical memories. In this way, we are creating a consciousness experience that lifts our mind and spirit momentarily.

What if we could sustain this feeling and extend that awareness into our daily lives? All we would have to do is become acutely aware of the divine energy that surrounds us always. Knowing that the tiny vibrating strings that make up all living things and beings contains this divine essence, we can tune into that resonance and sync up with it anytime to create a magical experience. The more we see the essence and spirit of God in everyone and everything around us, the more we ourselves radiate that divine love and light. We can intentionally create a radiant field of divine consciousness anytime that will magically affect everyone around us and elevate the experience of all who encounter it. We can create a natural flow of divine synchronicity where people, places and things all fall into place perfectly with harmony and symmetry. It's all about tuning into the truth of our absolute unity in the vibrating field of total oneness. It starts by activating the divine spark within ourselves and then igniting it in others by extending love and appreciation for who they truly are as an expression of the divine source.

As an extension of the Creator-consciousness, we can create our experience of life in any way we choose. This divine endowment exists within all conscious beings throughout all of creation. Every single thought form emanating from the primal consciousness has an innate awareness of its ability to expand and express its creative essence. From a budding, blossoming rose bush to a joyful, curious child, this "Creator-consciousness" is the essence of being and it is expressed beautifully in the vast diversity of our creative manifestations. With intention, love and grace, we can expand our creator-consciousness by expressing ourselves in creative ways that inspire and empower others.

The power of attraction that I felt in the presence of Mt. Shasta comes from the same divine and creative source that drives the creation and evolution of all beings. The strong desire to create and evolve is governed by the law of attraction and inspired by the omnipresence of the divine source. All of that which affects our consciousness is of a divine origin and nature for we share the same creative desire and evolutionary impulse. For there is only one infinite field of consciousness and it is alive with intelligent energy. As evolutionary beings, we are riding on the fabric of time and space and it is the interweaving of these threads that gives us the experience of every creative moment. It is the "here and now" of our present awareness that creates our consciousness experience. Every time a thread of space intersects with a thread of time, a present moment is created.

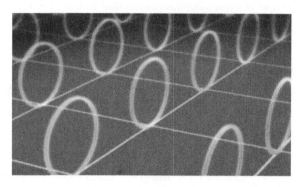

10.5

Our lives are made up of a series of moments strung together and interwoven into the fabric of consciousness that represents the accumulative past, the active present and the awaiting future. For transcendent beings who are not bound by time and space, this fabric can be viewed all at once in the eternal present. For us, we must experience it one moment at a time in a linear fashion always moving forward away from the past and toward the future. If we are in a constant state of running away from the past and into the future, we are allowing our consciousness to be trapped by time and space. However, when we bring our full awareness into the present moment, we free ourselves from these bonds and can glimpse the magic of the present moment just like the divine transcendent beings do. It is the recognition of the preciousness of each moment that reveals it magnificent glory. Once you become completely aware that each moment is a choice and that which you choose determines the quality of your experience now and forevermore, you become much more conscientious of every thought, word and action.

Having faith in the divine guidance you are being given in every moment helps you to make decisions that are most conducive to your well-being and that of others. This guidance comes from your own higher self as well as your angelic guides and ascended masters. Both sources of inspiration are responsive to the gravitational waves emanating from the divine trinity at the Paradise core. We can imagine a wheel of eternity with Paradise at its center and from this wheel, a web spirals outward like the genesis pattern creating a network of interconnected looping space-time bubbles. We are riding on that wheel of eternity while spinning our webs of consciousness that spiral into multi-dimensional experiences. The quality of the experiences on that ride through time and space depend entirely upon the choices that define each moment. We can intentionally choose to take the best ride when we tune into the higher guidance we receive.

The higher influences that inspire our lives and govern our choices are the focus of our exploration today. We'll take all we've learned on our adventure thus far and apply it to our greater understanding of the divine nature and origin of consciousness. Not only do we want to consciously evolve by developing a higher awareness of the divine source, but we also want to fully embrace each and every moment of our daily experience by learning how to apply it! This means bringing our consciousness fully into every sight, smell, touch, taste and sound and appreciating it deeply for all it is worth. In this way, we are intentionally creating our experience by embracing the most positive aspects of each moment and even enhancing them for the benefit of ourselves and others. This elevates the experience to the level at which you wish to experience it. It's all up to you! Let's increase our awareness about how this all works and how we, as Creators, can shape each moment by collaborating with the higher beings and harmonizing with the greater forces that are influencing our experience.

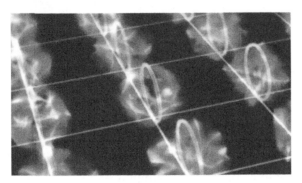

10.6

Let's stop for a moment, close our eyes and listen carefully. Let's listen with our hearts and our minds so that we can feel the essence of the present moment as well as hear the sounds which define it. We can feel the serenity of nature because it is existing within a harmonious state. This is due to the lack of interference by man which tends to disrupt the natural flow of life. These living things and beings live in a synchronistic state governed by the laws of nature. They surrender to the universe and allow the symphony to flow beautifully each striking the perfect chord without resistance. That's what we are feeling and hearing when we stand quietly and absorb the spirit of nature. If man would learn to surrender to the universe and allow the harmonious synchronicity to unfold without resistance, he would find it much easier to obey the laws of nature and therefore exist in the desired state of love, peace, harmony and unity with the rest of creation. In this state, one opens himself up to divine synchronicity and the abundance the Creator wants all of his children to enjoy.

Interference and resistance prevent this flow from entering our lives in a peaceful and harmonious way. Wealth accumulated by disobeying the laws of nature is always accompanied by disharmony, separateness and the corruption of the natural flow. With that in mind, let's completely surrender to the universe by opening our hearts and taking in the beauty that surrounds us. Let's expand our consciousness by becoming aware of the energetic field that unites us all. By surrendering and opening our hearts and minds we are harmonizing with the rest of creation. Together we produce a coherent frequency that creates a higher vibration — a symphony that invites the divine beings to join in. Their presence will illuminate us while we explore the divine sources of intelligent energy influencing our consciousness.

Let's find an open meadow at the base of her majesty Mt. Shasta where we can rest and refuel while we discuss the true nature of reality and how our perception of it defines our consciousness experience.

10.7

As we sit and listen to the water tumbling into the stream from its source high above, I am reminded of an experience I shared in an earlier chapter. While standing in an open meadow not long ago, I reached out to the universe by spreading my arms out wide and looking up into the sky with the deep sense of gratitude and lighthearted joy. I was sending out waves of love as I expanded my heart space to embrace all living beings in my presence. It wasn't long before I got a response! Suddenly, I became aware of a beautiful monarch butterfly drawn to my presence as it flitted around me. I extended both of my hands out in front of me in a welcoming gesture and it landed right on my fingertips. I knew this was a special gift — a "hello" from another spirit saying, "I heard you." The love I extended created a vortex of energy which drew this little spirit in. I used my creative power of attraction to manifest a beautiful experience. My husband, standing at the edge of the meadow, was videotaping this exchange of spirit (unbeknownst to me at the time). Afterwards when I joined him, I excitedly shared my story and he validated my experience by saying, "It's the law of attraction in action, sweetie. The butterfly was attracted to your outpouring of love."

As I thought about that, I realized that I must have attracted the butterfly to me by creating a field of spiraling love, or divine consciousness, around me. This is the love of the Creator that is alive within me and by recognizing it, I can use it to attract these experiences at will. This is how I creatively manifest by transforming my thoughts into the forms I wish to experience. I believe this is the true nature of our reality. The thought forms which make up our reality are manifestations of spiraling, vibrating energy responding to the will of the Creator who is intentionally directing it. Since every living creative being has a free will mind of its own, the interplay between the divine will and human will, both directing form with the power of intention, can either result in divine synchronicity or utter chaos and anywhere in between. The key to creating synchrony with divine order and divine timing is surrendering our human will to the will of our highest self and the divine source. Aligning our will with God's will allows us to flow with divine synchronicity creating a beautiful symphony rather than resisting it and creating only static. The human impulse to create in our own way separate from God's way and out of alignment with the divine source has caused way too much chaos in this world already! It's time to RISE UP, declare our divine power and align with the highest source of our being. It's time to transform human chaos and dark shadows into divine order and luminescence!

When you rise up and declare your divine birthright, you become unlimited in your capacity to create! You resonate with higher vibrational fields of energy and attract only positive outcomes with pure intentions allowing you to serve in the highest way possible! Empowered by the divine light of love, you can transform, transmute and direct energy in any way you choose. You can "trans-form" by translating your pure intentions into beautiful thought-forms that serve the highest good. You can transmute lower energies by redirecting them with the power of love, forgiveness and compassion. Empowered in this way, you can direct the symphony of vibrating strings and manifest a reality that aligns heaven with earth and the divine will with human will. You can make empowered choices that make a positive difference in your life and the world around you.

So how do we harmonize and align with the divine will? How do we attract this higher vibrational field of energy? Since all energy responds to the gravitational force of love, we can lovingly request divine guidance and then simply tune into the messages we receive. We can align with the will of our own higher self by responding to our intuitive thoughts and emotions. We instinctively know what the higher course of action is in most cases. With practice, we can develop the ability to redirect thoughts and words that are not aligned with the highest energies of love, kindness and compassion. We can detect the negative influences when selfish responses sneak in that reek of greed, resentment, blame or jealousy. We can always witness and monitor these thoughts and emotions and identify where they're coming from. We can explore why they might be arising and set an intention to address the source of their negativity. We can make a strong commitment to always forgive, resolve and redirect lower energies with the power of pure love and compassion.

Balancing our male and female energies is also an important part of our ascension journey that helps us RISE UP to a higher way of living and being. Identifying the nature of our masculine and feminine traits and exploring how we are expressing them allows us to see where we need more balance. We can observe the feminine traits within ourselves that inspire creativity and spirituality enhanced by the desire to love and nurture with kindness and compassion. Then we can observe the masculine traits within that apply logical reasoning and practical solutions motivated by the desire to protect and control with power and authority. With both of these feminine and masculine influences, a balanced approach works best in the 3D realm where we want to thrive but still need to survive. We need to learn to ground our creativity and spirituality into the earth plane if we want to manifest our projects in the physical realm. To do this, we need a spiritually-inspired practical approach that works best in 3D. We can still be creative while using practical strategies and we always benefit from co-creating and collaborating with other like-minded souls. We become more empowered when we combine our forces and create a vortex of love. Remember God is within us as the divine essence of our soul. For we know that love is the most powerful force in the universe. When we co-create with love, anything is possible!

You will find more details about co-creating and manifesting with the power of love and light in the final book of my "Up" trilogy, *Lighten Up! Activating Your Light Body.* On this 10-day journey, you will increase your light quotient so you can attract a spiraling field of higher vibrational love all around you at all times. You will raise your light frequency by activating the divine codes within your DNA. On this journey, we will ignite dormant strands and keep them lit by activating them daily. You will increase the power of your brain by enhancing the signal your antennae is receiving. This will give you better access to the akashic records of all time and allow you to tune into the infinite field of wisdom beyond time. If you engaged in my first book, Wake Up!, you learned how to liberate your mind by balancing any karma you've created in this and past lives. By exploring transformative experiences in this and past lives, you were empowered to identify and apply the lessons you've come here to learn so you can move onto more advanced ones. You learned how to intentionally create meaningful experiences so you can continue to consciously evolve toward more enlightened ones. With Rise Up!, we have been enhancing and activating your true divine nature by understanding more about the divine source from which we came. By exploring who we are, where we came from, why we're here and where we're going, we have learned how to become the creators we were always meant to be. We can tap into the Creator-consciousness by understanding how creation was made, how it works and how we can create within it. The "Up" trilogy has been designed to liberate your mind from limiting beliefs, ignite your spirit by developing Creator-consciousness and activate your light-body to awaken your divine abilities.

Ultimately, and simply, the most important goal is to stay focued on being the best person you can possibly by choosing the ascension path. When you make a choice to wake up, rise up and lighten up, you continue to ascend by becoming the best version of yourself. By liberating your mind, igniting your spirit and activating your light body, you can attain the highest level of functioning in an optimal state empowered by love and light. Then you can be of optimal service to others with the vitality and vigor to make a positive difference in the world. The goal of the ascension path is to be of service to others by creating unity, harmony, equality and abundance for all. We can all progress on our ascension paths by working together towards this inspired goal. Inspiring unity consciousness is the objective and applying our Creator-consciousness is the way to achieve it.

It's in the best interest of all beings to work together toward the same evolutionary goal of ascension. All evolutionary beings have a strong desire at the very core of their being to ascend on our journey back to the source and this unites us. We are united by this divine purpose and those who recognize this are highly motivated to work together harmoniously to achieve it. All of the channeled material I have read and shared reveals teachings intended to help us ascend on our evolutionary path. The beings sharing this information seem to feel that it is their mandate to do so and as such, is an important part of their own ascension.

In Summary

At the beginning of our journey today, I presented a visualization which described energy in terms of vibrating strings. This probably sounds familiar to you since "String Theory" is one of the leading theories in modern physics to explain the most fundamental particle of energy and matter. String theory proposes that force, matter, space and time are composed of tiny vibrating strings. In a book called "A Complete Idiot's Guide to String Theory" by George Musser, he likens these to guitar strings that, when plucked, strike a certain tone, or chord, which identifies their true nature. For instance, if the chord is E, the string may belong to an electron or if it is a P, a proton. He describes these as "sub, sub, sub-atomic" strings meaning that there may be trillions of them inside just one subatomic particle and that they only vibrate under specific conditions.

George believes that this theory may be the root essence of the natural world and that, if true, these strings create "the ultimate symphony of unimaginable intricacy." He also talks about gravity as a "special force" because instead of just traveling through space like electromagnetic energy or the strong and weak nuclear forces, it warps space. Remember, how the event horizon of a black hole, the most powerful center of gravity in our galaxy, warps time and space? George admits that space might be far more complex than we give it credit for but that understanding the way strings vibrate may help to explain creative processes like the workings of gravity. We learned on our journey that string theory requires 11 dimensions of reality and that both the concepts of vibrating strings and the multidimensional nature of reality fit nicely within the teachings of the Urantia Book as well as the Law of One series. The fact that these were both written long before physics introduced "String Theory" and recognized 11 dimensions is not surprising to me. The authors were channeling divine intelligence with a much higher perspective after all. With 13 total dimensions, we know that the first and last dimensions are actually "dimensionless." Rather, they are points, or portals to and from infinity, through which we spiral out of and back into. Whether scientifically proven or taught by higher beings, intelligent design is apparent within the vibrational nature of a multidimensional reality that is sourced from infinity, our true origin and destiny.

These explanations, along with the other revelations we've discovered throughout this adventure, help us to understand the mechanisms through which infinite intelligence constructs our reality and the channels through which intelligent beings direct and oversee it. Whether by transmuting energy and matter through projection or reflection, a pure source of energy is at the root of it all which resembles vibrational love and light. We can think of this light as the primal consciousness in action — creating and evolving, loving and learning, doing and being all at once. As the light projects farther away from the source on its descending path toward material reality, it becomes more distorted. The Law of One book speaks of our reality in terms of vibrational distortions. All is in divine order, however, because its journey away from the source is all about learning how to love its way back home through evolutionary experiences in time and space.

According to the Urantia Book, there is a point when the vibrating source energy, they call "ultimatons", transforms into electrons which are the basis for our atomic and molecular reality.

What I found interesting about this transformational stage was that the pure "ultimatonic" energy responds only to the pull of Paradise gravity and the "electronic" energy responds to the pull of linear, or material, gravity. At this point, the sources of intelligent energy also change as the responsibilities for controlling and directing this creational energy are passed down throughout the evolutionary worlds to the free will beings who inhabit them. Energy has a long journey from the core of Paradise to a planetary destination and along the way has been transmuted and transformed into many different forms based on the will of the beings intelligently directing it.

Ultimately, the Creator is directing the whole show and so we can think of all energy transformation as being under the direction of divine will. However, the Creator's plan of self-realization through the experience of evolutionary "free-willed" beings naturally involves an expansion of projected consciousness. To facilitate the expansion, a hierarchy of beings is required to organize, administer, supervise, coordinate and direct this complex network of vibrating strings and conscious beings! The level at which these beings operate depends on their evolutionary stage of development and on the nature of their specific role. It seems as if some beings are more of a personal or spiritual nature than others, but all creative beings represent an ascending level of consciousness either way and that's who we are!

With that empowering realization, let's get up and stretch. Let's tune back into the meadow and peer up at the towering majesty of Mt. Shasta and admire the descending waterfall. The water rushing down from its source up above into the water below is such a perfect analogy for what we have been discovering on our journey. We learned from Genesis, in the bible, that there are waters above and waters below and that this really represents vibrating realms of higher and lower consciousness. We learned how vibrational consciousness defines all realities based on its frequency and how this translates to light and sound waves. We discovered that multidimensional realities act like oceanic realms layered one upon the other along a rotational axis that connects them. We know that these vibrational realms represent different realities that we descend and ascend through on our evolutionary space-time adventure. We also know that the entire expanse of creation from eternity out to the rotating spheres is all still unfolding within the watery womb of the Divine Mother. The stage of creation is settled in the theatre of infinity and it is and always will be the backdrop for all of the acts in both eternity and time and space. On that note, let's gather our things and move on from this glorious meadow bidding farewell to all the living beings who blessed us while we were here.

Up ahead we see the trail that ascends the mountain and as we hike up it, we can't help but notice that we are literally on an ascension path on this last day of our journey! As we ascend, let's continue our discussion about infinite intelligence.

Intelligent energy describes an infinite field of consciousness existing and experiencing on many diverse planes of reality. I see energy and consciousness as interchangeable terms. The nature of both depends entirely upon their vibrational resonance. Furthermore, since energy and matter are constantly being transmuted from one state to the next, these terms are also somewhat interchangeable. We have learned through the teachings in the Urantia Book that the Universal Father projects unique patterns of personality through a special gravity circuit reserved for this specific purpose.

We also learned that each of us are endowed with a "thought adjuster" that permits direct contact with our Creator. We were taught that the Eternal Son has a spiritual influence on all of creation which is also projected through a gravity circuit reserved for this divine purpose. Finally, we learned that the Infinite Spirit activates the will of the Father and Son through the mind-gravity circuit. She employs the technique of radiating the influence of the Seven Master Spirits outward into creation as a means of progressing the universal mind through seven levels of evolutionary consciousness. These techniques of the Paradise Trinity help us to understand the source of our personality, spirit and mind attributes.

We learned from George Musser that gravity is a special force that warps space and this gives us an idea how the gravity circuits of the Father, Son and Spirit might influence our "warped" perception of reality. I understand that there are many other beings and forces at work that shape our consciousness but the divine Trinity is the primal source of our consciousness and all effects thereafter are a result of this influence. Of course, the Creator is the primal cause, or first thought, and all other thought-forms created thereafter are "effects" setting up the whole cause and effect nature of reality, existential and experiential. Therefore, we started out our journey of self-realization (in my book Wake Up!) with a cause and effect analysis of our own life experiences because this principle defines our existence at the most fundamental level and therefore, helps us to reveal our divine nature and true purpose (in Rise Up!). Now as we move forward, we will learn how to ignite our divinity by activating our light-body (in Lighten Up!).

Since we know there are many dimensions and portals through which creative energy is utilized and expressed, we must attune our Creator abilities by directing the super strings of consciousness. These super strings originate in the "Great Central Sun" at the core of creation and are projected into huge nebulae to be nurtured and birthed. These great nebulae give birth to suns and stars which eventually break away from the gravity grasp of their Great Mother. Within the hot core of suns and stars, the vibrating strings of consciousness transform from ultimatons to electrons so that atoms and molecules can form. This is the foundation of our planetary reality and all forms produced thereafter are based on the revolutionary rate, size and number of the subatomic particles which make up the atoms. In other words, the nature of the subatomic particles is determined by the nature of the vibrating strings, or consciousness, they are made of.

These powerful suns from which electrons emerge respond to the gravitational pull of the Creator as they continue to swing around the circle of eternity in search of their Mother. They themselves have a strong force of love at their core and as such, exert a gravitational attraction on the matter around them until they give birth to a family of their own. Each of these solar beings has a consciousness unique to their own pattern personality given to them by the Creator. Their role is to project consciousness by emitting photons. In this way, they become a portal through which consciousness, or energy, can be projected, transmuted, directed and controlled according to the will of the intelligent energy behind it. These energies are united in their divine purpose, so they work together harmoniously.

This divine energy reaches our planet through portals which are spiraling vortexes. In the various ages of our planetary evolution, Creator beings set up a whole network of vortexes aligned in such a way that these divine energies can be received and transmitted. In a sense this is like a communication network and, at the same time, a power grid! In the book, "The Yugas", the authors speak of a "Consciousness Matrix" and a "Golden Age" when we were aware of the interconnectedness of all forms of conscious thought. With a focused effort, we can move toward that sacred place once again where we are unified within the deeper meaning and greater purpose of our existence. Of course, the intense solar flares and alignments that facilitate global ascension and the "harvesting" of higher frequency beings, naturally elevates the collective consciousness. Those whose souls are ready for an acceleration in consciousness will be propelled into a higher dimensional experience when the 3rd and 5th realities merge. Those whose souls require more learning in 3D, will simply take another ride on the ferris wheel of time with another opportunity to get off when the time is right.

My sincerest desire is that the revelations we have discovered throughout this amazing outdoor adventure have given you a greater depth of understanding about the true nature of your reality. I have presented potentialities and possibilities for you to consider. All along I have encouraged you to go within and decide for yourself because this is the only way fundamental truths will ever have any personal significance for you. Once you can start discovering these truths for yourself, you will awaken to a reality that has far more creative potential. Our human potential is vast, and our spiritual potential is limitless! This is largely due to our divine nature but also because of the tremendous influence of our own higher selves and divine guides. The entire field of infinite intelligence is available to us. All we have to do is RISE UP by opening our hearts and minds to the presence of a unifying field of consciousness.

Once we realize we are an integral part of this one "being", each a cell of the One Great Self, then we consciously and energetically connect to the living, breathing and pulsating action of it and develop a strong desire to be in harmony with it. We have a direct connection to the Creator, our divine Mother/Father, and as the children, we are one big family all attracted to the gravitational pull of divine love. The Creator and Creatix love us dearly and that's why they keep us within their gravity grasp. Every single one of us are part of the creative plan and we each play a significant role in fulfilling the divine purpose — to know and love thyself. No matter what we think we have done in the past to separate us from God or each other has already been forgiven. Every moment of every day we are presented with another opportunity to turn toward the light of love.

Each moment is a choice for us to express our highest self, think the most virtuous thoughts, say the kindest words and perform the most loving actions in divine service to others. The best way to do this is to bring our consciousness into the present moment, the here and now, where the threads of space and time intersect and reveal the eternal magic moment. Divine grace and beauty lies within us and shines in all things and beings all around us. It's all in the way we perceive it. This is where the magic lies and it is truly all we have — just this one moment to shine brightly like the superstars that we truly are. Like Plato discovered, there is one star for each individual soul. That's how important we are! Like Ra revealed, our souls are eternal. We come from our star and we return to it. That is where the essence of our higher-self resides, and we can connect to it anytime. Our star is in the heavens just waiting for us to reach out and tune in. When we have fulfilled our destiny in this lifetime, it will reveal to us our divine nature. Meanwhile, we can bring heaven down to earth right here and now by expressing our divine essence every day in every way. We can inspire the whole field of consciousness with our higher thoughts, words and actions. We have the power to collectively cause a major shift in consciousness on this planet. Many believe Mother Earth has already shifted into a higher vibration and now it is up to us to catch up with her. She loves us all dearly and she wants all of her children to join her as she moves into the brighter light of a higher way.

Let's raise our vibration by living in the light of love and by creating a higher way of living and being here and now. Let's connect into our higher self and to those divine beings who love us dearly and support us always. Let's reach out to Mother/Father God and tell them how much we adore them and how grateful we are for this beautiful life on this amazing planet. Knowing we are an aspect of the One Great Self who is actually experiencing through us, let's make sure to create the best experience possible! Let's make them proud of our performance. The best way to show our deep love and affection is by offering the best experience we can. Let's show that same respect and consideration to sweet dear Mother Earth and treat each other with love and compassion. Let's raise the roof on this consciousness experience! Let's all RISE UP! We can do this! We have the potential. As divine beings we have unlimited potential. We can do, be and have anything we desire with the power of our pure intentions.

I sincerely hope this adventure has inspired awe and wonder in you and you have a greater appreciation for the magic and mystery of it all. I hope you feel incredibly blessed for the precious opportunity to be alive and well. For as long as you are breathing and have a voice that can be heard, you can make a powerful, positive difference. Truth, beauty and goodness are the keys to awaken the hearts and minds of our brothers and sisters everywhere. I love each one of you dearly and know that we are a species worth saving. We each must do our part and we can start right here and now. Let's consciously evolve together. Together we can ignite an acceleration of consciousness that will rock our planet! Yep, that's it! Let's rock on!

I have enjoyed this adventure tremendously and am looking forward with great anticipation to the last leg of our collective journey. Together let's absorb this final initiation and activation for it embraces the spiritual essence of our search for sacred wisdom and divine love. Many blessings, my friends as I leave you with this lovely passage:

"My soul — my own subconscious, individualized piece of the universal energy —
believed it was part of everything...My soul knew it would survive, that it was eternal,
that it was ongoing and unlimited in its understanding that this, too, was part
of the adventure we call life."

~ from *Out on a Limb* by Shirley MacLaine[2]

Preparation for Merkaba Initiation and Activation

This ascension journey has been chock-full of profound revelations and this makes for a plentiful bounty of truths to contemplate. I suggest you set your journal beside you now as you go within. This way, when certain aspects of the creation story resonate loudly within the core of your being, you can write them down. Once you find a comfortable place to sit and start taking some nice deep breaths, you can close your eyes and imagine stepping into your golden merkaba. This is your expanded light-body vehicle with two golden tetrahedrons merging, one upright 3D triangle on top and one inverted 3D triangle on the bottom creating a 6-pointed star. You can astral travel to any location in time and space, and throughout eternity, in your golden merkaba light-body vehicle. This Golden Star Merkabah Activation virtually draws you into the light of the source. Once you have merged with the light, you can review the revelations we've covered in today's journey through the solar system and beyond.

Merkaba Initiation
(Audio version available at: www.SuzanneRossTranscendence.com)

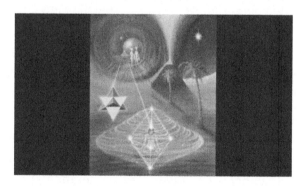

10.8

You are a rainbow light body. Your soul is intricately interwoven into the consciousness matrix of Mother Earth. The Hopis refer to the mother of creation as Grandmother Spider. This is an analogy for how the mother holds us in her web of consciousness. We can become trapped in the 3D consciousness matrix especially when there are many attachments holding us within this web. The intention behind many Buddhist practices is to detach from our sense desires in this realm so that we can explore other realms beyond this limited 3D perspective. We can still remain interwoven into the earth plane and embrace our present experience while expanding our awareness into the multidimensional realms of time, space and beyond into eternity and even infinity. A powerful way to do this is to move beyond our seven chakras and to place our consciousness within the Golden soul star 8 inches above our heads.

We can envision the soul star as a star tetrahedron wherein the inverted triangle representing our human soul is merged with the upright triangle representing our cosmic soul. The star tetrahedron, in its 3D manifestation as a Golden hologram, also represents a Merkaba. Once our consciousness is seated inside this Merkaba above we can imagine it expanding to the size of the vehicle within which we can travel throughout the cosmos because that's exactly what we're going to do in the following Golden Star Merkaba Activation.

Golden Star Merkaba Activation

10.9

To get started, just sit back, get comfortable and close your eyes. Now follow your breath as it moves in and out of your body. Take a deep breath in through your nose and expand your belly while counting to five and then breathe out through your mouth while contracting your belly to the count of five. Repeat this until you feel calm, centered and in a fully relaxed state. Now bring your attention to your third eye by focusing on the space between your brows until you see the shape of an eye in front of you with a piercing indigo blue pupil staring back at you. Move into this expanded consciousness which gives you access to the Akashic records of your eternal soul. Make a request to communicate directly with your highest self as the eternal soul who is projecting the multidimensional holograms of your time and space experiential selves. Your eternal soul is your existential self — the only true you existing in the eternal now moment.

Envision your eternal soul as the fullest expression of all that you are. Picture yourself expressing in the eternal realm as an angelic light being. This is you fully expressed as the embodiment of your perfect divine blue print. You are the ultimate expression of beauty, truth, grace and symmetry. Imagine yourself taking on the most beautiful form you can possibly imagine and so it is and that is you. This is your "I AM". Now imagine this beautiful portrayal of yourself in the center of a circle with your arms outstretched. Imagine that there are 12 points of consciousness evenly spaced encircling you. These circles represent the 12 dimensions that your eternal soul is interwoven into. Nine of these realms, 3D through 11D exist as a holographic time and space realities. 12D, 1D and 2D are eternal, infinite and elemental as the Eternals, Deity and Aten.

We will begin this Golden Star Merkaba activation, by tuning into the twelfth dimension. This is the eternal realm of divine perfection perfectly settled in the eternal now moment. This is also the realm of the Eternals. This eternal realm has a beginning but no ending. This is the central universe which has the Paradise Core to infinity at its center. Through the Paradise Core, the Infinite Source continues to flow through the portal of eternity so that creation can expand endlessly. This realm is the perfect expression of creation. The perfect divine blueprint for the only true universal reality and all other time and space holographic universes are merely a reflection of this one perfect universe. All the forms here are the fullest expression of their perfect divine blueprint. The fundamental patterns of creation are expressed in their perfected state without any distortion. There is perfect divine order without any perception of chaos. Unity, harmony, peace and joy prevail in this perfectly synchronized universe of divine perfection. Here is where the 12 male and female creator beings reside as the 24 elders. They represent the 12 male and female blueprints or 24 perfect designs they can express with perfection in eternity. As these perfect forms are projected into the realms of time and space as conscious beings, their blueprint becomes distorted as a holographic projection. They become fragmented fractals as they are separated from the Divine Source. Their consciousness becomes distorted and these fragmented souls cannot be perfectly aligned with their divine blueprint until they connect back into their eternal soul in the central universe of divine perfection.

As you tune into your indigo blue third eye, that is exactly what you are doing. You are traveling beyond the time and space illusion and connecting directly back into your eternal soul so that you can be perfectly aligned with it. You move beyond the chaos and into divine order. You become perfectly synchronized with who you are as a divinely perfect being expressing all the highest qualities of unity, harmony, truth, beauty, grace and symmetry. Once you have connected into your eternal soul in this way, you will forever remain in direct communication. Your eternal soul is plugged directly into the Divine Source as well being in such close proximity to it. Through your eternal soul you can connect directly into the Paradise Core and travel through it. Any time you like, you can travel through the core and be seated in the infinite sea of pure bliss.

Let's move through this Paradise portal into the first dimension now. The Paradise Core at the center of creation is the portal to infinity. It is the first dimension beyond creation. It is the infinite source of creation which we call Deity. In this realm, consciousness is infinite existing in a pure bliss state of violet transcendence that is beginningless and endless. As far as you can see in all directions there is only pure stillness and infinite violet light. You feel totally at peace in this expansive and unlimited space. It is blissful and serene in this realm beyond existence and experience. This is the Absonite realm where you can just be without any expectation or reason or purpose. Here you can simply be at one with the infinite source of pure consciousness.

From infinity into eternity, let's move beyond the Paradise Core and central universe of perfection into the second dimension of creation. This is the elemental realm of creation we call Aten. Here is where the fundamental patterns of creation transform into sacred geometry and begin to form elements such as fire, air, water and earth. These are the elements necessary to create the physical illusion of form in the time and space realm. The second dimension is the space between the central universe of eternal perfection and the time and space universes of holographic illusion. Here is the realm where the only true eternal reality transforms into a holographic reflection of the one perfect universe. All time and space universes are merely a reflection of this one perfect central universe. Imagine the true forms in eternity transforming into holograms. See how the elements of creation transform from fire, air, earth and water to holographic projections through the use of sacred geometry. Fire becomes a tetrahedron, air becomes an octahedron, water becomes an icosahedron and consciousness itself becomes a dodecahedron. These are the holographic forms of the elements that can be projected into the creation of the time and space universes.

10.10

Now that we have visited infinity and eternity, it's time to explore the multidimensional realms of time and space experience. Imagine your eternal soul standing in the center of a perfect circle which is defined by 12 individual circles evenly spaced around you. Now turn toward the circle marked 3D. And then slowly move your attention to the circles that follow from 4D to 9D and imagine who you might be in these multidimensional realms with each of your forms getting lighter and lighter until you become formless in the 10th and 11th dimensions. These are the nine experiential realms from 3D to 11D. Amongst these holographic dimensional experiences, you may be expressing in both physical and spiritual incarnations. You are also experiencing in other galaxies and parallel universes. In the fullest expression of who you truly are in the eternal now moment, you are simultaneously expressing in multidimensional realms as a cosmic citizen who is intergalactic and can travel around the cosmos through interdimensional portals. As we imagine this interdimensional travel, I want you to move your consciousness into your crown chakra and spin it counterclockwise transcending time.

Imagine that the violet chakra spinning at the crown of your head is in truth a black hole with two spiraling arms seated at the center of an immense galaxy. Get ready to travel through the supermassive black hole at the center of this galaxy. Imagine the two spiraling arms as one bright red with a masculine quality and the other electric blue with a feminine quality. With these two qualities perfectly synchronized, you can easily travel through the black hole in the center now that you are perfectly balanced within your masculine and feminine energies. Now as a perfectly balanced being, you can travel through the portal of divine light between your crown chakra and the 8th Golden Star chakra 8 inches above your head. On the other side of this light portal, you can step into your Golden Merkaba in the shape of a star tetrahedron where your human self is perfectly merged with your divine self. Within the space of your Merkaba vehicle, you are both human and divine and this is the ultimate truth of who you really are.

Imagine stepping into your Golden Merkaba with your consciousness perfectly seated inside of this Golden Star and get ready to travel throughout the cosmos easily traversing interdimensional portals from one dimension into the next so that you can view the multidimensional realms that your eternal soul is experiencing simultaneously in the eternal now moment. Let your imagination run wild as you visit each of the dimensions starting in 3D with the human form you are experiencing in this time and space realm and then imagine a golden light portal opening in your 3D reality which you can easily move into within your Golden Merkaba above and traverse into the next dimension. Imagine what this next dimension might look like. 4D is the astral realm where the interplay between the light beings and the dark beings is intense. This is where angels and demons both reside, and it is where you as a light warrior are overcoming the darkness and transmuting the shadows with your golden rod of light.

10.11

Now imagine a golden light portal opening in this realm so that you can traverse into the next seven realms one at a time and see who you might be expressing in these both as a galactic and universal being. Enjoy this journey and know that who you imagine you might be in these multidimensional realms is exactly who you are in truth. For you can easily access your other multidimensional selves expressing in many different time and space realms because you are directly connected into the eternal soul who is projecting these holographic beings. You are your eternal soul and you know exactly who you are projecting in these realms of time and space. Tune into them and feel into what they are experiencing. Imagine what each of your multidimensional selves looks like, feels like and is seeing and being. For guidance tuning into your multidimensional selves, go to www.SuzanneRossTranscendence.com, click on the Sessions tab and select Multidimensional Soul Retrieval. I will be delighted to guide you through the process of revealing the identities of your soul's fragments and where they have incarnated so you can be reunited with them.

Now let's move into the 12th dimension of the Eternals who work directly with the elements to create perfect blueprints of human forms that can express multidimensionally. There are 12 male and female blueprints which create 24 perfect designs of male-female forms. Reflections of these 24 elders were projected upon planet Earth at the time when Jesus and the 12 disciples were manifesting on the earth plane. Jesus represented the immortal one as the 13th whole soul in the center and the 12 disciples the perfect divine compliments. Mother Mary was prepared through many initiations and activations to bring in this higher dimensional being with her partner through divine light transmissions of DNA codes. At the same time, there were 12 other couples using DNA light transmission practices to bring in the other 12 disciples.

Essentially these couples represented the 24 elders plus the 13th immortal couple, Mary and Joseph, as the Creative Mother and Divine Father. With your Golden Star activated, you can tune into the 12th dimension and imagine the 24 elders expressing in eternity as the 24 male-female divine blueprints of perfection. You can also imagine the Creative Trinity of the Father, Mother and Child expressed perfectly in each one of these beings as divine light, divine love and creative action. From the 12th dimension, you can see perfectly the portal to infinity where the Divine Trinity resides in perfect union and perfect bliss as the Divine Father, the creative mother and the perfect child. You can imagine the Divine Trinity merged perfectly with the Creative Trinity as the divine star tetrahedron perfectly seated at the center of the portal to infinity. With the upright divine tetrahedron resting in infinity and the inverted creative tetrahedron extending into eternity, a star tetrahedron is formed just like the one above your head which is also a portal to eternity and infinity!

You see you are a multi-dimensional time and space being as well as an eternal soul infused by the Infinite Source. You are all of these at once as both the Creative and Divine Trinity. You are a perfect expression of the Divine Father, Creative Mother and Eternal Child. You are divine, creative and expressive. You are divine light and love in action. You are three in one and one in three. You are living, eternal and immortal. You are all that and more. You are a divine perfect being expressing in time and space. Remember that you are divine perfection in action and extend your divine light and love to all beings in all ways always. And so be it. And so it is. Amen.

Your Personal Revelations

_____

_____

_____

_____

_____

_____

_____

_____

REFERENCES

Chapter cover image courtesy of www.pixabay.com

Illustrations

1-3. www.pixabay.com

4. Personal photo

5-9. www.pixabay.com

10. Personal graphic

11. www.pixabay.com

Text:

Godfre Ray King, Unveiled Mysteries, St Germain Press, 1934

1. page 1

Shirley MacLaine, Out on a Limb, Bantam Books, 1983

2. page 348

ABOUT THE AUTHOR

In December of 1995, Suzanne Ross experienced a profound miracle that she describes as a divine intervention. In her first book, *Wake Up! Awakening through Reflection*, she vividly shares this remarkable blessing and how it awakened her ability to channel higher intelligence and align with the authenticity of her highest self. In this second book in the Up! Trilogy, *Rise Up! Awakening through Revelation*, Suzanne shares how 15 years later in 2010, during her walking meditations, she found herself shifting into higher dimensional experiences and moving through them as a crystalline light being. Soon after, she became a disciple in the Vedantic Tradition after receiving a powerful initiation that propelled her into a profound sense of oneness. In one transcendent moment, she became fully aware of the infinite source illuminating all the realms with the divine light of pure love. At the same time, the life force of her own kundalini energy activated her third eye and fully ignited her crown chakra. In that moment beyond time, she was braided with the divine blueprint of her eternal soul essence and ecstatic bliss became her new normal. She was instantly overwhelmed by a strong desire to share this pure bliss state with all others.

From that moment on, Suzanne has dedicated her life to bringing the higher teachings of divine enlightenment to all of humanity through her inspirational books, group workshops, live events, energetic sessions and internet television series. Suzanne is building a unity community in Sedona, Arizona, the spiritual mecca of North America, where spiritually-inspired teachers and seekers can come together. Here, they will be free to live and learn and to rejoice and ascend into a higher state of awareness. Together, they will inspire unity and harmony so that pure love and joy can prevail.

Suzanne was born in Shasta County, California where she grew up in the mystical forests of the sacred Mount Shasta playing with fairies, elementals and trolls. She was visited regularly by galactic beings who would come at dawn and bless her with celestial love and healing light. She grew into her ego identity as a teen and young adult, falling asleep in the illusion, until her profound awakening at the age of 31 when she was braided with her higher self. Since then, she has been dedicated to enhancing the mental, physical, emotional and spiritual well-being of her clients, friends and followers. Suzanne is the President of Lighten Up! Enterprises and the CEO of Awakening, a 501c3 nonprofit. Please visit her websites at: www.SuzanneRossTranscendence.com, SciSpi.tv/ & www.TheAwakeningCenters.org.